Threat Hunting in the Cloud

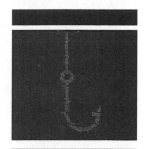

Threat Hunting in the Cloud

Defending AWS®, Azure® and Other Cloud Platforms Against Cyberattacks

Chris Peiris
Binil Pillai
Abbas Kudrati

WILEY

This book is dedicated to my mother, Shantha, and my father, Christopher, who taught me that hard work, passion, and curiosity will overcome any obstacle in life. Thank you for the support and courage you provided me to take on the world. . .and to my youngest son, Deven, who teaches me to venture out of my comfort zone and challenge the status quo every day. This is for you.

— Dr. Chris Peiris

I dedicate this book to my dad, Capt. Aravindakshan Pillai, my mom, Ambika Devi, my sister, Beena Pradeep, and my school teachers, not only for their love and care but also for their support during my childhood socialization, which helped shape how I view the world around me and learn the importance of respecting others, regardless of their race, ethnicity, religion, gender, age, etc.

— Binil Pillai

I dedicate this book to my dad, Shabbir Hussain, whom I role model in many ways, and to my mom, Zahra, who keeps me in her everyday prayers.

— Abbas Kudrati

About the Authors

 Dr. Chris Peiris's information technology career spans over 25 years, the last 15+ years dedicated to cybersecurity. Chris is an avid publisher and a thought leader in the cybersecurity, enterprise architecture, and cloud integration spaces. He has advised Fortune 500 companies, federal and state governments, and defense and intelligence entities across the U.S., Asia Pacific Japan, Middle East Africa, Australia, and New Zealand.

Chris is a published author of 10 books on multiple technologies, including cybersecurity, cloud computing, web services, C#, and Java topics. These books have been translated into nine languages and are available in 30+ countries. He is also an academic researcher at Monash University and University of Canberra. Chris was awarded an Associate Professorship (Adjunct) fellowship at the University of Canberra in recognition of academic research contributions to cybersecurity and cloud computing. He has multiple tertiary qualifications from Harvard University, the University of Canberra, and Monash University. He is an author of multiple academic research journals and frequent speaker at professional IT conferences.

Chris was the Director of Cybersecurity for Microsoft, Asia Pacific Japan, and Australia. He was also the National Security Lead for Avanade (Accenture and Microsoft joint venture) and an advisor to multiple defense and intelligence think tanks. Chris has assisted in creating "government wide secure threat management frameworks" in Taiwan, Singapore, New Zealand, and Australia. He also created incident response, security operations center/cyber fusion center, advisory services, and threat intelligence capabilities across Asia Pacific Japan, Middle East Africa, and Americas.

Binil Pillai is a strategic-thinking business development professional with 23 years of multifaceted experience building relationships, cultivating partnerships, retaining customers, and growing profit channels by establishing trust. As Global Director of Security, Compliance and Identity (SCI) at Microsoft, Binil focuses on the small, medium, and corporate segment and works with corporate executives to evangelize security as a foundational capability to accelerate a secure digital transformation journey. Binil has experience in security product development, managed security product marketing, and led worldwide security go-to-market and sales activations. He was the business architect who designed and launched the Business Value Analysis (BVA) model to quantify security risk exposure for B2B customers. Before joining Microsoft, Binil worked as a regional practice manager for Deloitte Consulting's strategy and operations practice. His business strategy consulting experience spans business transformation, corporate strategy alignment, post-merger integration, adoption and change management, customer relationship management, IT strategic planning, and more, with a wide range of companies and government agencies.

Binil is passionate about establishing a coaching culture to improve learning and performance, make the most of the people's potentials and deliver sustainable results. As a PROCI-certified change management practitioner, Binil embraces the leadership accountability to take a step-by-step approach that helps the organization achieve success, no matter how complex the system, process, method, or culture need to affect or transform. Binil graduated from INSEAD in Business Strategy & Financial Acumen and has a master's in business administration. He is TOGAF certified enterprise architect and account-based marketing (ABM) professional from ITSMA.

He has also published many thought leadership documents. His recent publications are "How COVID-19 Changes Small Medium Enterprise (SME) Priority on Security," "Identity – Building Trust in a Digital World," "How Does Your Cybersecurity Posture Need To Change?," and "What Does It Take To Protect Your Workplace?"

Abbas Kudrati, a long-time cybersecurity practitioner and CISO, is Microsoft Asia's Chief Cybersecurity Advisor. Abbas works with customers on cybersecurity strategy, how Microsoft sees the threat landscape, how we are investing in the future of security at Microsoft, and how organizations can take advantage of Microsoft's security solutions to help improve their security posture and reduce costs.

In addition to his work at Microsoft, he serves as an executive advisor to Deakin University, LaTrobe University, HITRUST ASIA, EC Council ASIA, and many security and technology startups. He supports the broader security community through his work with ISACA chapters and student mentorship. He is also a part-time professor at Deakin University, Melbourne, Australia, and a regular speaker on Zero Trust, cybersecurity, cloud security, governance, risk, and compliance.

Abbas has received multiple industry awards, such as "Business Leader/Professional of the year 2021 by IABCA," "Top Security Advisor for APJ for the year 2020 and the year 2019," "Best Security Professional of the year 2018," "CISO 100 Award 2018," "Finalist for Australian CISO of the year 2015," "IT Governance Professional of the year 2014," and "Security Strategist of the year 2011."

He graduated from Gujarat University, India, with a bachelor's degree in Accounting and Auditing and is a certified Forrester Zero Trust Strategist, C|CISO, CISM, CISA, CGEIT, CPDSE, and CSX-P, among other professional certifications.

About the Technical Editors

 Sina Manavi is a cybersecurity evangelist and Senior Manager – Group Information Security Governance at AIA. Over the past decade, Sina has worked with different government agencies, in the banking and financial sectors, as well as for well-known companies such as EC Council in different roles, from penetration testing to threat hunting and intelligence, cyber incident response, data protection, third-party security, governance, risk and compliance, cloud security, and strategy planning and digital transition.

Sina also has been a regular keynote speaker at various conferences and webinars, supporting cybersecurity communities with the latest about the threat landscape. He has shared his knowledge and experience as a cybersecurity practitioner across the globe.

Sina started his career as a software developer and application security analyst while getting his B.Sc. in software engineering at Azad University Lahijan, Iran. After moving to Malaysia to get his Master of Computer science (Digital Forensics) at University Putra, Malaysia, Sina expanded his career to the next level. Due to his passion for teaching, he conducted penetration testing, secure code practice, digital forensics, incident response, and mobile security training for industry cybersecurity professionals.

 Madanraj Sadasivam (Madan) is an enterprising leader and planner with a strong record of contributions to information and communications technology strategy, architecture, systems and procedures, and organizational agility targeting senior-level assignments. Madan has 17+ years of hands-on software architecture experience involved in the architecture, design, and implementation of microservices architectures, service-oriented architectures, and distributed systems.

Madan currently serves the Australian federal government as an enterprise architect, with responsibilities and oversight of all architecture activities in the enterprise. His technical focus areas include future-proofing digital transformation with an API strategy. Madan is passionate about enabling API platforms for digital business, from designing and publishing APIs for developers to API traffic management, security, and analytics.

Madan graduated from the University of Madras, India, with a bachelor's degree in information technology and is a certified service-oriented architect. He is currently pursuing a world-leading executive MBA program with the Australian Graduate School of Management (AGSM) to enhance his analytical, strategic, and leadership skills.

Acknowledgments

From Chris: This book has been a personal "pet project" and a labor of love across multiple years. The concept, structure, and value proposition took several iterations to materialize with the help of numerous industry experts.

Frist of all, I like to call out both Binil and Abbas for their enthusiasm, collaboration, contribution, and teamwork. Thank you for delivering an exceptional product in light of their high-profile day jobs and burning the midnight oil while authoring the book. It was a very rewarding experience working with both and I hope this book will be the first of many best sellers they will go on to author in the future.

Technical editors Madan and Sina have been a delight to work with as technical reviewers. Both of them not only performed technical review responsibilities but also contributed to some content in several chapters. I hope both Madan and Sina will benefit from this experience and venture into the publishing world with their next best sellers.

A special thank you is directed at the Wiley Publishing team. It has been a privilege to work with Kenyon Brown, Kezia Endsley, Pete Gaughan, and the wider team. Ken has been managing the project from its inception. I remember vividly the first conversation I had with Ken evaluating the book proposal. The book subject matter was "unique and untested," and the book proposal was to address a gap in the market in relation to multi-cloud threat hunting. Ken and Wiley took a gamble on us and have been our partners throughout this journey. Thank you for your help on the book structure, marketing, and staying late to take our calls. Kezia did an exceptional job of project managing and keeping all our authors and tech editors focused and on schedule. Thank you, Kezia, for your guidance, diligence, flexibility, and your patience managing us scattered across Australia, North America, and Asia. Thank you also to the copy editors, graphics designers, and marketing teams at Wiley for making us look good.

This book would not be possible with out some other key contributions. Specifically, Nigel Wyatt for his initial screening of book topics, publishing options, and market analysis. Diana Kelley, for helping with our foreword for the book. We are thrilled to have you on board with this project, Diana. Thank you also for assisting to source GCP content and introducing us to Google subject matter experts. Abbas, thank you for facilitating and organizing Diana's contributions.

This book explores several cutting-edge unexplored topics across multiple technology platforms, such as Microsoft Azure, AWS, and GCP. We anticipated that we would encounter issues finding research material/content as a result. However, we were very fortunate to have leading industry authorities to guide and assist us along the way. Specifically, thank you to Mark Simos, for your long-standing contributions to Microsoft Reference Architecture and Azure subject matter. Dr. John Hildebrandt, thank you for guiding us through AWS content. You have been very generous with your time guiding Madan and myself through the AWS content. Also, thank you Dr. Anton Chuvakin for assisting with GCP content. I appreciate your time and dedication to assist us in light of time zone challenges and to facilitate short time frames.

Last but not least, thank you for my wife Kushanthi, and my sons, Keshera, Viira, and Deven, for their support throughout the authoring process. There have been some long nights and early mornings and thank you for your love, understanding, and patience.

From Binil: Socialization is a process that begins in childhood, by which individuals acquire the values, habits, and attitudes of a society that are later reinforced by various forces over time. I dedicate this book to my dad, Capt. Aravindakshan Pillai, my mom, Ambika Devi, my sister, Beena Pradeep, and my school teachers not only for their love and care but also for their support during my childhood socialization, which helped shape how I view the world around me and learn the importance of respecting others, regardless of their race, ethnicity, religion, gender, age, etc.

During the threat-hunting services product development in 2017, I realized the opportunity to write a book about threat hunting in the cloud. Having an idea and turning it into a book is as hard as it sounds. The experience is both internally challenging and rewarding. I want to thank the individuals that helped make this happen. It is my privilege to co-author this book with Dr. Chris Peiris and Abbas Kudrati, two exceptional professionals and leaders in the cybersecurity space. None of this would have been possible without our technical reviewers, Madan Raj Sadasivam and Sina Manavi, as well as the Wiley publishing team, Kenyon Brown and Kezia Endsley.

Most of my learnings that I shared in the book are based on my Microsoft work experience. I'm honored being part of Microsoft and humbled with the opportunity to learn plenty. Many colleagues, customers, and partners have allowed me to work on their business needs that bring so much personal pleasure, I thank all of you.

Finally, thanks to my beautiful wife Dhanya, and our children, Abhinand and Nayana, all of whom give meaning to my life. I am truly so grateful for all your support.

From Abbas: Writing a book is more challenging than I thought as compared to writing blogs and web articles. The experience was both internally challenging and rewarding. I especially want to thank my co-authors Chris Peiris and Binil Pillai; without them, my entry into the world of authors would not have been possible.

To my first computer teacher, Mr. Subham Mitra, who sparked my interest in the majestic world of computer science during my early school days, and to all my teachers, who have taught me so much.

I would also like to extend my appreciation to my friends and colleagues at Microsoft, from whom I learn every day. My special thanks to Microsoft Cybersecurity "Think Tank" Mark Simos. Our inspiring and passionate Microsoft Leadership team Hayete Gallot, Vasu Jakkal, Ann Johnson, Jonathan Trull, and Bret Arsenault. My manager/mentor/mate Avinash Lotke, all my APJ threat experts, aka Global Belt team Udeesh Millathe, Sharon Ko, Anil Malekani, and Iftekhar Hussain, all my peer Chief Security Advisors, all our product managers from whom I learn every day on the field. Also, our technical reviewers, Sina Manvi, Madan Raj Sadasivam, and Rahul Ramdas, who worked behind the scenes.

Finally, this list of acknowledgments would be incomplete without recognizing the support of my family, who provided the foundation to achieve all that I have in life. Thanks to my awesome wife, Fatema. She is my friend, philosopher, and guide for life and has always been on my side in thick and thin, our children Murtaza and Batool, who sacrificed many weekends so I can complete this book. With my most profound appreciation and gratitude to you all.

Contents at a Glance

Foreword   xxxi

Introduction   xxxiii

Part I   Threat Hunting Frameworks   1

Chapter 1   Introduction to Threat Hunting   3

Chapter 2   Modern Approach to Multi-Cloud Threat Hunting   35

Chapter 3   Exploration of MITRE Key Attack Vectors   63

Part II   Hunting in Microsoft Azure   99

Chapter 4   Microsoft Azure Cloud Threat Prevention Framework   101

Chapter 5   Microsoft Cybersecurity Reference Architecture
              and Capability Map   183

Part III   Hunting in AWS   241

Chapter 6   AWS Cloud Threat Prevention Framework   243

Chapter 7   AWS Reference Architecture   321

Part IV   The Future   371

Chapter 8   Threat Hunting in Other Cloud Providers   373

Chapter 9   The Future of Threat Hunting   391

Part V   Appendices   411

Index   489

Contents

Foreword   xxxi

Introduction   xxxiii

Part I   Threat Hunting Frameworks   **1**

Chapter 1   Introduction to Threat Hunting   **3**
          The Rise of Cybercrime   4
          What Is Threat Hunting?   6
          The Key Cyberthreats and Threat Actors   7
              Phishing   7
              Ransomware   8
              Nation State   10
          The Necessity of Threat Hunting   14
              Does the Organization's Size Matter?   17
          Threat Modeling   19
          Threat-Hunting Maturity Model   23
              Organization Maturity and Readiness   23
                  Level 0: INITIAL   24
                  Level 1: MINIMAL   25
                  Level 2: PROCEDURAL   25
                  Level 3: INNOVATIVE   25
                  Level 4: LEADING   25
          Human Elements of Threat Hunting   26
              How Do You Make the Board of Directors Cyber-Smart?   27
              Threat-Hunting Team Structure   30
                  External Model   30
                  Dedicated Internal Hunting Team Model   30
                  Combined/Hybrid Team Model   30
                  Periodic Hunt Teams Model   30

		Urgent Need for Human-Led Threat Hunting	31
		The Threat Hunter's Role	31
		Summary	33
Chapter 2		**Modern Approach to Multi-Cloud Threat Hunting**	**35**
		Multi-Cloud Threat Hunting	35
		Multi-Tenant Cloud Environment	38
		Threat Hunting in Multi-Cloud and Multi-Tenant Environments	39
		Building Blocks for the Security Operations Center	41
		Scope and Type of SOC	43
		Services, Not Just Monitoring	43
		SOC Model	43
		Define a Process for Identifying and Managing Threats	44
		Tools and Technologies to Empower SOC	44
		People (Specialized Teams)	45
		Cyberthreat Detection, Threat Modeling, and the Need for Proactive Threat Hunting Within SOC	46
		Cyberthreat Detection	46
		Threat-Hunting Goals and Objectives	49
		Threat Modeling and SOC	50
		The Need for a Proactive Hunting Team Within SOC	50
		Assume Breach and Be Proactive	51
		Invest in People	51
		Develop an Informed Hypothesis	52
		Cyber Resiliency and Organizational Culture	53
		Skillsets Required for Threat Hunting	54
		Security Analysis	55
		Data Analysis	56
		Programming Languages	56
		Analytical Mindset	56
		Soft Skills	56
		Outsourcing	56
		Threat-Hunting Process and Procedures	57
		Metrics for Assessing the Effectiveness of Threat Hunting	58
		Foundational Metrics	58
		Operational Metrics	59
		Threat-Hunting Program Effectiveness	61
		Summary	62
Chapter 3		**Exploration of MITRE Key Attack Vectors**	**63**
		Understanding MITRE ATT&CK	63
		What Is MITRE ATT&CK Used For?	64
		How Is MITRE ATT&CK Used and Who Uses It?	65
		How Is Testing Done According to MITRE?	65
		Tactics	67
		Techniques	67

Threat Hunting Using Five Common Tactics   69
   Privilege Escalation   71
     Case Study   72
   Credential Access   73
     Case Study   74
   Lateral Movement   75
     Case Study   75
   Command and Control   77
     Case Study   77
   Exfiltration   79
     Case Study   79
Other Methodologies and Key Threat-Hunting Tools to Combat
   Attack Vectors   80
   Zero Trust   80
     Threat Intelligence and Zero Trust   83
   Build Cloud-Based Defense-in-Depth   84
Analysis Tools   86
   Microsoft Tools   86
     Connect To All Your Data   87
     Workbooks   88
     Analytics   88
     Security Automation and Orchestration   90
     Investigation   91
     Hunting   92
     Community   92
   AWS Tools   93
     Analyzing Logs Directly   93
     SIEMs in the Cloud   94
Summary   95
   Resources   96

Part II   **Hunting in Microsoft Azure**   **99**

Chapter 4   **Microsoft Azure Cloud Threat Prevention Framework**   **101**
Introduction to Microsoft Security   102
Understanding the Shared Responsibility Model   102
Microsoft Services for Cloud Security Posture Management
   and Logging/Monitoring   105
   Overview of Azure Security Center and Azure Defender   105
   Overview of Microsoft Azure Sentinel   108
Using Microsoft Secure and Protect Features   112
   Identity & Access Management   113
   Infrastructure & Network   114
   Data & Application   115
   Customer Access   115
   Using Azure Web Application Firewall to Protect a Website
     Against an "Initial Access" TTP   116
   Using Microsoft Defender for Office 365 to Protect
     Against an "Initial Access" TTP   118

Using Microsoft Defender Endpoint to Protect
Against an "Initial Access" TTP   121
Using Azure Conditional Access to Protect Against
an "Initial Access" TTP   123
Microsoft Detect Services   127
Detecting "Privilege Escalation" TTPs   128
Using Azure Security Center and Azure Sentinel to Detect
Threats Against a "Privilege Escalation" TTP   128
Detecting Credential Access   131
Using Azure Identity Protection to Detect Threats
Against a "Credential Access" TTP   132
Steps to Configure and Enable Risk Polices (Sign-in Risk
and User Risk)   134
Using Azure Security Center and Azure Sentinel to Detect
Threats Against a "Credential Access" TTP   137
Detecting Lateral Movement   139
Using Just-in-Time in ASC to Protect and Detect
Threats Against a "Lateral Movement" TTP   139
Using Azure Security Center and Azure Sentinel to
Detect Threats Against a "Lateral Movement" TTP   144
Detecting Command and Control   145
Using Azure Security Center and Azure Sentinel to
Detect Threats Against a "Command and Control" TTP   146
Detecting Data Exfiltration   147
Using Azure Information Protection to Detect
Threats Against a "Data Exfiltration" TTP   148
Discovering Sensitive Content Using AIP   149
Using Azure Security Center and Azure Sentinel to
Detect Threats Against a "Data Exfiltration" TTP   153
Detecting Threats and Proactively Hunting with
Microsoft 365 Defender   154
Microsoft Investigate, Response, and Recover Features   155
Automating Investigation and Remediation with Microsoft
Defender for Endpoint   157
Using Microsoft Threat Expert Support for Remediation
and Investigation   159
Targeted Attack Notification   159
Experts on Demand   161
Automating Security Response with MCAS
and Microsoft Flow   166
Step 1: Generate Your API Token in Cloud App Security   167
Step 2: Create Your Trigger in Microsoft Flow   167
Step 3: Create the Teams Message Action in Microsoft Flow   168
Step 4: Generate an Email in Microsoft Flow   168
Connecting the Flow in Cloud App Security   169

Performing an Automated Response Using Azure
        Security Center   170
    Using Machine Learning and Artificial Intelligence in Threat
        Response   172
        Overview of Fusion Detections   173
        Overview of Azure Machine Learning   174
    Summary   182

**Chapter 5   Microsoft Cybersecurity Reference Architecture
               and Capability Map   183**
    Introduction   183
    Microsoft Security Architecture versus the NIST Cybersecurity
        Framework (CSF)   184
    Microsoft Security Architecture   185
        The Identify Function   186
        The Protect Function   187
        The Detect Function   188
        The Respond Function   189
        The Recover Function   189
    Using the Microsoft Reference Architecture   190
        Microsoft Threat Intelligence   190
        Service Trust Portal   192
        Security Development Lifecycle (SDL)   193
        Protecting the Hybrid Cloud Infrastructure   194
            Azure Marketplace   194
            Private Link   195
            Azure Arc   196
            Azure Lighthouse   197
            Azure Firewall   198
            Azure Web Application Firewall (WAF)   200
            Azure DDOS Protection   200
            Azure Key Vault   201
            Azure Bastion   202
            Azure Site Recovery   204
            Azure Security Center (ASC)   205
            Microsoft Azure Secure Score   205
        Protecting Endpoints and Clients   206
            Microsoft Endpoint Manager (MEM) Configuration
                Manager   207
            Microsoft Intune   208
        Protecting Identities and Access   209
            Azure AD Conditional Access   210
            Passwordless for End-to-End Secure Identity   211
            Azure Active Directory (aka Azure AD)   211
            Azure MFA   211
            Azure Active Directory Identity Protection   212
            Azure Active Directory Privilege Identity
                Management (PIM)   213

Microsoft Defender for Identity   214
Azure AD B2B and B2C   215
Azure AD Identity Governance   215
Protecting SaaS Apps   216
Protecting Data and Information   219
Azure Purview   220
Microsoft Information Protection (MIP)   221
Azure Information Protection Unified Labeling Scanner
   (File Scanner)   222
The Advanced eDiscovery Solution in Microsoft 365   223
Compliance Manager   224
Protecting IoT and Operation Technology   225
Security Concerns with IoT   226
Understanding That IoT Cybersecurity Starts with a Threat
   Model   227
Microsoft Investment in IoT Technology   229
Azure Sphere   229
Azure Defender   229
Azure Defender for IoT   230
Threat Modeling for the Azure IoT Reference Architecture   230
Azure Defender for IoT Architecture (Agentless Solutions) 233
Azure Defender for IoT Architecture (Agent-based solutions) 234
Understanding the Security Operations Solutions   235
Understanding the People Security Solutions   236
Attack Simulator   237
Insider Risk Management (IRM)   237
Communication Compliance   239
Summary   240

Part III   **Hunting in AWS**   **241**

Chapter 6   **AWS Cloud Threat Prevention Framework**   **243**
Introduction to AWS Well-Architected Framework   244
The Five Pillars of the Well-Architected Framework   245
Operational Excellence   246
Security   246
Reliability   246
Performance Efficiency   246
Cost Optimization   246
The Shared Responsibility Model   246
AWS Services for Monitoring, Logging, and Alerting   248
AWS CloudTrail   249
Amazon CloudWatch Logs   251
Amazon VPC Flow Logs   252
Amazon GuardDuty   253
AWS Security Hub   254
AWS Protect Features   256

How Do You Prevent Initial Access? 256
How Do You Protect APIs from SQL Injection Attacks Using API
  Gateway and AWS WAF? 256
    Prerequisites 257
    Create an API 257
    Create and Configure an AWS WAF 259
AWS Detection Features 263
How Do You Detect Privilege Escalation? 263
  How Do You Detect the Abuse of Valid Account to Obtain
    High-Level Permissions? 264
    Prerequisites 264
    Configure GuardDuty to Detect Privilege Escalation 265
    Reviewing the Findings 266
How Do You Detect Credential Access? 269
  How Do You Detect Unsecured Credentials? 269
    Prerequisites 270
    Reviewing the Findings 274
How Do You Detect Lateral Movement? 276
  How Do You Detect the Use of Stolen Alternate Authentication
    Material? 277
    Prerequisites 277
    How Do You Detect Potential Unauthorized Access to Your
      AWS Resources? 277
    Reviewing the Findings 278
How Do You Detect Command and Control? 280
  How Do You Detect the Communications to a Command and
    Control Server Using the Domain Name System (DNS)? 281
    Prerequisites 281
    How Do You Detect EC2 Instance Communication with a
      Command and Control (C&C) Server Using DNS 281
    Reviewing the Findings 282
How Do You Detect Data Exfiltration? 284
    Prerequisites 285
    How Do You Detect the Exfiltration Using an Anomalous
      API Request? 285
    Reviewing the Findings 286
How Do You Handle Response and Recover? 289
  Foundation of Incident Response 289
  How Do You Create an Automated Response? 290
    Automating Incident Responses 290
    Options for Automating Responses 291
    Cost Comparisons in Scanning Methods 293
  Event-Driven Responses 294
  How Do You Automatically Respond to Unintended
    Disabling of CloudTrail Logging? 295
    Prerequisites 296

Creating a Trail in CloudTrail   296
Creating an SNS Topic to Send Emails   299
Creating Rules in Amazon EventBridge   302
How Do You Orchestrate and Recover?   305
Decision Trees   305
Use Alternative Accounts   305
View or Copy Data   306
Sharing Amazon EBS Snapshots   306
Sharing Amazon CloudWatch Logs   306
Use Immutable Storage   307
Launch Resources Near the Event   307
Isolate Resources   308
Launch Forensic Workstations   309
Instance Types and Locations   309
How Do You Automatically Recover from
    Unintended Disabling of CloudTrail Logging?   310
    Prerequisites   311
    Aggregate and View Security Status in AWS Security Hub   311
    Reviewing the Findings   312
    Create Lambda Function to Orchestrate and Recover   314
How Are Machine Learning and Artificial
    Intelligence Used?   317
Summary   318
References   319

Chapter 7   AWS Reference Architecture   321
AWS Security Framework Overview   322
The Identify Function Overview   323
The Protect Function Overview   324
The Detect Function Overview   325
The Respond Function Overview   325
The Recover Function Overview   325
AWS Reference Architecture   326
The Identify Function   326
Security Hub   328
AWS Config   329
AWS Organizations   330
AWS Control Tower   331
AWS Trusted Advisor   332
AWS Well-Architected Tool   333
AWS Service Catalog   334
AWS Systems Manager   335
AWS Identity and Access Management (IAM)   337
AWS Single Sign-On (SSO)   338
AWS Shield   340
AWS Web Application Firewall (WAF)   340
AWS Firewall Manager   342

AWS Cloud HSM   343
AWS Secrets Manager   345
AWS Key Management Service (KMS)   345
AWS Certificate Manager   346
AWS IoT Device Defender   347
Amazon Virtual Private Cloud   347
AWS PrivateLink   349
AWS Direct Connect   349
AWS Transit Gateway   350
AWS Resource Access Manager   351
The Detect and Respond Functions   353
GuardDuty   354
Amazon Detective   356
Amazon Macie   357
Amazon Inspector   358
Amazon CloudTrail   359
Amazon CloudWatch   360
Amazon Lambda   361
AWS Step Functions   362
Amazon Route 53   363
AWS Personal Health Dashboard   364
The Recover Functions   365
Amazon Glacier   366
AWS CloudFormation   366
CloudEndure Disaster Recovery   367
AWS OpsWorks   368
Summary   369

Part IV   **The Future**   **371**

Chapter 8   **Threat Hunting in Other Cloud Providers** **373**
The Google Cloud Platform   374
Google Cloud Platform Security Architecture
alignment to NIST   376
The Identify Function   376
The Protect Function   378
The Detect Function   380
The Respond Function   382
The Recover Function   383
The IBM Cloud   385
Oracle Cloud Infrastructure Security   386
Oracle SaaS Cloud Security Threat Intelligence   387
The Alibaba Cloud   388
Summary   389
References   389

Chapter 9	**The Future of Threat Hunting**	**391**
	Artificial Intelligence and Machine Learning	393
	How ML Reduces False Positives	395
	How Machine Intelligence Applies to Malware Detection	395
	How Machine Intelligence Applies to Risk Scoring	
	in a Network	396
	Advances in Quantum Computing	396
	Quantum Computing Challenges	398
	Preparing for the Quantum Future	399
	Advances in IoT and Their Impact	399
	Growing IoT Cybersecurity Risks	401
	Preparing for IoT Challenges	403
	Operational Technology (OT)	405
	Importance of OT Security	406
	Blockchain	406
	The Future of Cybersecurity with Blockchain	407
	Threat Hunting as a Service	407
	The Evolution of the Threat-Hunting Tool	408
	Potential Regulatory Guidance	408
	Summary	409
	References	409
Part V	**Appendices**	**411**
Appendix A	**MITRE ATT&CK Tactics**	**413**
Appendix B	**Privilege Escalation**	**415**
Appendix C	**Credential Access**	**421**
Appendix D	**Lateral Movement**	**431**
Appendix E	**Command and Control**	**435**
Appendix F	**Data Exfiltration**	**443**
Appendix G	**MITRE Cloud Matrix**	**447**
	Initial Access	447
	Drive-by Compromise	447
	Exploiting a Public-Facing Application	450
	Phishing	450
	Using Trusted Relationships	451
	Using Valid Accounts	452
	Persistence	452
	Manipulating Accounts	452
	Creating Accounts	453
	Implanting a Container Image	454
	Office Application Startup	454
	Using Valid Accounts	455
	Privilege Escalation	456
	Modifying the Domain Policy	456
	Using Valid Accounts	457

Defense Evasion 457
  Modifying Domain Policy 457
  Impairing Defenses 458
  Modifying the Cloud Compute Infrastructure 459
  Using Unused/Unsupported Cloud Regions 459
  Using Alternate Authentication Material 460
  Using Valid Accounts 461
Credential Access 461
  Using Brute Force Methods 461
  Forging Web Credentials 462
  Stealing an Application Access Token 462
  Stealing Web Session Cookies 463
  Using Unsecured Credentials 464
Discovery 464
  Manipulating Account Discovery 464
  Manipulating Cloud Infrastructure Discovery 465
  Using a Cloud Service Dashboard 466
  Using Cloud Service Discovery 466
  Scanning Network Services 467
  Discovering Permission Groups 467
  Discovering Software 468
  Discovering System Information 468
  Discovering System Network Connections 469
Lateral Movement 469
  Internal Spear Phishing 469
  Using Alternate Authentication Material 470
Collection 471
  Collecting Data from a Cloud Storage Object 471
  Collecting Data from Information Repositories 471
  Collecting Staged Data 472
  Collecting Email 473
Data Exfiltration 474
  Detecting Exfiltration 474
Impact 475
  Defacement 475
  Endpoint Denial of Service 475
  Resource Hijacking 477

Appendix H   Glossary **479**

Index **489**

Foreword

 The book you're about to read fills a much-needed gap in cloud cybersecurity. A little over two years ago, a couple of cybersecurity experts stopped to grab a coffee after a long day at a technical conference in Las Vegas. As the conversation progressed, the friends realized one of the topics they most wanted to learn more about wasn't being addressed by any of the conference sessions: cross-cloud threat hunting.

How did they know it was a topic that needed to be covered? Because each of them had experienced the need first hand. Chris Peiris built an early cyber fusion center for Microsoft and joined Avanade to build out their fusion center with side-by-side Azure and AWS capability. Based in Australia, Chris now works with the AU DoD and has seen how multi-cloud security has gone from a business requirement to a regulatory one with new legislation in Australia that demands a multi-cloud approach to prevent vendor lock-in. As the Global Director, Strategy & Business Development for Security at Microsoft, Binil Pillai works with corporate executives and understands that true organizational security means being able to hunt for vulnerabilities and exposures across multiple different cloud providers. His experience with threat-hunting product development also contributed to build the concept of this book. As an award-winning CISO and Microsoft's Chief Cybersecurity Advisor for APAC, Abbas Kudratri knows first-hand the security challenges governments and large enterprises face as they transform from on-premise to cloud-based.

Based on their different experiences, the authors bring their own cross-cloud viewpoints to the book. They worked collaboratively to improve content and coverage: augmenting one another's knowledge to create a truly comprehensive text. And to keep it effective and focused, Chris, Binil, and Abbas have divided the book into multiple parts. The first part focuses on the big picture and how to make board members "cyber smart" about cross-cloud threat hunting. The authors carefully picked real-world examples and case studies that will really matter to executives and enumerate the key business drivers. They also provide guidance on whether or not an organization should staff and manage their own in-house threat-hunting team, or partner with an external provider for the best return on investment.

The latter part of the book provides a deep how-to technical guide for cross-cloud threat hunting. One of the challenges security experts face is a lack of normalization from one cloud to the next. Although most large cloud vendors have native tooling (such as Azure Defender and AWS GuardDuty), it can be quite confusing going from one to the other since interfaces are different, features are different, and each security models are different. In fact, even between services on the same provider, there can be differences. And when your company spans both clouds, you need a way to threat hunt across the entire environment. Since hunting in a vacuum isn't effective, the authors use the industry-leading MITRE ATT&CK Framework as a reference architecture against which hunting activities and progress can be mapped. The final chapter provides their insight about the future of threat hunting, leveraging current technology trends and the potential evolution of threat-hunting practices by cloud service providers.

After many months of work, a lot of late nights, and, yes, some additional caffeine, this book is ready for you. Whether you're a CISO who needs to explain cross-cloud threat hunting to the executive board, or a fusion center director looking to increase your teams' threat-hunting skills, there's something here to help bring your organization to a better security state. Multi-cloud deployments are here to stay, and you need this book to help you stay safe cross-cloud.

Diana Kelley

CTO & Co-Founder, SecurityCurve

www.securitycurve.com

Introduction

The rise of cybercrime has created an insatiable appetite for threat hunting. Many organizations take a reactive approach to cybersecurity. Often, the first indication that something is happening on their network is when they receive an alert about an attack in progress. However, by this point, it may already be too late to stop the attack. In today's challenging and rapidly changing environment, cyberthreat actors are becoming increasingly sophisticated, and many of them can remain undetected until they achieve their objectives. By taking a proactive approach to security, security teams can identify infections while they are still in the "stealth" phase, allowing them to be remediated before they do significant damage to the organization. To do this, the security team needs to learn to *threat hunt*.

Threat hunting is a critical focus area to increase the cybersecurity posture of any organization. Threat hunting can be performed in a proactive context (referred to as ethical hacking) or in a defensive context to combat bad actors from penetrating the organization's defenses. Several industry best practices provide a threat-hunting framework that can act as a set of guidelines for organizations. The MITRE ATT&CK (Adversarial Tactics, Techniques & Common Knowledge) Framework is highly regarded in the cybersecurity industry as one of the most comprehensive catalogs of attacker techniques and tactics. Threat hunters use this framework to look for specific techniques that attackers often use to penetrate defenses.

Testing that incorporates a comprehensive view of an environment's ability to monitor and detect malicious activity with the existing tools that defenders have deployed across an organization is critical to safeguard against cyberattacks. There are some practical questions we are presented with on a daily basis while implementing cloud cybersecurity solutions to expedite digital transformation projects globally. These questions are specifically:

- What are the critical business and technical drivers of a threat-hunting framework in today's rapidly changing cloud environments?
- Is there an industry-leading framework to ensure whether we address all known attack vectors?
- What are the human elements that organizations need to focus on for building internal capability or source threat-hunting capability from external cloud providers?
- What metrics are available to assess threat-hunting effectiveness irrespective of the organization's size—from enterprise or small- to medium-sized businesses?
- Is there a catalog or a reference architecture artifact that can assist both business and technical users in addressing each attack vector?
- How does threat hunting work with vendor-specific single cloud security offerings?
- How does threat hunting work on multi-cloud implementations?
- What do industry-leading cloud providers, such as Amazon Web Services (AWS) and Microsoft Azure, provide as building blocks to combat offensive and defensive threat-hunting capabilities?
- What is the future of threat hunting?

These questions were confronted by Dr. Chris Peiris in a real-world scenario when he was presented with an opportunity to build a "side-by-side" cybersecurity fusion center implementation on the Microsoft Azure and AWS technology platforms. He noticed there is a growing customer requirement to enable a "multi-cloud" strategy with enterprise customers. Chris, in collaboration with Binil and Abbas, started to address this growing, ever-increasing customer demand.

They noticed that the primary motivations for customer organizations to have a tailored cybersecurity risk framework are to avoid "vendor locking" to a specific technology platform and to meet regulatory compliance requirements. This approach ensures vendor neutrality and rapid disaster recovery for the organization from a risk-mitigation perspective. This will help organizations strategize their security posture and build a threat-hunting ecosystem that ensures long-term sustainability. Therefore, counter to the popular sentiment of Cloud Service Providers (CSPs) competing for market share, there is a growing "synergy framework" that enables the CSPs to work together to address customer requirements.

As a practical example, an email phishing attack can be detected by the Microsoft Defender for Office 365 tool via the organization's Azure or Windows assets. The same threat hunting can be achieved via Amazon's GuardDuty cloud-offering tool. It is practical to build a multi-cloud threat-hunting framework that can leverage the best of both worlds from multiple cloud providers to address the organization's specific cybersecurity risks.

This multi-cloud synergy framework enables a rich toolset for an organization to increase its security posture and leverage CSP's global threat intelligence assets. The organization can significantly improve its security postures by partnering with CSPs using this multi-cloud capability.

This book aims to present a threat-hunting framework that enables organizations to implement multi-cloud security toolsets to increase their security posture. We focus on the AWS and Microsoft security toolsets and address the most common threat vectors using the MITRE ATT&CK Framework as a reference architecture. We also address the future of threat hunting in relation to AI, machine learning, quantum computing, and IoT proliferation. This book is a practical guide for any organization aiming to build, optimize, and advance its threat-hunting requirements. It provides a comprehensive toolset to accelerate business growth with secured digital transformation and regulatory compliance activities.

What Does This Book Cover?

Many organizations are quickly discovering that threat hunting is the next step in the evolution of the modern Security Operations Center (SOC), but remain unsure of how to start hunting or how far along they are in developing their own hunting capabilities. We believe this book addresses a gap in the market. There are several books on threat-hunting frameworks and how to use them in on-premise environments (as opposed to cloud/CSP implementations). The threat-hunting capability on cloud assets is mainly unexplored. This book also addresses the people (the human element) and the business measurements to consider in order to successfully adopt a threat-hunting framework. There is practical guidance to implement a threat-hunting framework irrespective of the organization's size and maturity.

There are specific vendors' blog posts/articles and "how-to guides" to address individual threat vectors. However, there is no definitive guide on how threat hunting works on Microsoft or AWS to address all major attack vectors. That's where this book comes in.

Can an organization build a comprehensive threat-hunting framework addressing all the common attack vectors using cloud assets? This book attempts to address these key questions on the AWS and Microsoft cloud platforms.

The contents in the book are prepared to serve business decision makers like board members, CXOs, and CISOs, as well as a technical audience. Business users will find the technology-agnostic cloud threat-hunting methodology framework valuable to manage their cybersecurity risks. Technical users will benefit from the how-to guide on Microsoft Azure and AWS to address these risks. There are no other books in the market that address Microsoft Azure and AWS side by side. You will also get an opportunity to learn to use the best of both worlds in Microsoft Azure and AWS (i.e., you can create a solution where endpoint detection and response is addressed by Microsoft, with Microsoft Defender for Endpoint, and information management is done by AWS Macie).

We have structured the book in five parts:

- **Part I:** An introduction to threat-hunting concepts and industry frameworks that address threat hunting. This section is targeted toward business decision makers such as the board members, the CXOs, and the CISOs.

- **Part II:** How does Microsoft Azure address key threats? This section is targeted toward a technical audience.

- **Part II:** How does AWS address key threats? This is targeted toward a technical audience, similar to the previous section.

- **Part IV:** Other cloud threat-hunting platforms and the future of threat hunting. This is targeted toward business decision makers, technical professionals, and anyone who wants to learn the potential future threat-hunting trends.

- **Part V:** Appendices. These mainly contain MITRE ATT&CK Framework reference material that correlates to key attack vectors that the book explores.

Here is a further breakdown of chapter contents.

Part I: Threat Hunting Frameworks

Chapter 1: Introduction to Threat Hunting   This chapter sets the context of rising cybercrime, and the key threat attack vectors such as phishing, ransomware, and nation state attacks. The chapter further explores the necessity of threat hunting, how threat hunting affects organizations of all sizes, the threat-hunting maturity model, and the human elements of threat hunting. Finally, this chapter recommends a few priorities that can help any organization build a foundation to make the board of directors cyber-smart.

Chapter 2: Modern Approach to Multi-Cloud Threat Hunting   This chapter discusses multi-cloud and multi-tenant environments and how Security Operation Centers (SOCs) are designed to monitor their activities. We explore threat modeling and threat-hunting goals and objectives. The chapter provides fresh insights for organizations keen to learn about the skillsets required for threat hunting and the metrics available to measure the effectiveness of threat hunting.

Chapter 3: Exploration of MITRE Key Attack Vectors   This chapter explains how you can leverage ATT&CK tactics and techniques to enhance, analyze, and test your threat-hunting efforts. The objective is to illustrate how to prevent bad actors from penetrating defenses by focusing on a few key attack vectors in this chapter. We leverage privilege escalation, credential access, lateral movement, command and control, and exfiltration as these are essential methods and analyze in-depth with real-world examples (using case studies). We also discuss the Zero Trust Architecture Framework as a key enabler for threat prevention.

Part II: Hunting in Microsoft Azure

Chapter 4: Microsoft Azure Cloud Threat Prevention Framework   This chapter explores Microsoft's threat-hunting capabilities in detail. The chapter introduces Microsoft security concepts and discusses its relevance to the shared responsibility model. This is followed by a detailed how-to guide on preventing privilege escalation, credential access, lateral movement, command and control, and exfiltration Tactics Techniques, and Procedures (TTPs). It also explains how to automate some of your hunting tasks using Microsoft security services on Microsoft 365 and Azure capabilities.

Chapter 5: Microsoft Cybersecurity Reference Architecture and Capability Map   This chapter focuses on the Microsoft Cybersecurity Reference Architecture. The chapter explores the "wider Microsoft reference" architecture for all TTPs discussed in the MITRE ATT&CK Framework. We also discuss the NIST Framework's alignment to the Microsoft reference architecture.

Part III: Hunting in AWS

Chapter 6: AWS Cloud Threat Prevention Framework   This chapter covers AWS threat-hunting capabilities in detail. We address the five key threat TTPs (i.e., prevention of privilege escalation, credential access, lateral movement, command and control, and exfiltration) and include a how-to guide similar to Chapter 4. The objective is to expose the reader to the similarities as to how these threat vectors are addressed on multiple cloud platforms.

Chapter 7: AWS Reference Architecture   This chapter covers AWS Reference Architecture on threat hunting. We followed the same format as Chapter 5 to illustrate the similarities of multiple cloud platforms. The chapter explores wider threat-hunting capabilities available in AWS on top of the five TTPs discussed in Chapter 6.

Part IV: The Future

Chapter 8: Threat Hunting in Other Cloud Providers This chapter focuses on the threat-hunting capability stack that aligns to the MITRE ATT&CK Framework available from other major cloud platform service providers, such as Google Cloud Platforms (GCP), IBM, Oracle, and Alibaba (Ali Cloud). The chapter provides an overview of how these leading cloud platform providers of IaaS, PaaS, and SaaS have built or adopted threat-hunting capabilities to protect their customer's data.

Chapter 9: The Future of Threat Hunting This chapter explores the future of threat hunting and the technological advances challenging the current threat-hunting landscape. In this chapter, we discuss the importance of bringing all relevant capabilities together and integrating them. This includes artificial intelligence, machine learning, quantum proof cryptography, the Internet of things (IoT), operational technology, cybersecurity blockchain, threat hunting as a service, and regulatory compliance challenges.

Part V: Appendices

Appendix A: MITRE ATT&CK Tactics This appendix details the complete list of TTPs available in the MITRE ATT&CK Framework.

Appendix B: Privilege Escalation This appendix addresses an in-depth analysis of tactics and subtactics of the privilege escalation TTP.

Appendix C: Credential Access This appendix addresses an in-depth analysis of tactics and subtactics of the credential access TTP.

Appendix D: Lateral Movement This appendix addresses an in-depth analysis of tactics and subtactics of the lateral movement TTP.

Appendix E: Command and Control This appendix addresses an in-depth analysis of tactics and subtactics of the command and control TTP.

Appendix F: Data Exfiltration This appendix addresses an in-depth analysis of tactics and subtactics of the data exfiltration TTP.

Appendix G: MITRE Cloud Matrix This appendix addresses an in-depth analysis of the cloud matrix by the MITRE ATT&ACK Framework.

Appendix H: Glossary This appendix contains definitions of various industry terms used in the book.

Additional Resources

In addition to this book, here are some other resources that can help you learn more:

The MITRE ATT&CK Framework:

https://attack.mitre.org/

Microsoft Security:

https://docs.microsoft.com/security/

AWS Security:

https://aws.amazon.com/security/

Google Cloud Platform Security:

https://cloud.google.com/security/

How to Contact the Publisher

If you believe you've found a mistake in this book, please bring it to our attention. At John Wiley & Sons, we understand how important it is to provide our customers with accurate content, but even with our best efforts, an error may occur.

In order to submit your possible errata, please email it to our Customer Service Team at wileysupport@wiley.com with the subject line "Possible Book Errata Submission".

Threat Hunting Frameworks

In This Part

Chapter 1: Introduction to Threat Hunting
Chapter 2: Modern Approach to Multi-Cloud Threat Hunting
Chapter 3: Exploration of MITRE Key Attack Vectors

Introduction to Threat Hunting

What's in This Chapter

- The rise of cybercrime
- What is threat hunting?
- Key cyberthreats and threat actors
- Why is threat hunting relevant to all organizations?
- Does an organization's size matter?
- Threat modeling
- Threat hunting maturity model
- Human elements of threat hunting
- How do you make the board of directors cyber-smart?
- Threat hunting team structure
- The threat hunter's role

The Rise of Cybercrime

> **"If you protect your paper clips and diamonds with equal vigor. . .you'll soon have more paper clips and fewer diamonds."**
>
> *—Attributed to Dean Rusk, U.S. Secretary of State 1961–1969*

This quote was first mentioned decades ago in the context of the cold war. However, it still resonates today, especially with the rise of cybercrime we are currently experiencing. Modern cybercrime is a sophisticated business with complex supply-chain activities and multiple threat actors working together in synergy. The threat actors are practicing division of labor, where one team is deployed to penetrate defenses and another team is subsequently employed to exploit the data breach. This level of sophistication is possible due to the staggering rewards cybercriminals and organized crime syndicates are achieving.

In 2009, the cost of cybercrime to the global economy was USD 1 trillion according to McAfee, the Silicon Valley based cybersecurity vendor, in a presentation to the World Economic Forum (WEF) in Davos, Switzerland. McAfee has since announced that cybercrime is estimated to top USD 6 trillion by 2021, according to Cybersecurity Ventures. This has been a significant increase in the last few years. The Cybersecurity Ventures report continues to elaborate that "if cybercrime is a country, it will be the third largest economy after the U.S. and China in the context of Gross Domestic Product (GDP) comparisons."

Cybercriminals can be found globally and have different skillsets and motivations. Some types of cybercrime persist independent of economic, political, or social changes, while certain types are fueled by ideology and monetary gain. The cyber defenders and the industry face an extremely diverse set of criminal actors and their ever-evolving tactics and techniques. These threat actors are opportunistic in nature. These cybercriminals capitalize on disruptive events such as the COVID-19 pandemic. As COVID-19 spread globally, cybercriminals pivoted their lures to imitate trusted sources like the World Health Organization (WHO) and other national health organizations, in an effort to get users to click on malicious links and attachments.

The recent Solorigate nation state attack is another example of multi-layer sophisticated attacks. These attacks were driven by ideology, not pure monetary gain. We discuss this nation state attack in detail later in the chapter. These examples illustrate that cybersecurity is a key focus area for any organization in our modern cloud-centric world. The proliferation of private cloud, hybrid cloud, and public cloud has introduced another layer of sophistication/increased attack vectors for cyberattacks. Therefore, more focus should be on preventative methods to ensure "modern IT diamonds are secured" in relation to Dean Rusk's comments many decades earlier.

Email phishing in the enterprise context continues to grow and has become a dominant vector. Given the increase in available information regarding these schemes and technical advancements in detection, the criminals behind these attacks are now spending significant time, money, and effort to develop scams that are sufficiently sophisticated to victimize even savvy professionals. Attack techniques in phishing and business email compromises are evolving. Previously, cybercriminals focused their efforts on malware attacks, but they have shifted their focus to ransomware, as well as phishing attacks with the goal of harvesting user credentials. Human-operated ransomware gangs are performing massive, wide-ranging sweeps of the Internet, searching for vulnerable entry points. These vulnerable entry points will be controlled by sophisticated "command and control" systems to disrupt organizations via distributed denial of service (DDoS) attacks at the attacker's discretion. Defending against cybercriminals is a complex, ever-evolving, and never-ending challenge.

NOTE According to Cybersecurity Ventures, global cybercrime costs will grow by 15% per year over the next five years, reaching USD 10.5 trillion annually by 2025.

It is estimated that 50% of the world's data will be stored in the cloud infrastructure by 2025. This equates to approximately 100 zettabytes of data across public clouds, government-owned clouds, private clouds, and cloud storage providers. This exponential data growth provides incalculable opportunities for cybercriminals because data is the fundamental building block of the digitized economy. Chief Information Security Officers (CISOs) and security teams are burdened by conventional solutions that can't adapt to the cloud to effectively prevent cyberattacks. And pressures continue to mount as employees produce, access, and share more data remotely through cloud apps during disruptive events such as COVID-19.

NOTE The *IBM Cost of Data Breach Report 2020* reports the following:

- The average cost of a data breach is USD 3.86 million.
- The U.S. has the most expensive data breaches.
- Healthcare is the most vulnerable industry; the average cost is USD 7.13 million.
- The average time to identify and contain a breach is 280 days.

It's staggering to comprehend that an adversary could be "lurking" inside your enterprise for 280 days/9+ months before being discovered and contained. Organizations are required to combat these growing threats and increase their security posture. They have to be proactive in their defense strategies. They also have to react very quickly when the enterprise is under attack. Threat hunting is a key tool available for defenders to protect their digital assets against their adversaries.

What Is Threat Hunting?

There are many different approaches to increasing an organization's cybersecurity defenses against adversaries. One fundamental solution is known as *threat hunting*. Threat hunting provides a proactive opportunity for an organization to uncover attacker presence in an environment. While no formal academic definition exists for threat hunting, leading global cybersecurity authority SANS defines threat hunting as the "proactive, analyst-driven process to search for attacker tactics, techniques, and procedures (TTP) within an environment." Attacker TTP must be researched and understood to know what to search for in collected data. Information about attacker TTP most often derives from signatures, indicators, and behaviors observed from threat intelligence sources. This added context should include targeted facilities, what systems were affected, protocols manipulated, and any other information pertinent to better understanding an attacker's TTP.

> **"Knowledge is power. For security professionals to create successful defense strategies, they need more diverse and timelier insights into the threats they are defending."**
>
> —*Microsoft Cybersecurity Intelligence Report, 2020*

The threat hunt requires accurate threat intelligence to achieve success. The formal model for threat hunting ensures the focus of the hunt remains on the attacker's outlined purpose of the hunt. This also maximizes the usage of threat intelligence. The presented formal threat hunt model is also agnostic of the analytic techniques employed throughout the hunt, allowing the model flexibility to work with any hunting tools or techniques (i.e., artificial intelligence and machine learning tools, etc.). Threat hunting requires a formal process to protect the integrity and rigor of the analysis; it's similar to incident response in that it requires a formal process to handle an investigation rigorously.

The methodology employed by the adversaries is similar despite the sophistication and diversity of the attacks. It is irrelevant whether attackers use large-scale attacks for financial gain or targeted attacks to support geopolitical interests. A phishing email can be a generic campaign targeting millions of users or a targeted single user (i.e., referred to *spear phishing*, which we will discuss later in the next section) that represents a socially engineered campaign over many months.

Spoofed domains, referred to as *homoglyphs*, can be used to trick victims; for example, `Microsoft.com` and `Micr0soft.com`, where the first "o" is replaced by a zero digit and can be easily overlooked by human readers. This malicious domain, `Micr0soft.com`, then can be leveraged to distribute malware, steal credentials, or support a fraudulent website. Subsequently, the same malware can be used to create a *botnet* (an industry term for a "web robot") to facilitate a DDoS attack against an organization, distribute ransomware, or steal sensitive information in relation to a nation's critical infrastructure.

The defenders leverage threat hunting to combat adversary behavior to protect against cyberattacks. The defenders use multiple tools and methods to achieve this goal. The defenders investigate commonalities across various environments and ecosystems to understand and disrupt these attack vectors such as phishing, spear phishing, homoglyphs, etc. The defenders dismantle the criminals' infrastructure, sharing information gathered through the course of their investigations. These additional insights are shared globally through defender intelligence networks to increase the security posture of the global software ecosystem. Let's investigate the key cyberthreats and threat actors and explore the key attack vectors the adversaries leverage to penetrate an organization's defenses.

The Key Cyberthreats and Threat Actors

There are numerous threat hunting battlegrounds that cybercriminals utilize to penetrate the organization's defenses. We will discuss in detail a comprehensive set of techniques, tactics, and procedures (TTPs) via the MITRE ATT&CK frameworks in Chapter 3. Following are the most important key battlegrounds. We will discuss them further elaborating with TTPs in Chapter 3.

Phishing

It is estimated that more than 90% of all cyberattacks were initiated via phishing attacks. Phishing is defined by using email as the attack vector to inject malicious code or diverting the user to a "phony site" to harvest user credentials. This is a very popular attack vector leveraged by cybercriminals due to its low barrier to entry and high successful click-through rates by unsuspecting victims. Phishing is usually accredited to mass email campaigns. However, sophisticated cybercriminals target specific individuals and organizations exclusively. This is commonly referred to as *spear phishing*.

Spear phishing is an increasingly common form of phishing that uses information about a target to make attacks more specific and "personal." These attacks may, for instance, refer to their targets by their specific name or job position, instead of using generic titles like in broader phishing campaigns do.

> "Some 91% of cyberattacks begin with a spear phishing email. According to a Trend Micro report, 94% of targeted emails use malicious file attachments as the payload or infection source. The remaining 6% use alternative methods such as installing malware through malicious links."
>
> —*Antony Savvas at Computerworld UK*

According to Trend Micro, the most commonly used file types for spear phishing attacks, accounting for 70% of them, are .RTF (38%), .XLS (15%), and .ZIP (13%). Executable (.EXE) files were not as popular among cybercriminals since emails with .EXE file attachments are usually detected and blocked by firewalls and security intrusion detection systems. Trend Micro also suggests that 75% of email addresses for spear phishing targets are easily found through web searches or using common email address formats.

Figure 1.1 illustrates the credential phishing process. Cybercriminals begin by setting up a criminal infrastructure designed to steal an individual's credentials. Note that there are phishing kits available on the "dark web" to facilitate this process. Cybercriminals send malicious emails to the unsuspecting individual, who then clicks on a link within the email. The individual might then be taken to a fake web form that impersonates a real page (such as a bank login page) to enter their credentials, or the site might contain malware that's automatically downloaded to their device, capturing credentials stored on the device or in the browser memory. The victim's credentials are then collected by the cybercriminals, who use the credentials to gain access to legitimate websites or even to the victim's corporate network. This access can be temporary or turn the victim's machine into a zombie in persistent form, and they can receive commands from the Command and Control (C2) servers for the future gains.

Ransomware

There has been massive growth of ransomware in recent years. The bad actors are notorious for injecting ransomware into phishing emails to infect computers and mobile devices. This results in locking up files, and they often threaten complete destruction of data unless the organization pays the ransom.

NOTE   According to Cybersecurity Ventures, ransomware attacks are expected to hit businesses every 11 seconds and cost the world USD 20 billion by 2021.

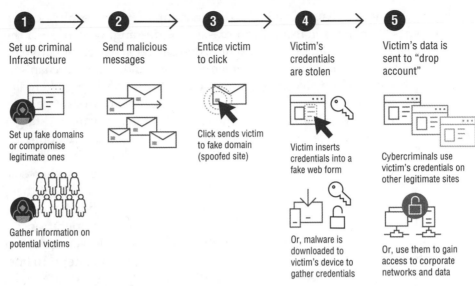

Figure 1.1: Phishing lifecycle implemented by cybercriminals

Note the ransomware damages are not limited to ransom payouts. The percentage of businesses and individuals who are paying via digital currencies (i.e., Bitcoin) to reclaim access to their data and systems are not accurately tracked. Therefore, the actual monetary impact of ransomware attacks could be seriously understated. Other ransomware costs include damage and destruction (or loss) of data, downtime, lost productivity, post-attack disruption to the normal course of business, forensic investigation, restoration and deletion of hostage data and systems, reputational harm, and employee training in direct response to the ransomware attacks.

Figure 1.2 illustrates the steady rise of ransomware from 2015 to 2021.

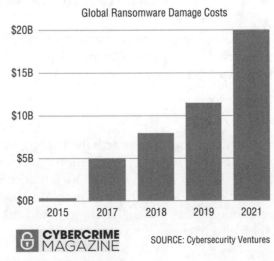

SOURCE: Cybersecurity Ventures

Figure 1.2: Global ransomware damage costs

Ransomware attacks have been increasing in complexity and sophistication over the years. Cybercriminals perform massive wide-ranging sweeps of the Internet to search for vulnerable entry points. Alternatively, they enter networks via "commodity Trojan malware" and leverage command and control mechanisms to attack at their discretion. Recently, commodity platforms are being offered in underground markets and the dark web with customizable ransomware tools (called *Ransomware-as-a-Service*), where one can build ransomware and target particular victims/organizations by subscribing to the service and customizing the payload based on the target vulnerabilities. As an example, cybercriminals used Dridex (a strain of banking malware that leverages macros in Microsoft Office) to gain initial access to networks, and then ransomed a subset of them with the DoppelPaymer ransomware during the 2019 Christmas holiday season.

WannaCry was one of the more sophisticated ransomware operations; it was targeted at many organizations, including but not limited to government agencies, utilities, and hospitals across the globe. During this incident, 16 hospitals in the UK were impacted and patients' lives were threatened due to the disruption and lack of access to their medical records.

As another example, cybercriminals exploited vulnerabilities in VPN and remote access devices to gain credentials, and then saved their access to use for ransoming hospitals and medical providers during the COVID-19 pandemic. Cybercriminals actively employ different tactics and change their tack based on the configurations they encounter in the network. They decide which data to exfiltrate, which persistence mechanisms to use for future access to the network, and ultimately, which ransomware payload to deliver.

> **"In some instances, cybercriminals went from the initial entry to ransoming the entire network in less than 45 minutes."**
>
> **—Microsoft Cybersecurity Intelligence Report**

Figure 1.3 shows an example of how various ransomware payloads are delivered according to the Microsoft Cybersecurity Intelligence Report. These attack vectors and tactics are explored in detail in Chapter 3.

Nation State

A nation state threat is defined as cyberthreat activity that originates in a particular country with the specific intent of furthering national interests. Nation state actors are well-funded, well-trained, and have more patience to play the "long game." These factors make the identification of anomalous activity very difficult. Similar to cybercriminals, they watch their targets and change techniques/tactics to increase their effectiveness.

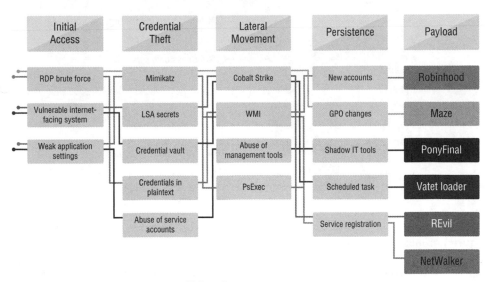

Figure 1.3: Ransomware tactics and lifecycle

The defenders investigate top-level trends in country-of-activity origin, targeted geographic regions, and the top nation state activity groups. According to the latest research, nation state activity is significantly more likely to target organizations outside of the critical infrastructure sectors. The most frequently targeted sector has been non-governmental organizations (NGOs). These are advocacy groups, human rights organizations, non-profit organizations, and think tanks focused on public policy, international affairs, or security. The nation state actors have these common operational aims regardless of the strategic objectives behind the activity:

- Espionage
- Disruption or destruction of data
- Disruption or destruction of physical assets

The most common attack techniques used by nation state actors are reconnaissance, credential harvesting, malware, and virtual private network (VPN) exploits. Advanced nation state adversaries invest heavily in the development of unique malware in addition to using openly available malicious code.

Surprisingly, nation state attackers have targeted "non-government" entities contrary to popular belief of focusing on government critical infrastructure. Figure 1.4 shows a breakdown of key industries that nation state attackers have focused on, according to the Microsoft Threat Intelligence Report.

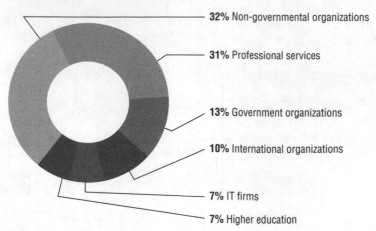

32% Non-governmental organizations

31% Professional services

13% Government organizations

10% International organizations

7% IT firms

7% Higher education

Figure 1.4: Industry breakdown of nation state attacks

> **NOTE**   According to the Microsoft Cybersecurity Intelligence Report, the country of origin of nation state attacks are Russia (52%), Iran (25%), China (12%), and North Korea and other (11%).
>
> Top targets are the U.S. (69%), United Kingdom (19%), Canada (5%), South Korea (4%), and Saudi Arabia (3%).

Combating nation state actors is a very complex process that involves both technology challenges and legal jurisdiction challenges. The Microsoft threat intelligence team published the threat actor report in Figure 1.5, which classifies each known threat actor (color-coded by nation state). Note the symbols of the periodic table are used to identify and classify the threat actors.

There are known threat actors (i.e., identified by Advanced Persistent Threat, or APT suffix) and other unique threat actors specifically engineered to bring down the defenses of the target nation.

The report continues to name the most common nation state threat actors, as shown in Figure 1.6.

Nation state attacks are "covert" in nature and are not exposed to public scrutiny. However, there have been some recent high-profile nation state attacks that captured the public's attention. The SolarWinds nation state attack (commonly referred to as *Solarigate*) was exposed in the late 2020 as one of these high-profile cyberattacks. Solorigate represents a modern cyberattack conducted by highly motivated actors who demonstrated they won't spare resources to reach their goal. The collective intelligence about this attack shows that, while hardening individual security domains is important, defending against today's advanced attacks necessitates a holistic multi-layer defense strategy. A summary of the key attack vectors is as follows:

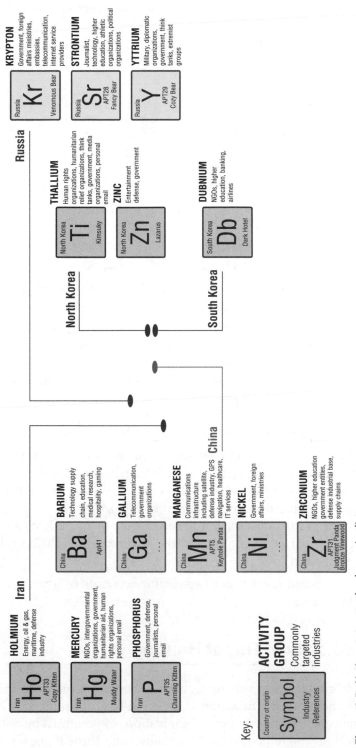

Figure 1.5: Nation state attack adversaries list

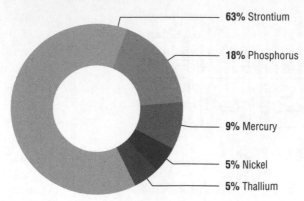

Figure 1.6: Breakdown of major nation state actors

- Compromise a legitimate binary (DLL file) belonging to the SolarWinds Orion Platform through a supply-chain attack.
- Deploy a backdoor malware on devices using the compromised binary to allow attackers to remotely control affected devices.
- Use the backdoor access on compromised devices to steal credentials, escalate privileges, and move laterally across on-premises environments to gain the ability to create Simple Access Mark-up Language (SAML) tokens. An intruder, using administrative permissions, gained access to an organization's trusted SAML token-signing certificate. This enabled them to forge SAML tokens that impersonate any of the organization's existing users and accounts, including highly privileged accounts.
- Initiate anomalous logins using the SAML tokens created by a compromised token-signing certificate, which can be used against any on-premises resources (regardless of identity system or vendor) as well as against any cloud environment (regardless of vendor), because they have been configured to trust the certificate. Because the SAML tokens are signed with their own trusted certificate, the anomalies might be missed by the organization.
- Access cloud resources to search for accounts of interest and exfiltrate data/emails.

The Necessity of Threat Hunting

In a digital climate that is changing at an incredibly rapid pace, it is unrealistic to believe that your organization will never be compromised. It is impossible to eliminate every threat to your organization, so you must be able to perform early detection and remediation. At the same time, think twice if you think your company is too small to be targeted by threat actors. Organizations are now going on the offensive and thinking about proactive ways to hunt for threats.

Three things are required before an adversary can be considered a threat: opportunity, intent, and capability to cause harm. No cybersecurity system is impenetrable or capable of recognizing or stopping every potential threat.

Hackers' tactics, weapons, and technologies are evolving so rapidly that by the time a new threat signature is learned, defenses may have already been compromised. Organizations are adopting the "assume breach" mentality to counter cyberattacks.

NOTE "Assume breach" is an approach that assumes that your enterprise is already breached and vulnerable. This is in contrast to stopping every cyberattack with the view of not being breached and accepting that the adversaries have already penetrated the enterprise. The focus is to change the security posture of the organization to be proactive, knowing adversaries are monitoring their digital assets.

An attacker's goal can change dramatically. This could be as simple as stealing valid login credentials to purchase Amazon goods or as sophisticated and dangerous as bringing down nuclear reactors, causing fatalities. Attackers use stolen credentials to carry out search-and-steal or search-and-destroy missions using tools and techniques unknown to end users. This enables them to go undetected and cause tremendous damage to intellectual property.

Threat hunting is necessary to counter the sophisticated techniques that cybercriminals use to evade detection by conventional means. Attackers are innovating at an alarming rate, creating new forms of attack. Organizations can't afford to wait weeks or months to learn about incidents. From the moment of intrusion, the cost, damage, and impact of an attack grows by the hour.

As a result, an increasing number of organizations are becoming proactive about threat hunting. Threat hunting focuses on identifying perpetrators who are already within the organization's systems and networks, and who have the three characteristics of a threat. Threat hunting is a formal process that is not the same as preventing breaches or eliminating vulnerabilities. Instead, it is a dedicated attempt to proactively identify adversaries who have already breached the defenses and found ways to establish a malicious presence in the organization's network.

NOTE The adoption of threat hunting signals a transition from reactive strategies to proactive ones, with companies looking for ways to tackle problems in a more timely and efficient way.

Threat hunting is human-driven, iterative, and systematic. Hence, it effectively reduces damage and overall risk to an organization. Its proactive nature

ensure all analysts are able to hunt and better protect critical business assets, regardless of their skill level.

The recommendation is to hire an outside security firm specialized in threat hunting for small and medium business organizations with no threat-hunting experience or for businesses without an IT department.

If your business lacks the budget to hire an external company, turn to software tools specializing in threat-hunting techniques. Some security software can automate the process to a degree.

Another area of focus is educating staff to prevent and recover from attacks. Cybercriminals leverage phishing emails to trick employees. Therefore, educate the organization's staff about the signs of phishing and other security best practices.

> **TIP**   For small businesses with limited resources, enlisting a threat-hunting service managed by an external security firm is an ideal approach. Before going that route, ensure your small business has taken steps to solidify your IT security:
>
> ■ Ensure company data is encrypted and backed up. Have one backup stored in the cloud.
> ■ Adopt a password-management service to require strong passwords and to avoid using the same passwords across accounts.
> ■ Go beyond traditional security software such as antivirus and firewalls. The best endpoint security software encompasses holistic protection features, including checks to determine if websites visited by your staff are safe.

Up-to-date IT defenses layered with threat hunting are a powerful combination. This puts your organization in a position to stop cyberattacks and keeps your business safe.

Many companies attempt threat hunting without establishing the right security foundations, which includes both technology (such as a well-managed network segmentation and access control) and mature security operations processes (such as incident response and log collection).

For small businesses, it's important to ensure that your organization is ready to threat hunt. You should have a fairly mature security setup capable of ingesting multiple sources of information and storing that information in a way that lets you access it.

Irrespective the size of the organization, businesses should assess their need to hunt threats in their environments, and then determine if they have the structure to support it.

Security leaders must consider the following three factors to determine whether threat hunting is for them:

■ Technology
■ Detection Process
■ People

Threat Modeling

Threat modeling is at the heart of threat hunting. There are different methodologies defined for threat modeling. Threat modeling should be improved over time by expanding the coverage and threat actors targeting the organization or same industry, and/or using similar platforms and attack applicability.

There are two prerequisites for threat modeling:

- Asset inventory with criticality levels should be defined.

- For each of those assets, security mitigation and defense controls, including but not limited to Firewall, IDS, Antimalware, Endpoint Detection Response (EDR), Data Leakage Prevention (DLP), Authentication, Authorization, and Encryption Controls should be listed.

Knowing what platforms, assets, and security controls are available helps threat-modeling and hunting teams define the scope and priorities of their planning. Depending on the maturity level, the scope should be started small and grow as the maturity level increases. Using the aforementioned items, threat-hunting finding and investigation should be prioritized based on its impact and likelihood. The threat model should be mapped based on the organization's assets.

Threat modeling is a systematic approach of proactively assessing the weakness of the IT environment and assets and, based on their criticality level and potential vulnerabilities, a remediation plan should be developed. Defining the scope plays a critical role as part of developing a successful threat-hunting program. The components outlined in Figure 1.7 are required before planning threat modeling.

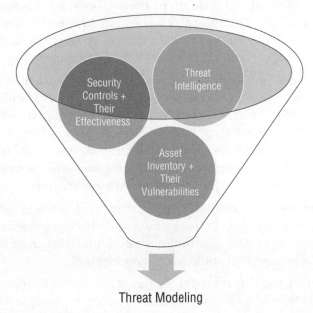

Threat Modeling

Figure 1.7: Components of threat modeling

There are several threat modeling methodologies available. One of the leading industry models is the Microsoft Security Development Lifecycle (SDL), as shown in Figure 1.8. It defines the threat modeling approach in the following five steps.

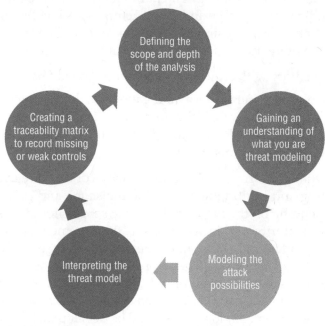

Figure 1.8: Microsoft Security Development Lifecycle

1. **Defining the scope and depth of the analysis.** At this stage, the scope and depth of threat hunting should be defined based on threat modeling. Obtaining a list of assets and their criticality assists with the rest of the process in scoping and defense and remediation planning.

2. **Gaining an understanding of what you are threat modeling.** At this stage, based on the collected system, threat hunters should understand the components of each asset. It helps them to profile the standard architecture and flag it in the future if suspicious changes and interconnections take place. Architecture diagrams at this stage should be gathered for further review. Furthermore, the business workflow gives the required insight to threat hunters for future behavioral analysis.

3. **Modeling the attack possibilities.** Defining a list of assets, existing security controls, and identified vulnerabilities and misconfigurations. In the next stage, a system architecture outlines a potential triggering threat agent or failing the control that could lead to an incident.

4. **Interpreting the threat model.** At this stage, threat hunters should wear their "hacker hats" and think similar to a hacker and analyze the possibilities.

Having the threat intelligence feeds at this stage helps to extract the required knowledge of threat actors and TTPs. Additionally, threat actors should constantly think of alternatives to bypass certain controls and be proactive.

5. **Creating a traceability matrix to record missing or weak controls.** At this point of threat modeling, based on the findings, mitigation control should be assessed:

   1. Threat agent
   2. Asset
   3. Attack surface
   4. Attach goal
   5. Impact

Threat hunters, by knowing these details and the threat landscape and current relevant threat actors and their TTPs, should also advise if any vulnerabilities need to be remediated or existing security controls are not sufficiently strong enough. This "risk rating" will be defined at this stage. If any of the aforementioned issues cannot be addressed at this point in time, the threat hunter should consider those issues as a high priority in their watch list.

Note that during this stage, business objectives and strategy should also be strongly considered. For instance, if it is a military organization, confidentiality and integrity are paramount. Applying this to a financial sector organization, availability should be added as an additional key concern.

The following questions should be answered regardless of what threat modeling techniques are leveraged:

- What is the defined scope? And what should be worked on?
- What are the odds? And what could fail or break?
- What is the action plan for them?
- Is our mitigation control effective enough?

There are various threat modeling tools and frameworks that could be utilized. Since our focus is on threat hunting, MITRE ATT&CK can be a better option to leverage (see Figure 1.9). The MITRE ATT&CK framework can be one of the key frameworks applied during the threat modeling process. However, it is important to take note that the MITRE ATT&CK focuses on potential attack vectors. Hence, during risk assessment, system criticality, threat impact, and the likelihood of modus operandi need to be considered. Therefore, participation of system and business owners are especially important during risk modeling when using the MITRE ATT&CK framework.

We will discuss the MITRE ATT&CK in detail in Chapter 3.

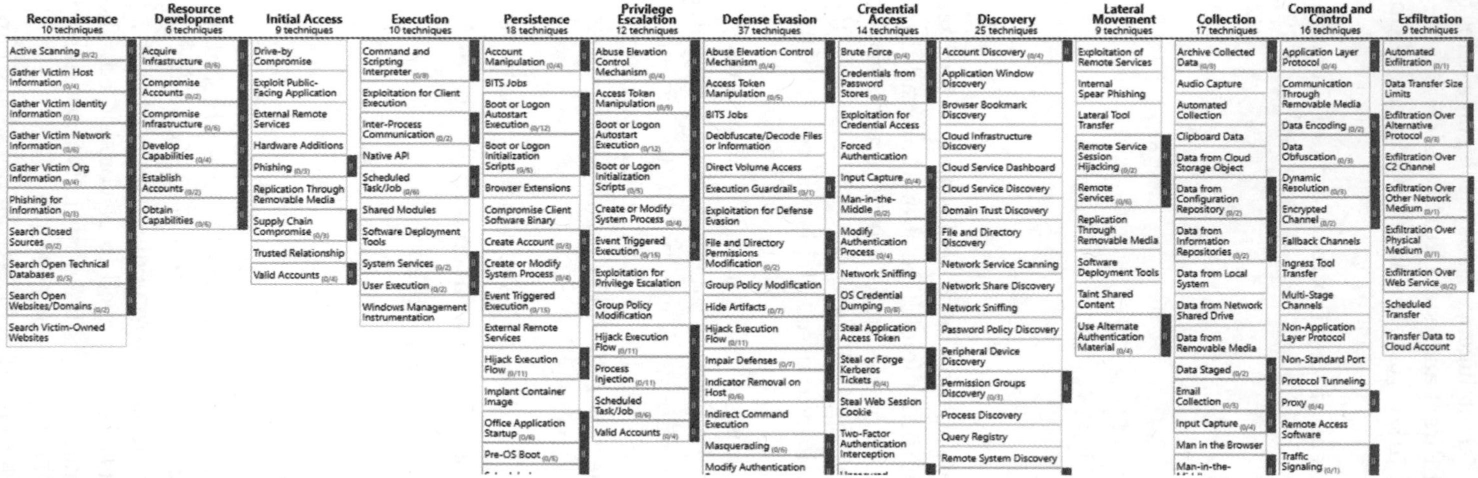

Figure 1.9: MITRE ATT&CK framework

Reconnaissance (10 techniques)	Resource Development (6 techniques)	Initial Access (9 techniques)	Execution (10 techniques)	Persistence (18 techniques)	Privilege Escalation (12 techniques)	Defense Evasion (37 techniques)	Credential Access (14 techniques)	Discovery (25 techniques)	Lateral Movement (9 techniques)	Collection (17 techniques)	Command and Control (16 techniques)	Exfiltration (9 techniques)
Active Scanning (0/2)	Acquire Infrastructure (0/6)	Drive-by Compromise	Command and Scripting Interpreter	Account Manipulation (0/4)	Abuse Elevation Control Mechanism (0/4)	Abuse Elevation Control Mechanism	Brute Force (0/4)	Account Discovery (0/4)	Exploitation of Remote Services	Archive Collected Data (0/3)	Application Layer Protocol (0/4)	Automated Exfiltration (0/1)
Gather Victim Host Information (0/4)	Compromise Accounts (0/2)	Exploit Public-Facing Application	Exploitation for Client Execution	BITS Jobs	Access Token Manipulation (0/5)	Access Token Manipulation	Credentials from Password Stores (0/5)	Application Window Discovery	Internal Spear Phishing	Audio Capture	Communication Through Removable Media	Data Transfer Size Limits
Gather Victim Identity Information (0/3)	Compromise Infrastructure (0/6)	External Remote Services	Inter-Process Communication (0/2)	Boot or Logon Autostart Execution (0/12)	Boot or Logon Autostart Execution (0/12)	BITS Jobs	Exploitation for Credential Access	Browser Bookmark Discovery	Lateral Tool Transfer	Automated Collection	Data Encoding (0/2)	Exfiltration Over Alternative Protocol (0/3)
Gather Victim Network Information (0/6)	Develop Capabilities (0/4)	Hardware Additions	Native API	Boot or Logon Initialization Scripts (0/5)	Boot or Logon Initialization Scripts (0/5)	Deobfuscate/Decode Files or Information	Forced Authentication	Cloud Infrastructure Discovery	Remote Service Session Hijacking (0/2)	Clipboard Data	Data Obfuscation (0/3)	Exfiltration Over C2 Channel
Gather Victim Org Information (0/4)	Establish Accounts (0/2)	Phishing (0/3)	Scheduled Task/Job (0/6)	Browser Extensions	Create or Modify System Process (0/4)	Direct Volume Access	Input Capture (0/4)	Cloud Service Dashboard	Remote Services (0/6)	Data from Cloud Storage Object	Dynamic Resolution (0/3)	Exfiltration Over Other Network Medium (0/1)
Phishing for Information (0/3)	Obtain Capabilities (0/6)	Replication Through Removable Media	Shared Modules	Compromise Client Software Binary	Event Triggered Execution (0/15)	Execution Guardrails (0/1)	Man-in-the-Middle (0/2)	Cloud Service Discovery	Replication Through Removable Media	Data from Configuration Repository (0/2)	Encrypted Channel (0/2)	Exfiltration Over Physical Medium (0/1)
Search Closed Sources (0/2)		Supply Chain Compromise (0/3)	Software Deployment Tools	Create Account (0/3)	Exploitation for Privilege Escalation	Exploitation for Defense Evasion	Modify Authentication Process	Domain Trust Discovery	Software Deployment Tools	Data from Information Repositories (0/2)	Fallback Channels	Exfiltration Over Web Service (0/2)
Search Open Technical Databases (0/5)		Trusted Relationship	System Services (0/2)	Create or Modify System Process (0/4)	Group Policy Modification	File and Directory Permissions Modification (0/2)	Network Sniffing	File and Directory Discovery	Taint Shared Content	Data from Local System	Ingress Tool Transfer	Scheduled Transfer
Search Open Websites/Domains (0/2)		Valid Accounts (0/4)	User Execution (0/2)	Event Triggered Execution (0/15)	Hijack Execution Flow (0/11)	Group Policy Modification	OS Credential Dumping (0/8)	Network Service Scanning	Use Alternate Authentication Material (0/4)	Data from Network Shared Drive	Multi-Stage Channels	Transfer Data to Cloud Account
Search Victim-Owned Websites			Windows Management Instrumentation	External Remote Services	Process Injection (0/11)	Hide Artifacts (0/7)	Steal Application Access Token	Network Share Discovery		Data from Removable Media	Non-Application Layer Protocol	
				Hijack Execution Flow (0/11)	Scheduled Task/Job (0/6)	Hijack Execution Flow (0/11)	Steal or Forge Kerberos Tickets (0/4)	Network Sniffing		Data Staged (0/2)	Non-Standard Port	
				Implant Container Image	Valid Accounts (0/4)	Impair Defenses (0/7)	Steal Web Session Cookie	Password Policy Discovery		Email Collection (0/3)	Protocol Tunneling	
				Office Application Startup (0/6)		Indicator Removal on Host (0/6)	Two-Factor Authentication Interception	Peripheral Device Discovery		Input Capture (0/4)	Proxy (0/4)	
				Pre-OS Boot (0/5)		Indirect Command Execution	Unsecured	Permission Groups Discovery (0/3)		Man in the Browser	Remote Access Software	
						Masquerading (0/6)		Process Discovery		Man-in-the-	Traffic Signaling (0/1)	
						Modify Authentication		Query Registry				
								Remote System Discovery				

One threat model cannot be applied for all systems since threat landscape and adversaries and TTPs may vary from one industry to another. The output of threat modeling is a list of threat-hunting procedures and processes customized for the organization. These procedures and processes should be automated where applicable.

Threat-Hunting Maturity Model

Many organizations are quickly discovering that threat hunting is the next step in the evolution of the modern Security Operations Center (SOC), but remain unsure of how to start hunting or how far along they are in developing their own hunting capabilities. How can you quantify where your organization stands in relation to effective hunting? With a general model that can map hunting maturity across organizations. Let's consider what constitutes a good hunting program with these questions in mind. There are three factors to consider when judging an organization's threat-hunting effectiveness program:

- The quality and quantity of the data they collect for hunting
- The tools they provide to access and analyze the data
- The skills of the analysts who actually use the data and the tools to find security incidents

Among these factors, the analysts' skills is probably the most important, since that allows them to turn data into "indicators of compromise (IOCs)." The quality and quantity of the data that an organization routinely collects from its IT environment is also a strong factor in determining the Hunting Maturity Model (HMM) level. The more data from around the enterprise (and the more different types of data) provided to an expert hunter, the more anomalies or IOCs they will discover. The toolsets you use will shape the style of your hunts and determine what kinds of hunting techniques you will be able to leverage.

> **"Threat hunting requires a lot of different data types and resources and needs special, expensive tools."**
>
> —*David Szili, SANS Institute, 2019*

Organization Maturity and Readiness

Threat hunting is one of the defense layers among other existing controls, tools, and processes to mitigate cyberthreats that is necessary for all organizations to have in place. However, CISOs and security strategists should also take note that efficient threat hunting will only be possible in a mature environment where required processes, technology, and people are in place.

An advanced state of the art of threat hunting is where Firewalls, Antivirus, EDR, DLP, and the Security Information and Event Management system (SIEM) are integrated and correlate the rich data. This will assist skillful security analysts leveraging the latest reliable threat intelligence IOC feeds and actionable tactics, techniques, and procedures coming together to find the potentially suspicious activity with minimum false positives. Threat hunting should be considered a "magic wand" that can resolve most of your security loopholes.

When threat intelligence was introduced, there was a misconception that the more threat feeds you had, the more you could protect. Many of those feeds were outdated and unreliable. On the contrary, loading a high volume of IOCs can slow down security appliances. Inspecting every single data packet against millions of IOCs is a very tedious task. Hence, the notion of "actionable and vetted IOCs" was introduced to streamline the threat-hunting process.

Analysts should perform gap assessments and understand the existing enterprise capabilities prior to launching a threat-hunting program. This will define their threat-hunting program, and investment in phases to reach to desired threat-hunting maturity level.

The HMM has five levels, as illustrated in Figure 1.10.

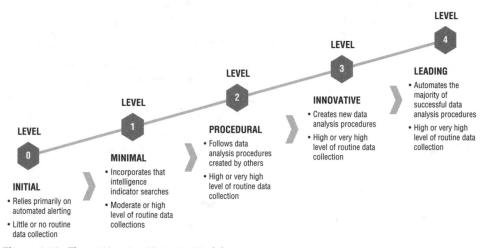

Figure 1.10: Threat Hunting Maturity Model

Level 0: INITIAL

At the foundation level, threat-hunting programs mainly rely on automated alerting tools and correlating tools such as WAF, antivirus, IDS, and SIEM. The collected information is not very comprehensive. Hence, threat hunting at this level is extremely limited and close to 0. No IT data is available at this stage.

Level 1: MINIMAL

Data collection scope is limited to the same automated alerting tools at level 1. However, IT data is included for daily incident response activity by leveraging threat intelligence feeds. Correlated data is usually pumped into the SIEM or into other log management tools. Security analysts at this stage can search based on the IOCs and TTPs for a number of malicious historical activities. However, it is still considered a poor threat-hunting capability.

Level 2: PROCEDURAL

Threat hunting at this level can usually start at the foundation level, where threat analysts and other researchers develop procedures and apply the same method in the organization. At this level, the organization's threat hunting is limited to procedures that are published or shared by other researchers or service providers. However, usually at this point, threat hunters are yet to develop their own customized or innovative procedure.

Level 3: INNOVATIVE

Threat hunters at this stage are more educated and skilled and have more practical knowledge of analysis techniques in order to identify malicious and suspicious activities. Additionally, they manage to obtain more data and use data visualization and machine learning techniques to develop their own procedures. They should be able to develop repeatable procedures. However, they may face challenges when the number of cases increases, and they cannot cope with the number of processes and events and analyze them in a timely manner.

Level 4: LEADING

In the previous section, it was mentioned that threat hunting is not an automated process by definition. At this level-4 stage, hunters should be able to automate the repetitive processes and tune the existing ones, and thanks to automation, they can dedicate more time to building new processes. While automation is increasing, it still requires hunters to frequently review existing cases to improve and build new ones. While there are commercial products that can help you with this automation process, automated services at this point can perform this high-quality human activity. Proper metrics are defined to monitor key performance indicators (KPIs) and Service Level Agreements (SLAs).

Automated risk scoring is leveraged using machine learning, with horizon scanning maintained for future technological developments. Hunts are occurring continuously, with successful analytics and discovered IOCs shared across the community, while the knowledge repository and workflows are integrated with the wider SOC. Data visibility is high across all relevant areas of the estate and is very well understood.

> **TIP** For organizations that are already hunting, the maturity model can be used both to measure their current maturity and provide a roadmap for improvement. Hunter teams can match their current capabilities to those described in the model, and then look ahead to develop/improve their skills and/or data collection abilities in order to achieve the next level of maturity. In order to get anywhere, you must first know where you are and where you are aiming to be.

Human Elements of Threat Hunting

> **NOTE** Threat hunting is a little bit of art, a little bit of science, and a little bit of technology. Human elements bring these all together with their knowledge and experience to mitigate the risk.

For thousands of years, humans have worked to collect intelligence from their enemies. Intelligence gathering is not a new practice; in fact, it is one of the oldest war tactics dating back to biblical times, when warlords and army commanders used it to gain advantages over their rivals.

> **"If you know the enemy and know yourself, you need not fear the results of a hundred battles."**
>
> —*The Art of War*, **Sun Tzu**

However, the methods and tactics have changed as new technologies and new forms of "warfare" have been developed. In recent years, cyberattacks have led to an entirely new host of intelligence challenges, especially for corporations, who are not accustomed to the practice of intelligence gathering the way governments are. Yet, CyberThreat Intelligence (CTI) can be critically important to how organizations defend against attacks and uncover their cyber adversaries.

There are many different forms of intelligence gathering, including Open-Source Threat Intelligence (OSINT), Machine Intelligence or Signals Intelligence (SIGINT), and Social Media Intelligence (SOCMINT). However, one source of intelligence that's often overlooked is Human Intelligence (HUMINT). HUMINT can be defined as the process of gathering intelligence through interpersonal contact and engagement, rather than by technical processes, feed ingestion, or automated monitoring. It's a risky practice that requires a very particular set of skills, but it can provide you with the most valuable intel. As threat actors' TTPs and attack strategies change, the one constant behind all attacks is that they are human-driven. Understanding an attacker's motives and tendencies can help organizations make the right strategic cybersecurity decisions.

A cyber intelligence program is all about uncovering who, what, where, when, why, and how behind a cyberattack. Tactical and operational intelligence can help identify the what and how of an attack, and sometimes the where and when. But it's difficult to discover the who and why behind an attack without human involvement and manual intelligence gathering. HUMINT can be used to support longer-term, strategic cybersecurity decisions, and should supplement any other intelligence gathering, feed ingestion, and cyber reconnaissance activities your team is doing. Therefore, manual and automated intelligence gatherings are not mutually exclusive, but rather complementary. Both are necessary for an advanced cybersecurity operation, which is why human-to-human research will always be a critical part of the threat-hunting process.

How Do You Make the Board of Directors Cyber-Smart?

As cyberthreats continue to escalate, boards of directors are becoming increasingly interested in cybersecurity and risk management. This is no surprise, as the board is ultimately held liable and responsible should a breach occur. And it's important because leadership sets the tone for the rest of the organization. They must lead by example when it comes to cybersecurity, and actively participate in, and be supportive of, the mission to be secure. As such, cybersecurity has made its way onto the agenda of many board meetings.

When it comes to threat hunting, the first question that every board of directors may ask is "why should we consider adding cyberthreat hunting to cybersecurity strategy?" This is a strategic question to ask. If your board of directors does not seem to be asking this question, they either are not fully aware of your broader cybersecurity strategy or they underestimate the risk of a potential cyberthreat. It is the responsibility of the CISO to educate the board of directors about the benefits of threat hunting, such as:

- Improve speed and accuracy of response
- Reduce actual breaches based on number of incidents detected thus minimize the reputational and financial damages
- Reduce exposure to external threats
- Reduce resources (i.e., staff hours, expenses) spent on responses

Many surveys conducted in the past show that the majority of organizations using threat-hunting tactics are recognizing measurable improvements in cybersecurity performance indicators.

Ultimately, the board of directors needs a basic education in threat hunting and its relationship to the cybersecurity strategy. It's up to you to provide them with the information that they need to know, so they can understand everything else. They simply can't wrap their minds around things they can't understand. If they don't have a foundation, the rest of the subject matter is going to be very difficult to understand. It's very important that they understand because you want them to approve the resources you need and the budget you want.

Here are a few ways that can help you build that foundation to make your board of directors cyber-smart:

- **Build cyber risk awareness:** Provide insights about the organization's critical information assets, how they are currently being protected and information about the primary risk that organization is facing.

- **Integrate cybersecurity into the enterprise-wide risk management and governance processes:** Organizations need to include Cybersecurity risks as part of their overall enterprise-wide risk management instead of looking at it as IT risk. Cybersecurity is a business priority and it impacts across the enterprise—inside and outside. Therefore, the enterprise level governance process can look at Cyber related risk and prioritize for action.

- **Educate about the importance of engaging attackers with active defense:** Threat hunting is a proactive technique that combines security tools, analytics, and threat intelligence with human analytics and instinct. There is a massive amount of information available about potential attacks—both from external intelligence sources and from an organization's own technology environment. The board of directors needs to know the value of threat-hunting capabilities to aggregate and analyze the most relevant information to proactively engage with attackers and tune defenses accordingly.

- **Keep them up-to-date:** Let them know what's going on in the threat environment. You can also include information on trends and future analysis. Be sure to touch on what your peers are doing as well.

- **Share success stories:** Let them know it's not all doom and gloom; that there are some positive things going on as well. It helps to buoy their spirits.

Cyberthreats are daunting. Not only are they complex and constantly evolving, they have the potential to impart significant financial and reputational damage to an organization. Plus, there's no way to be 100% protected. That's why cybersecurity is no longer just the responsibility of IT departments. Boards of directors are ultimately liable and responsible for the survival of their organizations, and in today's interconnected world, cyber resilience is a big part of that responsibility. That means that boards must take an active role in cybersecurity.

The boards of directors can take on the role of cybersecurity leaders within their organizations. The National Association of Corporate Directors (NACD)'s *Director's Handbook on Cyber-Risk Oversight* outlines five principles that all corporate boards should consider "as they seek to enhance their oversight of cyber risks:"

- **Directors need to understand and approach cybersecurity as an enterprise-wide risk management issue, not just an IT issue.** As much as we have been saying this, it's surprising how many organizations still associate information security or cybersecurity with IT. Even though most of the reporting structures come up through the IT department, it can't be the central focus because the impacts are organization-wide. The skillsets needed to manage the risks and deal with issues are organization-wide. The board needs to understand that a 1:1 with IT is a mistake, and it's been the underlying cause of many big breach events.

- **Directors should understand the legal and regulatory implications of cyber risks as they relate to their company's specific circumstances.** With responsibility comes accountability. Executive management and board members are being held accountable for many high-profile breaches, and in many cases losing their positions. Target CEO, President, and Chairman Gregg Steinhafel resigned from all his positions following the massive 2013 data breach. Equifax's CEO Richard Smith resigned following a backlash over the massive hack that compromised the data of an estimated 143 million Americans.

- **Boards should have adequate access to cybersecurity expertise and discussions about cyber risk management should be given regular and adequate time on the board's meeting agenda.** It's becoming more common to see board members who have a technological or security background. This expertise can really elevate a board's awareness. And more awareness is how we win against cybercriminals.

- **Directors should set the expectation that management will establish an enterprise-wide risk management framework with adequate staffing and budget.** The NACD handbook specifically mentioned the National Institute of Standards and Technology Cybersecurity Framework (NIST CSF), which was created to enable "organizations—regardless of size, degree of cybersecurity risk, or cybersecurity sophistication—to apply the principles and best practices of risk management to improving the security and resilience of critical infrastructure." When you're writing your policies or developing your program, having a framework to base it on is very helpful. There's no need to reinvent the wheel!

- **Board-management discussion of cyber risk should include identification of which risks to avoid, accept, mitigate, or transfer through insurance, as well as specific plans associated with each approach.** Effectively managing cybersecurity risk requires an understanding of the relative significance of organizational assets in order to determine the frequency by which they will be scrutinized for risk exposures. This is no small task. It takes considerable thought and effort, along with a great deal of cybersecurity expertise.

Threat-Hunting Team Structure

There are various structures for threat-hunting teams, and they depend more on an organization's culture and structure than on the size of the security team. The most common team structures are discussed in the following sections.

External Model

This model essentially outsources your threat-hunting activity and can introduce your organization to the concept and benefits of threat hunting. Nonetheless, an external team will never understand your environment like you do, and as a result, this model is less desirable in the long term.

Dedicated Internal Hunting Team Model

Typically, in large organizations and government entities, a small team of skilled, full-time employees are employed as threat hunters. They may have access to alerts from the organization's SOC. However, they are not spending most of their time on alert analysis. The drawback of this structure is creating silos between SOC analysts and hunt team members.

Combined/Hybrid Team Model

A team member might have a combined role of SOC analyst/threat hunter, incident responder/threat hunter, or security team member/threat hunter doing daily hunting in addition to their other duties. SOC analysts already have most of the skills required for threat hunting, so this is an obvious step forward for organizations. This is a typical model for smaller organizations or smaller teams with skilled analysts and strong detection capabilities. The risk in a combined role model is analysts might have other priorities, such as daily SOC operations, leaving no time for threat hunting at the end of the day.

Periodic Hunt Teams Model

In this model, security team members are periodically pulled away from other work to form a threat-hunting team. This might happen weekly, biweekly, or monthly, and it requires a clear plan with a specific task to be effective. This model works for large organizations with a large pool of SOC analysts as well as for smaller ones with a small security team, performing threat hunting just a few hours per week. It is important to rotate team members to give everyone exposure to threat hunting.

Urgent Need for Human-Led Threat Hunting

The most devastating cyberthreats generally involve human-led attacks, often exploiting legitimate tools and processes such as PowerShell. Hands-on live hacking enables attackers to modify their tactics, techniques, and procedures on the fly to bypass security products and protocols. Once inside a victim's network, attackers can move laterally, exfiltrate data, install malware and backdoors for future attacks, and deploy ransomware. While technology, particularly intelligent automated technology, has an important role to play, expert operators are still required. Stopping human-led attacks requires human-led threat hunting.

According to a Sophos survey of 5,000 IT managers, 48% already incorporated human-led threat hunts in their security procedures to identify attacker activity that may not be detected by security tools (e.g., SIEM, endpoint protection, firewall, etc.). See Figure 1.11. A further 48% plan to implement it. Respondents are also alert to the urgency of deploying human-led hunting, with virtually all (99.6%) respondents who want to implement it looking to do so within the next year.

The status of human-led threat hunting varies significantly by geography. Sixty-nine percent of respondents from China have already implemented this approach, closely followed by Spain (65%), India (61%), and South Africa (60%). Conversely, Turkey has been slowest to adopt human-led hunting with just 26% of respondents already doing it, with Nigeria (32%) and Poland (33%) only slightly ahead.

The Threat Hunter's Role

NOTE   There is a severe cybersecurity skills shortage. It is estimated that there were 3.5 million cyber jobs unfilled in 2020.

The rise of the threat hunter role creates some unique challenges related to the shortage of cybersecurity professionals. As more companies start to adopt security automation, the threat-hunting process steps outside of the box by requiring a highly trained human element.

Plans to incorporate human-led threat hunts

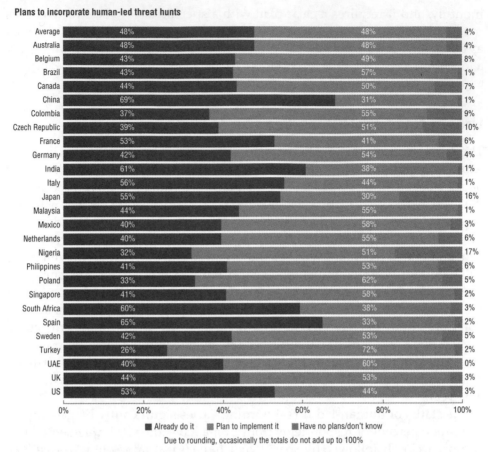

	Already do it	Plan to implement it	Have no plans/don't know
Average	48%	48%	4%
Australia	48%	48%	4%
Belgium	43%	49%	8%
Brazil	43%	57%	1%
Canada	44%	50%	7%
China	69%	31%	1%
Colombia	37%	55%	9%
Czech Republic	39%	51%	10%
France	53%	41%	6%
Germany	42%	54%	4%
India	61%	38%	1%
Italy	56%	44%	1%
Japan	55%	30%	16%
Malaysia	44%	55%	1%
Mexico	40%	58%	3%
Netherlands	40%	55%	6%
Nigeria	32%	51%	17%
Philippines	41%	53%	6%
Poland	33%	62%	5%
Singapore	41%	58%	2%
South Africa	60%	38%	3%
Spain	65%	33%	2%
Sweden	42%	53%	5%
Turkey	26%	72%	2%
UAE	40%	60%	0%
UK	44%	53%	3%
US	53%	44%	3%

■ Already do it   ■ Plan to implement it   ■ Have no plans/don't know
Due to rounding, occasionally the totals do not add up to 100%

Figure 1.11: Organizations show their willingness to implement human-led threat hunting

---

HOW CISO SHOULD APPROACH THREAT HUNTING

Threat hunting means you have moved past looking for indicators of compromise and are looking for patterns of compromise.

There are no "blue team" operations or "red team" operations. If you think about it that way, you will build silos when you are required to build barns. It is all about the network and endpoint.

You only have so many resources, and you only have so much time. Closely watch your security team to make sure nobody is burning out and maintain a good work/life balance. Train your people so they work for the best outcome.

While tier-1 and tier-2 analysts rely on alerts from systems and some combination of manual and automated workflow to escalate and respond to security events, the threat-hunting process hinges on an expert's ability to create hypotheses and to hunt for patterns and indicators of compromise in data-driven networks. Usually, that means tier-3 security analysts with the experience and creativity to proactively discover tactics, techniques, and procedures employed by advanced threats.

Threat analyst activities require awareness of attackers' TTPs, understanding of threat intelligence and data analysis, knowledge of forensics and network security, and plenty of time to carry out these tasks. With tier-3 analysts in short supply, who is going to fill these roles? The skills dilemma may depend on how organizations structure their SOC. We discuss the skillsets required for threat hunting in Chapter 2.

Summary

- The rise of cybercrime has created an insatiable appetite for threat hunting.
- Organizations should apply threat modeling techniques to derive their custom threat-hunting methodology. Frameworks such as MITRE ATT&CK can provide a solid baseline for this.
- One of the fundamental problems with cybersecurity is that organizations often do not realize when they have been compromised. Traditional incident response methods are typically reactive, forcing security teams to wait for a visible sign of an attack. The problem is that many attacks today are stealthy, targeted, and data-focused. Traditional methods of defense revolve around reactive security—waiting for visible signs of a breach and taking appropriate actions in response. Modern attacks are much more advanced and sophisticated. These types of attacks rarely show signs and often go undetected for months or years. Proper threat hunting offers sufficient network visibility to help security professionals detect malicious activity and respond accordingly.
- The Threat Hunting Maturity Model (HMM) helps organizations map their current maturity and helps them set a target maturity to achieve in a reasonable time frame.
- Businesses should assess their need to hunt threats based on risk exposure, and then determine if they have the structure to support this.
- Threat-hunting solutions involve a unique combination of people, processes, and technologies. Organizations put people at the forefront of threat hunting, which means they are supported by robust technology and processes for better visibility into their network. This allows them to detect and respond to malicious activity.

Modern Approach to Multi-Cloud Threat Hunting

What's in This Chapter

- Multi-cloud threat hunting
- The building blocks of the Security Operations Center (SOC)
- Cyberthreat detection, threat modeling, and the need for proactive threat hunting in SOC
- Cyber resiliency and the organization's culture
- Metrics for assessing the effectiveness of a threat-hunting program

Multi-Cloud Threat Hunting

According to Flexera's state of the cloud report from 2020 (`https://info.flexera.com/SLO-CM-REPORT-State-of-the-Cloud-2020`), shown in Figure 2.1, demand for a multi-cloud strategy has been high compared to single public and single private strategies, and since 2018, the trend is going higher as well.

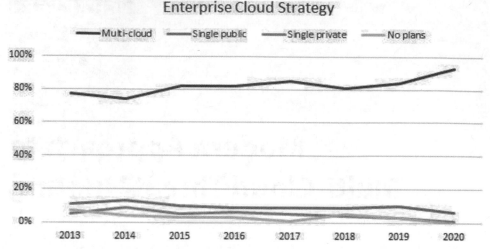

Figure 2.1: Flexera's state of the cloud report

Multi-cloud environments usually refer to the distribution of cloud assets, software, application, infrastructure, and resources across several cloud-hosting environments/providers. Typically a multi-cloud architecture utilizes two or more public clouds as well as multiple cloud service providers (CSPs) with the aim of eliminating the dependency and achieving a higher level of resiliency within the environment.

Each of the CSPs is responsible for a particular activity; for instance, one serves as an IaaS, another one as a PaaS, and another one is a SaaS service. Considering that each of these CSPs is a third-party vendor, they carry a number of risks with different pros and cons. Figure 2.2 demonstrates a simplified vision of the multi-cloud environment.

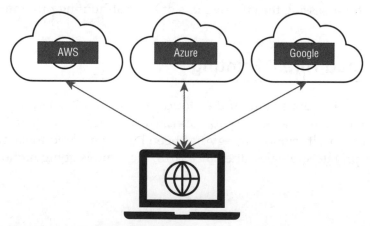

Figure 2.2: Simplified multi-cloud environment

Multi-cloud computing enables organizations to reduce the downtime and/or prevent data loss. It is always advised to avoid a single point of failure, and using this approach helps if one CSP failed, because organizations still can operate resiliently. There are many CSPs around the globe and each has its technological, geological, and regulatory requirements. Using multi-cloud environment also allows one to leverage competitive pricing.

There are several advantages of deploying a multi-cloud architecture, including reducing reliance on any single vendor, cost-efficiencies, increasing flexibility through choice, adherence to local policies, and compliances requiring organizations to host certain types of data in a specific country or a geographical location.

Due to advanced and integrated technologies and the need to comply with a variety of customers and regulators, it could be claimed that many of the CSPs' security postures are more reliable and mature compared to many legacy organizations. However, it is important to perform due diligence and due care to find the gaps and work together to resolve them.

One of the challenges with a multi-cloud environment is obtaining a single source of truth of current security controls and asset inventories, different workflow management and dashboards, and provisioning or deprovisioning the assets where and when needed.

Another challenge that organizations face during cloud migration to a multi-cloud environment is that data will be shared among different parties, which may concern the data protection and privacy issue.

Roles and responsibilities should be clearly defined between each party of CSPs and the organizations with respect to each security implementation, maintaining the compliance state, and for governing the security posture regularly.

To meet these requirements, CSPs need to provide a high level of transparency, where an organization's stakeholders (such as the CISO and CIO) can confidently engage the CSPs. Lack of sufficient transparency can be one of the challenges an organization will face during this migration. In a multi-cloud environment, the key challenge for security teams is to have an integrated vision of the full IT environment. CISOs need to ensure that threat-detecting systems can operate on all platforms and preferably send information to one integrated dashboard. There are other multi-cloud challenges that are beyond this chapter.

After migrating to the cloud, an organization should deploy required security controls and precautionary action, including but not limited to the following:

- **Asset inventory:** Identifying asset inventories on the cloud, especially crown jewels to help threat hunters identify the threat actors, their TTPs, and defined use cases.

- **Configuration management and patching:** Threat hunters should monitor misconfigured VMs and workloads. Special use cases should be defined to identify those new assets that have recently joined the network, especially if they have high targeted vulnerabilities or are being used by relevant threat actors.

Another area that threat hunters need to invest more time in is identifying exposed instances or APIs that integrate multiple clouds. This section requires extensive threat modeling to know what APIs are in place, what the mitigation controls are, and where they can fail, as well as which area requires additional monitoring by threat hunting.

- **Authentication and authorization:** Administrator activity and privileged users' activity are also important to monitor via threat hunters. Due to the nature of the cloud, whereby assets are accessed remotely, secure remote connection and monitoring is crucial. Being remotely accessible ideally invites curious devils and insiders to start digging for a hole to get access.

- **Threat-hunting solutions:** After deploying all related security hygiene, the SecOps (Security Operations) team should plan for readiness of the threat hunting to kick off, as discussed in Chapter 1. While we have discussed threat hunting mainly in the on-premise environment, the SecOps team should choose their threat-hunting solution to resolve the challenges that they may face.

While the stored data in CSPs may contain other customer data as well, the threat-hunting solution should be able to filter the unnecessary info and only obtain the metadata for data processing purposes.

Multi-Tenant Cloud Environment

Threat hunting helps reduce the operation overload as well as boosts identifying threats in an on-premises environment and prioritizes remediation planning.

Cloud computing is more common than ever, not only for organizations using different cloud services, but also using multiple CSPs, which is also known as a multi-cloud environment. In other words, you have one organization or community using several CSPs in once place. These CSPs could be private, public, or even hybrid cloud. On the contrary, one cloud provider serves a variety of organizations and each organization or customer is known as the tenant; this is called a multi-tenant environment.

In this section, we discuss the common risks in multi-cloud and multi-tenant environments and how threat hunting helps to address these risks.

Multi-tenant is defined as multiple customers or organizations accessing the same CSP, whereby different systems (IaaS, PaaS, SaaS) from different companies are hosted on one pool of physical servers. Multi-tenant architectures apply to both public cloud and private cloud environments, allowing each tenant's data to be separated from each other. There are several multi-tenancy model types, all with varying levels of complexity and costs. Multi-tenancy is one of the main criteria in defining cloud computing, where different customers access the secured and isolated, abstracted system without interfering with each other or even noticing other users. One benefit of multi-tenanting is that many users can get access to one server and use the resources at maximum level with lower costs, all at the same time.

In a multi-tenant environment, customers enjoy the affordable cost and integration via APIs with other applications. Most of the asset maintenance and updating/upgrading is under the CSP roles and responsibilities. It is important that the shared responsibility model be discussed at the contract level. On the contrary, multi-tenant offers limited customization, security changes, and upgrades dependencies and the vendor lock-in issue.

In a nutshell, if customers need a particular customization or security features to be applied, it depends on CSP approval and their roadmap. Other CSPs might provide the same customization, maybe with a lower cost on demand without waiting for the CSP roadmap.

In addition to these operational challenges, there are a number of cyber risks and compliance issues that led to many organizations being hesitant to adopt this new approach and migrate to the cloud. Many of the cyber risks in the multi-tenant (single CSP) environment also exist in a multi-cloud environment, which is discussed in the next section.

Such challenges drive many customers and organizations to look into the multi-cloud environments that address such limitations.

Threat Hunting in Multi-Cloud and Multi-Tenant Environments

An organization should know the risk of migrating to the cloud, be it multi-cloud or multi-tenant cloud, in advance, such as data security and privacy, shared model responsibility, increased dependencies on vendors, poor configuration, and access management, especially on admin and privileged users, unpatched VMs and platforms/infra, and many more. Of course, many security controls have been put in place, such as separation of duties, network security tools, integration and single management console and dashboard, IDS, IPS, encryptions, and other next-generation fantasy stuff.

However, if there is no proper monitoring considered, regardless of how secure the CSPs and on-premise platforms are, it will be difficult to reduce the cyber risk and identify them before an incident takes place or identify the APT attacks that could potentially be in the environment.

As discussed earlier in this chapter, threat hunting and threat modeling should be applied in the cloud environment as well.

As organizations migrate from a physical infrastructure/on-premise environment to a cloud environment, threat identification will be more challenging due to difficulties in compliance and configuration transparency, remote data sources and infrastructures, core security capabilities, and the number of APIs. In a nutshell, as the attack surface is expanding, threat hunting requires more attention, so the challenges related to threat hunting in a multi-cloud and/or multi-tenant environment must be discussed.

Now consider the challenges of a multi-tenant environment whereby different customer data types are hosted; the threat hunter could possibly breach the data privacy if certain data protection controls as well as role-based access controls (RBAC) are not in place.

On the other hand, threat-hunting complexity increases on a multi-cloud environment when you have heterogeneous infrastructures, services, vendors with different security postures, unbalanced security postures, different security controls in place where proper integration might not be in place, and more. Poor visibility on data at rest, in transit, and in process prevents the threat hunters from performing the threat hunting at all levels, and this is limited based on the access provided by the CSP and customers.

While customers can define application logs to be pumped into the SIEM or log collectors for threat hunting and incident management correlation, a number of the logs such as hypervisor logs, packet details, or system logs might not be shared with the customers.

Another challenge that threats hunters usually face in a modern cloud environment is that many organizations are moving to containerization and serverless approaches, whereby the instance constantly turns off and on whenever needed. This is typically a case where the organization is heavily invested in DevOps tools.

One of the main benefits of the cloud is you pay as you go. While the customer only pays for the amount of resources used, such as bandwidth, data, and processing resources, threat hunters should choose the required data carefully, as it will impact cost.

There are different types of threat-hunting commercial products and services offered by different vendors and service providers that could meet these challenges. Security-as-a-Service is one such approach that allows customers to subscribe and deploy into their multi-tenant cloud environment to boost their incident response and threat-hunting capabilities.

During threat-hunting maturity readiness, it is advisable that you build a successful threat-hunting program by starting small. As the maturity level increases, you then expand the scope of threat hunting to avoid overwhelming your hunters with thousands of events. In a multi-cloud or multi-tenant environment, the number of alerts received by log collectors and hunters increases tremendously over a period of time. Using the reliable threat source, you will now have an opportunity to use automation in threat-hunting for building and maintaining various use cases and hypothesis in a timely manner.

Building Blocks for the Security Operations Center

> "There are lot of benefits to cloud SIEM. . . stability, providing additional load without performance tradeoff, scalability, and maintenance."
>
> *—IDG Report SIEM Shift: "How the Cloud Is Transforming Security Operations," May 2020*

First, let's understand the two main concepts in cybersecurity—SOC and SIEM—and discuss the main differences between the two.

A Security Operations Center (SOC) is an organization function or a centralized unit with various security roles, such as Security Analyst, Threat Hunter, Red Team/Blue Team members, etc. It deals with defending and protecting the organization against various security-related issues using a variety of tools. One of the main tools used by the SOC team is Security Information and Event Management (SIEM).

So, the SIEM tool collects, normalizes, and analyzes application logs and events against the set of correlation rules. When these rules are triggered, they create a series of events that human analysts analyze and respond to.

NOTE   The *SIEM* term was coined by Mark Nicolett and Amrit Williams of Gartner in 2005.

Usually, you will not find an SOC without an SIEM but may find an organization with an IT team with a mature security understanding using an SIEM tool without a dedicated SOC unit. You will also often find that many organizations typically outsource their SOC capability to a third-party vendor that specializes in providing such cybersecurity services.

NOTE   If the SOC was a supermarket, the SOC security analyst would be the retail assistant working at the point of sale and the SIEM would be the point of sale.

An SOC is composed of many entities used for cybersecurity incidents and event monitoring within an organization technology environment, such as people, processes, procedures, security tools, and software like Firewall, CASB, Proxy, WAF, etc.

To build an SOC, you must understand that there are many moving parts and you must think of them as sections and treat each as a threat modeling exercise. At the end of the day, the main objective of having an SOC is to manage the threat.

Setting up a modern SOC is not an easy task and choosing the right people, processes, and technologies can be a real challenge. Table 2.1 compares the SIEM, SOC, and threat-hunting processes.

Table 2.1: Comparing SIEM, SOC, and Threat Hunting

	SIEM	SOC	THREAT HUNTING
Use case	Use SIEM for basic security control and for automating log analyses.	SOC can extend and maximize security control above and beyond an SIEM. One key differentiator is the processes that run within an SOC.	Threat hunting is used to further identify highly sophisticated attacks, patterns, and indicators of compromise.
Example	An SIEM can detect multiple failed login attempts due to brute force attacks.	If an SOC team detects a failed login attempt, they take further action by calling the employee, locking the account, and further investigating the reason for the lockout.	Threat hunting is an extended capability within SOC and uses the same infrastructure. Threat hunting uses behavior analysis to identity the pattern, such as: Was any admin account created after multiple login failures? Is the geolocation of the user the same as the login attempt logs? Is there a mismatch in the user's normal time of login?

Let's divide the decision-making process into logical steps, i.e., elements of a modern SOC.

The elemental pillars include the people, process, and technology aspects required to support and defend the organization (see Figure 2.3). By utilizing these elements in SOC, you can improve existing functions and develop those that are lacking, creating both opportunity and advantages for the SOC that end in desired results for the organization.

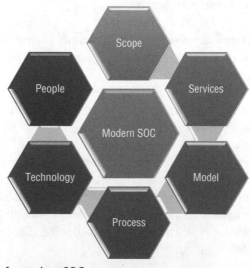

Figure 2.3: Elements of a modern SOC

Scope and Type of SOC

There is no one-size-fits-all approach when it comes to establishing and creating an SOC. An SOC should be scaled to either the global footprint of the organization or to the span of control for the business sector that operates the SOC.

Many large corporations have a main SOC, called a Global Security Operations Center (GSOC), which could be supported by smaller (child) SOCs around the globe.

These smaller SOCs also provide alerts and threat feeds to the main GSOC. There is always some redundancy built into SOCs, so if one is offline, another one can manage the load and sustain operations.

Services, Not Just Monitoring

Define all your SOC requirements and then develop a roadmap. Which services do you want to create within your SOC? It's not just about monitoring a few logs and events from your infrastructure, which used to be the case in a traditional SOC.

Modern SOCs provide a number of proactive services, which are resource-intensive operation tasks. This includes:

- Security management and event monitoring
- Security orchestration, automation, and response (SOAR)
- Log management
- Incident response
- Vulnerability management and penetration testing
- Managed defense and red team/blue team service
- Threat hunting and threat monitoring
- ICS and SCADA security monitoring
- Business resiliency
- Controls and compliance reporting based on certain regulatory requirements, such as PCI-DSS, HIPAA, SOX, and FISMA

SOC Model

The SOC model can include an onsite (in-house) dedicated SOC, outsourced (remote) SOC, or both.

Today's cybersecurity market is full of small, medium, large, and boutique managed service providers who offer you specific services for your security monitoring based on your specific needs. This includes threat hunting, penetration testing, red team/blue team, etc.

Each model has its own pros and cons. You choose from remote monitoring and analysis, a dedicated SOC center operated on your premises, or, for maximum security and cost effectiveness, a hybrid solution, which combines both.

Define a Process for Identifying and Managing Threats

This is the most crucial step and a key process one must embark upon when building an SOC, which is a threat modeling exercise. Threat modeling entails answering the following questions:

- Which threats are applicable to my organization and do I care the most about?
- What do these threats look like and for which sets of assets?
- How does SOC identify, detect, and block these threats?
- What run book and playbook do I need to create?

Once these questions are answered, playbooks are built in order to document how to respond, set severity, and escalate these specific threat types. Other important processes to consider are shift time and models.

Tools and Technologies to Empower SOC

The tooling in the SOC (see Figure 2.4) is a mixture of centralized breadth capabilities and specialized tools that enable high-quality alerts and an end-to-end investigation and remediation experience.

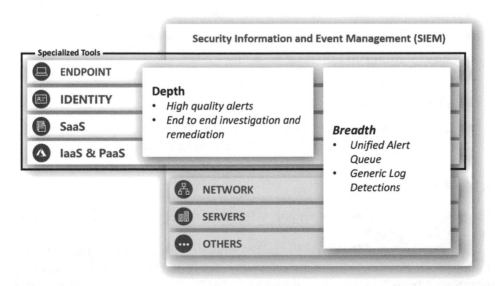

Figure 2.4: SOC tooling

One key element for managing an SOC is to ensure that the technology and platforms sync well with the information systems. You want to build a tool chest of software that can perform security audits, log analysis, penetration tests, and port scans. There are many commercial systems that can provide intrusion prevention, intrusion detection, and analyses.

You should have a good service/help desk ticketing system, documentation system, and inventory system. You should also stay on top of all the security trends by connecting to websites and security threat feeds that will update you on current events and on the threat landscape.

People (Specialized Teams)

You need to organize the SOC with specialized teams, allowing them to better develop and apply deep expertise, which supports the overall goals of reducing time to acknowledge and remediate threats.

> **"A dedicated team handling threat intelligence is not a requirement, but the function is critical to the success of an SOC. Without it, you can only protect against yesterday's threats."**
>
> —*Darren Lawless, Senior Manager, Threat Monitoring, IBM Security*

Figure 2.5 represents the key SOC functions within Microsoft: threat intelligence, incident management, and SOC analyst tiers.

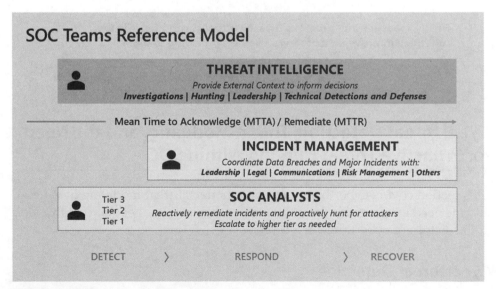

Figure 2.5: SOC teams reference model

You need a highly trained team of security analysts who are familiar with security-based alerts and scenarios. As security threats are constantly changing, analysts need to adapt and think outside the box when it comes to solving problems. Attacks can come in a variety of different forms and types, so having people who can learn on the fly is important.

Finding the right people can be challenging. You may need to evaluate other options, such as outsourcing (via managed security service providers, known as MSSPs) or even hiring specialists to provide surge incident response (IR) support. I believe a hybrid of these options functions quite effectively.

In a SANS Incident Response report, 61% of respondents called upon their own surge staff to manage serious incidents and 58% had a specialized response team.

"If you want a successful SOC, you need to simplify, prioritize, automate, and measure.

Simplify your stack. You don't need one of every tool on the market. What you do need, are capabilities that work together to achieve your goals.

Prioritize capability improvements. If everything is important then nothing is important. Create a prioritized roadmap based on the goals of your business.

Automate processes based on criticality and impact of the threat, as well as confidence in the data. Any processes that are repetitious and can be automated, should be automated.

Finally, measure your progress. Give the business confidence in the continued improvement of services you are providing to them."

—Mario Chiock, Fellow and CISO Emeritus, Schlumberger

Cyberthreat Detection, Threat Modeling, and the Need for Proactive Threat Hunting Within SOC

This section covers cyberthreat detection models, threat modeling in general, and the need for proactive threat hunting within an SOC. Let's start with a look at the history of cyberthreat detection.

Cyberthreat Detection

The first cybercrime took place many decades ago, when Bob Thomas developed the first computer worm in 1971. It showed a popup message on victims' computers that read "I'm the creeper, catch me if you can." Following that, cybercrimes started to take place one after another. The first Denial of Service (DOS) attack happened in 1989, by launching a worm attack and slowing the Internet for a few days. The estimated damage was about $100,000, up to $10mil.

During those early days, organizations were always looking for a way to fix the unknown and unpredicted incident. Gradually, software and security vendors come up with patches and hot fixes and anti-hacking, antivirus, and malware software and hardware was invented.

Over time, with advancing technologies, threat detection improved, using known attacks and viruses, malware signatures, and indicators of compromise (IOCs). All companies invested in signature-based detection control mechanisms. A lot of security products and server providers made a great deal of money by selling the latest signatures.

Following that, the speed and accuracy of identifying the known signature and IOCs became the winning point. That is where Intrusion Detection and Prevention Systems (IDPS) came in. Soon, organizations realized that while signature-based methods are perfectly accurate and fast enough (thanks to high-speed processors and memories), they could only mitigate against known signatures and IOCs. Hackers (and even script kiddies with minor changes in their code) could manage to penetrate the network and perform their malicious activity. See Figure 2.6.

Thereafter, threat detection from signature-based options changed to behavior and anomaly based detection. Technologies expanded and a variety of detection methods were introduced by security researchers.

Threat detection is no longer about identifying IOCs; in fact, now it's all about hunting the threats in the wild. Not to mention that regardless of the amount of investments and complex technologies and creative and strategic security defense controls, intruders can still manage to break into your network and remain undetected. Threat hunting allows you to proactively look for known and unknown threats and the modus operandi to mitigate the risk and prevent another headline in the news. Threat hunters constantly look for suspicious activity, codes, and unauthorized activity prior to data exfiltration, ransomware attacks, or Advanced Persistent Threats (APTs).

To avoid operational day-to-day activity and meeting the OPs deadline and SLAs, this role should be absolutely separate from operational duties and mainly focus on data collection and hunting. It should define and refine new procedures and automate and maintain them to increase efficiency.

Threat hunters may be part of SecOps organization, which may also depend on the size of an organization. They may also sit between the SecOps and enterprise and security architects teams and the business units.

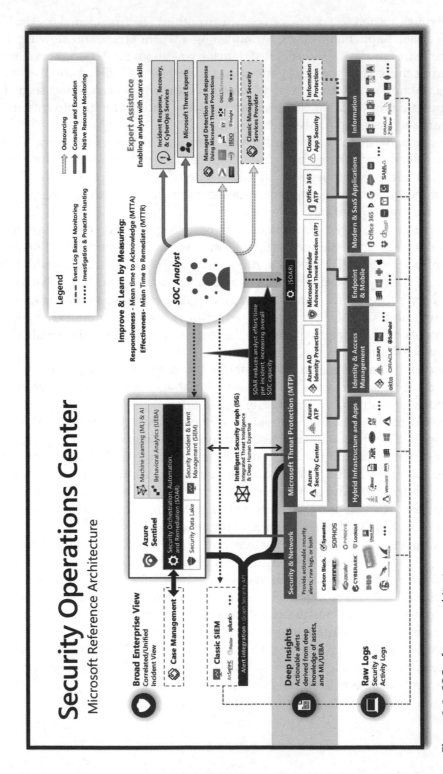

Figure 2.6: SOC reference architecture

Threat-Hunting Goals and Objectives

Threat hunting is like fishing in a big ocean. You need to know which ocean you are in and how much you know about it—how deep can you go, what type of fish are you planning to fish, what is your existing equipment, how skillful are you, and more. However, knowing what fish you are looking for is as important as knowing what type of threats you are looking for in your environment to hunt.

Threat hunting has been introduced to meet different goals and objectives. For instance, based on my experience, there is no organization that can claim they are running with fully 100% patched systems free of any vulnerabilities or misconfigurations. Not to mention that there are, from time to time, unknown assets in organizations that just pop up like mushrooms. On the other hand, there are many companies running on legacy infra and apps that are EOL and EOS. Businesses have accepted the risk and are running the operation by relying on existing mitigation controls.

One of the main objectives of the CISO should be to get to know the crown jewels and vulnerable systems and prioritize them based on system criticality. Then, based on threat modeling, prepare the hunting objectives and scope. Scoping is discussed in more detail in "Threat Modeling and the SOC" later in the chapter.

The next objective is to reduce the false positives and noise in the SOC and prioritize the events by relying on threat hunting and threat intelligence IOCs. Security Operations Centers usually receive thousands of false and true positive events and alerts. Threat hunting helps the SOC team prioritize which events to investigate and respond to. In complex and large organizations with heterogeneous software, applications and middleware, databases, operating systems and mainframes, and hardware and network devices, there are tons of patches to be deployed. Threat hunting, with the aid of reliable IOCs and TTPs, helps the threat and vulnerability management team prioritize which security patch should be deployed first and which vulnerability should be remediated.

Threat hunting helps the incident response and digital forensics team identify where the first compromise was initiated, what other machines are involved in this series of exploits, and when, how, and what the modus operandi was.

CISOs and security operations teams should take into account the lesson-learned strategy and define the goal of threat hunting. There is a saying that all companies have been compromised, the only difference is whether they know it or not.

Research and news show that many cyberattacks take place when the cyber-criminal and attackers had presence in the organization network months in advance. While some attackers may act noisy and launch ransomware and DDOS attacks, either destroying the assets or being caught by security control systems, many APTs successfully evade such security controls and silently coexist in the environment without raising a flag or alarm. Threat hunters, using the

TTP and known vulnerabilities and recent attack news and intel, should look for possible incidents and inform the CISO by taking precautionary action.

The output of such goals helps the remediation team to know, among reams of the missing patches, which patch and vulnerability should be prioritized, which system configuration should be fixed first, and identify the gap in process documents and standards. Hence, threat hunting is not just another checkbox for regulatory requirements or best practices to check. It requires a certain level of skill, organization security defense maturity, and the right equipment in place.

Senior management should also understand that the effectiveness of threat hunting is based on the available visibility, maturity level, and defined scope. Hence, it's best to define the scope based on the crown jewels and relevant threat actor present in their industry. As maturity levels improve, the visibility and coverage should be expanded. In that case, the ROI will be more justifiable.

Threat Modeling and SOC

Threat modeling is an important task when planning and building a successful SOC. Think about threat modeling as a practice to understanding your adversaries, their methods for attacking your organization, and how you will identify and respond to the attacks. Threat modeling will help you define scope, determine interesting log sources, select appropriate tools and technologies, and many other aspects to make SOC successful.

Make threat modeling exercises a standard practice to model and remodel threats. In the absence of proper threat modeling, you will end up wasting significant time, money, and energy in collecting irrelevant logs and investigating events that don't matter much. Threat modeling will also help you create appropriate use cases and filter out noise. Threat modeling details are covered in the following sections.

The Need for a Proactive Hunting Team Within SOC

Cybersecurity can often feel like a game of whack-a-mole. As our tools get better at stopping one type of attack, our adversaries innovate new tactics. Sophisticated cybercriminals burrow their way into network caverns, avoiding detection for weeks or even months, as they gather information and escalate privileges. If you wait until these advanced persistent threats become visible, it can be costly and time-consuming to address. It's crucial to augment reactive approaches to cybersecurity with proactive ones. Human-led threat hunting, supported by machine learning–powered tools like Microsoft Azure Sentinel, can help you root out infiltrators before they access sensitive data.

Assume Breach and Be Proactive

Traditional cybersecurity is *reactive*. Endpoint detection tools identify potential incidents, blocking some and handing off others to people to investigate and mitigate. This works for many of the routine, automated, and well-known attacks—of which there are many. However, our most sophisticated adversaries understand how these security solutions work and continuously evolve their tactics to get around them. The goal of the attackers is to remain undetected so they can gain access to your most sensitive information. To stop them, first you must find them.

Threat hunting is a proactive approach to cybersecurity, predicated on an "assume breach" mindset. *Assume breach* is a mindset that guides security investments, design decisions, and operational security practices. Assume breach limits the trust placed in applications, services, identities, and networks by treating them all—both internal and external—as not secure and probably already compromised. Just because a breach isn't visible via traditional security tools and detection mechanisms doesn't mean it hasn't occurred. Your threat-hunting team doesn't react to a known attack, but rather tries to uncover indications of attack (IOA) that have yet to be detected. Their job is to outthink the attacker.

Invest in People

Because threat hunting is concerned with emerging threats rather than known attack methods, people take the lead. It's therefore important that they have the time and authority to research and pursue hypotheses. This isn't possible if they are bogged down with security alerts. Many SOCs, including those at Microsoft, establish a three-tier model to address known and unknown threats. Tier-1 and Tier-2 analysts respond to alerts. Tier-3 analysts conduct research focused on revealing undiscovered adversaries. See Figure 2.7. You can learn more about how Microsoft organizes its SOC in "Lessons Learned From The Microsoft SOC—Part 2a: Organizing People."

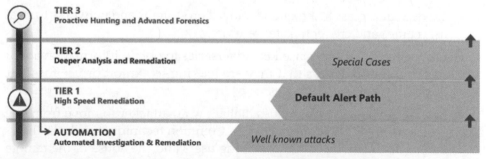

Figure 2.7: SOC using a three-tier approach: Tier 1 addresses high-speed remediation, Tier 2 performs deeper analysis and remediation, and Tier 3 conducts proactive hunts.

Develop an Informed Hypothesis

Threat hunting starts with a hypothesis. Threat hunters may generate a hypothesis based on external information, such as threat reports, blogs, and social media. For example, your team may learn about a new form of malware in an industry blog and hypothesize that an adversary has used that malware in an attack against your organization. Internal data and intelligence from past incidents also inform hypothesis development.

Once the team has a hypothesis, they examine various techniques and tactics to uncover artifacts that were left behind. A great tool for helping with hypothesis development and research is the MITRE ATT&CK (adversarial tactics, techniques, and common knowledge) framework.

These adversary tactics and techniques are grouped within a matrix and include the following categories:

- **Initial access:** Techniques used by the adversary to obtain a foothold within a network, such as targeted spear-phishing, exploiting vulnerabilities, or configuration weaknesses in public-facing systems.

- **Execution:** Techniques that result in an adversary running their code on a target system. For example, an attacker may run a PowerShell script to download additional attacker tools and/or scan other systems.

- **Persistence:** Techniques that allow an adversary to maintain access to a target system, even following reboots and credential changes. An example of a persistence technique would be an attacker creating a scheduled task that runs their code at a specific time or on reboot.

- **Privilege escalation:** Techniques leveraged by an adversary to gain higher-level privileges on a system, such as local administrator or root.

- **Defense evasion:** Techniques used by attackers to avoid detection. Evasion techniques include hiding malicious code within trusted processes and folders, encrypting or obfuscating adversary code, or disabling security software.

- **Credential access:** Techniques deployed on systems and networks to steal usernames and credentials for re-use.

- **Discovery:** Techniques used by adversaries to obtain information about systems and networks that they are looking to exploit or use for their tactical advantage.

- **Lateral movement:** Techniques that allow an attacker to move from one system to another within a network. Common techniques include "Pass-the-Hash" methods of authenticating users and the abuse of the remote desktop protocol.

- **Collection:** Techniques used by an adversary to gather and consolidate the information they were targeting as part of their objectives.

- **Command and control:** Techniques leveraged by an attacker to communicate with a system under their control. One example is that an attacker may communicate with a system over an uncommon or high-numbered port to evade detection by security appliances or proxies.

- **Exfiltration:** Techniques used to move data from the compromised network to a system or network fully under control of the attacker.

- **Impact:** Techniques used by an attacker to impact the availability of systems, networks, and data. Methods in this category would include denial of service attacks and disk- or data-wiping software.

Cyber Resiliency and Organizational Culture

Cyber resilience is the ability to prepare for, respond to, and recover from cyberattacks. It helps organizations protect themselves from cyber risks, defend against and limit the severity of attacks, and ensure that business operations continue to function. See Figure 2.8.

Cyber resiliency should be part of a holistic approach to security that takes all aspects of the business into consideration, from employees and partners to the board of directors. Improving security is not a one-time project, but a program of continuous improvement.

The U.S. National Institute of Standards and Technology (NIST) defines cyber resiliency as "the ability to anticipate, withstand, recover from, and adapt to adverse conditions, stresses, attacks, or compromises on systems that include cyber resources." More realistically, cyber resiliency is also about establishing a policy and process that help an organization survive and continue to execute its long-term strategy in the face of evolving security threats.

To become cyber resilient, enterprises must strike a balance between protecting critical assets, detecting compromises, and responding to incidents. Making the IT landscape cyber resilient requires investments in areas such as infrastructure, design, and development of systems, applications, and networks. At the same time, organizations must create and foster a resilience-conscious culture, of which security, security operations, and threat management are all essential parts.

Cybersecurity resiliency includes starting with the right mindset, technology, approach, focus on hygiene, and measurement of success. First and foremost, security initiatives and priorities must be aligned with the organization's business strategy to avoid wasting effort on unrelated activities and neglecting critical business assets.

Resiliency starts with the right "assume breach" mindset. Organizations must first accept the fact that attackers will successfully compromise resources in their environment. If an organization falsely assumes that they can be fully immune to all attacks, their investment choices are typically much less effective.

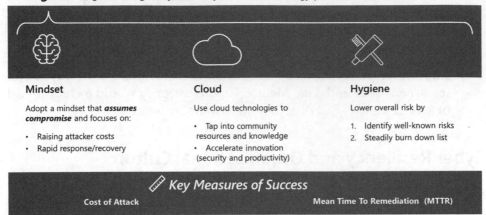

Figure 2.8: Cyber resilience is the ability to prepare for, respond to, and recover from cyberattacks.

The same cloud technologies that are inspiring business transformations can also be used to transform security strategy and operations.

Security organizations aim to increase their resilience by tapping into vast resources, investments, and knowledge using cloud technology (including threat intelligence). They rapidly provision new security capabilities from the cloud provider to enable rapid adaptation to attacker innovations.

Organizations made decisions about how to architect and operate their IT environments prior to cybersecurity being a significant priority. These legacy decisions represent a "technical debt" that organizations must pay down over time. By identifying these security hygiene risks, prioritizing them, and investing in remediating them, an organization can significantly lower their risk to both known attacks as well as likely future attacks.

Organizations should focus on measuring how difficult/expensive it is to attack them (especially for well-known attack patterns) as well as their ability to rapidly boot out attackers that successfully attack them.

Skillsets Required for Threat Hunting

To avoid similar misconceptions, bear in mind that threat hunting is not only an automated process that you can reactively live your life on. It requires constant tuning, remediation, and removing of false positives. This requires security analyst experience and proactive investigations.

Manual and automated penetration testing tools require experienced penetration testers to fine tune them and increase their efficiency. Furthermore, threat hunters are not incident responders that jump on and fix the incidents.

Rotate SOC analysts into the threat-hunting team for learning and development purposes.

Their main job is to obtain events, alerts, packets, and other relevant feeds to understand what was or could potentially be happening. Depending on the size of the company, the data size might vary. In small organizations and/or at the early stage of setting up the foundation of threat hunting, spreadsheets could be enough; as the maturity level increases and the amount of data increases, the size of the dataset will increase drastically as well.

That is where data analytics tools and skillset may require more. It is important not to define the threat-hunting scope so large as to cover the entire organization at this early stage. Instead, expand the coverage as the maturity level improves. Always start small and grow over time.

TIP When it comes to threat hunting, always think big, start small, and grow over time.

Just because it is about data analysis, does not mean that data scientists can become threat hunters. While their knowledge in analyzing data is useful, train your security analyst with data analysis courses or train your data analysts with security analysis arsenals.

Good threat hunters have an eye for detail and a sharp analytics mindset. They are proactive and out-of-the-box thinkers and have patience to look at the bigger picture.

"Hackers don't break in – they log in."

— *Bret Arsenault, Microsoft CISO*

As part of the maturity assessment and planning process when developing a threat-hunting program, the security analyst team requires a wide range of skillsets and knowledge.

Security Analysis

Threat hunters should be able to understand and work with network packets, parse the IOC feed, work with log correlation tools and SIEM, use security appliances such as firewall and IDS, reverse engineering malware, and know about exploits. They must constantly update their knowledge of threat actors, attack tools, and tactics. Similar to any other security analyst role, they must know how different operations work, what their critical files and processes are, and what their basic network protocols and services run. For instance, a threat hunter should be able to profile every department's normal behavior, like working hours, usual activities, and required tools, especially administrative tools such as PowerShell. By knowing what is considered "normal," anomalies can be identified with a minimum of false positives.

Data Analysis

Threat hunters should be able to know how to combine different data together in a structured and unstructured manner. They need visual demonstrations, machine learning tools, elastic searches, and relevant skills. Due to the high volume of data that hunters deal with, experience and knowledge in Machine Learning (ML) helps them by training the ML tools about normal behavior, cluster the known, bad, and questionable activities, and finally group them for further profiling and investigations.

Programming Languages

With most IT and security roles, basic skills in programming and scripting is always in good demand. However, if you are expecting your team to be able to customize and automate the procedures, reverse engineer and perform data analysis, having knowledge of scripting languages such as Python, Perl, and C/C++ is mandatory.

Analytical Mindset

Hunters should have an analytical mindset to be able to develop different hypotheses and build various use cases. They need to analyze the output and tune their processes and procedures.

Soft Skills

Threat hunters need to talk with different technical and nontechnical coworkers from time to time. Soft skills help them build an efficient relationship and obtain the required info and support. Threat hunters also present reports to management about the latest states. Knowing how to write technical and nontechnical reports tailored for different audiences is highly desirable. Based on the seniority level of this role, deep knowledge and practical hands-on skills may vary.

Outsourcing

Many organizations, due to a lack of security talent pools, prefer to outsource managed security services. While managed services provide advanced technologies and rich intel feeds, human factors play a critical role in threat hunting. CISOs need to ensure that threat hunting is not a one-day contract kind of job. Consultants can't simply walk in, set up the platforms, run the exercise, wash their hands, and walk away. It requires the constant presence of hunters who know the business and IT environment and work on cases and artifacts 24/7.

NOTE   The threat-hunting team is recognized as a great place to work and is seen as a leader in the field by other organizations.

To summarize, based on my experience, threat hunters require the following core skills:

- A mindset of curiosity
- Log analysis and general analytical skills
- Understanding of normal network behavior
- Understanding of normal endpoint user and application behavior
- Understanding the threat landscape and the use of CTI
- System administrator experience across Windows/Linux/common security products

Threat-Hunting Process and Procedures

There are different methods and processes for finding malicious users in your organization. There are three common methods that most threat-hunting teams leverage on their day-to-day jobs, all of which fully require skilled human-base analysis with the aid of relevant tools and services. See Figure 2.9.

Figure 2.9: Threat-hunting data collection steps

- **Hypothesis-based method:** Hypothesis-based is one of the most common and most preferred approaches. Threat hunters should always have a hypothesis that hackers are already in their organizations and should find a way to identify them by coming up with different hypotheses and testing that.

- **IOC- and TTPS-based method:** Another approach is relying on threat intelligence feeds—such as indicators of compromise (IOC) and tactics, techniques, and procedures (TTP)—by searching existing data. This approach depends greatly on your threat intel feed quality and accuracy.

- **Data-driven method:** The third approach takes advantage of identifying the suspicious leads using data scientific arsenals, including but not limited to machine learning and data visualization to prepare the initialization so experienced threat hunters can further investigate them.

Regardless of the method you choose, these steps help formalize the threat-hunting process and lead to a repeatable and reliable expected output. The stability of this level helps you to reach a higher maturity level.

Metrics for Assessing the Effectiveness of Threat Hunting

No information security program can be effective and successful without proper metrics and tracking. Metrics help management strategize their planning, prioritize their investments, and keep things accountable.

Metrics should be defined based on the key risk indicators (KRI), key performance indicators (KPI), and service level agreements (SLAs) mapped with organization policy and standards. For instance, the organization defined the remediation time of critical vulnerabilities on critical systems within a certain time. The KRI should be defined according to the indicated SLA in the Information Security Policy of the company and get the thresholds approved by senior management. Presenting the defined metrics could be quantitative or qualitative. Finally, to ensure that the performance meets the defined requirements, defined KPIs are required.

If you cannot measure it, you cannot manage it, and consequently you cannot secure it. Defining strong and comprehensive metrics helps the management ensure that the Return of Security Investment (ROSI) is justifiable and successful and the organizational goals and objectives have been achieved. Successful programs should detect a number of incidents prior to them happening, hunts where existing controls have limitations, the coverage increase over time, number of false positive SOCs received decrease, number of automated procedures increase, and they are reviewed and addressed in a timely manner.

Foundational Metrics

- **Scope:** One of the key metrics that needs to be defined is the total number of organizational assets and the number of included assets into the threat-hunting scope. You can break down this metric into critical and very important systems and others. In that case management always has a proper overview of their crown jewels. To demonstrate the improvement and expanding of the scope over time, always keep the trend liner charts.

- **Visibility:** Visibility metrics are important. Dropping the number of assets from what have been defined could be a red flag. Threat hunters need to keep the number in mind at all times, and if there are any changes, take the required action.

■ **Functionality metrics:** Installed security tools and sensors should function correctly and maintain a healthy state on all assets. For instance, say the antivirus or EDR agent is not working properly, meaning it either failed to report back to the console, didn't get the latest update signature, or couldn't send back the logs to the server or execute the administrative commands. This metric is one of the important ones, because security tools not functioning could be a sign of compromise as well. Many hackers not only bypass security tools, but they also sometimes disable them to avoid making any noise at the SOC level.

Low compliance rate of any of these metrics leads to inaccurate threat-hunting reports.

Operational Metrics

■ Number of hunted items vs. number of incidents

■ Number of open hunting investigation vs. number of closed based on defined SLAs

■ Number of hunted items based on environment and business criticality

■ Detecting time

■ Number of total hypothesized vs. verified hypothesis

■ Number of hunts based on the threat intelligence feeds

■ Number of automated procedures vs. manual procedures

■ Duration of each hunting process end to end (categorized based on automated and manual)

■ Total relevant threat actors specific to an industrial, directly targeted the organization vs. number of defined procedures and used cases

■ Total number of reported hunts vs. number of open and closed issues based on hunting (remediation)

■ Duration of remediation from the time the hunt has been reported

■ Used technique for hunting (% of technique's effectiveness)

■ Data source used for each hunt

■ Type of finding and root cause analysis (e.g., broken process, system malfunction, human error, misconfiguration, data breach, and other cyber incident categories)

■ Type of vulnerabilities

These metrics can be used for different purposes. In addition to having oversight and monitoring the threat-hunting program, they also show how effectively the program is serving the organization. On the other hand, they can help the CISO obtain strategic oversight as well. For instance, most of the reports show the number of security agents having a malfunction, which would be an alarming message to infra and the SecOps team. The following section explains how threat hunting can help the effectiveness of other compliance functional and operational reports.

On the other hand, the total number of reported hunts in comparison to timely remediation of them shows how proactively another team is acting. Reporting hunts does not prevent the cybercriminals; remediation does.

The total number of use cases and procedures demonstrates how the threat-hunting team operates—passively or proactively. Similar to SOCs, many of the defined use cases are outdated and obsolete with invalid signatures and nonexistent IPs, focusing on low-risk items.

Meeting the investigation SLA, threat-hunting lead, SOC, and CISO should determine whether automation is in place and if the number of resources and staff are adequate enough to meet the objective.

The patch compliance report shows the overall patch deployment state, representing most identified compromise could potentially demonstrate the accuracy and effectiveness of the patch management program as well. This same strategy can be applied to security configuration or vulnerability management reports as well.

The number of human errors, such as initiated cyber incidents, is identified due to social engineering or phishing attacks. Maybe the information security awareness program is not proactive enough and should be revised (see Table 2.2).

Table 2.2: Example of Threat-Hunting Metrics

METRIC DESCRIPTION	METRIC TYPE
Number of incidents identified proactively (vs. reactively)	Trend, Comparison
Number of vulnerabilities identified proactively (vs. vulnerability assessments)	Trend, Comparison
Dwell time of proactively discovered incidents (vs. reactively)	Trend, Comparison
Containment time of proactively discovered incidents (vs. reactively)	Trend, Comparison
Effort per remediation of proactively discovered incidents (vs. reactively)	Trend, Comparison
Data coverage (data types and coverage of estate)	Percentage
Hypotheses per MITRE ATT&CK tactic	Pie Chart
Hunts per MITRE ATT&CK tactic	Pie Chart
Incidents per MITRE ATT&CK tactic	Pie Chart

Table 2.2 (*continued*)

METRIC DESCRIPTION	METRIC TYPE
Percentage of successful hunts that result in a new detection analytic or rule	Service Level
Sensitivity and specificity of analytics or rules derived from hunts (true & false positive rates)	Service Level

Ultimately, the value of any metric is how useful it is to the recipient, often a senior manager such as a CISO, so all metrics should be developed in collaboration between the threat-hunting team and its relevant senior managers.

Adopt organizationally relevant metrics, such as Table 2.2, to drive improvements and show the return on security investment (ROSI) over time.

Threat-Hunting Program Effectiveness

As discussed, there are many elements that help a company's threat-hunting efforts meet the objectives and goals and become successful. CISO and the SecOPs team, prior to establishing any threat-hunting program, need to take into account these items, especially considering the maturity and readiness of the organization.

In a nutshell, successful threat hunting requires the elements outlined in Figure 2.10.

Figure 2.10: Threat hunting components

Educating stakeholders and staff is particularly important, because lack of proper training at each level could lead to a cyber incident. The training could be awareness programs for staff and senior management and cyber drills to refresh the readiness of the incident responders. It should include educating privileged users with admin accounts, high-risk staff who have access to sensitive information, and IT people who are responsible for setting up the IT environment for business.

Summary

- Threat hunting over a multi-cloud architecture is a complex activity, so it's important to understand the scope of the cloud services involved.

- Sophisticated and modern attacks use stealthy or novel techniques designed to bypass automated monitoring and detection. Continuous threat hunting is the best way to detect and prevent sophisticated or persistent attacks.

- While technology is clearly critical in the fight to detect and stop intrusions, the end user remains a crucial link in the chain to stop breaches.

- Well-trained staff can be an asset in combating the continued threat of phishing and related social engineering techniques.

- Continue to train your threat-hunting team and rotate your analyst role within your security operation.

CHAPTER 3

Exploration of MITRE Key Attack Vectors

What's in This Chapter

- Understanding the MITRE ATT&CK framework, its tactics, techniques, and case studies
- Threat hunting using five common techniques
- Analyzing the Zero Trust and defense-in-depth approaches
- Exploring the key threat-hunting tools to combat attack vectors
- Exploring the popular tools for analysis such as SIEM and SOAR

Understanding MITRE ATT&CK

Today, organizations are digitally evolving by choosing among diverse technology options to store business-critical data. On the other hand, the cyberthreat landscape is expanding geographically and constantly looking for vulnerabilities in the security layers to perform security compromises. Cyberattackers are consistently staying a step ahead of the security measures taken by organizations and succeeding in their data breach menace.

> **NOTE** The MITRE ATT&CK framework can increase visibility and improve an organization's security efforts.

To address today's challenges, the threat-hunting team needs to build a set of techniques to investigate and create a hypothesis of how attacks would work. This includes determining what artifacts are in the logs and the other parts of the systems such as volatile memory, Registry, bootloader, etc., that need to be analyzed. Organizations with an offense-focused team, like a pen-test group or a red team, have in-house experts who research and practice attacker techniques. Others may need to rely on researching published materials on attack techniques to create new hypotheses. For example, the MITRE ATT&CK framework, first released in 2013, is growing in popularity among researchers and security companies.

Regardless of what threat modeling techniques you pick up, the following questions should be answered:

- What is the defined scope and what should be worked on?
- What are the odds and what could fail or break?
- What is the action plan for them?
- Is our mitigation control effective enough?

MITRE ATT&CK is a globally accessible knowledge base of adversary tactics and techniques based on real-world observations. The ATT&CK knowledge base is used as a foundation for the development of specific threat models and methodologies in the private sector, in government, and in the cybersecurity product and service community.

With the creation of ATT&CK, MITRE is fulfilling its mission to solve problems for a safer world—by bringing communities together to develop more effective cybersecurity. ATT&CK is open and available to any person or organization for use at no charge.

The MITRE ATT&CK framework has gained a lot of attention and popularity in recent years. The ATT&CK framework is a series of matrices that break the hacking process down into tactic categories, based on the stages of the cyber kill chain. However, many companies are still navigating how to use it and what its implementation looks like. Initial questions may include those in the following sections.

What Is MITRE ATT&CK Used For?

Being a reference framework, ATT&CK is used to identify the root causes and data sources in an environment that, if prevented, would reduce the likelihood and capability of a successful hack. It's also a great starting point to get multiple teams on the same page, using the same terminology regarding a security-testing outlook. The framework includes information on threat actor groups, successful techniques they have previously executed in real-world breaches, information about software used in hacks, mapping of security vendors' software back to tactic detection and protection, and ultimately the data source where information on each tactic can be found in a network.

How Is MITRE ATT&CK Used and Who Uses It?

ATT&CK is a means of communication. It doesn't just give red and blue teams common terms, but it is also a conduit for other teams to interface with the security team. Using ATT&CK, security teams can easily explain strengths and weaknesses to leadership. In addition, they can learn to protect against something that they don't know about. If the security controls are reasonably mature, how does an organization determine how they would stand up to a real attack scenario?

How Is Testing Done According to MITRE?

ATT&CK is a tool to use when threat hunting for the unknown. It helps gauge a baseline to judge your current alerts to bridge the gap from what attackers are using and what the IDS/IPS is seeing. If you know certain techniques should be identified or blocked, you can verify that it is actually happening using that tool.

ATT&CK can be useful to cyberthreat intelligence as it describes adversarial behaviors in a standard fashion. Actors can be tracked with associations to techniques and tactics in ATT&CK that they have been known to utilize. This gives a roadmap to defenders to apply against their operational controls to see where they have weaknesses against certain actors and where they have strengths. Creating MITRE ATT&CK navigator entries for specific actors is a good way to visualize the environment's strengths and weaknesses against those actors or groups.

ATT&CK is valuable in a variety of everyday settings. Any defensive activities that reference attackers and their behaviors can benefit from applying ATT&CK's taxonomy. Beyond offering a common lexicon for cyber defenders, ATT&CK also provides a foundation for penetration testing and red teaming. This gives defenders and red teamers a common language when referring to adversarial behaviors.

What's most important to remember about implementing the MITRE ATT&CK Framework is that it is not a one-stop security shop. More squares filled in does not equal more protection, and technique visibility should always be verified with testing.

A list of tools that can help you accomplish this is available at MITRE ATT&CK® (https://attack.mitre.org). See Figure 3.1.

MITRE has techniques and sub-techniques. Techniques represent the broad action an adversary takes to achieve a tactical goal, whereas a sub-technique is a more specific adversary action.

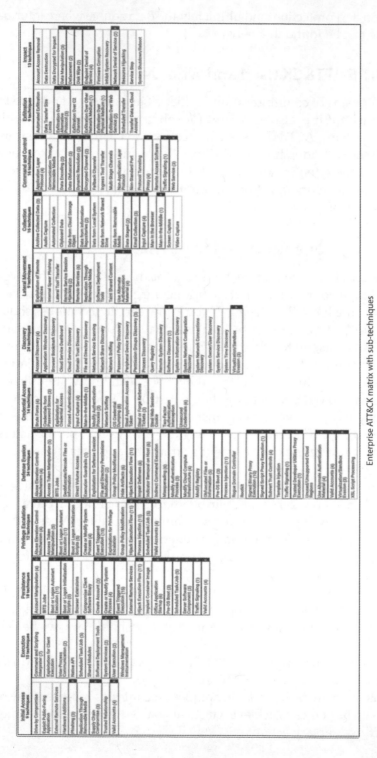

Enterprise ATT&CK matrix with sub-techniques

Figure 3.1: Enterprise ATT&CK matrix with sub-techniques

Tactics

The highest level of organization in ATT&CK is *tactics*. The strategic goal of an attacker may be to extort ransom, steal information, or simply destroy an organization's IT environment. But attackers must reach a series of incremental, short-term objectives to achieve their ultimate, strategic goal.

MITRE ATT&CK® (`https://attack.mitre.org`) assigned a reference ID [`TA*`], representing different tactics and sub-tactics, which you can find at `https://attack.mitre.org/tactic`. Most attacks begin with trying to gain Initial Access (TA0001). Then other fundamental tactics, including Execution (TA0002) and Persistence (TA0003), are usually necessary intermediate goals no matter the end goal of the attack. An attacker trying to steal information will need to accomplish Collection (TA0009) and finally Understanding MITRE ATT&CK™ Exfiltration (TA0010). Attackers may engage many other tactics in order to reach their goal, such as hopping from system to system or account to account through Lateral Movement (TA0008) or attempting to hide from your monitoring through Defense Evasion (TA005).

Attackers may engage many other tactics in order to reach their goal. It's important to understand, though, that tactics are a classification and description of short-term intent. Tactics describe what the attacker is trying to do at any given phase of the attack—not how they are specifically going about it.

Techniques

While tactics specify what the attacker is trying to do, *techniques* describe the various technical ways attackers have developed to employ a given tactic. Similar to the tactics, techniques also carry a reference ID as [`T*`], which represents different techniques, which you can find at `https://attack.mitre.org/techniques/enterprise`). For instance, attackers usually want to maintain their presence in your network over reboots or logon sessions. This is Tactic TA0003: Persistence. But you can achieve persistence many ways. For instance, on Windows systems, you can leverage certain keys in the registry whose values are executed as system commands in connection with predictable events, such as system start or logon (which is the T1060 - Registry Run Keys/Startup Folder technique). Or you can simply install your malicious program as a system service using technique T1050: New Service. Another technique is T1103: AppInit DLLs, which is a way of getting every process that loads `user32.dll` to also load your malicious DLL. There are many more techniques, and others will be developed in the future, but they all revolve around giving the attacker persistent access to the victim's system or network. Hence, they are all grouped under the same tactic.

Some techniques help facilitate more than one tactic, and this is reflected in ATT&CK. For instance, T1050: New Service is listed under two tactics—Persistence

and Privilege Escalation. For each technique, ATT&CK lists the applicable platforms (e.g., Windows and Linux), the permissions perquisite to exploiting the
technique, sources of data for detecting the technique (e.g., logs), and a cross-
reference to any related attack patterns in CAPEC, which is a related catalog of
common attack patterns focused on application security.

Let's take a look at an example of how some of these changes demonstrate
themselves in the latest version of the MITRE ATT&CK framework.

Figure 3.2 shows "Initial Access," which is a tactic found on the ATT&CK
Framework. In the previous version of the framework, Spear Phishing Attachment, Spear Phishing Link, and Spear Phishing via Service were techniques, and
in the new version, they are all sub-techniques and consolidated under Phishing,
which now exists at the Technique level. You can also see that Supply Chain
Compromise and Valid Accounts added new sub-techniques that were not there
previously. New sub-techniques were required across the entire framework to
properly scale and respond to threats as they evolve.

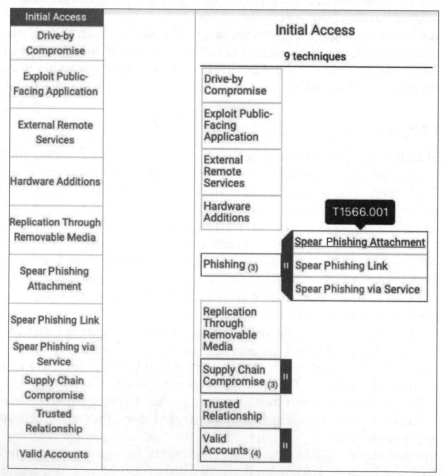

Figure 3.2: The Initial Access tactic, found on the ATT&CK Framework

By combining existing similar sub-techniques into groups and developing new sub-techniques across the entire framework, MITRE has solved a problem with granularity and built a new framework that can continue to evolve and scale for years to come. ATT&CK's growth has resulted in techniques at different levels of granularity: some are very broad and cover a lot of activity, while others cover a narrow set of activity. They wanted to address the granularity challenge while also giving the community a more robust framework to build onto over time.

Applying ATT&CK tags to threat intelligence enables you to classify, correlate, and derive meaningful conclusions to help you prioritize responses and make better decisions. Incorporating ATT&CK into ThreatConnect Playbooks lets you automate how the framework is utilized in your workflow. You can find the public GitHub repository at `https://github.com/ThreatConnect-Inc/threatconnect-playbooks`. For example, notify your Security Operations team and add indicators to blocklists when incidents associated with tactics and techniques relevant to your organization occur.

The MITRE Enterprise matrix includes all tactics and techniques relevant to on-premise and cloud solutions. The MITRE framework also provides tactics and techniques that are relevant only to cloud solutions.

Figure 3.3 shows the tactics and techniques representing the MITRE ATT&CK Matrix for Enterprise covering cloud-based techniques. The matrix contains information for the following platforms: AWS, GCP, Azure, Azure AD, Office 365, and SaaS. Within the Cloud Matrix, you can go even further and pick up a specific cloud solution, such as O365.

Refer to Appendix G to learn more about the definitions of the MITRE Cloud Matrix tactics and its techniques.

Threat Hunting Using Five Common Tactics

NOTE Attackers and defenders constantly respond to each other, which means, on either side, what works today might not tomorrow.

In this section, we discuss the following five ATT&CK tactics and techniques because of their prevalence in attacks.

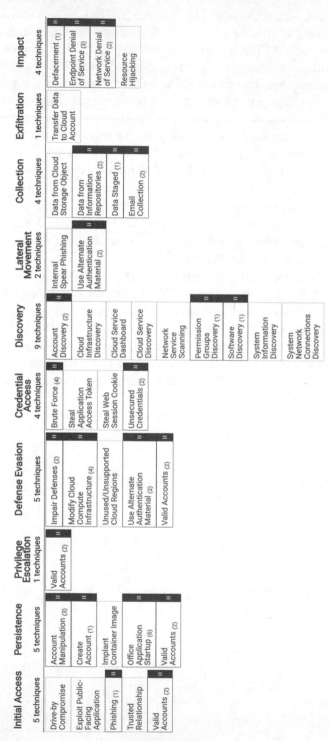

Figure 3.3: Tactics and techniques representing the MITRE ATT&CK® Matrix for Enterprise covering cloud-based techniques

ID	TACTIC	TOP THREE TECHNIQUES
TA0004	Privilege Escalation	■ Access Token Manipulation ■ Bypass User Account Control ■ DLL Search Order Hijacking
TA0006	Credential Access	■ Credential Dumping ■ Password Cracking ■ Man in the Middle
TA0008	Lateral Movement	■ Pass the Hash ■ Application Access Token ■ Pass the Ticket
TA0011	Command and Control	■ Connection Proxy ■ Non-standard Ports ■ One-way Communication
TA0010	Exfiltration	■ Automation Exfiltration ■ Exfiltration Over Alternative Protocol ■ Transfer Data to Cloud Account

Refer to Appendixes B to F to learn more about the definitions of these five ATT&CK tactics and techniques.

Many organizations are already collecting the logs and information that match the data sources necessary to detect these techniques. Explore each one of these techniques in-depth, highlighting how the attackers use them and how you can detect them. Identify which logs you need to collect and what you need to look for in those logs.

Privilege Escalation

Privilege escalation is a common way for attackers to gain unauthorized access to systems within a security perimeter. Attackers start by finding weak points in an organization's defenses and gaining access to a system. In many cases, that first point of penetration will not grant attackers with the level of access or data they need. Especially nowadays, removing the local admin is one of the best practices to reduce the attack surface. Hence, attacks need to escalate the privilege from a normal user to a higher privilege or admin in order to gain more permissions or obtain access to additional, more sensitive systems.

In some cases, attackers attempting privilege escalation find the "doors are wide open"—inadequate security controls, or failure to follow the principle of least privilege, with users having more privileges than they actually need. In other cases, attackers exploit software vulnerabilities, or use specific techniques to overcome an operating system's permissions mechanism.

Privilege escalation consists of techniques that adversaries use to gain higher-level permissions on a system or network. Adversaries can often enter and explore a network with unprivileged access but require elevated permissions to follow through on their objectives. Common approaches are to take advantage of system weaknesses, misconfigurations, and vulnerabilities.

There are many privilege escalation methods in Windows operating systems. Here is a brief review of the top three common methods.

- **Access Token Manipulation:** Adversaries may modify access tokens to operate under a different user or system security context to perform actions and bypass access controls. Windows uses access tokens to determine the ownership of a running process. A user can manipulate access tokens to make a running process appear as though it is the child of a different process or belongs to someone other than the user that started the process. When this occurs, the process also takes on the security context associated with the new token.

- **Bypass User Account Control:** Adversaries may bypass UAC mechanisms to elevate process privileges on a system. Windows User Account Control (UAC) allows a program to elevate its privileges (tracked as integrity levels ranging from low to high) to perform a task under administrator-level permissions, possibly by prompting the user for confirmation. The impact to the user ranges from denying the operation under high enforcement to allowing the user to perform the action if they are in the local administrators group and click through the prompt or allowing them to enter an administrator password to complete the action.

- **DLL Search Order Hijacking:** Adversaries may execute their own malicious payloads by hijacking the search order used to load DLLs. Windows systems use a common method to look for required DLLs to load into a program. Hijacking DLL loads may be for the purpose of establishing persistence as well as elevating privileges and/or evading restrictions on file execution.

Refer to Appendix B to learn more about the definitions of the Privilege Escalation tactic and its techniques.

Case Study

A leading organization in Asia produces and sells passenger tickets with a magnetic strip to their train and bus commuters. Customers can buy unregistered tickets directly from a retail store, or from the train or bus station. Customers can register the card online using a unique ID such as email address and bank account details (credit or debit card number), which can also automatically add money when the card balance meets a certain threshold.

A hacker somehow stole unique customer ID and bank details from the organization's database. The hacker used that stolen information to top up unregistered zero-balance tickets that he purchased from a retail store. He started selling these topped-up tickets in retail stores and online at a discounted price. For example, the hacker added $100 to an unregistered ticket using someone else's credit or debit card and sold the ticket with a 20% discount, i.e., $80. In the customer's bank transaction, there was a record reflecting the credit or debit card transaction; however, they did not initiate it. The hacker carried out this activity for a while until the organization realized the large volume of customers that were impacted.

The ticket was a genuine one, and the organization was liable to its customers, including financial loss. The organization had a substantial financial loss and reputational damage, as customers were worried about the data breach of their identity and payment details.

The organization realized the cause of the compromise in their infrastructure related to API and the web server. The use of information technology applications and services without explicit IT department approval also caused this compromise. They decided to implement security testing and the software development cycle that includes the API.

Credential Access

Credential access consists of techniques for stealing credentials like account names and passwords. Techniques used to get credentials include keylogging or credential dumping. Using legitimate credentials can give adversaries access to systems, make them harder to detect, and provide the opportunity to create more accounts to help achieve their goals.

Here is a brief review of the top three common credential access methods.

- **Credential Dumping:** Adversaries attempt to dump credentials to obtain account login and credential information, normally in the form of a hash or a cleartext password, from the operating system and software. Credentials can then be used to perform lateral movement and access restricted information.

- **Password Cracking:** Adversaries may use password cracking to attempt to recover usable credentials, such as plaintext passwords, when credential material such as password hashes are obtained. OS credential dumping is used to obtain password hashes, which may only get an adversary so far when pass the hash is not an option. Techniques to systematically guess the passwords used to compute hashes are available, or the adversary may use a precomputed rainbow table to crack hashes. Cracking hashes is usually done on adversary-controlled systems outside of the target network. The plaintext password resulting from a successfully cracked hash may be used to log in to systems, resources, and services.

- **Man in the Middle:** Adversaries may attempt to position themselves between two or more networked devices using a man-in-the-middle (MiTM) technique to support follow-on behaviors such as network sniffing or transmitted data manipulation. By abusing features of common networking protocols that can determine the flow of network traffic (e.g., ARP, DNS, LLMNR, etc.), adversaries may force a device to communicate through an adversary-controlled system so they can collect information or perform additional actions.

Refer to Appendix C to learn more about the definitions of the Credential Access tactic and its techniques.

Case Study

Credential stuffing is a brute force technique and a common type of attack that many popular brands have been caught up in. In credential stuffing, adversaries may use credentials obtained from breach dumps of unrelated accounts to gain access to target accounts through credential overlap. Occasionally, large numbers of username and password pairs are dumped online when a website or service is compromised, and the user account credentials accessed. The information may be useful to an adversary attempting to compromise accounts by taking advantage of the tendency for users to use the same passwords across personal and business accounts.

Uber was severely punished following its deception over a data breach that occurred in 2016. The company was fined a total of $1.2 million from separate regulators in the UK and the Netherlands, although both penalties resulted from the same incident.

An investigation from the UK's Information Commissioner's Office (ICO) found that an attacker gained access to Uber's data storage through credential stuffing. They used an Uber employee's previously exposed credentials from other websites to access their GitHub account.

Once inside this account, the attacker found login details to the Amazon Web Service S3 buckets where Uber's data was stored. This allowed them to steal data for 57 million Uber users, including both drivers and riders. The attackers then reached out to Uber and demanded a $100,000 payment for information on how they were able to access the S3 buckets. Uber paid up, making the payment seem as though it was part of their bug bounty program, but it did not make the matter fully public. The company didn't end up revealing the details of the breach until about a year later, in late 2017. The hacking incident and its resulting cover-up led to Uber being punished for several different reasons: for poor security practices, for late notification, and for being deceptive about the so-called bug bounty.

Despite the seemingly low rate of success, the sheer scale of credential stuffing makes it incredibly effective for hackers and devastatingly costly for users and companies.

Lateral Movement

Lateral movement consists of techniques that adversaries use to enter and control remote systems on a network. Following through on their primary objective often requires exploring the network to find their target and subsequently gaining access to it. Reaching their objective often involves pivoting through multiple systems and accounts to gain control. Adversaries might install their own remote access tools to accomplish lateral movement or use legitimate credentials with native network and operating system tools, which may be stealthier.

Adversaries may use alternate authentication material, such as password hashes, Kerberos tickets, and application access tokens, to move laterally within an environment and bypass normal system access controls. Here is a brief review of the top three common methods:

- **Pass the Hash:** Adversaries may "pass the hash" using stolen password hashes to move laterally within an environment, bypassing normal system access controls. Pass the hash (PtH) is a method of authenticating as a user without having access to the user's cleartext password. This method bypasses standard authentication steps that require a cleartext password, moving directly into the portion of the authentication that uses the password hash. In this technique, valid password hashes for the account being used are captured using a Credential Access technique. Captured hashes are used with PtH to authenticate as that user. Once authenticated, PtH may be used to perform actions on local or remote systems.

- **Application Access Token:** Adversaries may use stolen application access tokens to bypass the typical authentication process and access restricted accounts, information, or services on remote systems. These tokens are typically stolen from users and used in lieu of login credentials.

- **Pass the Ticket:** Adversaries may "pass the ticket" using stolen Kerberos tickets to move laterally within an environment, bypassing normal system access controls. Pass the ticket (PtT) is a method of authenticating to a system using Kerberos tickets without having access to an account's password. Kerberos authentication can be used as the first step to lateral movement to a remote system.

Refer to Appendix D to learn more about the definitions of the Lateral Movement tactic and its techniques.

Case Study

A recent attack from the PARINACOTA group, known for human-operated attacks that deploy the Wadhrama ransomware, is notable for its use of multiple methods for lateral movement (see Figure 3.4). After gaining initial access to an Internet-facing server via RDP brute force, the attackers searched for additional vulnerable machines in the network by scanning on ports 3389 (RDP), 445 (SMB), and 22 (SSH).

The adversaries downloaded and used Hydra to brute force targets via SMB and SSH. In addition, they used credentials that they stole through credential dumping using Mimikatz to sign into multiple other server machines via Remote Desktop. On all additional machines they were able to access, the attackers performed mainly the same activities, dumping credentials and searching for valuable information.

Notably, the attackers were particularly interested in a server that did not have Remote Desktop enabled. They used WMI in conjunction with PsExec to allow remote desktop connections on the server and then used netsh to disable blocking on port 3389 in the firewall. This allowed the attackers to connect to the server via RDP.

They eventually used this server to deploy ransomware to a huge portion of the organization's server machine infrastructure. The attack, an example of a human-operated ransomware campaign, crippled much of the organization's functionality, demonstrating that detecting and mitigating lateral movement is critical.

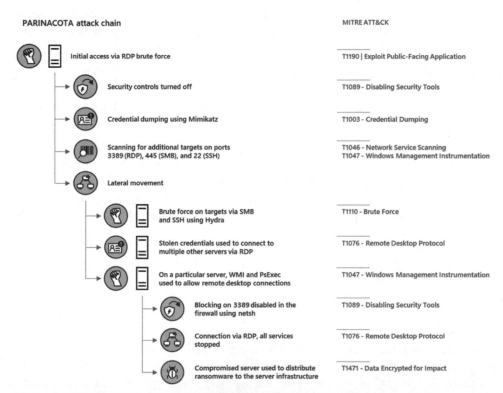

Figure 3.4: PARINACOTA attack with multiple lateral movement methods

Command and Control

Command and control consists of techniques that adversaries may use to communicate with systems under their control within a victim network. Adversaries commonly attempt to mimic normal, expected traffic to avoid detection. There are many ways an adversary can establish command and control with various levels of stealth depending on the victim's network structure and defenses:

- **Connection Proxy:** This technique is used by attackers to facilitate the Command-and-Control Tactic (TA0011), which represents how adversaries communicate with systems under their control within a target network. There are many ways an adversary can establish command and control with various levels of covertness, depending on system configuration and network topology. Due to the wide degree of variation available to the adversary at the network level, only the most common factors were used to describe the differences in command and control. There are still a great many specific techniques within the documented methods, largely due to how easy it is to define new protocols and use existing, legitimate protocols and network services for communication.

- **Non-standard Ports:** Adversaries may communicate using a protocol and port paring that are typically not associated. For example, HTTPS over port 8088[1] or port 587[2] as opposed to the traditional port 443. Adversaries may make changes to the standard port used by a protocol to bypass filtering or muddle analysis/parsing of network data.

- **One-way Communication:** Adversaries may use an existing, legitimate external web service as a means for sending commands to a compromised system without receiving return output over the web service channel. Compromised systems may leverage popular websites and social media to host command and control (C2) instructions. Those infected systems may opt to send the output from those commands back over a different C2 channel, including to another distinct web service. Alternatively, compromised systems may return no output at all in cases where adversaries want to send instructions to systems and do not want a response.

Refer to Appendix E to learn more about the definitions of the Command and Control tactic and its techniques.

Case Study

The professional service firm, which is the second-most targeted industry for cybersecurity attacks, was using SaaS solutions for business productivity. They did not deploy multifactor authentication across all employees except the IT department. They realized they had not received payment from a couple of customers to whom they issued invoices. First, they validated with the bank to ensure any delay from the bank side to reflect the amount if the customer had already paid. Their bank confirmed that they had not received payments from the customers. Then the professional service firm reached out to the customer's finance department. The customer finance team confirmed they paid based on the invoice and new account details provided. The professional service firm's finance team ensured that no account change was initiated from their end. So, they launched a full investigation of this incident.

Although there was a security policy to change the password every 90 days, a senior executive in the firm requested an exception overruling this policy. Around 20 senior executives got a similar exception. During the cyber team investigation, they found the executive's password was leaked to multiple sites. It was evident that a hacker dumped the executive's password. The hacker accessed the Practice Lead's email account, for which he had not changed his password for the past couple of years. The hacker set up "forward rule" in the senior executive's email account so that all emails that the senior executive received were forwarded to the hacker's personal email. As the executive did not attempt to change the password for more than two years, the hacker spent ample time waiting for the right opportunity to strike.

The senior executive sent invoices to customers. When the firm's finance team sent invoices to the senior executive by email attachment, they were forwarded to the hacker's email. The hacker picked a few emails with the invoice attached and amended the account information where the customer was expected to make the payment. The hacker logged in to the senior executive's email account and sent the invoice with altered account information and called out the account number change in the email. The customer had no reason to be suspicious as the email they received was from the genuine source that they regularly work with.

As a result of this incident, the professional service firm had to report to the local privacy commissioner. The challenge was that they could not determine the scope of the impact, as they had no idea how long the hacker was active in the network and whether other user credentials were compromised. The incident was exposed to the market and the professional service firm had to send one-to-one communication to around 2,000 customers to explain the situation. In addition to financial and reputational damage, it was an embarrassing situation for the professional service firm, as they tell their customers about the importance of security measures, but failed to implement a strict and universal security policy within their own organization.

NOTE Two Factor Authentication (2FA) can prevent hacker access to emails even if dumped passwords are used.

Exfiltration

Exfiltration consists of techniques that adversaries use to steal data from your network. Once they've collected data, adversaries often package it to avoid detection while removing it. This can include compression and encryption. Techniques for getting data out of a target network typically include transferring it over their command and control channel or an alternate channel and may also include putting size limits on the transmission.

- **Automation Exfiltration:** Adversaries may exfiltrate data, such as sensitive documents, through the use of automated processing after being gathered during collection.

- **Exfiltration Over Alternative Protocol:** Once an attacker obtains the desired information, the attacker must get that data out of the victim's network without being noticed. This is part of the Exfiltration Tactic (TA0010) and a common technique is the Exfiltration Over Alternative Protocol, where the exfiltration is performed with a different protocol from the main command and control protocol or channel. The data is likely to be sent to an alternate network location from the main command and control server. Alternate protocols include FTP, SMTP, HTTP/S, DNS, or some other network protocol. Different channels could include Internet web services such as cloud storage.

- **Transfer Data to Cloud Account:** Adversaries may exfiltrate data by transferring the data, including backups of cloud environments, to another cloud account they control on the same service to avoid typical file transfers/ downloads and network-based exfiltration detection. A defender who is monitoring for large transfers outside the cloud environment through normal file transfers or over command and control channels may not be watching for data transfers to another account within the same cloud provider. Such transfers may utilize existing cloud provider APIs and the internal address space of the cloud provider to blend into normal traffic or avoid data transfers over external network interfaces.

Refer to Appendix F to learn more about the definitions of the Data Exfiltration tactic and its techniques.

Case Study

An oil and gas facility had two high-tech exercise bicycles that were connected to the Internet and communicating through insecure methods. These were not segmented from corporate IT resources and thus presented the attacker with a network path to the organization's critical assets.

Awake Security identified that the two exercise bikes were sending unencrypted HTTP traffic to the Internet, and used basic authentication (a weak authentication method that exposes the username and password). Both machines were sitting on the corporate network and exfiltrating data out to the Internet. Additionally, they appeared to be unpatched, leaving the facility wide open to attack. (See https://awakesecurity.com/case-studies/iot-unsecured-iot-devices-used-for-data-exfiltration/.)

The firm's IT and security teams were completely unaware of these devices being on the network, since existing security and configuration management tools were blind to these unmanaged IoT devices.

Awake automatically looks for weak and insecure authentication mechanisms, the use of cleartext credentials, and for sensitive data leaving the network. These activities triggered an adversarial model in the Awake Security Platform, which alerted the security team about the insecure IoT devices.

The MITRE ATT&CK Framework is growing in popularity among researchers and security companies. It provides a detailed explanation of the hows and whys of specific attacker techniques. ATT&CK describes the purpose of the technique, the types of platforms, potential mitigations, and references to online reports.

Other Methodologies and Key Threat-Hunting Tools to Combat Attack Vectors

In this section, we discuss other leading methodologies and key threat-hunting tools to combat attack vectors outside of MITRE ATT&CK Framework tactics and techniques. We explicitly look at the Zero Trust and the cloud-based Defense in Depth strategy, and we introduce the Microsoft and AWS threat-hunting tools to analyze events and logs.

Zero Trust

Before the Internet, we created networks protected by firewalls, using a methodology called *castle defenses*. But then the Internet started to enable us to really transform how we did things. Now, in an organization, user population spans across employees, partners, and contractors, and they are all bringing their own devices. They store sensitive data in transformative cloud services. They connect devices deployed in our supply chains, dealers, factories, vehicles, and buildings. They even share users, devices, apps, and data with our partners and vendors. Furthermore, the bolt on security tools added over the years to combat new threats is now aging and not able to keep up with the new and emerging threats. We can see this simply by seeing the number of data breaches. So, Microsoft and many other industry players are leading a new approach to modernize cybersecurity using a comprehensive Zero Trust model adapt to the changing world and protect assets, data, and customers wherever they are.

We're living in a new reality. Those old assumptions will not keep us secure in the new world. We can no longer believe everything behind the corporate firewall is safe. We need new principles to protect us.

- **Verify explicitly.** Always authenticate and authorize based on all available data points, including user identity, location, device health, service or workload, data classification, and anomalies.

- **Use least privileged access.** Limit user access with Just In Time and Just Enough Access (JIT/JEA) to protect both data and productivity.

- **Assume breach.** Minimize blast radius for breaches and employ security strategy to prevent lateral movement.

Zero Trust is a security methodology that requires all users, even those inside the organization's enterprise network, to be authenticated, authorized, and continuously validating security configuration and posture, before being granted or keeping access to applications and data (Figure 3.5). Zero Trust is not simply a tool or product. It packages a set of existing technologies and processes like multi-factor authentication, identity and access management, and data analytics to provide defense-in-depth to thwart adversaries even after they've breached networks.

Next Generation Defense in Depth = Zero Trust

Figure 3.5: Zero Trust is a security methodology with several aspects.

To cut through the complexity, simply put, Zero Trust is next-generation defense-in-depth risk-based security—a journey toward intelligent security for an organization where we move away from a trust-by-default perspective to a trust-by-exception one.

An integrated capability to automatically manage those exceptions and alerts is important so you can more easily find and detect threats, respond to them, and prevent or block undesired events across your organization. This provides visibility across your environment and allows leveraging automation to make intelligent risk-based access decisions. It's not a point solution, but a holistic modular approach that adapts and grows with you and your business.

Zero Trust is one of the most effective ways for organizations to control access to their networks, applications, endpoints, identity, infrastructure, and data. It combines a wide range of preventative techniques including identity verification, micro segmentation, endpoint security, and least privilege controls to deter would-be attackers and limit their access in the event of a breach.

This added layer of security is critical as companies increase the number of endpoints within their network and expand their infrastructure to include cloud-based applications and servers. Both of these trends make it more difficult to establish, monitor, and maintain secure perimeters. Furthermore, a borderless security strategy is especially important for those organizations that have a global workforce and offer employees the ability to work remotely.

By segmenting the network and restricting user access, Zero Trust security helps the organization contain breaches and minimize potential damage. This is an important security measure as some of the most sophisticated attacks are orchestrated by internal users.

Zero Trust is targeted at both outside attackers that have already breached the network and malicious insiders, and is designed to prevent them from moving laterally through the network as they seek out sensitive data. For example, Edward Snowden had legitimate credentials to operate as a subcontractor within the National Security Agency's network. There was no way to know, however, that he was downloading top-secret material about NSA surveillance programs because there wasn't an additional micro-perimeter that prevented downloads without proper authentication. Zero Trust would have hypothetically uncovered or prevented his activities through the principle known as least privilege, which gives users the least network privileges they need to access the data, applications, and services necessary to do their job.

> **"Zero Trust architecture (ZTA) has the ability to fundamentally change the effectiveness of security and data sharing across DoD networks."**
>
> *—stated the Defense Innovation Board's July 2019 report entitled, "The Road to Zero Trust (Security)"*

Cloud deployments are excellent candidates for implementing Zero Trust concepts. If the cloud infrastructure itself is ever compromised, a Zero Trust–compliant architecture provides protection from adversaries seeking to entrench themselves in our virtual network. Different organizational requirements, existing technology implementations, and security stages affect how the Zero Trust model implementation takes place. Integration between multiple technologies, like endpoint management and SIEM, helps make implementations simple, operationally efficient, and adaptive.

While commercial clouds offer an excellent opportunity to scale capability and control costs, they pose risks since we do not control the infrastructure and there may be delays in communicating compromises. The assumption Zero Trust makes—that you are compromised—is particularly suited to cloud infrastructures.

Threat Intelligence and Zero Trust

Threat intelligence provides two main benefits to organizations:

- It helps inform organizations about threats.
- It gives you a language for communicating threats and their impact within your organization.

Threat intelligence as a Zero Trust control is about helping you understand the specific threats that you need to protect for the specific environments that you're protecting. Once you've deployed Zero Trust controls, you're going to have network segments that have different purposes or serve the business in different ways. Each of these is going to face different risks. For example, in a network or in a server environment, you're not likely to have users opening and clicking phishing emails, but in a user environment, it's quite likely you will.

Having a better know-how for the different tactics, techniques, and procedures that are being leveraged against your organizations within your region are going to help you protect these individual siloed environments and prioritize your mitigation strategy for each of them. In many ways, threat intelligence provides you the justification for your security budget.

As you mature in your journey, you are going to realize the need for specific types of intelligence about more specific types of threat; this is where you will now need to subscribe to paid or open-source threat intel feed or from a specific technology vendor. Organizations will likely engage with many different sources of threat intelligence. This is key to building a foundation of understanding, and again, the language for communicating internally and the risks that your organization faces.

The most important thing to understand when you're dealing with threat intelligence is that it's collected from many disparate sources (open sourced and paid). The analysis and outcome and, truly, even the confidence in what you receive may vary greatly.

Build Cloud-Based Defense-in-Depth

The last section outlined three principles of Zero Trust—verify explicitly, least privilege access, and assume breach. The guiding principle is *assume breach*, which is an extension of the defense-in-depth strategy. By constantly challenging the security capabilities, organizations can stay ahead of emerging threats.

There is no perfect defense. Even cutting the network cables between systems isn't enough to stop attackers from getting in. Attackers are strongly motivated to invent new ways to sneak or smash their way into our networks and steal our stuff. The better strategy we need is to assume breach and realize that any control can be overcome. See Figure 3.6.

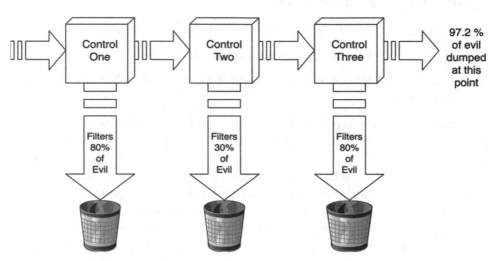

Figure 3.6: Control number filters

Say you've got a hundred attacks coming into your organization at a given moment. Control One filters out 80% of threats to give you only 20 attacks to worry about. Not bad. And then Control Two whacks nearly a third of those. Now the total has dropped to 13. Not a great control, but it still reduced things a bit. Finally, Control Three takes another 80% off that, dropping the number of attacks to just 3. By overlapping these three limited controls, you've created a single control that's 97% effective.

In today's cloud-enabled world, the perimeter of the network is an increasingly blurry line. Defense-in-depth involves defining a clear separation of "inside" and "outside" network operations and building multiple lines of defense separating the two. While some security controls are not applicable to implementing defense-in-depth in the cloud, it is possible to apply a variety of requirements. While a cloud consumer cannot implement physical controls (due to lack of physical access to cloud servers), they can implement both technical and administrative controls based upon the type of cloud architecture in use. Controls can be classified as external or internal to the cloud environment:

- **External Cloud Security:** The first step in implementing cloud-based defense-in-depth is identifying the use of each cloud resource and the associated level of appropriate security and trust. For example, an IaaS cloud environment such as AWS, and Azure being used to host a public website has very different requirements than environments hosting databases containing sensitive or confidential information. The security needs of each resource should be considered separately, and the controls applied to each environment must be commensurate with the level of risk associated with an exposure. Ideally, public-facing and internal resources should be kept in cloud environments completely isolated from one another unless absolutely necessary to do otherwise. If isolation is impossible, strictly defined interconnections should be utilized and can be implemented using both the tools available within the CSP's management interface as well as third-party tools, which can be integrated into the environment. An important part of external cloud security is locking down access to the cloud systems. One of the advantages of the cloud is that it can be accessed from anywhere; however, this also presents security concerns. Regardless of the technology implemented, all organizations should implement strong authentication controls, including multifactor authentication. Organizations with multiple cloud presences should implement a Cloud Access Security Broker (CASB) tool to ensure Identity and Access Management controls are applied consistently across all cloud resources.

- **Internal Cloud Security:** Cloud resources should also have strong internal security. "Compartmentalization" is often used to segregate data and services that do not need to be stored in the same location or accessed by the same groups of individuals. Within a virtual machine, access should be limited based upon the principles of need-to-know and least privilege to minimize the impact of a potential breach. For example, Amazon S3 buckets should always be set to private with access granted on an individual basis—a very common misconfiguration enables S3 buckets, often containing sensitive information, to be accessed by anyone. Sensitive information should be encrypted whether "at-rest" (being stored) or "in-transit" (being transmitted) with keys stored within the organizational network, not on cloud servers. All connections to cloud resources should use encrypted protocols like SSH and HTTPS or be tunneled using a VPN connection if possible.

> **NOTE** Implementing cloud security using defense-in-depth involves treating the cloud as an extension of the organization's internal network. By using secure connectivity, configuring cloud virtual machines to deny any other connections, an organization can apply their existing protections to their cloud infrastructure as well. Isolation of backend systems from public-facing ones and implementing access management strategies like least privilege and need-to-know decrease the impact of a potential breach.

Monitoring the cloud for potential threats will help you stay situationally aware of when your defense strategies fail so you can quickly mitigate a threat before it becomes a compromise.

There is no cut-and-copy checklist on what controls and defenses to leverage. It's going to vary based on an organization's business, technological infrastructure, culture, and relevant threats. The key is analyzing and understanding the threats you face and the assets you care about, and then applying divergent but overlapping controls to remediate as much risk as you can. The good news is that a coordinated collection of useful but imperfect defenses is not only more effective than a single bulletproof control, it's a lot more attainable.

Analysis Tools

Threat hunters can bring a wide range of tools to bear to analyze complex datasets from multiple sources, from scripts parsing raw data, to a full Security Information and Event Management (SIEM) that provides ad hoc and complex searching, reporting, and investigations. The decision is usually about setup complexity, cost, and the need to scale as the team grows. In the following section, two common threat-hunting platforms offered by Microsoft and Amazon are introduced for the benefit of starting points in collecting all relevant events and logs for further threat hunting and analytics.

Microsoft Tools

Microsoft Azure Sentinel (see Figure 3.7) is a scalable, cloud-native SIEM and Security Orchestration, Automation, and Response (SOAR) solution. Azure Sentinel delivers intelligent security analytics and threat intelligence across the enterprise, providing a single solution for alert detection, threat visibility, proactive hunting, and threat response.

Azure Sentinel is your bird's-eye view across the enterprise alleviating the stress of increasingly sophisticated attacks, increasing volumes of alerts, and long resolution time frames. You can:

- Collect data at cloud scale across all users, devices, applications, and infrastructure, both on-premises and in multiple clouds.

- Detect previously undetected threats and minimize false positives using Microsoft's analytics and unparalleled threat intelligence.

- Investigate threats with artificial intelligence and hunt for suspicious activities at scale, tapping into years of cybersecurity work at Microsoft.

- Respond to incidents rapidly with built-in orchestration and automation of common tasks.

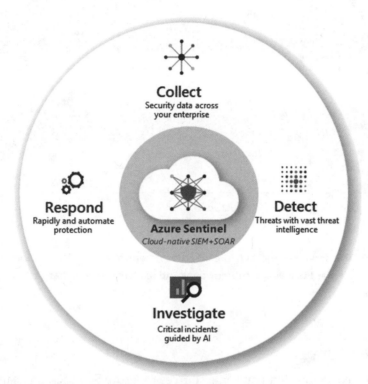

Figure 3.7: Microsoft Azure Sentinel

Building on the full range of existing Azure services, Azure Sentinel natively incorporates proven foundations, like log analytics and logic apps. Azure Sentinel enriches your investigation and detection with AI and provides Microsoft's threat intelligence stream and enables you to bring your own threat intelligence.

Connect To All Your Data

To on-board Azure Sentinel, you first need to connect to your security sources. Azure Sentinel comes with a number of connectors for Microsoft solutions, available out-of-the-box and providing real-time integration, including Microsoft 365 Defender (formerly Microsoft Threat Protection) solutions, and Microsoft 365 sources, including Office 365, Azure AD, Microsoft Defender for Identity (formerly

Azure ATP), Microsoft Cloud App Security, and more. In addition, there are built-in connectors to the broader security ecosystem for non-Microsoft solutions. You can also use common event format, Syslog, or REST-API to connect your data sources with Azure Sentinel. See Figure 3.8.

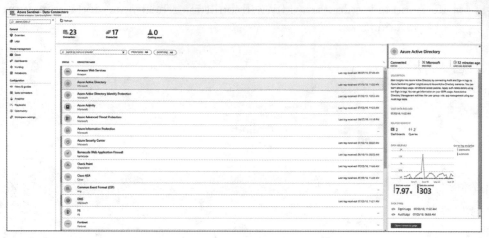

Figure 3.8: Azure Sentinel Data Connectors

> **NOTE**   This service supports Azure Lighthouse, which lets service providers sign in to their own tenant to manage subscriptions and resource groups that customers have delegated.

Workbooks

After you have connected your data sources to Azure Sentinel, you can monitor the data using the Azure Sentinel integration with Azure Monitor Workbooks, which provides versatility in creating custom workbooks (see Figure 3.9). While Workbooks are displayed differently in Azure Sentinel, it may be useful for you to see how to create interactive reports with Azure Monitor workbooks. Azure Sentinel allows you to create custom Workbooks across your data, and also comes with built-in workbook templates to allow you to quickly gain insights across your data as soon as you connect a data source.

Analytics

To help you reduce noise and minimize the number of alerts you have to review and investigate, Azure Sentinel uses analytics to correlate alerts into incidents. Incidents are groups of related alerts that together create an actionable possible

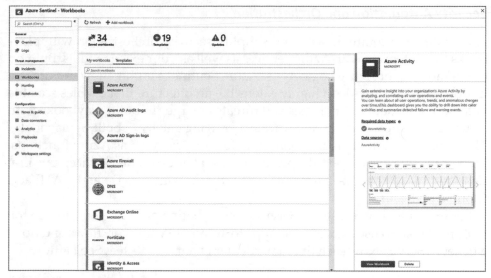

Figure 3.9: Azure Sentinel Workbooks

threat that you can investigate and resolve (see Figure 3.10). Use the built-in correlation rules as-is, or use them as a starting point to build your own. Azure Sentinel also provides machine learning rules to map your network behavior and then look for anomalies across your resources. These analytics connect the dots, by combining low-fidelity alerts about different entities into potential high-fidelity security incidents.

Figure 3.10: Azure Sentinel Incidents

Security Automation and Orchestration

Automate your common tasks and simplify security orchestration with play-books that integrate with Azure services as well as your existing tools. Built on the foundation of Azure Logic Apps, Azure Sentinel's automation and orches-tration solution provides a highly extensible architecture that enables scalable automation as new technologies and threats emerge. To build playbooks with Azure Logic Apps, you can choose from a growing gallery of built-in playbooks. These include more than 200 connectors for services such as Azure functions. The connectors allow you to apply any custom logic in code, ServiceNow, Jira, Zendesk, HTTP requests, Microsoft Teams, Slack, Windows Defender ATP, and Cloud App Security.

For example, if you use the ServiceNow ticketing system, you can use the tools provided to use Azure Logic Apps to automate your workflows and open a ticket in ServiceNow each time a particular event is detected. See Figure 3.11.

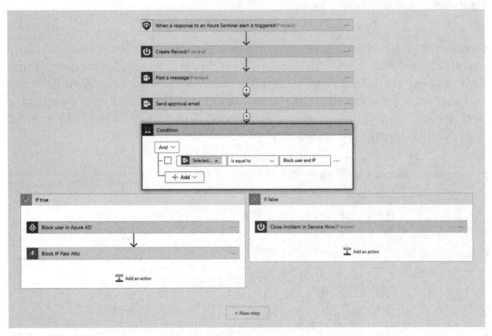

Figure 3.11: Security Orchestration Playbook

Threat hunting is all about proactive analysis of data to detect the anomalous behavior that is undetectable by the security products. As the threat-hunting team's analytics become more sophisticated, it may begin developing a set of repeatable analytics, enrichments, or data gathering steps. If it's repeatable and articulate, it can be automated. SOAR leverages the data storage and enrichment of the SIEM, understands basic rules of infrastructure integration, and allows the easy buildout of playbooks to automate a course of action. Gathering potential logs to analyze and automating the enriching processes when necessary could save threat hunters tedious and repetitive work. It could also help provide quicker triage. The SIEM with a SOAR could significantly improve speed to analysis. Taking the playbook a step further, it's possible to use data pushed to the SIEM and SOAR, such as the SQL injection detection logs from the WAF, and initiate an action.

This automated response action allows the team to limit what passive data has to be managed, and makes it easier to correlate the process logs returned with the suspicious SQL injection attacks.

Investigation

Currently in preview, Azure Sentinel's deep investigation tools help you to understand the scope and find the root cause of a potential security threat. You can choose an entity on the interactive graph to ask interesting questions for a specific entity, and drill down into that entity and its connections to get to the root cause of the threat. See Figure 3.12.

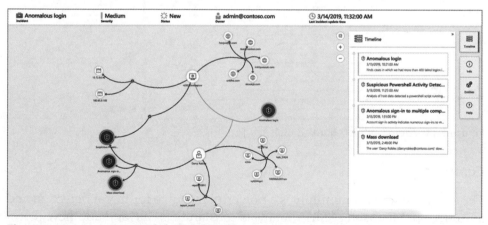

Figure 3.12: Interactive Graph for Investigation

Hunting

Azure Sentinel's powerful hunting search-and-query tools, based on the MITRE framework, enable you to proactively hunt for security threats across your organization's data sources, before an alert is triggered (see Figure 3.13). After you discover which hunting query provides high-value insights into possible attacks, you can also create custom detection rules based on your query, and surface those insights as alerts to your security incident responders. While hunting, you can create bookmarks for interesting events, enabling you to return to them later, share them with others, and group them with other correlating events to create a compelling incident for investigation.

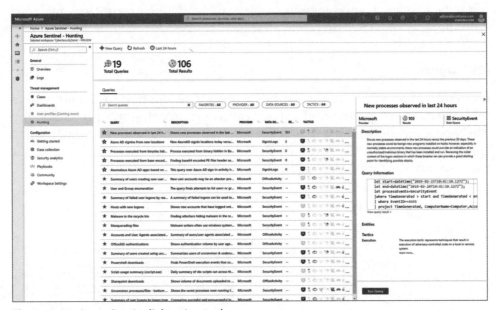

Figure 3.13: Azure Sentinel's hunting tools

Community

The Azure Sentinel community is a powerful resource for threat detection and automation. Microsoft security analysts constantly create and add new workbooks, playbooks, hunting queries, and more, posting them to the community for you to use in your environment. You can download sample content from the private community GitHub repository to create custom workbooks, hunting queries, notebooks, and playbooks for Azure Sentinel. See Figure 3.14.

Figure 3.14: Azure Sentinel Community

AWS Tools

Amazon Web Services (AWS) provides several services that can be used and chained together for scripts and analytical use.

Analyzing Logs Directly

Amazon CloudWatch is the core service for monitoring an AWS environment, because it is easy to get up and running and provides basic metrics, alarming, and dashboards (Figure 3.15). Amazon CloudWatch and AWS CloudTrail can be used together to interact directly with collected data. AWS offers methods of exporting Amazon CloudWatch logs, collected from custom applications to Amazon S3, AWS Lambda, or the Amazon ElasticSearch Service.

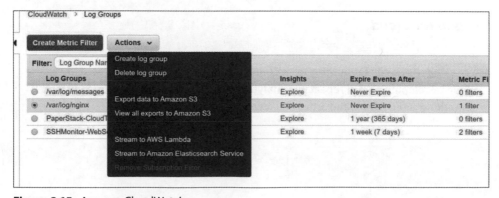

Figure 3.15: Amazon CloudWatch

AWS provides another service called Amazon Athena, which runs SQL queries against data in an Amazon S3 bucket (Figure 3.16). Customers build virtual tables that organize and format the underlying log data inside the bucket objects. It takes time to ensure that data is formatted and managed. Amazon GuardDuty is a managed service that is evaluating a growing number of findings that detect adversary behaviors and alerting the customer. Amazon GuardDuty evaluates potential behaviors by analyzing Amazon Virtual Private Cloud (VPC) Flow Logs. A similar real-time VPC flow logs analysis engine can be created using AWS Lambda, Amazon Kinesis, Amazon S3, Amazon Athena, and Amazon QuickSight.

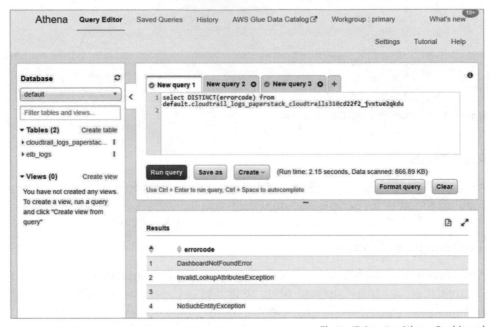

Figure 17. Amazon Athena Dashboard

Figure 3.16: The Amazon Athena service

SIEMs in the Cloud

> **NOTE** As the threat-hunting team's analytics become more sophisticated, they may begin developing a set of repeatable analytics, enrichments, or data gathering steps. If something is repeatable and articulate, it can be automated.

As a threat-hunting team starts to build a corpus of analytics that it wants to run repeatedly, or as its investigating, monitoring, and reporting needs become more comprehensive, a full SIEM is likely of interest. Several cloud-specific services, as well as traditional on-premises SIEMs, work with cloud infrastructure. The threat-hunting team should focus on developing and managing a tactical SIEM, which could be different from the SIEM an SOC might use. The tactical SIEM will likely have unstructured data, a shorter retention policy than the SOC's SIEM, and the ability to easily determine what the infrastructure looked like in the recent past.

In the cloud, good data management strategy should be implemented to be cost-effective, with pay-per-usage pricing. Generally, free or open source solutions tend to take more time and expertise to set up and maintain, but they are more customizable and cost little or nothing. Commercial solutions may cost more, but may come with better support, easy access to purpose-built connectors, and more reporting options.

After the tactical SIEM is stood up; the data is gathered, translated, and enriched; and mechanisms for analytics and reporting are in place, the threat-hunting team will start to discover repeated steps, analytics, or actions. The emerging service that integrates with the SIEM, called Security Orchestration Automation and Response (SOAR), can be helpful there.

ElasticSearch, a favorite of the open source community, boasts a significant user base and supports plug-ins for data importing, translating, and easy displaying with the Kibana application. AWS provides a managed Amazon ElasticSearch Service to make it easy to set up and run the search engine without having to do all the management heavy lifting. The company behind ElasticSearch, Elastic, has released a new app called the Elastic SIEM that is more focused on the security operations. Other products, such as ones from Sumo Logic and Splunk, also integrate directly with AWS and provide even richer and more full-featured analytic platforms.

Summary

- ATT&CK can be used many different ways to improve cybersecurity efforts. This chapter focused on explaining how you can leverage ATT&CK tactics and techniques to enhance, analyze, and test your threat-hunting efforts.

- We are in the early days of threat hunting, specifically in cloud environments. Organizations are moving away from traditional server-based infrastructure into serverless, event-driven architectures that rely on native cloud services.

- Threat hunters adapt their processes, tools, and techniques to identify and neutralize the threats in the cloud infrastructure landscape. Proper strategy ensures the right data is collected, enriched, and available to the tools the threat-hunting team uses to tease out suspicious anomalies from the vast and ever-changing infrastructure.

■ Your threat-hunting process is always growing and adapting to new information, increasing experience, and the changing threat landscape.

Resources

Understanding MITRE ATT&CK References:

■ `https://attack.mitre.org/`

■ `https://www.cynet.com/network-attacks/privilege-escalation/`

■ `https://www.sisainfosec.com/downloads/Case-Study/mitigating-privilege-escalation-attack-by-user-behaviour-analysis-and-threat-hunting.pdf`

Case Study References:

■ `https://awakesecurity.com/case-studies/iot-unsecured-iot-devices-used-for-data-exfiltration/`

■ `https://gallery.logrhythm.com/independent-white-papers/uws-using-mitre-attack-in-threat-hunting-and-detection-white-paper.pdf`

■ `https://www.comparitech.com/blog/information-security/credential-stuffing-attacks/`

■ `https://www.microsoft.com/security/blog/2020/06/10/the-science-behind-microsoft-threat-protection-attack-modeling-for-finding-and-stopping-evasive-ransomware/`

AWS Tools Reference:

■ `https://pages.awscloud.com/rs/112-TZM-766/images/How-to-Build-a-Threat-Hunting-Capability-in-AWS_Whitepaper.pdf`

Zero Trust References:

■ `https://breakingdefense.com/2020/01/disa-embraces-zero-trust-might-stop-the-next-snowden/`

■ `https://www.crowdstrike.com/epp-101/zero-trust-security/#:~:text=Zero%20Trust%20also%20prevents%20attacks,and%20minimizes%20the%20attack%20surface`

Defense-in-depth References:

- `https://www.f5.com/labs/articles/cisotociso/build-defense-in-depth-with-dissimilar-protections`
- `https://www.avertium.com/cloud-security-using-defense-in-depth/`

Microsoft Tools Reference:

- `https://docs.microsoft.com/en-us/azure/sentinel/overview`

Hunting in Microsoft Azure

In This Part

Chapter 4: Microsoft Azure Cloud Threat Prevention Framework
Chapter 5: Microsoft Cybersecurity Reference Architecture and Capability
Map

Microsoft Azure Cloud Threat Prevention Framework

What's in This Chapter

- Introduction to Microsoft Security
- Understanding the Shared Responsibility Model
- Microsoft Services for Cloud Security Posture Management and Logging/ Monitoring
  - Enabling Azure Security Center
  - Enabling Azure Defender
  - Enabling Azure Sentinel
- Microsoft Secure and Protect Features
  - How to use Azure Web Application Firewall to protect a website against "Initial Access" TTP
  - How to use Microsoft Defender for Office 365 for protection against "Initial Access" TTP
  - How to use Microsoft Defender Endpoint for protection against "Initial Access" TTP
  - How to use Azure Conditional Access for protection against "Initial Access" TTP
- Microsoft Detect Features
  - Detecting privilege escalation

- Detecting credential access
- Detecting lateral movement
- Detecting command and control
- Detecting data exfiltration

- Microsoft Respond and Recover Features

  - Automating investigation and remediation with Microsoft Defender for Endpoint
  - Using Microsoft Threat Expert support for remediation and investigation
  - Automating Security Response with MCAS and Microsoft Flow
  - How to perform an automated response using Azure Security Center
  - Using Machine Learning and Artificial Intelligence in Threat Response
  - Overview of Fusion Detection
  - Overview of Azure Machine Learning

This chapter focuses on using Microsoft services for cloud threat protection in alignment with the MITRE ATT&CK framework and the NIST Cybersecurity framework.

Introduction to Microsoft Security

Threats can come from anywhere—whether from bad actors trying to compromise systems due to poor security hardening and patching, lack of security controls, or employees not following their organization's best practices or falling into social engineering traps.

Organizations should manage their threat landscape from end to end using the integrated and comprehensive security, compliance, and identity management solutions. Microsoft has an arsenal of tools and technologies to bring all these capabilities together, whereby it allows developers to natively integrate individual layers of protection to improve end-user experiences, decrease SecOps inefficiencies, and reduce the risk of costly data breaches and compliance violations. See Figure 4.1.

Understanding the Shared Responsibility Model

Understanding the shared responsibility model is essential for those who want to take advantage of Cloud Security. Cloud providers such as Microsoft and AWS offer considerable advantages for security and compliance efforts, but they do not absolve the customer from protecting their users, applications, and service offerings.

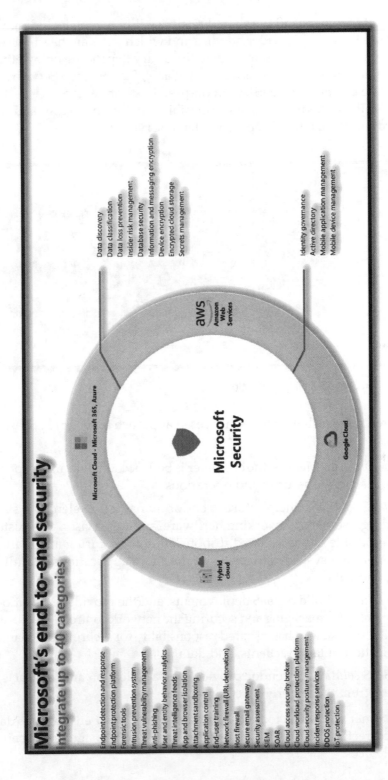

Figure 4.1: Microsoft's end-to-end integrated security features

It is critical to understand the shared responsibility model, including which security tasks the cloud provider handles and which tasks are handled by you as the customer. The workload responsibilities vary depending on whether the workload is hosted on Software as a Service (SaaS), Platform as a Service (PaaS), Infrastructure as a Service (IaaS), or in on-premises datacenters.

Figure 4.2 illustrates the areas of responsibility between the user and Microsoft, according to the type of deployment and services.

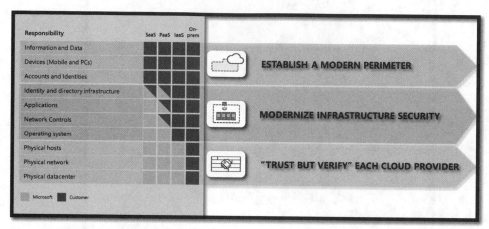

Figure 4.2: Shared responsibility on the cloud

In a shared responsibility model, a layered approach to security is described as follows:

- For *on-premises solutions*, the customer is both accountable and responsible for all aspects of security and operations.

- For *IaaS solutions*, the platform vendor manages the elements such as buildings, servers, networking hardware, and hypervisor. The customer is responsible or has a shared responsibility for securing and managing the operating system, network configuration, applications, identity, clients, and data.

- *PaaS solutions* build on IaaS deployments, and the provider is additionally responsible for managing and securing the network controls. The customer is still responsible or has a shared responsibility for securing and managing applications, identity, clients, and data.

- For *SaaS solutions*, a vendor provides the application and abstracts customers from the underlying components.

The customer continues to be accountable; they must ensure that data is classified correctly, and they share a responsibility to manage their users and endpoint devices.

Microsoft Services for Cloud Security Posture Management and Logging/Monitoring

According to the NIST Cybersecurity Framework, organizations need to develop and implement the necessary protections to restrict or mitigate the effect of a possible cybersecurity incident.

One of the primary strategies to manage cloud resources is to have an end-to-end visibility in terms of cloud security posture, threat, alerts, logging, and monitoring.

This section includes a quick summary of Azure services—Azure Security Center and Azure Defender, which is Microsoft's Cloud Security Posture Management (CSPM), and Azure Sentinel, which is Microsoft's cloud-native SIEM and SOAR technology (see Figure 4.3).

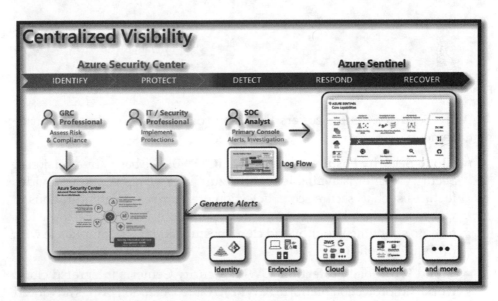

Figure 4.3: Azure Security Center vs. Azure Sentinel

Overview of Azure Security Center and Azure Defender

Azure Security Center (ASC) is focused on the protection and governance of Azure Workloads by assessing risk to them, reducing attack surface, and generating alerts on potential threats using advanced threat detection technologies. The roles who use ASC will typically include security engineers and GRC professionals that report risk to the CISO (Figure 4.4).

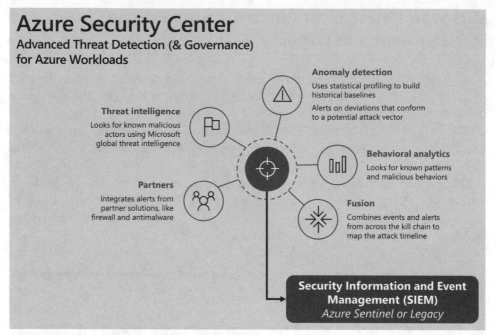

Figure 4.4: Azure Security Center overview

Azure Security Center covers the two broad pillars of cloud security management:

- **Cloud Security Posture Management (CSPM):** The basic/free version of Security Center is available for all Azure users. This version provides features such as secure score, detection of security misconfigurations in your Azure machines, asset inventory, and more. You can use these features to strengthen your hybrid cloud posture and track compliance with the built-in policies.

- **Cloud Workload Protection (CWP):** Security Center's integrated cloud workload protection platform (CWPP), Azure Defender, brings advanced and intelligent protection to your Azure and hybrid resources and workloads. Azure Defender allows you to get a range of additional security features such as vulnerability assessment, Just in Time and Just Enough Access, and many more. In addition to the built-in policies, you can also add custom policies and initiatives. You can add regulatory standards—such as NIST and Azure CIS—as well as the Azure Security Benchmark for a truly customized view of your compliance.

Prerequisites to enable Azure Security Center include:

- Paid or free subscription of Microsoft Azure
- Azure Defender subscription with the Owner, Subscription Contributor, or Security Admin role

Follow these steps to enable Azure Security Center:

1. Sign in to the Azure portal by visiting `https://portal.azure.com`.

2. From the portal's menu, select Security Center.

3. Security Center's overview page opens. See Figure 4.5.

Figure 4.5: The ASC overview dashboard

You can view and filter the list of subscriptions by selecting the Subscriptions menu item. Security Center will adjust the display to reflect the security posture of the selected subscriptions. After launching ASC the first time, you will be able to see:

■ Secure Score and Recommendations to improve your connected resources security posture.

■ An inventory of your resources that are now being assessed by Security Center, along with the security posture of each resource.

Azure Defender provides threat protection capabilities for your Azure, multi-cloud, and hybrid workloads within your subscription containing the applicable workloads. Enabling it at the workspace level doesn't enable just-in-time VM access, adaptive application controls, and network detections for Azure resources.

In addition, the only Azure Defender plans available at the workspace level are Azure Defender for servers and Azure Defender for SQL servers on machines. You can enable Azure Defender for SQL or Storage accounts at either the subscription level or resource level; however, you can enable Azure Defender for open source relational databases at the resource level only.

Figure 4.6 shows the Azure Defender dashboard in the Security Center, which provides visibility and control of the CWP features.

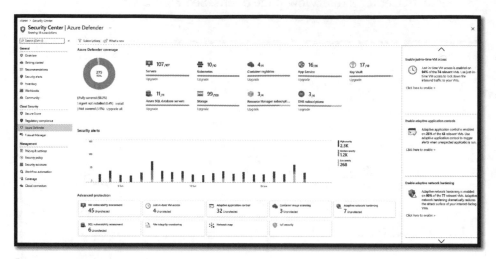

Figure 4.6: The Azure Defender dashboard

Follow these steps to enable Azure Defender:

1. From Security Center's main menu, select Pricing & Settings.
2. Select the subscription or workspace that you want to protect.
3. Select Azure Defender On to upgrade.
4. Click Save. See Figure 4.7.

For detailed steps and set up guide, visit `https://docs.microsoft.com/en-us/azure/security-center/`.

Overview of Microsoft Azure Sentinel

Microsoft Azure Sentinel is a scalable, cloud-native, Security Information Event Management (SIEM) and Security Orchestration, Automation, and Response (SOAR) solution. Azure Sentinel can provide many capabilities to SOC teams such as intelligent security analytics, threat hunting, single view of threats, and single solution for alerts detections, threat visibility, and threat response across the entire enterprise estate.

Figure 4.7: Azure Defender plans

It also allows for monitoring alerts and security-related events from any source (Microsoft security solutions, third parties, costume rules). See Figure 4.8.

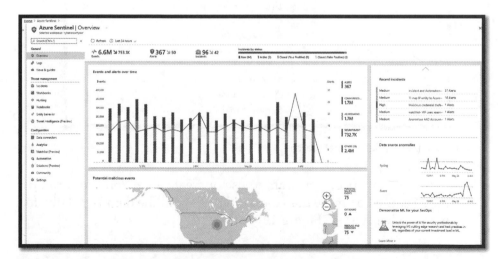

Figure 4.8: Azure Sentinel Overview

Azure Sentinel is designed to simplify the application of advanced technologies like Machine Learning and User and Entity Behavior Analytics (UEBA), to the variety of datasets you monitor and is complemented by other Microsoft Threat Protection solutions that provide a specialized investigation of hosts, email, identity attacks, and more. These can be helpful to both security analysts and SOC managers (Figure 4.8).

Here are the prerequisites for on-boarding Azure Sentinel:

- Active paid or free Azure subscription
- Log Analytics workspace
- Paid or Trial Subscription with a Contributor or a Reader permissions. Additional permissions may be required for you to connect specific data sources.

Follow these steps to enable Azure Sentinel:

1. Sign in to the Azure portal by visiting `https://portal.azure.com`.
2. Select the subscription in which Azure Sentinel is to be created.
3. Search for and select Azure Sentinel and then click Add. See Figure 4.9.

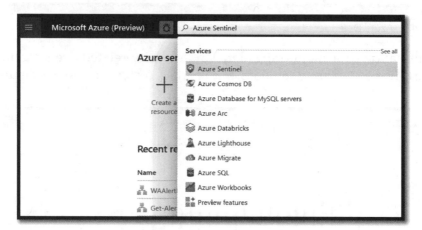

Figure 4.9: Azure Sentinel search

4. Select the workspace you want to use or create a new one. You can run Azure Sentinel on more than one workspace, but the data is isolated to a single workspace. See Figure 4.10.

Figure 4.10: Add Sentinel to a workspace

5. After enabling Azure Sentinel from the main menu, select Data Connectors. This will open the Data Connectors gallery. Select a data source and then open a connector page button. See Figure 4.11.

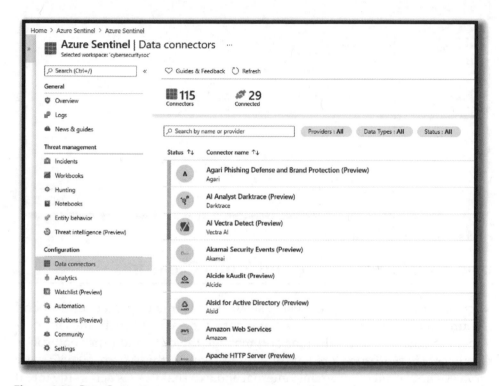

Figure 4.11: Data Connectors

6. The Next steps tab on the connector page shows relevant built-in workbooks, sample queries, and analytics rule templates that accompany the data connector. You can use these as is or modify them. Either way you can immediately get interesting insights across your data. This data will help you with investigation and hunting, which is discussed later in this chapter.

7. To view all the out-of-the-box detections, go to Analytics and then Rule templates. This tab contains all the Azure Sentinel built-in rules. See Figure 4.12.

For detailed steps and a setup guide, visit `https://docs.microsoft.com/en-us/azure/sentinel/quickstart-onboard`.

Figure 4.12: Built-in Analytics rule

Using Microsoft Secure and Protect Features

Microsoft provides comprehensive security features to protect end-to-end resources. They offer a wide array of security tools and capabilities for customers to create secure solutions and manage the data and other enterprise resources. These features are part of Azure as well within Microsoft 365; these services allow protection against internal and external threats across the threat kill chain. See Figure 4.13.

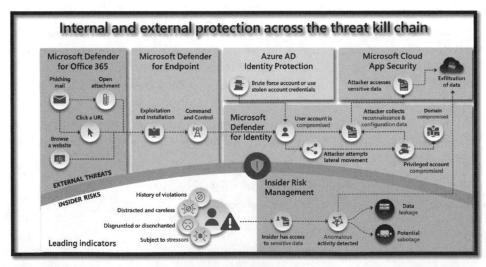

Figure 4.13: Threat kill chain protection with M365

The security and preventions security services from Azure, as shown in Figure 4.14, allow you to implement a layered, defense-in-depth strategy across identity, hosts, networks, and data. This security services and capabilities collection provides a way to understand and improve your security posture across your Microsoft and Azure environments.

Microsoft Security and Prevention Services			
Identity and Access Management	**Infrastructure and Network**	**Data and Application**	**Customer Access**
Azure Active Directory (AD)	Azure DDOS Protection Standard	Azure Backup	Azure AD External Identities (B2B, B2C)
Conditional Access	Azure Front Door	Azure Storage Service Encryption	
Domain Services	Azure Firewall and WAF	Web Application Firewall (WAF)	
Privileged Identity Management (PIM)	Azure Key Vault, Azure Service Bus	Azure Service Bus	
Multi Factor Authentication	Key Vault Managed, HSM, Azure Confidential Computing	Azure Confidential Computing	
Azure AD Identity Protection	Azure Private Link and Service Endpoints, Azure Information Protections	API Management and Azure Information Protection	
	Azure Application Gateway	Azure DevOps	
	VPN Gateway		
Azure Security Center / Azure Defender			

Figure 4.14: Microsoft Security and Prevention Services with Azure

The following sections briefly explain each of these services to understand what capabilities they provide under each domain of Identity & Access Management, Infrastructure & Network, Data & Application, and Customer Access.

Identity & Access Management

- **Azure Security Center:** ASC and Azure Defender is a unified infrastructure security management system that strengthens your datacenter's security posture and provides advanced threat protection across your hybrid, on-premises, and multi-cloud environment.

- **Azure Active Directory (AD):** AAD is Microsoft's cloud-based identity and access management services with many built-in security services and features to securely manage the identities.

  - Conditional access is the tool used by Azure AD to bring identity signals together, make decisions, and enforce organizational policies. This is a core service used for implementing Zero Trust Access Architecture.

- Domain Services is the tool used by Azure AD to provide managed domain services such as domain join, group policy, Lightweight Directory Access Protocol (LDAP), and Kerberos/NTLM authentication.

- Privileged Identity Management (PIM) is a service in Azure AD that enables you to manage, control, and monitor access to important resources in your organization.

- Multi-factor authentication is the tool used by Azure AD to help safeguard access to data and applications by requiring a second form of authentication.

- **Azure AD Identity Protection:** This tool allows organizations to automate the detection and remediation of identity-based risks, investigate risks using data in the portal, and export risk detection data to third-party utilities for further analysis.

Infrastructure & Network

- **VPN Gateway:** Virtual Private Network gateway is used to send encrypted traffic between an Azure virtual network and an on-premises location over the public Internet and to send encrypted traffic between Azure virtual networks over the Microsoft network.

- **Azure DDoS Protection Standard:** Provides enhanced DDoS mitigation features to defend against DDoS attacks. It is automatically tuned to help protect your specific Azure resources in a virtual network.

- **Azure Front Door:** A global, scalable entry point that uses the Microsoft global edge network to create fast, secure, and widely scalable web applications.

- **Azure Firewall:** A managed, cloud-based network security service that protects your Azure Virtual Network resources. It's a fully stateful firewall as a service with built-in high availability and unrestricted cloud scalability.

- **Azure Key Vault:** A secure secrets store for tokens, passwords, certificates, API keys, and other secrets. Key Vault can also be used to create and control the encryption keys used to encrypt your data.

- **Key Vault Managed HSM:** A fully managed, highly available, single-tenant, standards-compliant cloud service that enables you to safeguard cryptographic keys for your cloud applications, using FIPS 140-2 Level 3 validated HSMs.

- **Azure Private Links:** Enables you to access Azure PaaS Services (for example, Azure Storage and SQL Database) and Azure hosted customer-owned/partner services over a private endpoint in your virtual network.

- **Azure Application Gateway:** An advanced web traffic load balancer enables you to manage traffic to your web applications. Application Gateway can make routing decisions based on additional HTTP requests, such as URI path or host headers.

- **Azure Service Bus:** A fully managed enterprise message broker with message queues and publish-subscribe topics. Service Bus is used to decouple applications and services from each other.

- **Web Application Firewall:** WAF provides centralized protection of your web applications from common exploits and vulnerabilities. WAF can be deployed with Azure Application Gateway and Azure Front Door.

Data & Application

- **Azure Backup:** Provides simple, secure, and cost-effective solutions to back up your data and recover it from the Microsoft Azure cloud.

- **Azure Storage Service Encryption:** Allows you to encrypt data before storing and decrypts the data when you retrieve it automatically.

- **Azure Information Protection:** A cloud-based solution enables organizations to discover, classify, and protect documents and emails by applying labels to content.

- **API Management:** A way to create consistent and modern API gateways for existing backend services.

- **Azure Confidential Computing:** This service allows you to isolate your sensitive data while it's being processed in the cloud.

- **Azure DevOps:** Your development projects benefit from multiple layers of security and governance technologies, operational practices, and compliance policies when stored in Azure DevOps.

Customer Access

- **Azure AD External Identities:** With External Identities in Azure AD, you can allow people outside your organization to access your apps and resources, while letting them sign in using whatever identity they prefer. It also allows you to share your apps and resources with external users via Azure AD B2B collaboration.

  - Azure AD B2B lets you support millions of users and billions of authentications per day, monitoring and automatically handling threats like denial-of-service, password spray, or brute force attacks.

We will explore how Microsoft 365 services and Azure security services can help protect, detect, respond, and recover against MITRE ATT&CK Tactics, Techniques, and Procedures (TTP).

Using Azure Web Application Firewall to Protect a Website Against an "Initial Access" TTP

Azure Web Application Firewall (WAF) on Azure Application Gateway provides centralized protection of your web applications from common exploits and vulnerabilities. Web applications are increasingly targeted by malicious attacks that exploit commonly known vulnerabilities. SQL injection and cross-site scripting are among the most common attacks.

Follow these steps to create a WAF policy for preventing web-based attacks:

1. On the upper-left side of the portal, select Create a Resource. Search for WAF, select Web Application Firewall, then click Create.

2. On the Create a WAF Policy page, from the Basics tab, enter or select the following information. Accept the defaults for the remaining settings, and then select Review + create. Enter the appropriate Project Details, such as Policy for, Subscription, and Resource Group. See Figure 4.15.

Figure 4.15: WAF policy window

3. Provide detail for Instance details, such as Policy name, Location, Policy state, and select Policy mode as Prevention. Click Next : Managed Rules; see Figure 4.16.

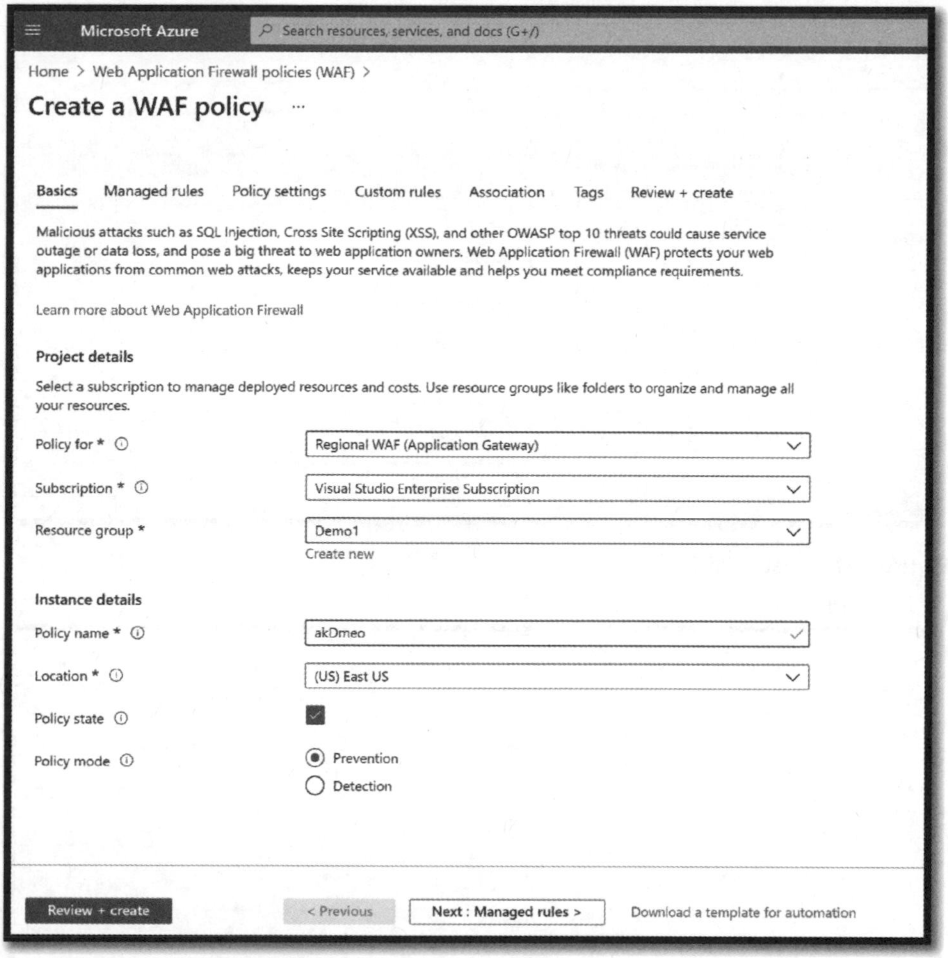

Figure 4.16: Create WAF Policy

4. Under Managed rules, select the rule set OWASP 3.2 or 3.1 from the drop-down menu.

5. Azure-managed OWASP rules are enabled by default. To disable an individual rule within a rule group, expand the rules within that rule group, select the check box in front of the rule number, and select Disable on the tab. See Figure 4.17.

6. To create a custom rule, select Add Custom Rule under the Custom Rules tab. This opens the custom rule configuration page. Figure 4.18 shows an example custom rule configured to block a request if the query string contains the text *blockme*.

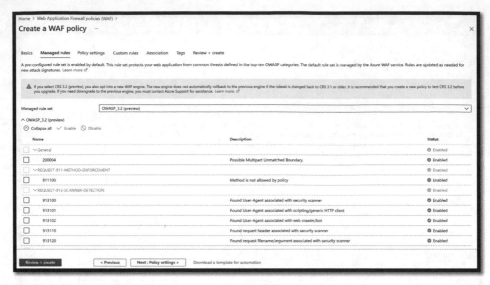

Figure 4.17: Create WAF Rule Set

Figure 4.18: Custom Rule Configuration page

Using Microsoft Defender for Office 365 to Protect Against an "Initial Access" TTP

Phishing is considered a top threat. Phishing is an email attack that tries to steal sensitive information in messages that appear to be from legitimate or trusted senders. There are a few specific types of phishing attack:

- **Spear phishing** uses focused and customized information specific to target individuals.

- **Whaling attacks** are directed at high-value individuals such as executives for a maximum effect.

- **Business email compromises** use a forged trusted sender such as a CFO requesting payment from a customer or a CEO asking a CFO to make an immediate payment.

Microsoft Defender for Office 365 can protect an organization with these different types of phishing emails using a number of security capabilities such as:

- Anti-phishing policies in Exchange Online Protection can be quickly turned on or off to block spam and spoofed senders.

- Spoof Intelligence can be used to gain insight and review the detected spoofed senders in the message.

- Implicit email authentication can help enhance standard email authentication checks for all inbound email with sender reputation, history, and behavioral analysis.

To create anti-phishing and anti-malware policies using Security and Compliance Center, follow these steps:

1. In the Security & Compliance Center (`https://security.microsoft.com/`), go to Email & Collaboration > Policies and rules > Threat policies > Anti-phishing. See Figure 4.19.

Figure 4.19: Create an anti-phishing policy

2. On the Anti-phishing page, click Create. The Create a New Anti-Phishing Policy wizard opens. On the Name your policy page, configure the following settings:

   ▪ **Name:** Enter a unique, descriptive name for the policy.

   ▪ **Description:** Enter an optional description for the policy.

3. When you're finished, click Next. On the next page, Users, groups, and domains, enter the required details:

   ▪ **The Users is:** Specifies one or more mailboxes, mail users, or mail contacts in your organization.

   ▪ **The Groups is a member of:** Specifies one or more groups in your organization.

   ▪ **The recipient domain is:** Specifies recipients in one or more of the configured accepted domains in your organization.

4. When you're finished, click Next. On the Phishing Threshold & Protection page, select the phishing email threshold as required and check/uncheck other options as shown in Figure 4.20.

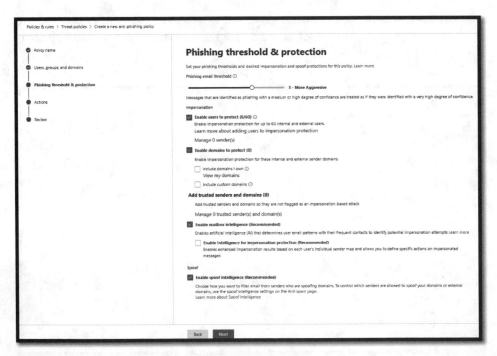

Figure 4.20: Set the phishing threshold and other settings

5. When you're finished, click Next.

6. On the Actions page, select the options as required and click Next.

7. On the Review Your Settings page that appears, review your settings. You can click Edit on each setting to modify it.

8. When you're finished, click Submit.

9. Click Done when the confirmation page appears.

You can create a custom anti-phishing policy in the M365 Security Center (`https://security.microsoft.com/`) and the associated anti-phishing policy at the same time using the same name for both.

Using Microsoft Defender Endpoint to Protect Against an "Initial Access" TTP

Microsoft Defender for Endpoint is an enterprise endpoint security platform designed to help enterprise networks prevent, detect, investigate, and respond to advanced threats.

Defender for Endpoint uses a number of built-in technologies of the Windows 10 operating system and a combination of other Microsoft cloud services. Figure 4.21 shows some of these services, which are discussed in the following list.

Figure 4.21: Microsoft Defender for Endpoint services

- **Threat & Vulnerability Management:** This feature allows you to scan, discover, prioritize, and remediate the endpoint vulnerabilities and misconfigurations.

- **Attack surface reduction:** This feature comes along with a number of other built-in capabilities to reduce the attack surface of an endpoint.

These capabilities include network protection, web protection, hardware-based isolation, application controls, control over specific folder access, and many more.

- **Next-generation protection:** This feature is also known as Microsoft Defender Antivirus, which comes with advanced capabilities such as behavior-based, heuristic, and real-time antivirus protection.

- **Endpoint detection and response:** Endpoint detection and response capabilities are put in place to detect, investigate, and respond to advanced threats. Their hunting capabilities let you proactively find breaches and create custom detections.

- **Automated investigation and remediation:** This feature offers automatic investigation and remediation capabilities that help reduce the volume of alerts in minutes at scale.

- **Microsoft Threat Experts:** Microsoft Defender for Endpoint's new managed threat-hunting service provides proactive hunting, prioritization, and additional context and insights that further empower Security Operation Centers (SOCs) to identify and respond to threats quickly and accurately.

Follow these steps to enable Microsoft Defender for Endpoint:

1. Sign in to the Microsoft Endpoint Manager admin center (`https://endpoint.microsoft.com/`).

2. Select Endpoint security > Microsoft Defender for Endpoint, and then select Open the Microsoft Defender Security Center. See Figure 4.22.

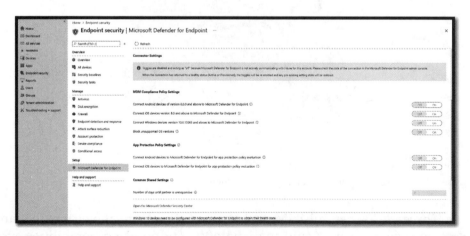

Figure 4.22: Microsoft Defender for Endpoint console

3. In Microsoft Defender Security Center:

   ▪ Select Settings > Advanced features.

   ▪ For Microsoft Intune connection, choose On.

   ▪ Select Save preferences.

4. Return to Microsoft Defender for Endpoint in the Microsoft Endpoint Manager admin center. Under the MDM Compliance Policy Settings, depending on your organization's needs:

   ▪ Set Connect Android devices to Microsoft Defender for Endpoint to On.

   ▪ Set Connect iOS devices to Microsoft Defender for Endpoint to On.

   ▪ Set Connect Windows devices to Microsoft Defender for Endpoint to On.

   When these configurations are ON, applicable devices that you currently manage with Intune, and devices you enroll in the future, are connected to Microsoft Defender for Endpoint for compliance.

5. Select Save.

Using Azure Conditional Access to Protect Against an "Initial Access" TTP

With the change in computing to a more cloud-centric model, it has become difficult to control access to the documents and data that an enterprise uses to run the business.

Formerly, all IT teams needed to keep content behind the corporate firewall, and access was governed by who had access to the network, and computers on the network were always company-owned and company-controlled.

In the current model, devices may be owned by the company, the user, or third parties such as vendors, partners, and contractors. In such scenarios, granular access control is the best defense.

Zero Trust is a MITRE-recommended security approach because it creates access limits that deter attacks. By placing security resources as close as possible to the end user, zero trust stops most adversaries at the reconnaissance stage. This means that with zero trust, bad actors and adversaries never enter the network.

Reconnaissance is the first stage in the MITRE framework. Zero trust prevents active scanning and gathering host information by cloaking the network and blocking perpetrator visibility. Preventing cyberattackers from progressing to the next phases significantly reduces the attack surface of any organization implementing zero trust.

For example, in case of initial access, many attackers tunnel into enterprise networks through VPNs. By replacing VPNs, zero trust minimizes the attack surface. In addition, zero trust blocks the ability to use stolen credentials by adding MFA and real-time monitoring.

In the Microsoft environment, Azure Conditional Access works with the Office 365 suite of products and SaaS apps configured in Azure Active Directory. Conditional access is a set of policies and configurations that control which devices or identities access various services and data sources. See Figure 4.23.

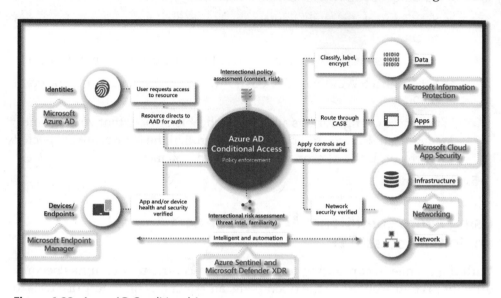

Figure 4.23: Azure AD Conditional Access

Conditional Access relies on signals from either the corporate AD Domain or Microsoft Intune, which is the Mobile Device Management and Mobile Application Management service by Microsoft.

Intune can inform the system about its state and trustworthiness before the device gains access to the data. Mobile devices (iOS, Android, Windows) must be enrolled in Intune, which provides security policy settings and verifies that it is not rooted or jail-broken.

End-user devices must be joined to the enterprise AD domain, where policies and governance are enforced centrally.

Suppose a user's device is not compliant with these policies. In that case, conditional access will guide the user on how to get the device into compliance so access to requested data may be enabled. This allows the users to self-serve their enrollment, so no help-desk call or IT intervention is required.

Let's look at an example of preventing initial access per GPS-based named location using Azure Conditional Access Service.

Admins can refine their Conditional Access policies by determining a user's location with even more precision. GPS-based named locations allow you to restrict access to certain resources to the boundaries of a specific country. Due to VPNs and other factors, determining a user's location from their IP address is not always accurate or reliable.

Leveraging GPS signals enables admins to determine a user's location with higher confidence. This is especially helpful if you have strict compliance regulations that limit where specific data can be accessed.

Users will be prompted to share their GPS location via the Microsoft Authenticator app during sign-in when the feature is enabled.

There are two simple steps:

1. Create a GPS-based named location.

2. Create or configure Conditional Access with this named location.

You'll first need to create the countries named location and select the countries where you want the policy to apply. Configure the named location to determine the location by GPS coordinates instead of by IP address. See Figure 4.24.

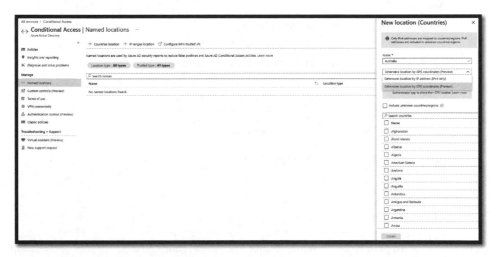

Figure 4.24: Azure Conditional Access

The next step is to create a Conditional Access policy to restrict access to selected applications for sign-ins within the boundaries of the named location, as shown in Figure 4.25.

Now, test the location-sharing experience using the Microsoft Authenticator App. Do make sure that the Authenticator app is installed and configured with your test account.

You will be prompted to share your Authenticator app's geolocation when trying to access the files or data. See Figure 4.26.

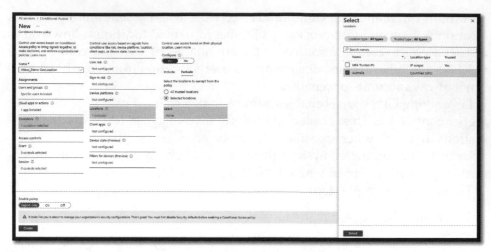

Figure 4.25: Set Conditional Access in Azure AD

Figure 4.26: Grant permission on Authenticator App when prompted to share your geolocation

Further, you may receive the prompt shown in Figure 4.27 the first time. In that case, when prompted, you will need to grant location permission to the Authenticator app.

Your location will be silently shared once per hour from your device, and location sharing will continue for the next 24 hours, so you will not be required to grant permission again unless you have disabled them.

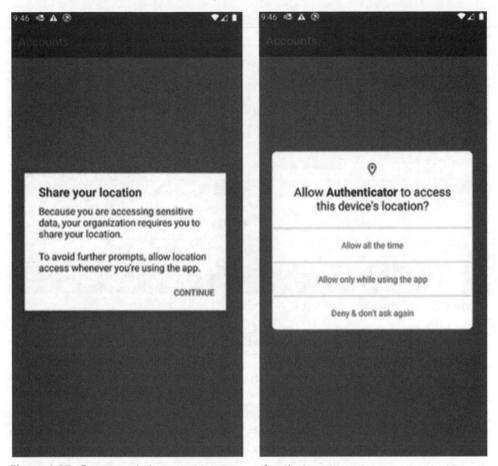

Figure 4.27: Grant permission prompt on your authenticator app

Microsoft Detect Services

Microsoft Detect services help identify suspicious activities and further facilitate mitigating threats such as Privilege Escalation, Credentials access, Lateral Movement, Detecting commands and Controls, and Data exfiltration (see Figure 4.28).

- **Azure Defender:** Azure Defender, part of Azure Security Center, brings advanced and intelligent protection across the Azure and hybrid resources and workload. Azure Defender provides security alerts and advanced threat protection for virtual machines, SQL databases, containers, web applications, your network, and more.
- **Azure Sentinel:** Covered in the beginning of this chapter.

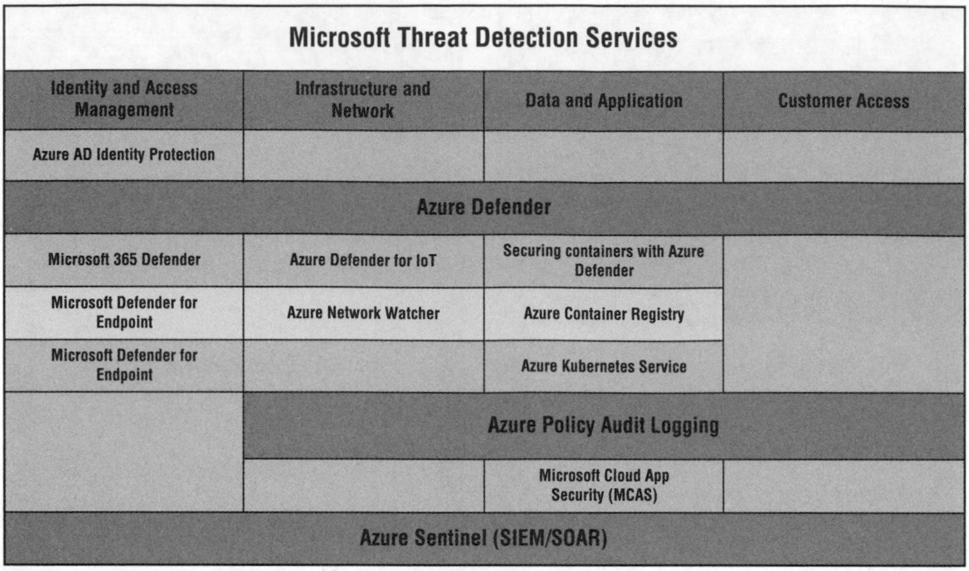

Microsoft Threat Detection Services			
Identity and Access Management	Infrastructure and Network	Data and Application	Customer Access
Azure AD Identity Protection			
Azure Defender			
Microsoft 365 Defender	Azure Defender for IoT	Securing containers with Azure Defender	
Microsoft Defender for Endpoint	Azure Network Watcher	Azure Container Registry	
Microsoft Defender for Endpoint		Azure Kubernetes Service	
	Azure Policy Audit Logging		
		Microsoft Cloud App Security (MCAS)	
Azure Sentinel (SIEM/SOAR)			

Figure 4.28: Microsoft Detect Services

Detecting "Privilege Escalation" TTPs

Privilege escalation can be defined as an attack that involves gaining illicit access of elevated rights, or privileges, beyond what is intended or entitled for a user. This attack can involve an external threat actor or an insider. This attack involves a key stage of the cyberattack chain and typically involves the exploitation of a privilege escalation vulnerability, such as a system bug, misconfiguration, or inadequate access controls.

There are five primary methods attackers used to make privilege escalation work: credential exploitation, vulnerabilities and exploits, misconfigurations, malware, and social engineering.

Using Azure Security Center and Azure Sentinel to Detect Threats Against a "Privilege Escalation" TTP

Let's explore how we can leverage and use Azure Security Center to detect alerts on privilege escalation:

1. On the Azure Portal, click the Azure Security Center tab, as shown in Figure 4.29.

Figure 4.29: Security Center service in Azure Portal

2. Click Security Alerts and select Add Filter with MITRE ATT&CK tactics, as shown in Figure 4.30.

Figure 4.30: Security Alert and Filter in ASC

3. Select the alert and click View Full Details for further investigation, as shown in Figure 4.31.

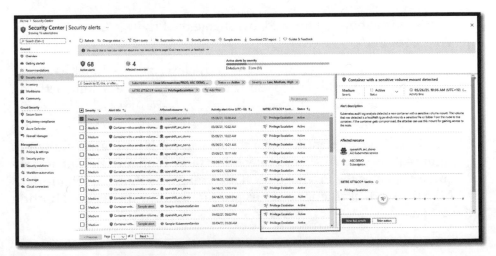

Figure 4.31: View Full details option in ASC

4. Review the alert detail and Take Action as required, as shown in Figure 4.32.

Figure 4.32: Detail Security Alert

Now let's look at how to hunt and investigate the Privilege Escalation tactic using Azure Sentinel:

1. Visit `https://ms.portal.azure.com` and select Azure Sentinel, as shown in Figure 4.33. Visit this link to learn how to set up Azure Sentinel services: `https://docs.microsoft.com/en-us/azure/sentinel/quickstart-onboard`.

2. Within the Azure Sentinel workspace, select Hunting, as shown in Figure 4.34. You can now select any Mitre Tactics and run relevant hunting queries such as the Privilege Escalation query, as shown in Figure 4.34. All Mitre Attack Tactics queries are pre-built in the Azure Hunting section.

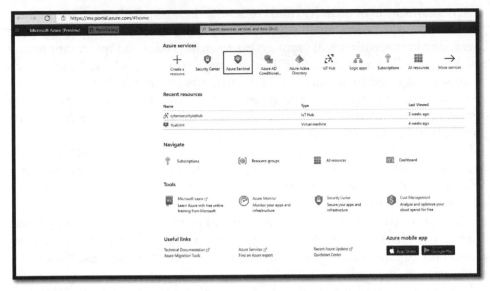

Figure 4.33: Azure Sentinel Service

Figure 4.34: Azure Sentinel Hunting feature

Detecting Credential Access

Credential-based attacks occur when attackers steal credentials to gain access or bypass an organization's security measures to abuse the resources or to steal critical data.

Commonly, attackers use phishing for credential theft as it's a fairly cheap and highly efficient tactic. The effectiveness of credential phishing relies on human interaction to deceive employees, unlike malware and exploits, which rely on weaknesses in security defenses.

An organization or an individual credential theft is usually a targeted effort. Attackers harvest social media sites such as LinkedIn, searching for specific users whose credentials will grant access to critical data and information. The phishing emails and websites utilized in corporate credential theft are much more sophisticated than those used for consumer credential theft.

There are many other ways and types of Credential Access abuse tactics; credentials can be stolen via brute force, although that is a noisy attack for anyone paying the slightest attention to their systems.

Password spraying is another variant of what is known as a brute force attack. In a traditional brute force attack, the perpetrator attempts to gain unauthorized access to a single account by guessing the password repeatedly in a very short period of time.

There are also many examples of stealing hashed passwords and either passing the hash or cracking them offline. Finally, the last set of techniques revolves around an attacker stealing cleartext passwords stored in cleartext files, databases, or even the registry.

Having an endpoint detection and protection solution such as Microsoft Defender for Endpoint deployed with your digital estate can help combat many attack tactics such as Credential Access.

The logs and alerts from your EDR can then be further ingested in your SIEM for detailed analysis.

Using Azure Identity Protection to Detect Threats Against a "Credential Access" TTP

Whether your assets are hosted on-premises or in the cloud, the security perimeter that separates users and data from outside threats can no longer be drawn using network lines. The perimeter is now drawn by identity components of authentication and authorization that span across all your devices, services, hosts, and networks.

While the network perimeter keeps a basic security role, it can no longer guide the security defense strategy because:

- Adversaries have demonstrated a consistent and ongoing ability to penetrate network perimeters using phishing attacks.

- Organizational data, devices, and users often exist and operate outside traditional network boundaries (whether sanctioned by IT or not).

- Port and protocol definitions and exceptions have failed to keep up with the complexity of services, applications, devices, and data.

- Organizations need to adopt different security philosophies and mindsets that are based on rigorous management of authentication and authorization, not firewall rules and exceptions.

Administrators are in control and need protection. The most important identities to protect are the administrators of on-premises and cloud systems, especially identity systems like Active Directory and Azure Active Directory. These administrators have access to all the data hosted on their systems and should be protected, monitored, and restricted appropriate with their high level of responsibility.

Identity Protection allows organizations to accomplish three key tasks:

- Automate the detection and remediation of identity-based risks.
- Investigate risks using data in the portal.
- Export risk detection data to third-party utilities for further analysis.

Identity Protection uses the learnings Microsoft has acquired from their position in organizations with Azure AD, the consumer space with Microsoft Accounts, and in gaming with Xbox to protect your users. Microsoft analyzes trillions of signals per day to identify and protect customers from threats.

The signals generated by and fed to Identity Protection can be further fed into tools like Conditional Access to make access decisions, or fed back to a Security Information and Event Management (SIEM) tool for further investigation based on your organization's enforced policies.

Azure Active Directory Identity Protection includes three default policies that administrators can choose to enable. These policies include limited customization but are applicable to most organizations. All of the policies allow for excluding users such as your emergency access or break-glass administrator accounts. See Figure 4.35.

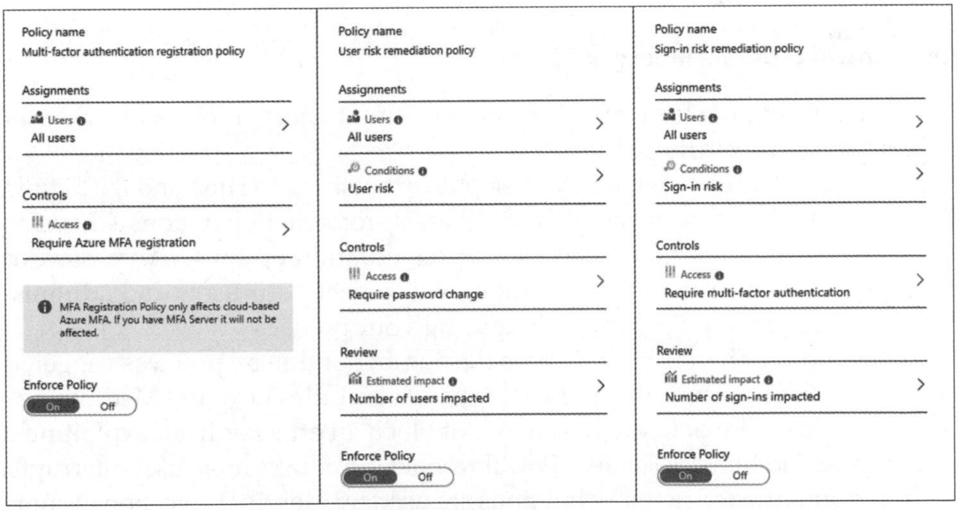

Figure 4.35: Identity Protection policies examples

Steps to Configure and Enable Risk Polices (Sign-in Risk and User Risk)

Both policies (Sign-in Risk Policy and User Risk Policy) work to automate the response to risk detections in your environment and allow users to self-remediate when risk is detected. See Figure 4.36.

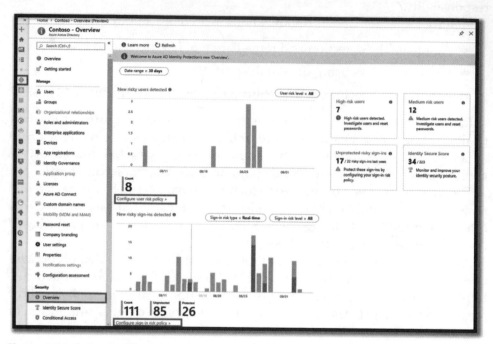

Figure 4.36: Policy Dashboard in Identity Protection

Choosing Acceptable Risk Levels

You must decide the level of risk you are willing to accept for balancing user experience and security posture.

It is recommended to set the user risk policy threshold to High and the Sign-in Risk policy to Medium and above and allow self-remediation options. Choosing to block access rather than allowing self-remediation options, like password change and multi-factor authentication, will impact your users and administrators. Weigh this choice when configuring your policies.

Choosing a High threshold reduces the number of times a policy is triggered and minimizes the impact to users. However, it excludes Low and Medium risk detections from the policy, which may not block an attacker from exploiting a compromised identity. Selecting a Low threshold introduces more user interrupts.

Configured trusted network locations are used by Identity Protection in some risk detections to reduce false positives.

Risk Remediation

Organizations can choose to block access when risk is detected. Blocking sometimes stops legitimate users from doing what they need to. A better solution is to allow self-remediation using Azure AD Multi-Factor Authentication (MFA) and self-service password reset (SSPR).

When a user risk policy triggers: Administrators can require a secure password reset, requiring Azure AD MFA to be done before the user creates a new password with SSPR, resetting the user risk.

When a sign in risk policy triggers: Azure AD MFA can be triggered, allowing the user to prove it's them by using one of their registered authentication methods, resetting the sign-in risk.

Exclusions

Policies allow for excluding users such as your emergency access or break-glass administrator accounts. Organizations may need to exclude other accounts from specific policies based on the way the accounts are used. Exclusions should be reviewed regularly to see if they're still applicable.

Enable Policies

There are two locations where these policies may be configured—Conditional Access and Identity Protection. Configuration using Conditional Access policies is the preferred method, providing more context including:

- Enhanced diagnostic data
- Report-only mode integration
- Graph API support

Follow these steps to Configure User Risk with Conditional Access:

1. Sign in to the Azure portal as a global administrator, security administrator, or Conditional Access administrator.

2. Browse to Azure Active Directory > Security > Conditional Access.

3. Select New Policy. See Figure 4.37.

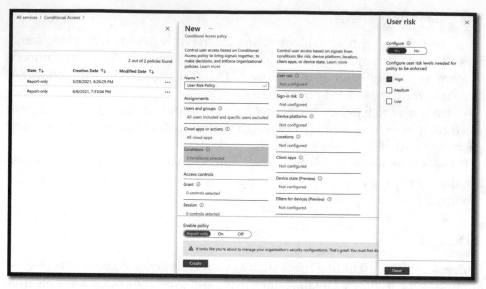

Figure 4.37: User risk policy

4. Give your policy a name. We recommend that organizations create a meaningful standard for the names of their policies.

5. Under Assignments, select Users and groups. Under Include, select All users. Under Exclude, select Users and groups and choose your organization's emergency access or break-glass accounts.

6. Select Done.

7. Under Cloud apps or actions > Include, select All cloud apps. Under Conditions > User risk, set Configure to Yes. Under Configure user risk levels needed for policy to be enforced, select High, then select Done. Under Access controls > Grant, select Grant access, Require password change, and select Select.

8. Confirm your settings and set the Enable policy to On.

9. Select Create to enable your policy.

Follow these steps to configure Sign in Risk with Conditional Access:

1. Sign in to the Azure portal as a global administrator, security administrator, or Conditional Access administrator.

2. Browse to Azure Active Directory > Security > Conditional Access.

3. Select New policy. See Figure 4.38.

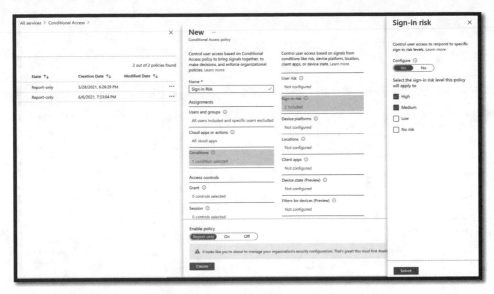

Figure 4.38: Sign in Risk Policy example

4. Give your policy a name. We recommend that organizations create a meaningful standard for the names of their policies.

5. Under Assignments, select Users and groups. Under Include, select All users. Under Exclude, select Users and groups and choose your organization's emergency access or break-glass accounts.

6. Select Done.

7. Under Cloud apps or actions > Include, select All cloud apps. Under Conditions > Sign-in risk, set Configure to Yes. Under Select the sign-in risk level this policy will apply to, select High and Medium.

8. Select Done.

9. Under Access controls > Grant, select Grant access, Require multi-factor authentication, and Select.

10. Confirm your settings and set the Enable policy to On.

11. Select Create to enable your policy.

Using Azure Security Center and Azure Sentinel to Detect Threats Against a "Credential Access" TTP

We can detect credential access alerts in Azure Security Center using similar steps as provided in privilege escalation. Change the filter to Credential Access, as shown in Figure 4.39.

Figure 4.39: Checking Credential Access alert in ASC

Similarly, we can hunt and investigate Credential Access tactics in Azure Sentinel, as shown in Figure 4.40.

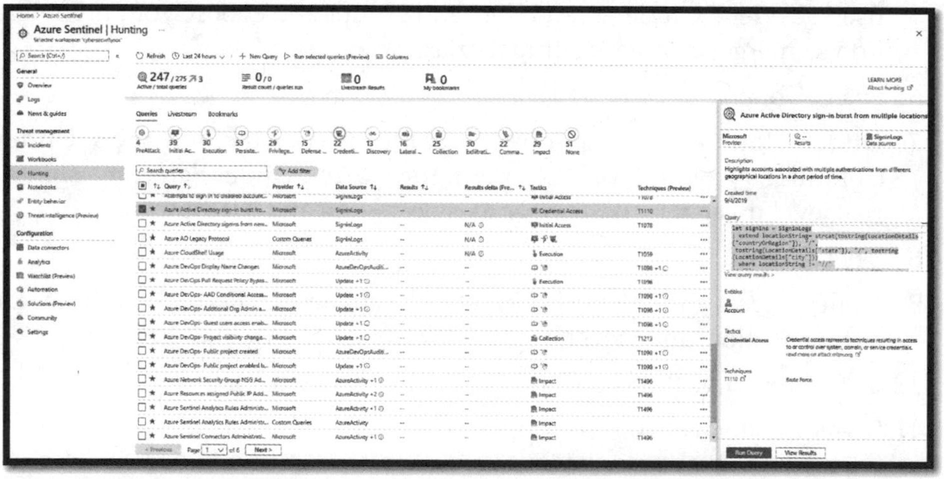

Figure 4.40: Hunting Credential Access Tactics Query in Azure Sentinel

Azure Sentinel can also correlate events based on many suspicious behaviors, such as:

- Deployment of executable files, such as remote access tools or password harvesting tools across an enterprise through network shares or removable media

- Deployment and use of remote execution of multi-purpose tools such as PSExec, PowerShell, and Windows Management Instrumentation clients in an enterprise
- Suspicious activity around Windows Administrative Shares
- Suspicious activity around Windows Remote Management
- The exploitation of remote services within the network
- Subverting logon scripts to establish persistence on endpoints and servers

Detecting Lateral Movement

Lateral movement is when an attacker uses non-sensitive accounts to gain access to sensitive accounts throughout your network. Attackers use lateral movement to identify and gain access to the sensitive accounts and machines in your network that share stored login credentials in accounts, groups, and machines. Once an attacker makes successful lateral moves toward your key targets, the attacker can also take advantage and gain access to your domain controllers.

The best way to prevent lateral movement exposure within your organization is to ensure that sensitive users only use their administrator credentials when logging in to hardened computers. In the event the admin needs access to the shared computer, then make sure they log in to the shared computer with a username and password other than their admin credentials.

Use of Privilege Access Workstation (PAW) or Secure Access Workstation (SAW) is another good practice to implement.

Implement a Least Privilege principal and verify that your users do not have unnecessary admin-level permission. Check if all the members in the shared group actually require admin-level rights.

Organizations can also deploy Microsoft Defender for Identity for protection against identity-based attack threats.

Defender for Identity is a cloud-based security solution that leverages your on-premises Active Directory signals to identify, detect, and investigate advanced threats, compromised identities, and malicious insider actions directed at your organization.

Threats signals from Microsoft Defenders for Identity are seamlessly shared with Azure Security Center and Azure Sentinel.

Using Just-in-Time in ASC to Protect and Detect Threats Against a "Lateral Movement" TTP

Threat actors actively hunt for accessible machines with open management ports, like RDP or SSH. If not secured, a virtual machine can be a potential target for an attack. When a VM is successfully compromised, it's used as the entry point to attack further resources within your environment.

As with all cybersecurity prevention techniques, the goal should be to reduce the attack surface. In this case, that means having fewer open ports, especially management ports. Legitimate users also use these ports, so it's not practical to keep them closed.

To solve this issue, Azure Security Center offers Just In Time (JIT). With JIT, you can lock down the inbound traffic to your VMs, reducing exposure to attacks while providing easy access to connect to VMs when needed.

When you enable just-in-time VM access, you can select the ports on the VM to which inbound traffic will be blocked. Security Center ensures "deny all inbound traffic" rules exist for your selected ports in the network security group (NSG) and Azure Firewall rules. These rules restrict access to your Azure VM's management ports and defend them from attack.

If other rules already exist for the selected ports, those existing rules prioritize the new "deny all inbound traffic" rules. If there are no existing rules on the selected ports, the new rules prioritize the NSG and Azure Firewall.

When a user requests access to a VM, Security Center checks that the user has Azure role-based access control (Azure RBAC) permissions for that VM. If the request is approved, Security Center configures the NSGs and Azure Firewall to allow inbound traffic to the selected ports from the relevant IP address (or range), for the amount of time that was specified.

After the time has expired, Security Center restores the NSGs to their previous states. Connections that are already established are not interrupted.

Follow these steps to enable and configure the JIT VM access in Azure Security Center:

1. Open the Azure Defender dashboard and, from the advanced protection area, select Just-in-time VM access. See Figure 4.41.

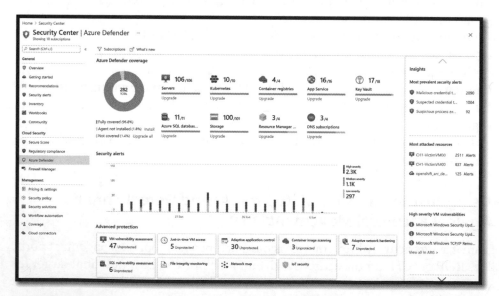

Figure 4.41: Just-in-time option in Azure Defender

The Just-in-time VM access page opens with your VMs grouped into the following tabs:

- **Configured:** VMs that have been already been configured to support just-in-time VM access. For each VM, the configured tab shows:
  - The number of approved JIT requests in the last seven days
  - The last access date and time
  - The connection details configured
  - The last user
- **Not configured:** VMs without JIT enabled, but that can support JIT. We recommend that you enable JIT for these VMs.
- **Unsupported:** VMs without JIT enabled and that don't support the feature. Your VM might be in this tab for the following reasons:
  - Missing network security group (NSG): JIT requires an NSG to be configured.
  - Classic VM: JIT supports VMs that are deployed through Azure Resource Manager, not classic deployment.
  - Other: Your VM might be in this tab if the JIT solution is disabled in the security policy of the subscription or the resource group.

2. From the Not Configured tab, mark the VMs to protect with JIT and select Enable JIT on VMs. See Figure 4.42.

Figure 4.42: Port configuration options

3. The JIT VM access page opens listing the ports that Security Center recommends protecting:
   - 22 - SSH
   - 3389 - RDP
   - 5985 - WinRM
   - 5986 - WinRM

4. To accept the default settings, select Save. To customize the JIT options:

- Add custom ports with the Add button.

- Modify one of the default ports, by selecting it from the list.

For each port (custom and default), the Add Port Configuration pane offers the following options:

- Protocol: The protocol that is allowed on this port when a request is approved

- Allowed source IPs: The IP ranges that are allowed on this port when a request is approved

- Maximum request time: The maximum time window during which a specific port can be opened

5. Set the port security to your needs, select OK, and then select Save.

Let's now discuss the steps to edit the JIT configuration on a JIT-enabled VM using Security Center. You can modify a VM's just-in-time configuration by adding and configuring a new port to protect for that VM, or by changing any other setting related to an already protected port. To edit the existing JIT rules for a VM:

1. Open the Azure Defender dashboard and, from the advanced protection area, select Adaptive Application Controls. See Figure 4.43.

Figure 4.43: Edit JIT option

2. From the Configured tab, right-click the VM to which you want to add a port and select Edit.

3. Under JIT VM access configuration, you can either edit the existing settings of a protected port or add a new custom port.

4. When you've finished editing the ports, select Save.

Here are the steps to request access to a JIT-enabled VM using ASC:

1. From the Just-in-time VM access page, select the Configured tab.

2. Select the VMs you want to access.
   The icon in the Connection Details column indicates whether JIT is enabled on the network security group or firewall. If it's enabled on both, only the firewall icon appears.
   The Connection Details column provides the information required to connect the VM, and its open ports.

3. Select Request access. The Request access window opens. See Figure 4.44.

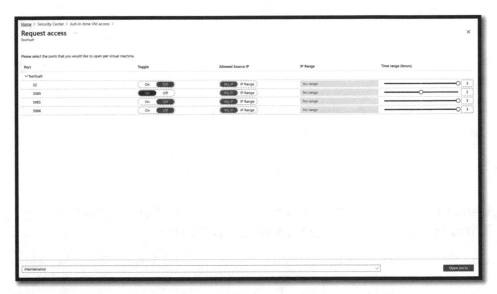

Figure 4.44: Request access window on ASC

4. Under Request access for each VM, configure the ports that you want to open and the source IP addresses that the port is opened on and the time window for which the port will be open. It will only be possible to request access to the configured ports. Each port has a maximum allowed time derived from the JIT configuration you've created.

5. Select Open ports. (If a user who is requesting access is behind a proxy, the option My IP may not work. You may need to define the full IP address range of the organization.)

Follow these steps to audit JIT access in ASC:

1. From Just-in-time VM access, select the Configured tab.

2. For the VM that you want to audit, open the ellipsis menu at the end of the row.

3. Select Activity Log from the menu. The activity log provides a filtered view of previous operations for that VM along with time, date, and subscription. See Figure 4.45.

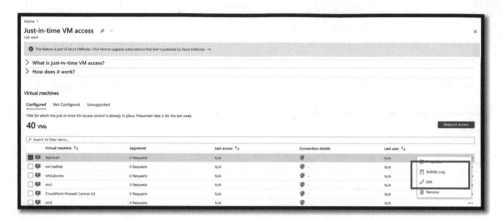

Figure 4.45: Download the activity log

4. To download the log information, select Download as CSV.

Using Azure Security Center and Azure Sentinel to Detect Threats Against a "Lateral Movement" TTP

Let's look at how we can detect lateral movement alerts in Azure Security Center using similar steps provided in previous tactics. Change the filter to Lateral Movement, as shown in Figure 4.46.

Similarly, we can hunt and investigate Lateral Movement tactics in Azure Sentinel, as shown in Figure 4.47.

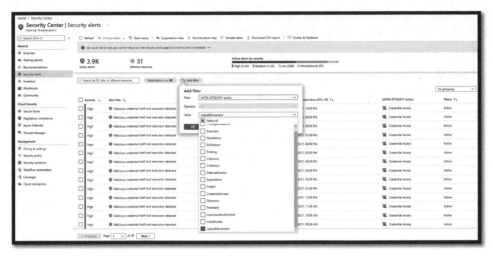

Figure 4.46: Selecting and detecting Lateral Movement alerts in ASC

Figure 4.47: Hunting Lateral Movement in Azure Sentinel

Detecting Command and Control

The *command and control* tactic (called C2 or C&C) represents how adversaries communicate with systems under their control within a target network. This is one of the most damaging attack methods that's often executed over the DNS.

In this method, an attack starts by infecting a server or computer, which may be behind a corporate firewall; the attacker may execute such an attack in a few different ways, such as:

- Sending a phishing email to trick the user into following a link to a malicious website or opening an attachment that executes malicious code.
- Using password spray attacks to gain access to the environment.
- Through any security vulnerability in the end-user browser plug-ins.
- Via infected and compromised software.

After gaining access to an environment with the C2 technique, the attacker then accomplishes data theft, shuts down the servers or critical infrastructure, reboots the systems, or performs Distributed Denial of Services.

Using Azure Security Center and Azure Sentinel to Detect Threats Against a "Command and Control" TTP

Let's look at as how we can detect Command and Control alerts in Azure Security Center using similar steps as provided in previous tactics. Change the filter to Command and Control, as shown in Figure 4.48.

Figure 4.48: Checking Command and Control Alert in ASC

C&C often uses many different forms of communication such as Beacon, Command, Exfiltration, or Connectivity Checks. A good logging and event correlations system can help detect this type of attack by analyzing different types of log sources such as DNS, Endpoint, Servers, Network Firewalls, WAF, and VPN logs.

Azure Sentinel can be used to hunt and investigate Command and Control tactics, as shown in Figure 4.49.

Figure 4.49: Hunting Command & Control Tactic in Azure Sentinel

Detecting Data Exfiltration

Data exfiltration is a technique used by malicious actors to target, copy, and transfer sensitive data. Data exfiltration can be done remotely or manually and can be very difficult to identify and detect, given it often resembles a normal behavior on the network traffic.

Some of the most common attack techniques used by the attacker are social engineering, phishing attacks, physical theft of data from a USB thumb drive, smartphone, laptop, etc., or human error.

It is not possible to protect your data from exfiltration using just a single solution. An organization will be required to implement a layered defense approach such as a DLP solution, CASB, EDR solution, web filtering solution, and a good data governance practice for identifying and classifying the data.

The Microsoft Cloud App Security (MCAS) dashboard can provide lots of information to detect data leakage, risky users, risky applications, and many more; (see Figure 4.50).

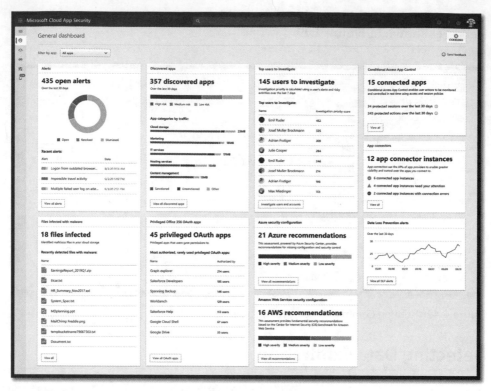

Figure 4.50: Microsoft Cloud App Security (MCAS) dashboard

Using Azure Information Protection to Detect Threats Against a "Data Exfiltration" TTP

Azure Information Protection (AIP) is a foundational technology that enables a variety of other Microsoft features, like Office 365 Message Encryption (OME), Office 365 Data Loss Protection (DLP), and others.

With AIP, a customer can protect files or other resources via encryption at that object level. The file might be stored anywhere, but the ability to open the file is protected by AIP and the access controls specified. This means that system administrators (or even those with physical access) of the file storage do not have access to the file.

This technology provides protection against most breach scenarios and is excellent for confidential data. Since access requires an Azure AD–issued access token, you must have Internet connectivity to access an AIP-protected file. Because all access is brokered via a centrally issued token, there is definitive auditing and tracking of AIP protected files—and you can easily revoke access to a given file regardless of where the file is stored. The technology provides enterprise data recovery options so when access to a given file is lost, highly trusted individuals can recover the file.

Azure Information Protection allows you to gain greater control over the security and compliance of your business information via its robust protection via classification and encryption model without the need to ask users to complete complex security tasks during their working day. By automating the permissions process as a native action within SharePoint, AIP ensures that information is secured in a structured, predictable manner, automatically.

Because Azure Information Protection is embedded in other product features, there are several general scenarios where it might be in use:

- Used directly via the Azure Information Protection client. Users apply labels to files, which trigger application of policies that protect the file.

- Used indirectly via Office 365 features like OME or DLP. Users apply policies that Office 365 administrators have determined are commonly needed.

- Used indirectly via bulk classification/labeling engines. System administrators for a file server might apply rules that result in protection of files.

If you're working within a Microsoft Office 365 environment, Azure Information Protection provides you with a deeper understanding—as well as granular control of—where your content is being distributed and how it is being used. This level of visibility helps to:

- Prevent illicit modification, storage, and distribution of business-critical data

- Remove the challenge of unauthorized users viewing sensitive content

- Gain greater control of information by monitoring which users are interacting with content and how they are doing so

- Meet regulatory data protection and compliance standards

To protect your organization from data exfiltration threats, it is crucial to first identify and discover your sensitive content. The following section will help you discover sensitive content using Azure Information Protection.

Discovering Sensitive Content Using AIP

You'll need an Azure subscription that includes Azure Information Protection. Make sure that you can sign in to the Azure portal with a supported administrator account, and have protection enabled. Supported administrator accounts include: Compliance administrator, Compliance data administrator, and Security administrator or Global administrator.

You'll need the Azure Information Protection unified labeling client and scanner installed, as well as the Network Discovery service. Follow these detailed steps if you haven't yet completed this process: `https://docs.microsoft.com/en-us/azure/information-protection/quickstart-deploy-client`.

To run the scanner, you'll need SQL Server installed on the scanner machine. When working with a standard, cloud-connected environment, your domain account must be synchronized to Azure Active Directory. This isn't necessary if you're working offline. If you're not sure about your account, contact one of your system administrators to verify the sync status.

You must have created sensitivity labels and published a policy with at least one label to the Microsoft 365 compliance center, for the scanner service account.

Follow these steps to create a network scan job:

1. Sign in to the Azure portal as a supported administrator, and navigate to the Azure Information Protection area.

2. In the Scanner menu on the left, select Network Scan Jobs.

3. Select + Add to add a new job. In the Add a New Network Scan Job pane, enter a meaningful name, such as Quickstart, and an optional description.

4. Select your cluster name from the drop-down list.

5. Select the row to open the Choose IP ranges pane. There, enter an IP address or IP range to scan.

6. Keep the default value of One Time.

7. Calculate the current UTC time, considering your current time zone, and set the start time to run within five minutes from now. See Figure 4.51.

Figure 4.51: Add Network scan job example in Azure Information Protection

8. Select Save at the top of the page.

9. Return to the Network scan jobs (Preview) grid and wait for your scan to start running. The grid data is updated as your scan completes, as shown in Figure 4.52.

Figure 4.52: Scan job status in AIP

Once your network scan job is complete, you can check for any risky repositories found. For example, if a repository is found to have both read and write public access, you may want to scan further and confirm that no sensitive data is stored there.

To add risky repositories to your content scan job, follow these steps:

1. Sign in to the Azure portal as a supported administrator and navigate to the Azure Information Protection pane.

2. In the Scanner menu on the left, select Repositories. See Figure 4.53.

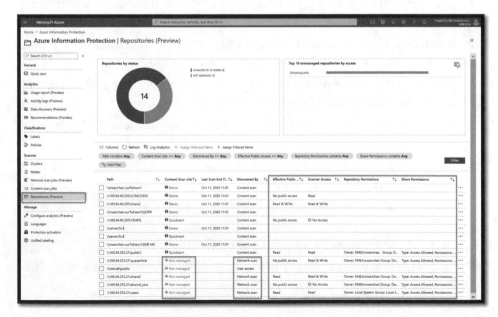

Figure 4.53: Azure Information Protection Repositories

3. In the grid below the graphs, locate a repository that is not yet managed by the scanner. Not being managed by the scanner means that they are not included in a content scan job and are not being scanned for sensitive content. Select the row, and then above the grid, select Assign Selected Items.

4. In the Assign to Content Scan Job pane that appears on the right, select your content scan job from the drop-down list, and then select Save. See Figure 4.54.

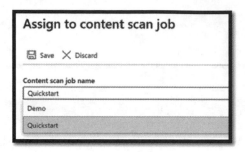

Figure 4.54: Assign to content scan job option in AIP

The next time your content scan job runs, it will now include this newly discovered repository, and identify, label, classify, and protect any sensitive content found, as configured in your policy.

Follow these steps to define and run your content scan job:

1. Use the content scan job you prepared with the tutorial prerequisites to scan your content.

2. If you don't have a content scan job yet, perform Configure Initial Settings in the Azure portal, and then return here to continue.

3. Sign in to the Azure portal as a supported administrator and navigate to the Azure Information Protection pane.

4. In the Scanner menu on the left, select Content Scan Jobs and then select your content scan job.

5. Edit your content scan job settings, making sure that you have a meaningful name and optional description.

6. Keep the default values for most of the settings, except for the following changes:

    ▪ Treat recommended labeling as automatic. Set to On.

    ▪ Configure repositories. Ensure that there is at least one repository defined.

    ▪ Set Enforce to On.

7. Select Save and then return to the Content Scan Jobs grid.

8. To scan your content, go back to the Content Scan Jobs area and select your content scan job.

9. In the toolbar above the grid, select Scan Now to start the scan.

10. When the scan is complete, continue with View scan results. See Figure 4.55.

If your results are empty and you would like to run a meaningful scan, create a file named Payment Info in one of the repositories included in your content scan job. Save the file with the following content: Credit card example: *2384 2328 5436 3489*. Then run your scan again to see the difference in the results.

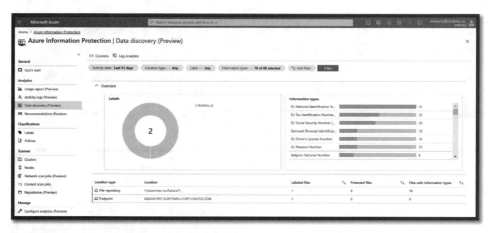

Figure 4.55: Network Content Scan result window

Using Azure Security Center and Azure Sentinel to Detect Threats Against a "Data Exfiltration" TTP

Once an attacker has gained initial access in a network, they will be looking for ways to extract data from a system. In our fictitious example, the attacker has gained access to a local administrator account and is now looking to export all the user credentials stored in the Active Directory.

We can detect Data Exfiltration alerts in the Azure Security Center using similar steps as provided in previous tactics. Change the filter to Data Exfiltration, as shown in Figure 4.56.

With the introduction of Azure Sentinel, an organization can now view threats and alerts across their entire IT estate. They can also take advantage of incidents within Sentinel to correlate alerts and entities across all data sources to add contextual information that is meaningful to the investigation process.

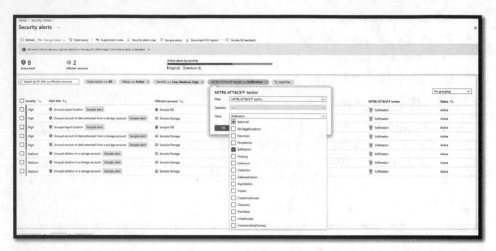

Figure 4.56: Checking Data Exfiltration Alert in ASC

MCAS and Microsoft Defender for Server and Identity events and logs can be seamlessly ingested in Azure Sentinel, and you can use Azure Sentinel to easily hunt and investigate Data Exfiltration, as shown in Figure 4.57.

Figure 4.57: Hunting Data Exfiltration tactic in Azure Sentinel

Detecting Threats and Proactively Hunting with Microsoft 365 Defender

Advanced hunting is a query-based threat-hunting tool that lets you explore up to 30 days of raw data. This allows you to proactively inspect events in your network and further helps you to locate threat indicators and entities.

You can use the same threat-hunting queries to build custom detection rules. These rules run automatically to check for and then respond to suspected breach activity, misconfigured machines, and other findings. See Figure 4.58.

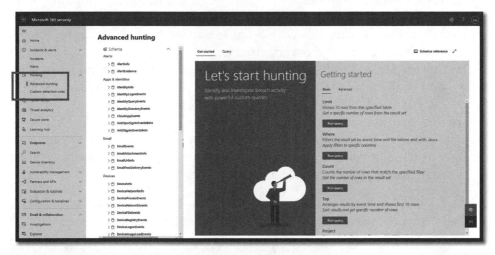

Figure 4.58: Microsoft 365 Security Advanced Hunting option

This capability is similar to advanced hunting in Microsoft Defender for Endpoint. Available in Microsoft 365 Security Center, this capability supports queries that check a broader dataset from:

- Microsoft Defender for Endpoint
- Microsoft Defender for Office 365
- Microsoft Cloud App Security
- Microsoft Defender for Identity

To use advanced hunting, visit `https://security.microsoft.com/`. You must have Admin or Security Admin rights.

To learn more about advanced hunting with Microsoft 365 Defender, visit `https://docs.microsoft.com/en-us/microsoft-365/security/defender-endpoint/advanced-hunting-overview`.

Microsoft Investigate, Response, and Recover Features

For the Response domain, if a cyber incident occurs, the effects must be managed by organizations. To comply with this requirement, the company should create a response plan, identify communication lines among the relevant parties, collect and analyze information about the case, conduct all the activities necessary to eliminate the incident, and integrate lessons learned into revised response strategies.

For the Recover domain, organizations need to develop and implement effective activities to restore any capacity or services that have been impaired by a cybersecurity event. Your organization needs to have a recovery plan in place, coordinate recovery activities with outside parties, and incorporate lessons learned into your updated recovery strategy.

The investigate and respond services from Azure, as shown in Figure 4.59, allow you to pull logging data so you can assess a suspicious activity and respond to those alerts. We have covered many of these examples in the previous section of this chapter.

In this section, we cover the use of automation and orchestration. We will also see how artificial intelligence and machine learning can help Security Analyst and Threat Hunter quickly respond to threats and alerts.

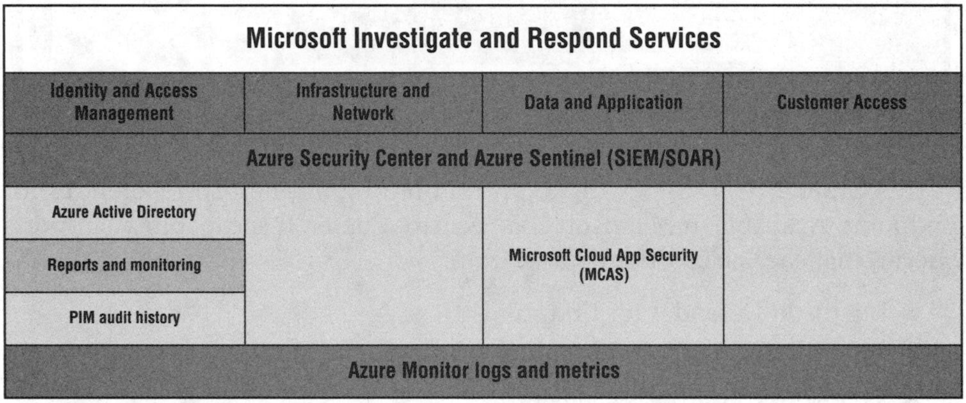

Microsoft Investigate and Respond Services			
Identity and Access Management	Infrastructure and Network	Data and Application	Customer Access
Azure Security Center and Azure Sentinel (SIEM/SOAR)			
Azure Active Directory		Microsoft Cloud App Security (MCAS)	
Reports and monitoring			
PIM audit history			
Azure Monitor logs and metrics			

Figure 4.59: Microsoft Investigate and Respond services

Let's look at each of these services briefly to understand what capabilities they provide under each domain of Identity and Access Management and Data and Application.

Core services:

- **Azure Security Center:** We covered this service in the previous section of this chapter.

- **Azure Sentinel:** We covered this service in the previous section of this chapter.

- **Azure Monitor logs and metrics:** This service delivers a comprehensive solution for collecting and analyzing and allows you to take action on telemetry from your cloud and on-premises environments. Azure Monitor collects and aggregates data from a variety of sources into a common data platform where it can be used for analysis, visualization, and alerting.

Identity & Access Management:

- **Azure AD reports and monitoring:** Azure AD reports provide a comprehensive view of activity in your Azure cloud environment. AD Monitoring lets you route your Azure AD activities logs to different endpoints.

- **Azure AD PIM audit history:** This audit history shows all roles, assignments and activations within the past 30 days of all the privileged roles.

Data & Application:

- **Microsoft Cloud App Security:** MCAS provides tools to gain a deeper understanding of what is happening in your cloud environment; it also helps you manage the risky apps, risky users, and data leakage.

Automating Investigation and Remediation with Microsoft Defender for Endpoint

You can save lots of quality time and effort of your Security Operation team by taking advantage of built in automation capabilities for investigation and remediation within Microsoft Defender for Endpoint.

To turn on automated investigation and remediation, follow these steps:

1. Go to the Microsoft Defender Security Center (`https://securitycenter .windows.com`) and sign in as a Global Admin or Security Administrator.

2. In the navigation pane, choose Settings.

3. In the General section, select Advanced Features.

4. Turn on both Automated Investigation and Automatically Resolve Alerts.

5. Set up device groups.

6. In the Microsoft Defender Security Center (`https://securitycenter .windows.com`), on the Settings page, under Permissions, select Device Groups.

7. Select + Add Device Group.

8. Create at least one device group, as follows:
   - Specify a name and description for the device group.
   - In the Automation Level List, select a level, such as Full – Remediate Threats Automatically. The automation level determines whether remediation actions are taken automatically, or only upon approval. To learn more, see Automation Levels in Automated Investigation and Remediation at `https://docs.microsoft.com/en-us/microsoft-365/ security/defender-endpoint/automation-levels?view=o365- worldwide#levels-of-automation`.

9. In the Members section, use one or more conditions to identify and include devices.

10. On the User Access tab, select the Azure Active Directory groups who should have access to the device group you're creating.

11. Select Done when you're finished setting up your device group.

Visit the Action Center at `https://security.microsoft.com/` to view pending and completed remediation actions (see Figure 4.60).

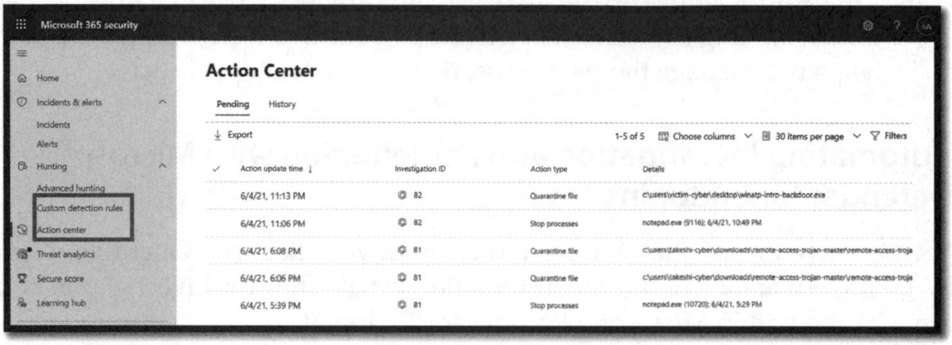

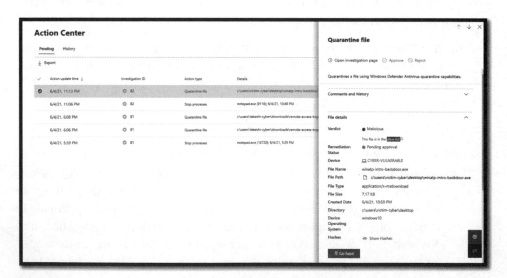

Figure 4.60: Review and approve pending actions in Action Center

The unified Action Center, as shown in Figure 4.61, brings together remediation actions across Defender for Endpoint and Defender for Office 365. It defines a common language for all remediation actions and provides a unified investigation experience.

Figure 4.61: Review and approve pending actions in Action Center

Using Microsoft Threat Expert Support for Remediation and Investigation

Microsoft Threat Experts is a managed threat-hunting service that provides your Security Operation Centers (SOCs) with expert-level monitoring and analysis to help them ensure that critical threats in your unique environments don't get missed.

Microsoft Threat Expert is a managed threat-hunting service that provides expert-driven insights and data through these two capabilities: Targeted Attack Notification and Access to Experts on Demand.

Targeted Attack Notification

Targeted Attack Notification provides proactive hunting for the most critical threats to your network, including human adversary intrusions, human operated ransomware, or advanced attacks like cyber-espionage.

These notifications show up as a new alert. Additionally, the managed hunting service includes:

- Threat monitoring and analysis, reducing dwell time and risk to the business
- Hunter-trained artificial intelligence to discover and prioritize both known and unknown attacks
- Identifying the most important risks, helping SOCs maximize time and energy
- Scope of compromise and as much context as can be quickly delivered to enable fast SOC response

Follow these steps to enable this service:

1. You must be an existing customer for Microsoft Defender for Endpoint.

2. You need to apply for Microsoft Threat Experts - Targeted Attack Notifications to get unique insights and analysis that help identify the most critical threats.

3. To enroll in Microsoft Threat Experts - Targeted Attack Notifications benefits, go to Settings > General > Advanced features > Microsoft Threat Experts - Targeted Attack Notifications to apply. Once accepted, you will get the benefits of Targeted Attack Notifications. See Figure 4.62.

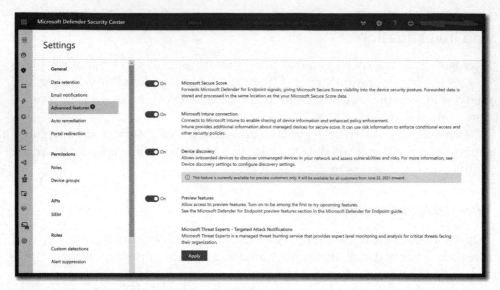

Figure 4.62: Microsoft Threat Experts

Contact your account team or Microsoft representative to subscribe to Microsoft Threat Experts - Experts on Demand to consult with Microsoft's threat experts on relevant detections and adversaries that your organization is facing.

1. Enter your name and email address so that Microsoft can get back to you on your application. See Figure 4.63.

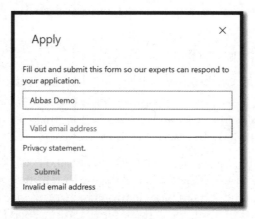

Figure 4.63: Microsoft Threat Expert Application Window

2. Read the privacy statement then click Submit when you're done. You will receive a welcome email once your application is approved, as shown in Figure 4.64.

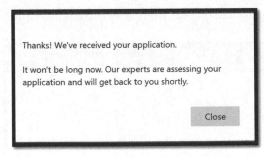

Figure 4.64: Microsoft Threat Expert Application Confirmation

3. When accepted, you will receive a welcome email, and you will see the Apply button change to a toggle that is on. In case you want to take yourself out of the Targeted Attack Notifications service, slide the toggle to off and click Save preferences at the bottom of the page.

4. You will be able to see the targeted attack notification from the MTE via the following sources:

   ▪ The Defender for Endpoint portal's Incidents page

   ▪ The Defender for Endpoint portal's Alerts dashboard

   ▪ OData alerting API and REST API

   ▪ DeviceAlertEvents table in Advanced hunting

   ▪ Your email, if you choose to configure it

Experts on Demand

Customers can engage Microsoft's security experts directly from within Microsoft Defender Security Center for timely and accurate responses. Experts provide insights needed to understand better the complex threats affecting your organization, from alert inquiries, potentially compromised devices, the root cause of a suspicious network connection, to additional threat intelligence regarding ongoing advanced persistent threat campaigns.

With this capability, you can:

▪ Get additional clarification on alerts, including root cause or scope of the incident

▪ Gain clarity into suspicious device behavior and next steps if faced with an advanced attacker

▪ Determine risk and protection regarding threat actors, campaigns, or emerging attacker techniques

Consult a threat expert is available in several places in the portal so you can engage with experts in the context of your investigation:

▪ From the Help and Support Menu, as shown in Figure 4.65.

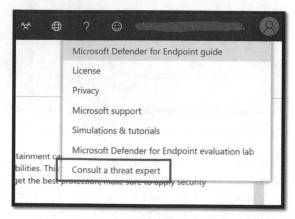

Figure 4.65: Consult a Threat Expert option under support menu

▪ From the Devices page action menu, as shown in Figure 4.66.

Figure 4.66: Devices action page in Microsoft Defender for Endpoint

▪ From the Alerts page action menu, as shown in Figure 4.67.

Figure 4.67: A left page action menu on Microsoft Defender for Endpoint

▪ From the File page action menu, as shown in Figure 4.68.

Figure 4.68: A left page action menu on Microsoft Defender for Endpoint

A popup screen opens. The screen in Figure 4.69 shows when you are on a trial subscription.

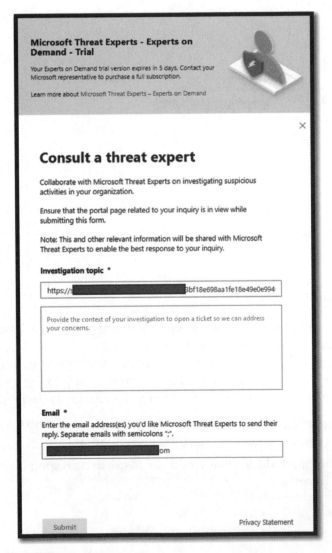

Figure 4.69: MTE screen

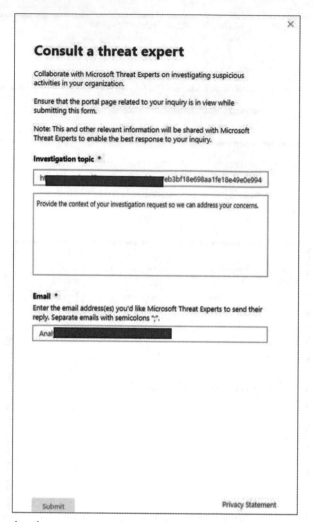

Figure 4.70: Consult a threat expert page

The screen in Figure 4.70 shows when you are on a full Microsoft Threat Experts - Experts on-Demand subscription.

The Investigation topic field is pre-populated with the link to the relevant page for your investigation request. For example, a link to the incident, alert, or device details page that you were at when you made the request.

- In the next field, provide enough information to give the Microsoft Threat Experts enough context to start the investigation.

- Enter the email address that you'd like to use to correspond with Microsoft Threat Experts.

The response from Microsoft Threat Experts varies according to your inquiry. However, they will email a progress report to you about your Consult a threat expert inquiry within two days, to communicate the investigation status from the following categories:

- More information is needed to continue with the investigation

- A file or several file samples are required to determine the technical context

- Investigation requires more time

- Initial information was enough to conclude the investigation

It is essential to respond quickly to keep the investigation moving to the next stage.

Finally, the following are a few sample investigation topics that you can consult with Microsoft Threat Experts - Experts on Demand.

Alert Information

- We see this alert: "Suspicious behavior by a system utility was observed." Can you please share more context on this?

- We see two similar attacks, which generate different alerts. One is "Suspicious PowerShell command line" and the other is "A malicious file was detected based on the indication provided by O365." What is the difference?

- We see a new type of alert for a living-off-the-land binary: [AlertID]. Can you us how to investigate this and share more details on this alert?

- I see a high number of failed login attempts on our executive-level employees device. I cannot find any further evidence around these sign-in attempts. How can Defender for Endpoint see these attempts? What type of sign-ins are being monitored?

Possible Machine Compromise

- Can you please confirm and clarify on this malicious activity "Unknown process observed?" This message or alert is seen frequently on many devices.

- Can you help validate a possible compromise on the following system on [date] with similar behaviors as the previous [malware name] malware detection on the same system in [month]?

Threat Intelligence Details

- I recently saw a [social media reference, for example, Twitter or blog] post about a threat targeting my industry. Can you help us understand what protection Defender for Endpoint provides against this threat actor, any IoC you can share?

- We detected a phishing email that delivered a malicious Microsoft Word document to a user. The malicious Word document caused a series of suspicious events, which triggered multiple Microsoft Defender alerts for [malware name] malware. Do you have any further information on this malware?

Microsoft Threat Experts' Alert Communications

- I received this targeted attack notification from Microsoft Threat Experts. We don't have our own incident response team. What can we do now, and how can we contain the incident?

- Can your incident response team help us address the targeted attack notification that we got?

- I received a targeted attack notification from Microsoft Threat Experts. What data can you provide to us that we can pass on to our incident response team?

Automating Security Response with MCAS and Microsoft Flow

Microsoft Flow is a low-code/no-code automation platform that allows you to create simple automated and integrated workflows and connections with a few clicks, as well as enable API integrations with just a bit of copy-and-paste. Similar to other task and workflow programs like Zapier and IFTTT, Flow has the benefit of being free for most Office 365 licenses and has deep integrations with most Office products.

Although you can tie any API into Flow, it is easiest to use with its hundreds of built-in connectors such as MS Word, Excel, SharePoint, Teams, Power BI, Salesforce, ServiceNow, and many others.

The prerequisites to connect Cloud App Security with Microsoft Flow are as follows:

- Verify licensing for Flow and MCAS (Cloud App Security)
- Create API token
- Create new flow
- Configure CAS trigger and select "when an alert is generated"
- Paste API token in authentication settings

For this use case, the flow is as follows: When a new alert is generated, post a message to a channel in Teams, create a new record (ticket) in ServiceNow, and send an email.

Step 1: Generate Your API Token in Cloud App Security

- Go to `https://portal.cloudappsecurity.com`. (You need to be logged in with an admin account.)
- Click the Settings icon in the upper-right corner.
- Select Security Extensions.
- The first tab is API Tokens. Click the blue + button on the upper-right corner of the token list.
- Name and save your token. See Figure 4.71.

Figure 4.71: Generate new token in MCAS

Step 2: Create Your Trigger in Microsoft Flow

- Go to `https://flow.microsoft.com`.
- Click My Flows in the left sidebar.
- Click the + New button in the upper-right corner.
- Select Create from Blank.
- In the splash screen, click Create from Blank again.
- In the connector search bar, search for Cloud App Security.
- Select Cloud App Security.
- Select the trigger called, "When An Alert Is Generated."
- When prompted, enter your API token.
- Click the New Step button.

Step 3: Create the Teams Message Action in Microsoft Flow

- Under Choose Action, search for Teams in the search bar.
- Click the Microsoft Teams icon.
- Under Actions, select Post Message.
- Select Team ID (it will pull information from your instance of Teams).
- Select Channel ID (it will also pull information from Teams).
- Enter your message.
- Once you click in the message box, you will be given a menu that lets you select Dynamic Content or Expressions.
- The dynamic content list gives you any information available from the CAS alert.
- Click Alert Display Name and Alert Category. (These will create blocks in the message box. You can enter any ancillary information you want here as well.)
- Click the New Step button. See Figure 4.72.

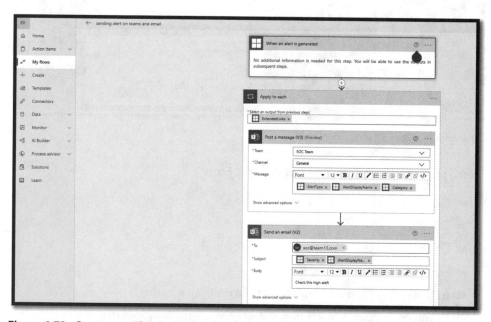

Figure 4.72: Create new Flow in Microsoft Flow application

Step 4: Generate an Email in Microsoft Flow

- Search for Outlook in the search bar.
- Select Office 365 Outlook.

- Under Actions, select Send an Email.
- Enter a recipient.
- Enter a subject.
- Enter the message body. Note: All fields here can use dynamic content.
- Click Save.
- Now that the flow is made and saved, you can rename it by clicking on the descriptor in the upper-left corner.

Connecting the Flow in Cloud App Security

- Go to `https://portal.cloudappsecurity.com`.
- Click Control in the left sidebar.
- Select Policies.
- Find the event/policy that you want to trigger the flow (or create a new Cloud App Security Policy) and select it.
- In the Alerts section, click the box next to Send Alerts to Flow.
- In the Select Playbooks drop-down, choose the name of the flow you created earlier.
- Click Update (see Figure 4.73).

Figure 4.73: Create new Policy Alert in MCAS

Performing an Automated Response Using Azure Security Center

This section focuses on ASC and Azure Sentinel features for automation in alert and threat response, including some of the automated hunting methods.

Scenario 1: Receive Only Defender Antimalware Alerts Using Azure Security Center Workflow Automation.

Here are the steps:

1. Open Azure Security Center, and on the left navigation pane, click Workflow Automation.

2. On the Workflow automation blade, click the + Add Workflow Automation button. The blade shown in Figure 4.74 appears.

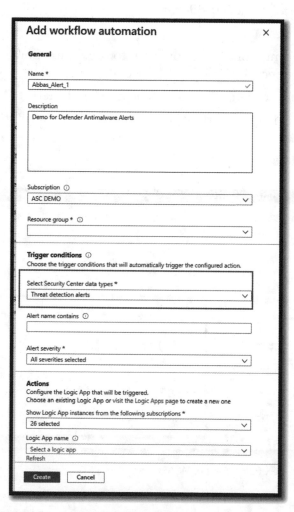

Figure 4.74: Workflow automation tab in ASC

3. Under Triggers conditions, you can see that the automation can be triggered by alerts or recommendations. Under Alert severity (see Figure 4.75), you can also select the severity level that you want to target.

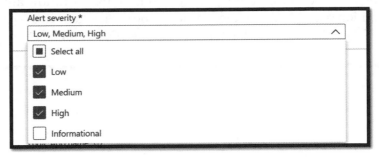

Figure 4.75: Alert Severity selection in Add workflow automation

4. For this use case and scenario, we need to build a workflow automation that will trigger only when Antimalware Detection arrives in ASC. To accomplish this, we will leverage the Logic App Designer, as shown in Figure 4.76.

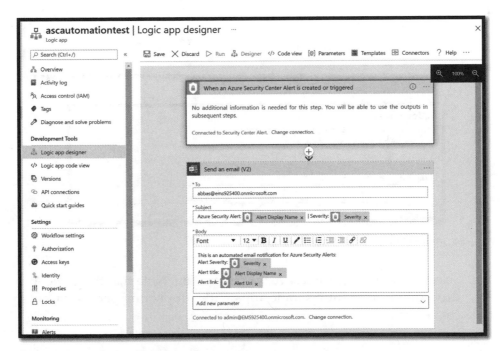

Figure 4.76: Logic App Designer

Create the workflow automation using Logic App Designer by selecting the trigger points such as Send an Email for a specific type and severity of alert.

5. After you've defined your logic app, return to the workflow automation definition pane (Add Workflow Automation). Click Refresh to ensure your new Logic App is available for selection. See Figure 4.77.

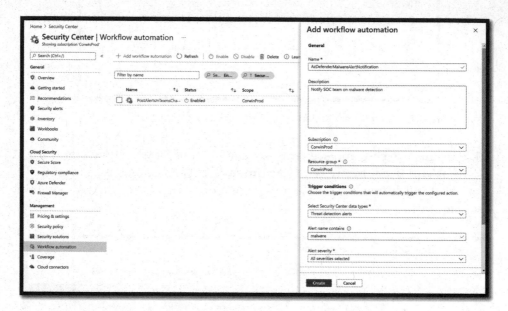

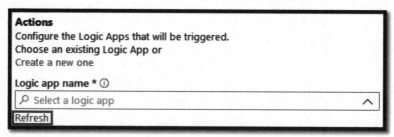

Figure 4.77: Adding workflow automation in ASC

6. Select your logic app and save the automation. Note that the Logic App drop-down only shows logic apps with supporting Security Center connectors.

Using Machine Learning and Artificial Intelligence in Threat Response

Machine learning (ML) is now an essential toolkit in security analytics to detect new and advanced variants of attacks that escape the traditional rules-based system. However, a scarce ML talent pool makes it difficult for security organizations to staff applied security data scientists. To democratize the ML toolkit tailored to the security community's needs, Microsoft has introduced built-in ML within many services, including ASC and Azure Sentinel. One such service is *Fusion Detections*.

Overview of Fusion Detections

Fusion detections using ML combines low- and medium-severity alerts from Microsoft and third-party security products into high-severity incidents. By design, these incidents are low-volume, high-fidelity, and high-severity.

Fusion is enabled by default. Because the logic is hidden and therefore, not customizable, you can only create one rule with this template.

Microsoft recently released 32 new Fusion detections reaching 90 Fusion incident types and Build Your Own Machine Learning framework within Azure Sentinel.

Figure 4.78 shows how a Fusion incident looks in Azure Sentinel portal.

Figure 4.78: Example of a Fusion incident in Azure Sentinel

To enable Fusion detections, select the Analytics blade in the Azure Sentinel portal. In your Active Rules view, a built-in rule of Fusion rule type named "Advanced Multistage Attack Detection" is enabled by default for all Sentinel workspaces. See Figure 4.79. You can disable this any time when it's not required.

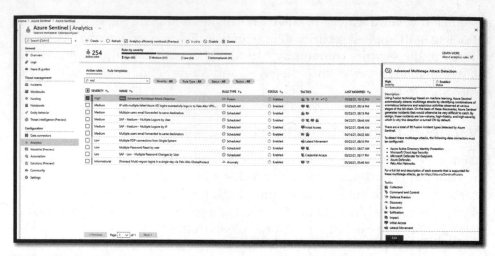

Figure 4.79: Enable/disable Fusion detections rule in Azure Sentinel

Overview of Azure Machine Learning

You can either bring your raw data directly to the Azure Databricks ML environment via EventHub or Azure Blobs or you can use the capabilities provided with Azure Sentinel to export the data from Azure Sentinel Log Analytics tables.

Regardless of the export methods used for raw data, you can use the libraries provided by the BYO-ML framework to import the ML model scoring back into Sentinel Log Analytics tables for further processing and creating incidents.

Azure ML is an end-to-end machine learning platform that enables users to build and deploy models faster on Azure. Azure ML allows you to run Jupyter Notebooks on a VM or a shared cluster computing environment.

Let's look at the steps to create an Azure ML workspace in Azure Sentinel:

1. From the Azure portal, navigate to Azure Sentinel > Threat management > Notebooks and then select Launch Notebook. See Figure 4.80.

2. Select individual notebooks to view their descriptions, required data types, and data sources. See Figure 4.81.

3. Create the ML Workspace by selecting and entering the required details, such as your subscription, resource group, etc., and select Review + Create. See Figure 4.82.

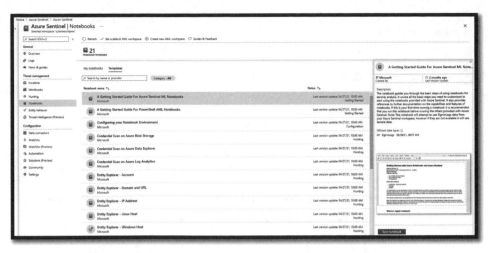

Figure 4.80: Example of Notebooks

4. After Validation is passed, select Create. See Figure 4.83.

5. Wait for the deployment to complete. Your ML workspace is ready for use once it's completed. See Figure 4.84.

6. From the Azure portal, navigate to Azure Sentinel > Threat management > Notebooks, where you can see notebooks that Azure Sentinel provides. Select the notebook you want to use, and then select Launch Notebook to clone and configure the notebook into a new Azure Notebooks project that connects to your Azure Sentinel workspace. When the process is complete, the notebook opens within Azure Notebooks for you to run, as shown in Figure 4.85.

7. After selecting Launch Notebook, choose a compute instance. If you don't have a compute instance, select the plus sign (+) to start the Create Compute Instance wizard, as shown in Figure 4.86.

8. On the Select Virtual Machine page, provide the required information, and then select Next. See Figure 4.87.

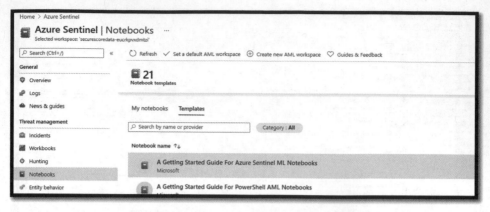

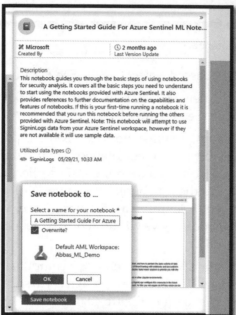

Figure 4.81: Selection of Notebook ML Template in Azure Sentinel

9. On the Configure Settings page, provide the required information, and then select Create. See Figure 4.88.

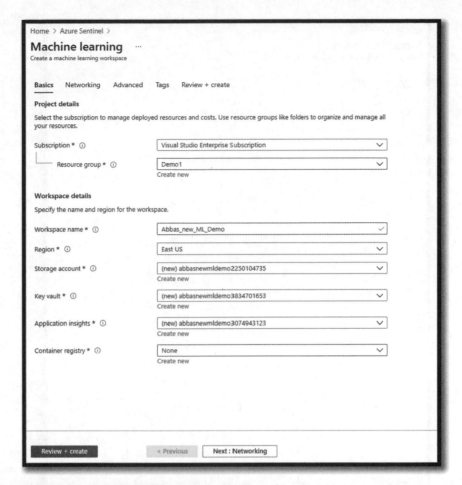

Figure 4.82: Create the ML Workspace in Azure Sentinel

10. Once your notebook server is created, within each cell, select the Run icon to execute code in the notebooks. See Figure 4.89.

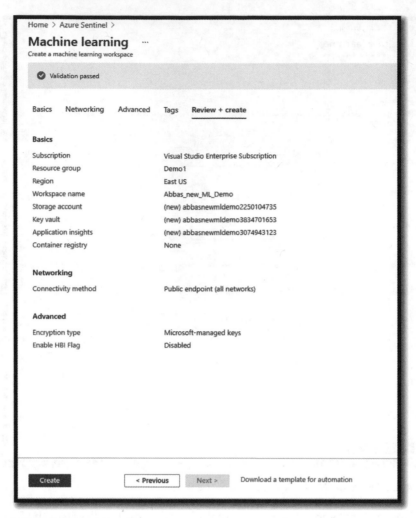

Figure 4.83: Validation pass window

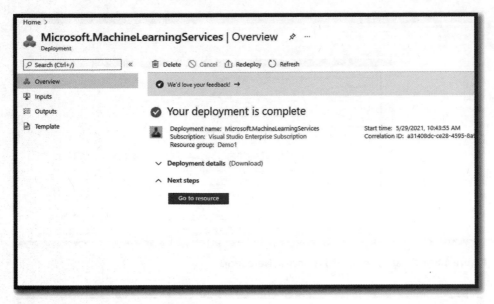

Figure 4.84: Confirmation window

Figure 4.85: Selection of Notebooks in Azure Sentinel

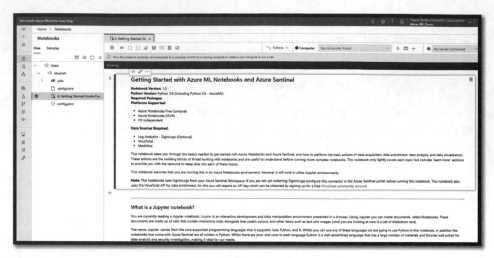

Figure 4.86: Create a compute instance in Notebooks

Figure 4.87: Create Compute instance for Microsoft ML

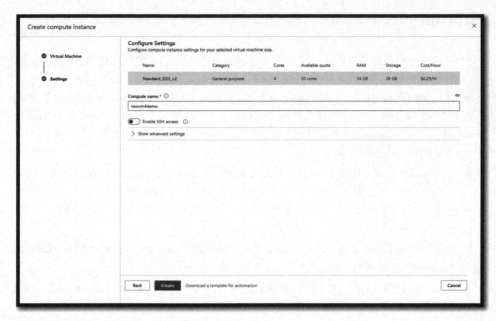

Figure 4.88: Configuration settings window

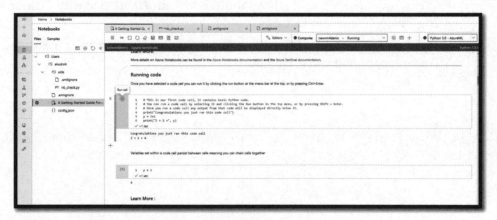

Figure 4.89: Run Code window in Azure Notebook

Summary

- Microsoft has a wealth of information for automation and orchestration. Use the technology that best meets your organization's needs.

- Azure Conditional Access within Azure AD can provide a number of options for preventing initial access to your environment such as using MFA, IP-base location block, GSM-based location block, and Identity Threat and Risky User.

- Azure Sentinel is a cloud-powered SIEM, giving you breadth of insight across all your tools in one place and providing several options for automation, orchestration using machine learning run book, playbook, notebook, and AI-based capabilities.

- Microsoft Defender offers a depth of insight into your modern workplace and cloud infrastructure.

- Microsoft leverages MITRE ATT&CK Framework to detect and hunt threats using Azure Security Center, Azure Defender, and Azure Sentinel.

- Workflow automation can help in reducing alert fatigue for your SecOps.

- You can leverage ML and AI capabilities within Azure Security Center using Fusion Detection tactics.

- You can bring your own ML within Azure Sentinel by creating your own ML workspace and using Notebook.

Microsoft Cybersecurity Reference Architecture and Capability Map

What's in This Chapter

- Understanding how the Microsoft Security architecture aligns with the NIST Cybersecurity Framework (CSF)
- Understanding the Identify, Protect, Detect, Respond, and Recover functions attributed to Microsoft Security
- Using the Microsoft Reference Architecture

  - Protecting the hybrid cloud infrastructure
  - Protecting endpoints and clients
  - Protecting identities and access
  - Protecting SaaS apps
  - Protecting data and information
  - Protecting IoT and operation technology
  - Understanding security operations
  - Understanding people security

Introduction

Most organizations have several challenges in managing their IT environment, especially when managing a hybrid cloud environment that includes IaaS, PaaS, and SaaS services. Cybercriminals are also constantly evolving their techniques and tools and CISOs and cyber defenders are continuously deploying new security controls and technologies and adding new layers of security controls. As the number of technologies and connectivity increases, managing the integration, monitoring, and data flow becomes more complicated.

Prior to defining and designing a threat-hunting program, CISOs need to assess the existing capabilities, security controls, and tools, as well as understand the data flow and organization architecture.

This chapter focuses on the Microsoft Cybersecurity Reference Architecture (MCRA) to obtain a better understanding of the Microsoft Azure environment as well as its capabilities and security tools, dashboards, sensors, and log connectors, which help cyber defenders and threat hunters identify gaps and remediate security loopholes (configurations, patches, as well as people as the weakest link).

Microsoft Security Architecture versus the NIST Cybersecurity Framework (CSF)

The NIST Cybersecurity Framework (CSF) was originally published in February 2014 in response to Presidential Executive Order 13636, "Improving Critical Infrastructure Cybersecurity," which called for the development of a voluntary framework to help organizations improve the cybersecurity, risk management, and resilience of their systems. NIST conferred with a broad range of partners from government, industry, and academia for over a year to build a consensus-based set of sound guidelines and practices.

While intended for adoption by the critical infrastructure sector, the foundational set of cybersecurity disciplines comprising the CSF have been supported by government and industry as a recommended baseline for use by any organization, regardless of its sector or size. Industry is increasingly referencing the CSF as a de facto cybersecurity standard.

In this chapter, we discuss how Microsoft 365 security solutions address each category within four NIST CSF core actions: Identify, Protect, Detect, and Respond. Regardless of the size of your business, this framework will guide you in deploying security solutions that are right for your organization.

This chapter will help you get started with your Microsoft 365 security solutions. It discusses how these products work together in the greater enterprise environment and provides insight into the most effective security scenarios you can enable for your organization.

In the later part of the chapter, we also discuss the overall Cybersecurity Reference Architecture from Microsoft.

The NIST Framework Core consists of five concurrent and continuous functions: Identify, Protect, Detect, Respond, and Recover. When considered together, these functions provide a high-level, strategic view of the lifecycle of an organization's management of cybersecurity risk.

Microsoft has aligned the security capabilities in Microsoft 365 to four of these core functions as shown in Figure 5.1.

Although Microsoft offers some guidance and tools to help with certain Recover functions (data backup and account recovery, for example), Microsoft 365 doesn't specifically address this function; it's covered under Azure services such as Azure Back Up and Azure Site Recovery.

Functions	Identify	Protect	Detect	Respond
Categories	Asset Management	Identity Management and Access Control	Anomalies and Events	Response Planning
	Business Environment	Awareness and Training	Security Continuous Monitoring	Communications
	Governance	Data Security	Detection Processes	Analysis
	Risk Assessment	Protective Technology		Mitigation
	Risk Management Strategy	Information Protection Processes and Procedures		Improvements
	Supply Chain Risk Management	Maintenance		

Figure 5.1: Microsoft 365 Security services aligned with NIST CSF

The Microsoft 365 security solutions philosophy is built on four pillars: Identity and Access Management, Threat Protection, Information Protection, and Security Management, as shown in Figure 5.2.

Microsoft Security Architecture

This section explores the Identify, Protect, Detect, Respond, and Recover functions attributed to Microsoft 365 Security solutions.

Identity & access management	Threat protection	Information protection	Security management
Protect users' identities & control access to valuable resources based on user risk level	*Protect against advanced threats and recover quickly when attacked*	*Ensure documents and emails are seen only by authorized people*	*Gain visibility and control over security tools*
Azure Active Directory	**Microsoft Defender for Endpoint**	**Azure Information Protection**	**Azure Security Center**
Conditional Access	**Microsoft Windows Security Defender**	**Office 365 Data Loss Prevention**	**Azure Defender**
Windows Hello and Authenticator App	**Microsoft Office 365 Defender**	**Microsoft Cloud App Security**	**Microsoft XDR**
Windows Credential Guard	**Microsoft XDR**	**Microsoft Intune**	**Azure Sentinel**
Microsoft Defender for Identity			**Microsoft Office 365 Defender**

Figure 5.2: Microsoft 365 Security solutions

The Identify Function

This section addresses the six categories that comprise the Identify function: Asset Management, Business Environment, Governance, Risk Assessment, Risk Management Strategy, and Supply Chain Risk Management. They "develop an organizational understanding to manage cybersecurity risk to systems, people, assets, data, and capabilities."

- **Asset Management:** Microsoft 365 security solutions help identify and manage key assets such as user identity, company data, PCs and mobile devices, and cloud apps used by company employees.

- **Business Environment:** Every business environment is different, and your users and organizational structure, mission, and leadership are also unique. You know best how to manage security technology within your business environment.

- **Governance:** Microsoft 365 security solutions include tools and resources to help you manage risk and meet regulatory, privacy, and operational (e.g., incident response) requirements.

- **Risk Assessment:** Capabilities in Microsoft 365 can help your organization understand cybersecurity risk related to your users, devices, apps, cloud services, and data through a variety of built-in tools and guidance. Microsoft is committed to ensuring that its customers have visibility into the risk assessments for their cloud services and provides guidance on a number of risk assessments of Microsoft cloud services.

- **Risk Management Strategy:** Using Microsoft 365 risk assessment capabilities can help your organization establish a risk management strategy. Microsoft can help you execute this strategy as it pertains to your priorities, constraints, risk tolerances, and assumptions. In addition, because security is an ongoing endeavor, Microsoft can help you decide on the fundamental steps that will have the most potent and lasting effect.

- **Supply Chain Risk Management:** The key example of supply chain risk management is Azure Active Directory business-to-business (B2B) collaboration, which enables any organization using Azure AD to work securely with users from any other organization, whether or not they use Azure AD.

The Protect Function

This section addresses the six categories that comprise the Protect function: Access Control, Awareness and Training, Data Security, Information Protection Processes and Procedures, Maintenance, and Protective Technology. The section also highlights Microsoft 365 solutions that you can leverage to align to this function.

- **Identity Management, Authentication, and Access Control:** The first safeguard against threats or attackers is to maintain strict, reliable, and appropriate access control. Your employees need to be able to reach the devices, apps, and data they need to be productive, balanced with the right level of access control. Microsoft 365 security solutions such as Azure AD Conditional Access can allow you to control access across devices, apps, and data.

- **Awareness and Training:** The organization's personnel and partners are provided cybersecurity awareness education and are trained to perform their cybersecurity-related duties and responsibilities consistent with related policies, procedures, and agreements. Microsoft's annual Digital Defense Report and Security Intelligence Reports are excellent sources of learning.

- **Data Security:** Microsoft 365 security solutions can help enable data protection in accordance with your organization's risk strategy. Through Microsoft 365 security solutions, data is controlled and protected at rest (e.g., in the cloud, server and workstation hard disk, shared drives, etc.), in use, and in transit. Bitlocker and Azure Information Protection (AIP) services help your organization with Data Security.

■ **Protective Technology:** Technical security solutions are managed to ensure the security and resilience of systems and assets, consistent with related policies, procedures, and agreements. We discussed a number of protective services in the previous chapter. These services include Azure Conditional Access, MAS, Microsoft Defender, and Azure Information Protection.

■ **Information Protection Processes and Procedures:** Security policies (that address purpose, scope, roles, responsibilities, management commitment, and coordination among organizational entities), processes, and procedures are maintained and used to manage protection of information systems and assets. Defining the security policies, processes, and procedures is an important step you will need to take to maintain the security management of your organization.

■ **Maintenance:** To better protect an organization from threats and data breaches, attention must be paid to the vulnerabilities that may not be visible during maintenance and repairs of industrial control and information system components, such as devices and servers. Performing these maintenances and repairs securely and consistent with policies and procedures will protect organizational users, devices, apps, and data. Microsoft 365 can help you mitigate the potential threats.

The Detect Function

This section addresses the three categories that comprise the Detect function: Anomalies and Events, Security Continuous Monitoring, and Detection Processes. We summarize the key Microsoft 365 and Azure solutions that you can leverage to align to this function.

■ **Anomalies and Events:** Many common types of threats target three key attack vectors: devices, email, and identity credentials. Microsoft 365 provides capabilities to detect attacks across these three attack areas. These solutions offer advanced threat protection, security and audit log management, and application whitelisting to ensure the security and resilience of systems and assets, consistent with related policies, procedures, and agreements.

■ **Security Continuous Monitoring:** Microsoft 365 and Azure security solutions offer continuous monitoring, threat detection, vulnerability assessment, and event logging. Some of these services include Microsoft Defender for Endpoint, Microsoft 365 Defender, Azure Defender, MCAS, Azure Security Center, and Azure Sentinel SIEM.

■ **Detection Processes:** The detection process is something an organization will be in charge of; Microsoft does take actions that help secure all organizations by adapting Assume Breach Strategy.

The Respond Function

This section addresses the five categories that comprise the Respond function: Response Planning, Communications, Analysis, Mitigations, and Improvements. We also summarize the key Microsoft 365 and Azure solutions that you can leverage to align to this function.

- **Response Planning:** Microsoft 365 security solutions can help an organization to plan a response to a threat, event, or security incident based on various visibility reports and insights. These services include Azure AD Access and usage report and Azure Defender.

- **Communications:** Educate your employees on security; whatever security tools you deploy to protect your company won't be effective if your employees don't use them properly or regularly. Ensure that all employees in your organization are aware of security threats and their role in protecting company assets.

- **Analysis:** Analysis is conducted to ensure adequate response and support recovery activities. Microsoft offers guidance and education on Windows security and forensics to allow organizations to investigate cybercriminal activity and more effectively respond and recover from malware incidents.

- **Mitigation:** Microsoft 365 security solutions provide tools to help with the incident response as part of an organization's risk mitigation strategy, including in-depth guides to respond to security IT incidents, whitepapers on how Microsoft responds to security incidents in Office 365, and built-in reports.

- **Improvements:** Using Microsoft 365 extensive reporting, logging, and insights, you'll be responsible for determining and implementing any improvements to your organization's security.

The Recover Function

This section addresses the three categories that comprise the Recover function: Recovery Planning, Improvements, and Communications. We also summarize the key Azure solutions that you can leverage to align to this function.

- **Recovery Planning:** Recovery processes and procedures are executed and maintained to ensure timely restoration of systems or assets affected by cybersecurity events. Azure Backup and Site Recovery are two such features that can help an organization with Recovery planning.

- **Improvements:** Recovery planning and processes are improved by incorporating lessons learned into future activities.

- **Communications:** Restoration activities are coordinated with internal and external parties, such as coordinating centers, Internet service providers, owners of attacking systems, victims, other CSIRTs, and vendors.

Using the Microsoft Reference Architecture

The Microsoft Cybersecurity Reference Architecture (MCRA) provides a single-page view of the various security solutions, which seamlessly work together in a highly integrated manner to drive simplicity and effectiveness. See Figure 5.3. The Reference Architecture can be used as a starting template for security architecture and for comparison of security capabilities. It also helps you understand the integration of different components in the Microsoft suite and their capabilities.

As organizations compete to migrate toward the cloud faster, poor architecture designs could open new loopholes and vulnerabilities. As a result, the demands of designing exhaustive architecture and integrating heterogeneous environments, especially hybrid clouds, are increasing.

MCRA describes Microsoft's cybersecurity capabilities and how they integrate with existing security architectures and capabilities.

MCRA covers M365 Security and Compliance Portal, Secure Score, MCAS (Microsoft Cloud Security Broker), Microsoft Defender and XDR, Microsoft Azure Defender, IoT and Operation Security, Security Operations, and People Security.

The entire Reference Architecture is built on some of the core foundations such as Microsoft Threat Intelligence, Microsoft Service Trust Portal (`https://aka.ms/stp`), Microsoft Security Development Lifecycle (SDL), GitHub Advance Security, and the Microsoft Security and Compliance Management Portal (see Figure 5.4).

Microsoft Threat Intelligence

Microsoft isn't the only company that invests in AI. However, Microsoft is in a unique position to create more powerful AI solutions. That's due in part to the massive volume and diversity of the signals they have access to, combined with their human expertise.

Like humans, intelligence requires expert guidance and data, or signals, to learn and get smarter. Microsoft analyzes trillions of signals with unparalleled diversity. These signals are collected from diversified sources and analyzed using AI and ML algorithms to get a unique insight into the various threats.

Across Microsoft platforms, billions of endpoints send anonymized telemetry from both the commercial and consumer worlds at multiple points up and down the stack. The data that Microsoft collects from the various sources passes through a strict privacy/compliance boundary to ensure that data is only being used in ways that their customers have agreed to. See Figure 5.5.

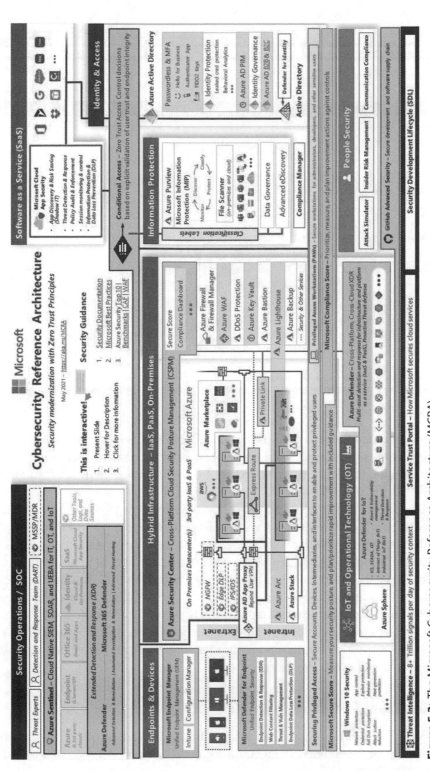

Figure 5.3: The Microsoft Cybersecurity Reference Architecture (MCRA)

Figure 5.4: Foundation of Microsoft Reference Architecture

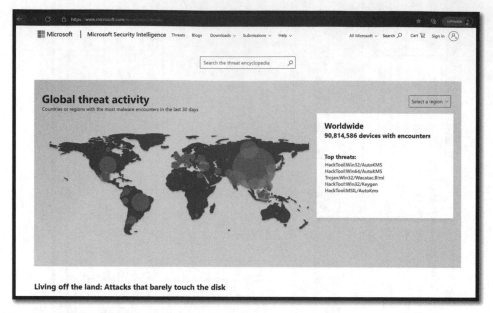

Figure 5.5: Microsoft's Global threat activity portal

The data sources include the product noted earlier, specialized security sources, insights from dark markets (criminal forums), and learnings from incident response engagements where Microsoft helps customers with investigations and remediates incidents.

The data then goes through a collection and analysis phase to normalize it, apply various analytics to identify relevant security insights and findings, and publish to an internal API.

Each of the Microsoft products then accesses the data to provide findings, context, insight, etc., relative to that capability and then automatically feeds new detections and insights into the graph to enrich other product findings.

Additionally, human teams are constantly working with the graph to hunt for adversaries in various environments (Azure, Office 365, Microsoft IT, Windows ATP Customers, etc.) and creating, tuning, and validating new analytics to improve the overall detection.

Service Trust Portal

The Service Trust Portal contains details about Microsoft's implementation of controls and processes that protect your cloud services and the customer data therein. See Figure 5.6.

Figure 5.6: Service Trust Portal

To access some of the resources on the Service Trust Portal, you must log in as an authenticated user with your Microsoft cloud services account (either an Azure Active Directory organization account or a Microsoft Account) and review and accept the Microsoft Non-Disclosure Agreement for Compliance Materials.

Existing customers can access the Service Trust Portal at `https://aka.ms/STP` with one of the following online subscriptions (trial or paid): Microsoft 365, Dynamics 365, or Azure.

Security Development Lifecycle (SDL)

The Microsoft SDL introduces security and privacy considerations throughout all phases of the development process, helping developers build highly secure software, address security compliance requirements, and reduce development costs. See Figure 5.7.

The guidance, best practices, tools, and processes in the Microsoft SDL are practices that Microsoft uses internally for building more secure products and services. Microsoft has updated the SDL practices as a result of growing experience with new scenarios, like the cloud, Internet of Things (IoT), and artificial intelligence (AI). To learn more, visit `https://www.microsoft.com/en-us/securityengineering/sdl/`.

Figure 5.7: Microsoft SDL portal

Protecting the Hybrid Cloud Infrastructure

Microsoft invests deeply in Azure platform security. The hybrid infrastructure model and the cloud security/networking controls are new to many security professionals, and hence there are frequently inadvertent configuration errors that expose hosted resources on the cloud environment.

Today, most organizations operate a multi-platform environment with Windows and Linux servers in the datacenters, application containers, and many different generations of applications to protect. Most organizations started security with a core set of security capabilities at the network edge/egress points to protect extranet and intranet resources.

MSFT provides different controls and dashboards such as Microsoft Secure Score, Azure Security Center, aka Azure Defender, which will be briefly discussed in this section. See Figure 5.8.

Azure Marketplace

On Azure, Microsoft invested in Azure Marketplace to ensure customers have access to capabilities from popular vendors, often used by customers to extend existing on-premises controls to the cloud. Azure Marketplace integrates existing capabilities and skills, Privilege Management for protecting against high-impact attacks against the privilege accounts, Azure AD App Proxy to move beyond a user's VPN and connect users to on-premises applications from the cloud. See Figure 5.9.

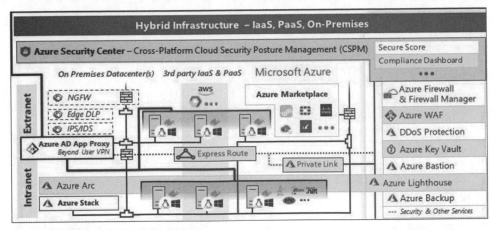

Figure 5.8: The Hybrid Infrastructure

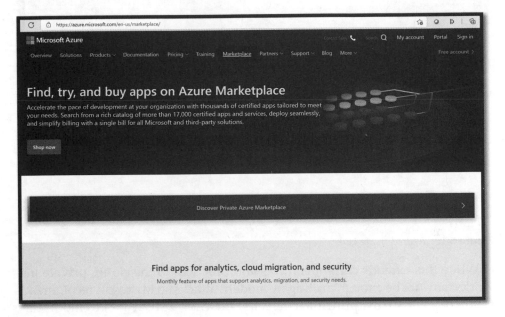

Figure 5.9: Azure Marketplace portal

Private Link

Microsoft provides Private Link support for Azure Services to help organizations extend private networks to the PaaS services used by applications. Azure Private Link enables an organization to access Azure PaaS Services (for example, Azure Storage and SQL Database) and Azure-hosted customer-owned/partner services over a Private Endpoint in your virtual network.

Traffic between your virtual network and the service traverses over the Microsoft backbone network, eliminating exposure from the public Internet. An organization can also create their own Private Link Service within their virtual network and deliver it privately to their customers. See Figure 5.10.

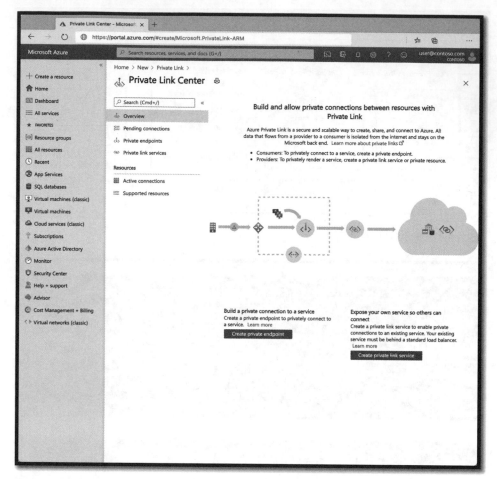

Figure 5.10: Azure Private Link

While this extends current controls and practices to the cloud, private networks may not be enough to mitigate modern attacks so Microsoft recommends following Zero Trust principles (`https://aka.ms/zerotrust`) to modernize your access control strategy using identity, network, application, data, and other controls.

Azure Arc

Microsoft has invested in a wide range of capabilities to help secure your hybrid multi-cloud environment and the workloads in it. These are built into Azure and several extend across your hybrid infrastructure estate (on-premises, AWS, GCP, and other clouds) using Azure Arc. See Figure 5.11.

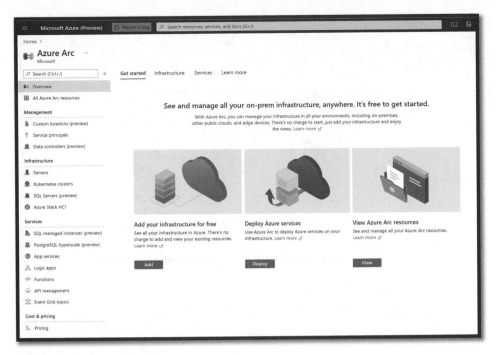

Figure 5.11: Azure Arc dashboard

Azure Arc simplifies governance and management by delivering a consistent multi-cloud and on-premises management platform. Azure Arc enables an organization to:

- Manage the entire environment, with a single pane of glass, by projecting your existing non-Azure, on-premises, or other-cloud resources into Azure Resource Manager.

- Manage virtual machines, Kubernetes clusters, and databases as if they are running in Azure.

- Use familiar Azure services and management capabilities, regardless of where they live.

- Continue using traditional ITOps, while introducing DevOps practices to support new cloud native patterns in your environment.

- Configure Custom Locations as an abstraction layer on top of Azure Arc–enabled Kubernetes cluster, cluster connect, and cluster extensions.

Azure Lighthouse

Azure Lighthouse provides cross-tenant support in Azure for services, often used by managed service providers and customers with multiple tenants. See Figure 5.12.

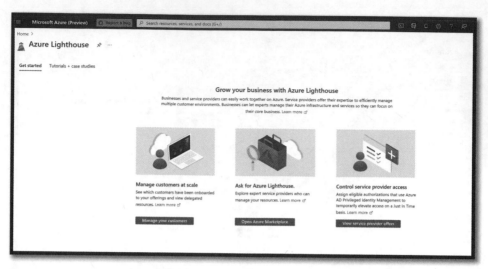

Figure 5.12: Azure Lighthouse portal

With Azure Lighthouse, service providers can deliver managed services using comprehensive and robust management tooling built into the Azure platform. As a result, customers maintain control over who can access their tenants, which resources they can access, and what actions can be taken. This service can also benefit enterprise IT organizations managing resources across multiple tenants. See Figure 5.13.

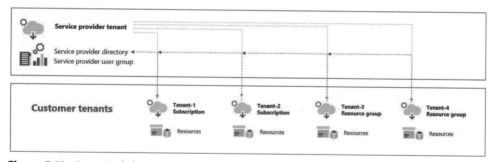

Figure 5.13: Azure Lighthouse architecture

Azure Firewall

Azure Firewall is a managed, cloud-based network security service that helps protect your Azure Virtual Network resources. See Figure 5.14.

- **Azure Firewall Premium:** A next-generation firewall with capabilities required for highly sensitive and regulated environments (TLS Inspection, IDPS, URL Filtering, Web Categories).

Figure 5.14: Azure Firewall

■ **Azure Firewall Manager:** A security management service that provides central security policy and route management for cloud-based security perimeters. See Figure 5.15.

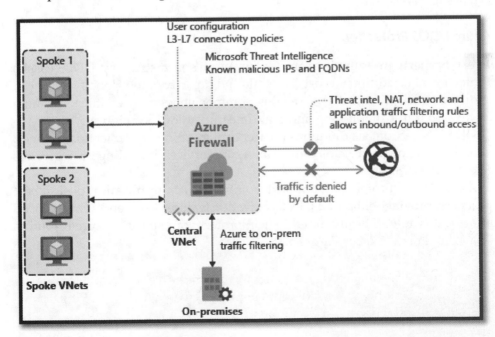

Figure 5.15: Azure Firewall architecture

Azure Web Application Firewall (WAF)

Azure WAF provides centralized protection of your web applications from common exploits and vulnerabilities. WAF on Application Gateway is based on Core Rule Set (CRS) 3.1, 3.0, or 2.2.9 from the Open Web Application Security Project (OWASP).

The WAF automatically updates to include protection against new vulnerabilities, with no additional configuration needed. WAF allows you to create separate policies for each site behind an organization's Application Gateway. See Figure 5.16.

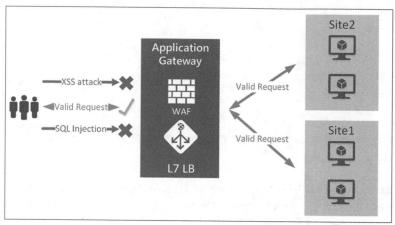

Figure 5.16: WAF design

Azure DDOS Protection

Every property in Azure is protected by Azure's infrastructure DDoS (Basic) Protection at no additional cost. The scale and capacity of the globally deployed Azure network provide defense against common network layer attacks through always-on traffic monitoring and real-time mitigation. See Figure 5.17.

DDoS Protection Basic requires no user configuration or application changes. DDoS Protection Basic helps protect all Azure services, including PaaS services like Azure DNS.

Azure DDoS Protection Standard, combined with application design best practices, provides enhanced DDoS mitigation features to defend against DDoS attacks. It is automatically tuned to help protect your specific Azure resources in a virtual network. See Figure 5.18.

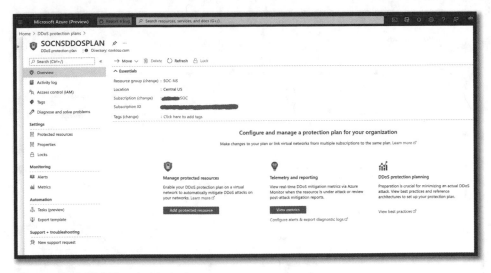

Figure 5.17: DDOS Plan dashboard

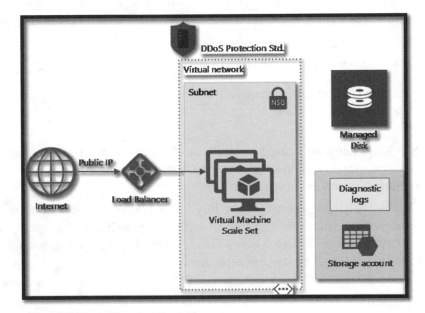

Figure 5.18: DDOS Protection Architecture

Azure Key Vault

Microsoft offers Azure Key Vault with two service tiers: Standard, which encrypts with a software key, and a Premium tier, which includes Hardware Security Module (HSM)–protected keys. See Figure 5.19.

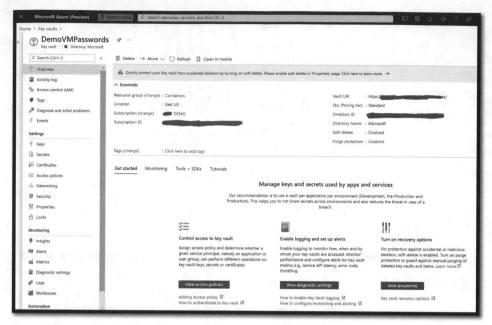

Figure 5.19: Azure Key Vault portal

Azure Key Vault can help an organization with the following problems:

- **Secrets Management:** Azure Key Vault can be used to securely store and tightly control access to tokens, passwords, certificates, API keys, and other secrets.

- **Key Management:** Azure Key Vault can also be used as a Key Management solution. Azure Key Vault makes it easy to create and control the encryption keys used to encrypt your data.

- **Certificate Management:** Azure Key Vault is also a service that lets you easily enroll, manage, and deploy public and private Transport Layer Security/Secure Sockets Layer (TLS/SSL) certificates for use with Azure and your internal connected resources.

Azure Bastion

Azure Bastion is a service that an organization can deploy to let their employees or contractors connect to a virtual machine using your browser and the Azure portal. The Azure Bastion service is a fully platform-managed PaaS service that you provision inside your virtual network. See Figure 5.20.

Figure 5.20: Example of Azure Bastion for Firewall

Azure Bastion provides secure and seamless RDP/SSH connectivity to your virtual machines directly from the Azure portal over TLS. When you connect via Azure Bastion, your virtual machines do not need a public IP address, agent, or special client software. Figure 5.21 shows the architecture of an Azure Bastion deployment.

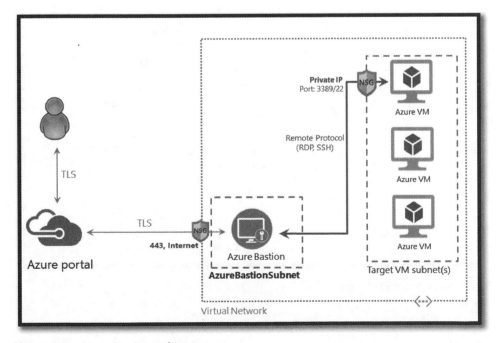

Figure 5.21: Azure Bastion architecture

The Bastion host in Figure 5.21 is deployed in the virtual network containing the AzureBastionSubnet subnet with a minimum /27 prefix.

- The user connects to the Azure portal using any HTML5 browser.
- The user selects the virtual machine to connect to.
- With a single click, the RDP/SSH session opens in the browser.
- No public IP is required on the Azure VM.

Azure Site Recovery

Using Azure Recovery, an organization can set up an Azure Site Recovery by simply replicating an Azure VM to a different Azure region directly from the Azure portal.

As a fully integrated offering, Site Recovery is automatically updated with new Azure features as they're released. An organization can minimize recovery issues by sequencing the order of multi-tier applications running on multiple virtual machines. It also ensures compliance by testing your disaster recovery plan without impacting production workloads or end users. And it keeps applications available during outages with automatic recovery from on-premises to Azure or Azure to another Azure region. See Figure 5.22.

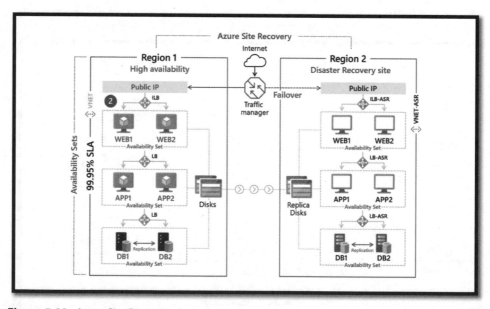

Figure 5.22: Azure Site Recovery

Azure Security Center (ASC)

ASC (see Figure 5.23) Microsoft Azure Defender (formerly known as Azure Security Center (ASC), not only helps organizations against distributed denial of service (DDoS), key management, ransomware-resistant backup archives, and confidential computing capabilities to protect data while it's being processed, but also is one of the key tools required to identify gaps and deficiencies and guide defender teams on how to remediate those issues in their cloud environment.

Azure Defender allows you to:

- Protect servers and workloads across multi-cloud (Amazon and Google Cloud) and on-premises datacenters.

- Perform vulnerability assessments.

- Detect and correct common misconfiguration issues such as

  - VMs exposed directly to the Internet

  - Missing Web Application Firewalls (WAFs) for web applications

  - Out-of-date patches and anti-malware signatures and many others

- Leverage cutting-edge capabilities in Azure like machine learning to suggest firewall rules and application whitelists (to allow/block which files can run on servers).

Figure 5.23: Azure Security Center (Azure Defender), view from the Azure portal

Microsoft Azure Secure Score

Microsoft Azure Secure Score (see Figure 5.24) is part of Azure Defender. It gives you reports on the deficiencies within the environment and the actions you may take to improve the environment. It also provides you with a list of tasks based on the impact and efforts needed to address the environment's gaps. It provides a granular level of information that is required for further understanding and investigation.

Figure 5.24: Azure Secure Score

Protecting Endpoints and Clients

Managing risk, health, and compliance across a broad spectrum of device platforms and ownership (BYODs, corporate devices, Macs, as well as unmanaged and mobile devices) is one of the most important priorities of the security and IT team (see Figure 5.25).

Many organizations take advantage of built-in Windows features and system management to provide basic security hygiene like patching and Active Directory account security and group policy.

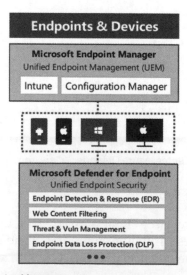

Figure 5.25: Microsoft Endpoint Manager

Microsoft Endpoint Manager (MEM) Configuration Manager

Microsoft provides cross-platform security, multi-cloud, and management (for Windows, Linux, Mac, iOS, and Android) using a single management portal, found at `https://endpoint.microsoft.com`. See Figure 5.26.

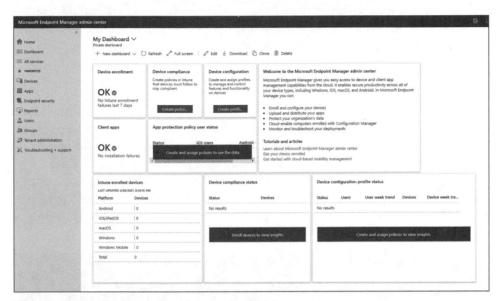

Figure 5.26: Microsoft Endpoint Manager Center

For the Endpoint Protection Platform (EPP) and Endpoint Detection and Response (EDR), Microsoft uses Microsoft Defender for Endpoint (see Figure 5.27).

Figure 5.27: Microsoft Defender for Endpoint

Microsoft Defender for Endpoint is a holistic, cloud-delivered endpoint security solution that includes risk-based vulnerability management and assessment, attack surface reduction, behavioral-based and cloud-powered next-generation protection, endpoint detection and response (EDR), automatic investigation and remediation, and managed hunting services.

These capabilities are underscored with APIs that enable access and integration with the platform. Microsoft Defender for Endpoint is easily deployed, configured, and managed with a unified security management experience.

Microsoft Intune

Microsoft Intune (formerly Windows Intune) is a Microsoft cloud-based management solution for mobile device and operating system management. It aims to provide Unified Endpoint Management of both corporate and Bring Your Own Device (BYOD) devices in a way that protects corporate data.

You control how your organization's devices are used, including mobile phones, tablets, and laptops. You can also configure specific policies to manage applications. For example, you can prevent emails from being sent to people outside your organization. See Figure 5.28.

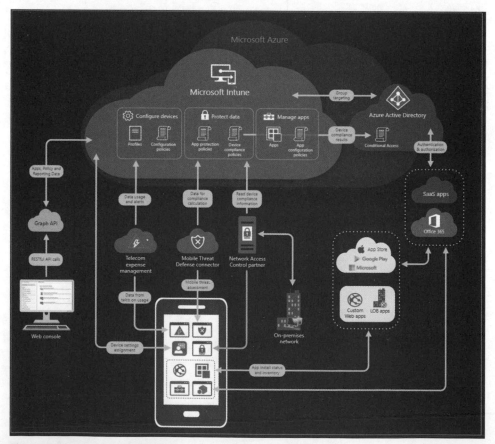

Figure 5.28: Intune architecture

Intune also allows people in your organization to use their personal devices for school or work. On personal devices, Intune helps make sure your organization's data stays protected and can isolate organization data from personal data.

Windows 10 Security includes an extensive set of platform capabilities and hardware security integrations to protect against ever-evolving attacks (see Figure 5.29).

Figure 5.29: Windows 10 Security

Protecting Identities and Access

Microsoft is taking a comprehensive approach to secure identities against the full range of threats and risks (see Figure 5.30).

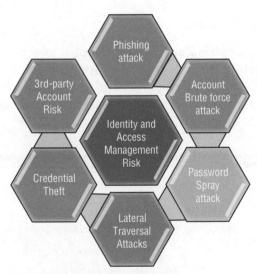

Figure 5.30: Threat and risk against identities and access

Microsoft's top services for identity protection include Azure Active Directory, Multi-Factor Authentication, Conditional Access, Azure AD Privilege Identity Management, Defender for Identity, Azure AD B2B and B2C services, and Identity Governance (see Figure 5.31).

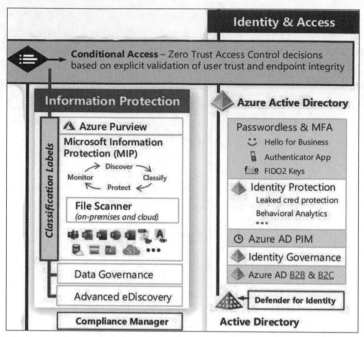

Figure 5.31: Identity and Access Management

Azure AD Conditional Access

Conditional Access applies Zero Trust principles to access control decisions by explicitly validating users' trust and endpoints requesting access to your resources. This helps build a de facto security perimeter around these modern resources with modern controls and provides simple, consistent policy enforcement across them. See Figure 5.32.

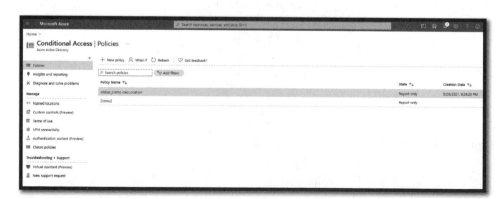

Figure 5.32: Azure Conditional Access Policies example

Policies have some of the most powerful capabilities within Azure Active. And you can scope these policies to meet just about any scenario required, including (or excluding) users/groups, apps, and other conditions such as risk, device platform and state, locations, and client application (browser, mobile, and desktop).

Passwordless for End-to-End Secure Identity

The Microsoft Authenticator app can be used to sign in to any Azure AD account without using a password. Microsoft Authenticator uses key-based authentication to enable a user credential that is tied to a device, where the device uses a PIN or biometric. Windows Hello for Business uses similar technology.

Windows Hello addresses the following problems with passwords:

- Strong passwords can be difficult to remember, and users often reuse passwords on multiple sites.

- Server breaches can expose symmetric network credentials (passwords).

- Passwords are subject to replay attacks.

- Users can inadvertently expose their passwords due to phishing attacks.

Azure Active Directory (aka Azure AD)

A fully managed multi-tenant service from Microsoft offers identity and access capabilities for applications running in Microsoft Azure and for applications running in an on-premises environment. Its name leads some to make incorrect conclusions about what Azure AD is. Therefore, to avoid any confusion with Windows Server Active Directory that you may already be familiar with in an on-premises environment, understand that Azure AD is not Windows Server Active Directory running on Virtual Machines in Microsoft Azure.

Azure AD is not a replacement for Windows Server Active Directory. If you already have an on-premises directory, it can be extended to the cloud using the directory integration capabilities of Azure AD. In these scenarios, users and groups on the on-premises directory are synced to Azure AD using a tool such as Azure Active Directory Sync (AAD Sync).

Azure MFA

Today, many organizations use on-premises multi-factor authentication systems to protect mission-critical data in their file servers and their critical Line of Business (LOB) applications. However, as these workloads (or parts of them) move to the cloud (at least in a hybrid manner), they need an effective and easy-to-use solution in the cloud for protection.

Microsoft published a whitepaper at `https://www.microsoft.com/en-us/download/details.aspx?id=39052` describing in depth how these workloads (or parts of them) move to the cloud (at least in a hybrid manner) in an effective and easy-to-use solution.

Azure Active Directory Identity Protection

One of Microsoft's benefits of having numerous clients utilizing its services is that Microsoft can use this information from those clients and apply some genuine machine learning on the information that comes from Azure AD, Microsoft accounts, and even Xbox services. See Figure 5.33.

Identity Protection allows organizations to accomplish three key tasks:

- Automate the detection and remediation of identity-based risks.
- Investigate risks using data in the portal.
- Export risk detection data to third-party utilities for further analysis.

Figure 5.33: Azure AD Identity Protection portal

Identity Protection uses Microsoft's learnings from their position in organizations with Azure AD, the consumer space with Microsoft Accounts, and in gaming with Xbox to protect your users. Microsoft analyzes over 8 trillion signals per day to identify and protect customers from threats.

The signals generated by and fed to Identity Protection can be further fed into tools like Conditional Access to make access decisions, or fed back to a Security Information and Event Management (SIEM) tool for further investigation based on your organization's enforced policies.

Azure Active Directory Privilege Identity Management (PIM)

Privileged Identity Management provides time-based and approval-based role activation to mitigate the risks of excessive, unnecessary, or misused access permissions on resources that you care about. It gives limited and secure admittance to clients or gatherings to certain Azure assets or to Azure AD jobs.

PIM provides time-based, restricted, MFA enforced, approved, and auditable roles to a user or group for some Azure resource or Azure AD role. For example, if your company hires a vendor for a project to do some high-level tasks on your Azure tenant, you cannot simply provide any role to him/her. See Figure 5.34.

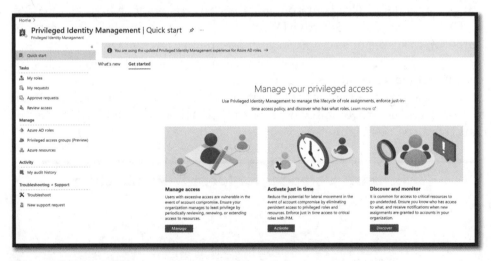

Figure 5.34: Azure PIM

Instead, you should be assessing the task first and providing a time-based access to your vendor until the project ends. When the project ends, the role is revoked, and that vendor will not have access to your Azure resource anymore. It means you are making the vendor "eligible" for doing some privileged tasks for a specific period. Here are some of the key features of Privileged Identity Management:

■ Provide just-in-time privileged access to Azure AD and Azure resources

■ Assign time-bound access to resources using start and end dates

- Require approval to activate privileged roles
- Enforce multi-factor authentication to activate any role
- Use justification to understand why users activate
- Get notifications when privileged roles are activated
- Conduct access reviews to ensure users still need roles
- Download audit history for internal or external audit

Microsoft Defender for Identity

Microsoft Defender for Identity (formerly Azure Advanced Threat Protection, also known as Azure ATP) is a cloud-based security solution that leverages an organization's on-premises Active Directory signals to identify, detect, and investigate advanced threats, compromised identities, and malicious insider actions directed at your organization.

It's designed for hybrid environments, such as customers who use Office 365, but still have on-premises Active Directory infrastructure in place. It detects and alerts you to suspicious activity in your on-premises Active Directory environment. As a post-breach alerting system, the assumption is that an attacker has already gained access to your environment.

Components of Defender for Identity include Defender for Identity Portal, Identity Sensor for Domain Controls and AD FS, and Defender for Identity cloud services. See Figure 5.35.

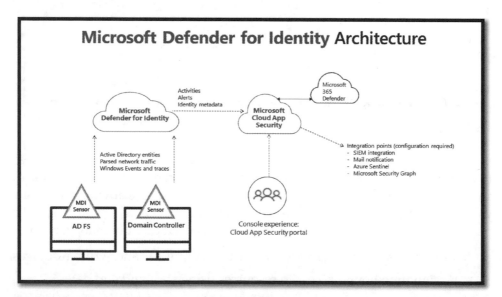

Figure 5.35: Microsoft Defender for Identity Architecture

Defender for Identity enables SecOp analysts and security professionals struggling to detect advanced attacks in hybrid environments to:

- Monitor users, entity behavior, and activities with learning-based analytics
- Protect user identities and credentials stored in Active Directory
- Identify and investigate suspicious user activities and advanced attacks throughout the kill chain
- Provide clear incident information on a simple timeline for fast triage

Azure AD B2B and B2C

Azure AD B2B collaboration can address the problem of sharing your applications with external users and is a feature of Azure AD rather than a standalone service.

These users could be suppliers, customers, partners, or any external user with whom you wish to collaborate. Again, this is more at the user level and not at the device level. See Figure 5.36.

Figure 5.36: Azure AD B2C portal

Azure AD Identity Governance

Azure Active Directory (Azure AD) Identity Governance allows you to balance your organization's need for security and employee productivity with the right processes and visibility. See Figure 5.37.

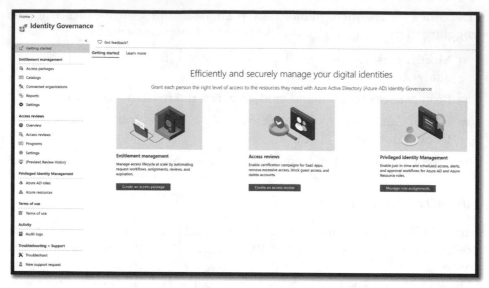

Figure 5.37: Identity Governance portal

In addition, it provides an organization with capabilities to ensure that the right people have the right access to the right resources. These and related Azure AD and Enterprise Mobility and security features allow you to mitigate access risk by protecting, monitoring, and auditing access to critical assets, while ensuring employee and business partner productivity.

Identity Governance gives organizations the ability to do the following tasks across employees, business partners, and vendors, and across services and applications, both on-premises and in clouds:

- Govern the identity lifecycle
- Govern the access lifecycle
- Secure privileged access for administration

Protecting SaaS Apps

Some of the common challenges faced with SaaS apps are concerning governance, risk, and compliance of those sprawling SaaS applications estate and unsanctioned Shadow IT applications. See Figure 5.38.

Microsoft has invested in secure and compliant SaaS services and helps its customers secure third-party Software as a Service (SaaS) with Microsoft Cloud App Security (MCAS), which provides Cloud Access Security Broker (CASB) capabilities, including XDR capabilities for SaaS applications as well as governance, threat protection, data protection, and more for these SaaS apps and the data stored within SaaS. See Figure 5.39.

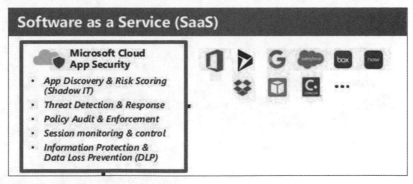

Figure 5.38: SaaS challenges

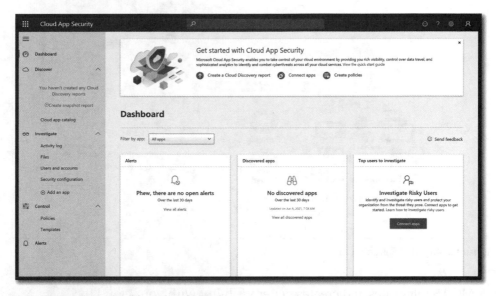

Figure 5.39: MCAS Dashboard and Portal

MCAS also natively integrates with leading Microsoft solutions and is designed with security professionals to provide simple deployment, centralized management, and innovative automation capabilities.

MCAS and MDE illustrate Microsoft's philosophy of a single agent (or control point) for resources that provide many security services. This helps reduce the performance impact of installing too many security agents.

It supports various deployment modes, including log collection, API connectors, and reverse proxy. In addition, it provides rich visibility, control over data travel, and sophisticated analytics to identify and combat cyberthreats across all Microsoft and third-party cloud services (see Figure 5.40).

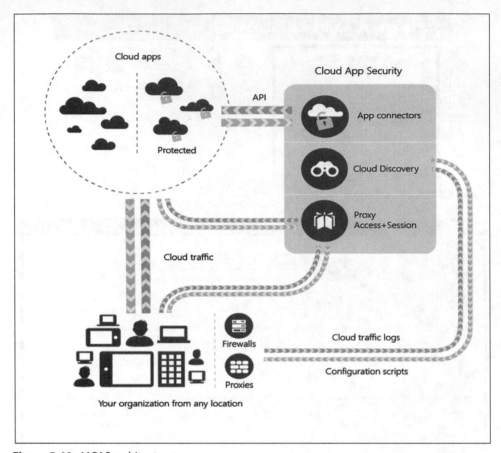

Figure 5.40: MCAS architecture

MCAS integrates and creates better visibility with your cloud by:

- Identifying cloud apps within your cloud environment using cloud discovery features.
- Helping you manage Shadow IT by sanctioning and unsanctioning apps in your cloud.
- Using easy-to-deploy app connectors that take advantage of provider APIs, for visibility and governance of apps that you connect to.
- Using Conditional Access App Control protection to get real-time visibility and control over access and activities within your cloud apps.
- Helping you have continuous control by setting, and then continually fine-tuning, policies.

Protecting Data and Information

Organizations today face a number of challenges concerning protecting and governing the data and information such as labeling, discovering, tracking information, and tracking data loss or manipulation of a file, and implementing and enforcing organization policy to protect different levels of sensitive data. For data classification, the biggest challenge is to discover and classify the data across on-premises, mobile devices, SaaS, and cloud infrastructure.

Data discovery and classification can be done through AIP scanner as an automated approach, or users can manually perform these tasks. Relying on users to identify the data and classifying them would be challenging and requires an extensive information security awareness and an educational program on how to identify the data as well as what control should be applied. Microsoft AIP could help an organization as a technology enabler to automate and manage this section. However, data classification criteria (e.g., highly confidential, confidential, restricted, public, etc.) and required security controls such as applying encryption, defining the right access of to who can access the classified documents, and others, should be defined at the data governance level and endorsed by senior management.

Microsoft is focused on providing strong data protection with an emphasis on persistently protecting the data anywhere it goes, and this contrasts with the typical industry approach, which relies solely on controls for devices/ storage/networks that are unable to protect the data created/copied outside the enterprise (see Figure 5.41).

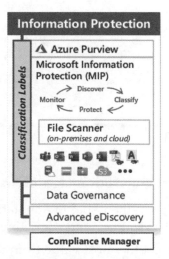

Figure 5.41: Protecting information and data

To overcome these challenges, Microsoft offers a range of services such as Azure Purview, Microsoft Information Protection (MIP), and Advanced eDiscovery.

> *"When we talk about assets on the balance sheet, data deserves its row."*
>
> *—Satya Nadella, Microsoft CEO*

Azure Purview

Microsoft Azure Purview is a fully managed, unified data governance service that helps you manage and govern your on-premises, multi-cloud, and SaaS data.

Purview creates a holistic, up-to-date map of your data landscape with automated data discovery, sensitive data classification, and end-to-end data lineage. As a result, Purview empowers data consumers to find valuable, trustworthy data.

It's built over Apache Atlas, an open-source project for metadata management and governance for data assets. Azure Purview also has a data share mechanism that securely shares data with external business partners without setting up extra FTP nodes or creating redundant large datasets.

Azure Purview does not move or store customer data out of the region in which it is deployed. The Purview service can be accessed from the Azure portal. See Figure 5.42.

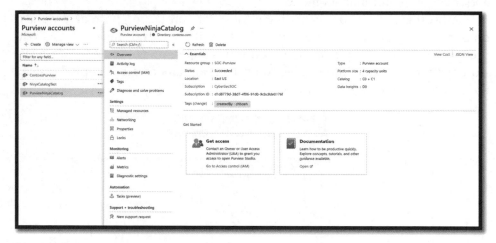

Figure 5.42: Azure Purview dashboard

Some of the business value and advantages of Azure Purview include:

- It is designed to address the issues of annotating data sources, creating documentation of data sources, and restricting access of data sources.
- It helps enterprises get the most value from their existing information assets. In addition, the catalog creation makes data sources easily discoverable and understandable by the users who manage the data.
- Provides a cloud-based service into which you can register data sources. During registration, the data remains in its existing location, but a copy of

its metadata is added to Azure Purview, along with a reference to the data source location. The metadata is also indexed to make each data source easily discoverable via search and understandable to the users who discover it.

■ After you register a data source, you can then enrich its metadata. Either the user who registered the data source or another user in the enterprise adds the metadata. Any user can annotate a data source by providing descriptions, tags, or other metadata for requesting data source access. This descriptive metadata supplements the structural metadata, such as column names and data types, that's registered from the data source.

■ Users can contribute to the catalog by tagging, documenting, and annotating data sources that have already been registered. They can also register new data sources, which are then discovered, understood, and consumed by the community of catalog users.

More details about this new service can be found at this link: `https://azure.microsoft.com/en-us/services/purview/`.

Microsoft Information Protection (MIP)

MIP helps an organization to discover, classify, and protect sensitive information wherever it lives or travels. These capabilities are included with Microsoft 365 Compliance, and it offers the tools to know your data, protect your data, and prevent data loss across the four elements of the information protection lifecycle, which are discover, classify, protect, and monitor.

MIP services can be accessed from the M365 Compliance portal at `https://compliance.microsoft.com`; (see Figure 5.43).

Figure 5.43: MIP service

AZURE INFORMATION PROTECTION VS. MICROSOFT INFORMATION PROTECTION

Azure Information Protection (AIP) labels, configured at the time using the AIP classic client in the Azure portal, enabled you to apply AIP labels. This enabled a more advanced subscription that let you apply a consistent classification and protection policy for documents and emails, whether they were stored on-premises or in the cloud.

Microsoft 365 only had built-in retention labels that enabled you to classify documents and emails for auditing and retention when that content was stored in Microsoft 365 services. See Figure 5.44.

In 2018, Microsoft introduced a unified labeling solution for Microsoft 365—Microsoft Information Protection (MIP)—that offered centralized management of labels and protection settings in the Security & Compliance Center.

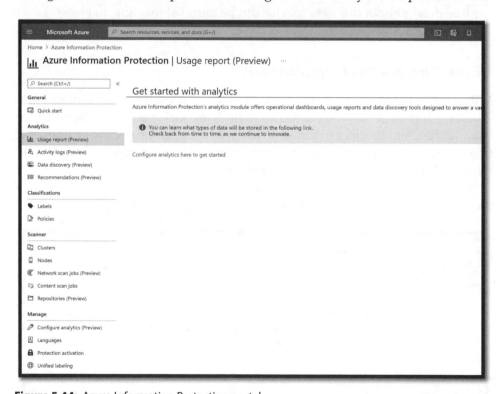

Figure 5.44: Azure Information Protection portal

Azure Information Protection Unified Labeling Scanner (File Scanner)

AIP File Scanner is used to discover and assess existing data in SharePoint sites and file shares. It runs as a Windows Server service and lets you discover, classify, and protect files on UNC paths (network shares) and SharePoint document libraries and folders.

The AIP scanner can inspect any files that Windows can index. If you've configured sensitivity labels to apply automatic classification, the scanner can label discovered files to apply that classification and optionally apply or remove protection. Figure 5.45 shows the AIP scanner architecture, where the scanner discovers files across your on-premises and SharePoint servers.

The scanner uses the Azure Information Protection client, and it can classify and protect the same types of files as the client.

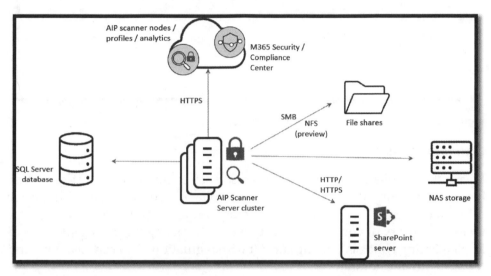

Figure 5.45: AIP File Scanner architecture

The Advanced eDiscovery Solution in Microsoft 365

Advanced eDiscovery builds on the existing Microsoft eDiscovery and analytics capabilities. Advanced eDiscovery provides an end-to-end workflow to preserve, collect, , review, analyze, and export content that's responsive to an organization's internal and external investigations. It also lets legal teams manage the entire legal hold notification workflow to communicate with custodians involved in a case.

You can use eDiscovery tools in Microsoft 365 to search for content in Exchange Online mailboxes, Microsoft 365 Groups, Microsoft Teams, SharePoint Online and OneDrive for Business sites, Skype for Business conversations, and Yammer teams. You can search mailboxes and sites in the same eDiscovery search by using the Content Search tool. And you can use Core eDiscovery cases to identify, hold, and export content found in mailboxes and sites.

If your organization has an Office 365 E5 or Microsoft 365 E5 subscription (or related E5 add-on subscriptions), you can further manage custodians and analyze content by using the Advanced eDiscovery solution in Microsoft 365. See Figure 5.46.

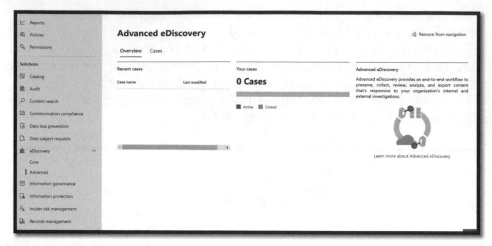

Figure 5.46: Core and Advanced eDiscovery portal

Compliance Manager

Microsoft Compliance Manager is a Microsoft 365 compliance center feature that helps you manage your organization's compliance requirements with greater ease and convenience. It can help you throughout your compliance journey, from taking inventory of your data protection risks to managing the complexities of implementing controls, staying current with regulations and certifications, and reporting to auditors.

With Microsoft Compliance Score, you can continuously assess and monitor data protection controls, get clear guidance on how to improve your score, reduce compliance risks, and leverage the built-in control mapping to scale your compliance effort across global, industrial, and regional standards.

- **Continuous assessments:** Microsoft Compliance Score can scan through your Microsoft 365 environments and detect your system settings, continuously and automatically updating your technical control status. For example, if you configured a compliance policy for Windows devices in the Azure AD portal, Microsoft Compliance Score can detect the setting and reflect that in the control details. Conversely, if you have not created the policy, Microsoft Compliance Score can flag that as a recommended action for you to take.

- With the ongoing control assessment, you can now proactively maintain compliance instead of reactively fixing settings following an audit.

- **Improve your score with recommended actions and solutions:** Microsoft Compliance Score provides you with improvement actions in different areas, such as information protection, information governance, device management, and more. This allows you to easily understand the contribution you are making toward organizational compliance by category.

Each recommended action has a different impact on your score, depending on the potential risk involved, so you can prioritize important actions accordingly.

Risk managers and compliance professionals can assess controls using the assessments view, which shows you the scores of GDPR, ISO 27001, ISO 27018, NIST CSF, NIST 800-53, HIPAA, FFIEC, and more. Microsoft Compliance Score helps make connections between each regulatory requirement and the solutions that can help you enhance your controls, thus increasing your overall score.

The Microsoft Compliance Score dashboard shows your current compliance score, helps you see what needs attention, and guides you to key improvement actions. Figure 5.47 shows an example of Compliance Manager dashboard with your compliance score.

Figure 5.47: Compliance Manager dashboard

Protecting IoT and Operation Technology

Organizations embrace the opportunity to reimagine and fundamentally transform their businesses using Internet of Things (IoT) technology.

The Internet of Things (IoT) can drive huge economic opportunities for industries and enable exciting innovations that reach across fields from childcare to eldercare, from healthcare to energy, from manufacturing to transportation. Diverse IoT in smart places—everything from remote monitoring, predictive maintenance, and smart spaces to connected products and customer-facing technologies like mobile apps—can reduce operational complexity, lower costs, and speed up time to market.

With technology pundits and analysts predicting even more expansive use of IoT devices and apps in the future, along with ever-evolving devices, services, and apps that touch the IoT space, organizations are often eager to take advantage of the business benefits. However, many companies are right to be cautious in their pursuit of the benefits of IoT solutions due to very real IoT security concerns. IoT deployments pose unique new security, privacy, and compliance challenges to businesses worldwide.

While traditional information cybersecurity revolves around software and how it is implemented, security for IoT adds an extra layer of complexity as the cyber and the physical worlds converge. A wide range of operational and maintenance scenarios in the IoT space rely on end-to-end device connectivity to enable users and services to interact, login, troubleshoot, send, or receive data from devices. Companies may want to take advantage of IoT efficiencies like predictive maintenance, for example, but knowing what IoT security standards to adhere to is essential, because operational technology (OT) is too important and valuable to risk in the event of breaches, disasters, and other threats.

Security Concerns with IoT

Although IoT devices may seem too small or too specialized to be dangerous, there is real risk in what are really network-connected, general-purpose computers that can be hijacked by attackers, resulting in problems beyond IoT security. Even the most mundane device can become dangerous when compromised over the Internet—from spying with video baby monitors to interrupted services on life-saving health care equipment. Once attackers have control, they can steal data, disrupt delivery of services, or commit any other cybercrime they'd do with a computer. Attacks that compromise IoT infrastructure inflict damage, not just with data breaches and unreliable operations, but also physical harm to the facilities, or worse—to the humans operating or relying on those facilities.

Concerns around security for IoT are also driven by:

- **Device heterogeneity or fragmentation:** Many companies use a large number of different devices running different software, using different chips, and may even use different methods to connect. This is what's known as device heterogeneity, and it creates a challenge to update and control all your different connected devices. For organizations with production IoT deployments, all these different devices create complexity—but software solutions do exist to simplify this process.

- **Connection to valuable operational technology (OT):** Many businesses would love to take advantage of the business benefits of connection, but can't risk the losses of revenue if facilities are attacked and go down, even for a few days. The good news is that there are trusted IoT cybersecurity companies that offer software solutions to help protect against attacks.

- **Challenges with legacy devices:** Some devices were designed before IoT existed and any connection was even possible. These devices have never been "hardened," the process for identifying and eliminating or mitigating vulnerabilities. Many other legacy devices are inexpensive or not designed with specific IoT security in mind, so they lack IoT cybersecurity features despite good intentions of the manufacturer.

Attackers try to compromise IoT solutions by identifying security weaknesses, so building security into every part of your IoT solution is essential for minimizing risks to your data, business assets, and reputation.

Because this new IoT connectivity covers such a large and often unfamiliar attack surface and IoT devices and apps can hold massive troves of personal, operational, and corporate data, IoT security pros need to go beyond the traditional information security requirements of confidentiality, integrity, and availability.

IoT cybersecurity pros are, of course, concerned with data breaches and other cyberattacks. But, because an IoT vulnerability has the potential to cause life-threatening physical danger or shutdown of profit-making operations, they must especially concern themselves with securing connectivity, device hardening, threat monitoring, and security posture management, as well as securing data on the backend in the cloud.

Understanding That IoT Cybersecurity Starts with a Threat Model

Microsoft has long used threat models for its products and has made the company's threat modeling process publicly available. The objective of threat modeling is to understand how an attacker might be able to compromise a system and then make sure appropriate mitigations are in place. Threat modeling forces the design team to consider mitigations as the system is designed rather than after a system is deployed. This fact is critically important, because retrofitting security defenses to myriad devices in the field is infeasible, error prone, and leaves customers at risk.

Many development teams do an excellent job capturing the functional requirements for the system that benefit customers. However, identifying non-obvious ways that someone might misuse the system is more challenging. Threat modeling can help development teams understand what an attacker might do and why. Threat modeling is a structured process that creates a discussion about the security design decisions in the system, as well as changes to the design that are made along the way that impact security. While a threat model is simply a document, this documentation also represents an ideal way to ensure continuity of knowledge, retention of lessons learned, and help new teams onboard rapidly. Finally, an outcome of threat modeling is to enable you to consider other aspects of security, such as what security commitments you wish to provide to your customers. These commitments in conjunction with threat modeling inform and drive testing of your Internet of Things (IoT) solution.

An IoT Cybersecurity attack can threaten:

- **Processes:** Threats to processes both under your control, such as web services, and threats from external entities, such as users and satellite feeds, that interact with the system, but are not under the control of the application.

- **Communication, also called data flows:** Threats around the communication path between devices, devices and field gateways, and device and cloud gateways.

- **Storage:** Threats to temporary data queues, operating systems (OS), and image storage.

An IoT attack can be broadly categorized in five different areas: spoofing, tampering, information disclosure, denial of service, and elevation of privilege. Spoofing and Information Disclosure:

- An attacker can manipulate the state of a device anonymously.

- An attacker may intercept or partially override the broadcast and spoof the originator (often called man-in-the-middle or MitM attacks).

- An attacker can take advantage of the vulnerability of constrained or special-purpose devices. These devices often have one-for-all security facilities like password or PIN protection, or rely on network shared key protections. When the shared secret to device or network (PIN, password, shared network key) is disclosed, it is possible to control the device or observe data emitted from the device.

Tampering:

- An attacker can tamper with any physical device—from battery drainage vulnerability or "sleep deprivation to random number generator (RNG) attacks made possible by freezing devices to reduce entropy.

- An attacker may partially or wholly replace the software running on the device, potentially allowing the replaced software to leverage the genuine identity of the device if the key material or the cryptographic facilities holding key materials were available to the illicit program.

Denial of Service:

- A device can be rendered incapable of functioning or communicating by interfering with radio frequencies or cutting wires. For example, a surveillance camera that had its power or network connection intentionally knocked out cannot report data, at all.

Information Disclosure:

- An attacker may eavesdrop on a broadcast and obtain information without authorization or may jam the broadcast signal and deny information distribution.
- An attacker may intercept or partially override the broadcast and send false information.

Elevation of Privilege:

- A device that does a specific function can be forced to do something else. For example, a valve that is programmed to open halfway can be tricked to open all the way.

Microsoft Investment in IoT Technology

Microsoft is investing in many technologies to manage and secure this ecosystem, including an end-to-end solution (called Azure Sphere) that's designed to provide highly secured, Internet-connected microcontroller (MCU) devices, and Azure Defender for IoT, which provides functionality such as asset and vulnerability management (see Figure 5.48).

Figure 5.48: IoT and Operational Technology challenges

Azure Sphere

Azure Sphere is a secured, high-level application platform with built-in communication and security features for Internet-connected devices. The platform integrates hardware built around a secured silicon chip; the Azure Sphere OS (operating system), a custom high-level Linux-based operating system; and the Azure Sphere Security Service, a cloud-based security service that provides continuous, renewable security.

Check out this URL to learn more about Azure Sphere: `https://azure .microsoft.com/en-us/blog/introducing-microsoft-azure-sphere-secure- and-power-the-intelligent-edge`.

Azure Defender

Defender currently covers the most highly used infrastructure services including servers/VMs, storage, databases, DNS, apps services, Kubernetes, container registries, key vault, and resource manager.

Azure Defender for IoT

For end-user organizations, Azure Defender for IoT offers agentless, network-layer security that is rapidly deployed, works with diverse industrial equipment, and interoperates with Azure Sentinel and other SOC tools that are deployed on-premises or in Azure-connected environments. For IoT device builders, Azure Defender for IoT offers lightweight agents to embed device-layer security into new IoT/OT initiatives.

Azure Defender provides threat detection for your cloud workload environments, while Azure Defender for IoT specifically helps protect IoT/OT devices from the specialized threats they face. Adversaries use different methods to target IT and IoT/OT networks. Azure Defender for IoT detects threats by analyzing the specialized protocols, devices, and machine-to-machine behaviors found in IoT/OT environments.

It also protects both managed and unmanaged IoT and operational technology (OT) devices with agentless, asset discovery, vulnerability management, and threat protection capabilities. This helps organizations to accelerate innovation with comprehensive security across all your IoT/OT devices. See Figure 5.49.

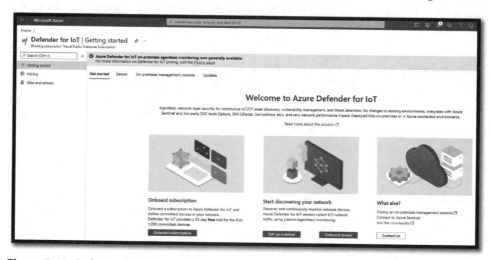

Figure 5.49: Defender for IoT

Additionally, this capability also protects IoT devices via lightweight micro agents that support standard IoT operating systems, such as Linux and RTOS. It can be deployed on-premises or in Azure-connected environments (see Figure 5.50).

Threat Modeling for the Azure IoT Reference Architecture

Microsoft uses the framework outlined previously to do threat modeling for Azure IoT. This section uses the concrete example of Azure IoT Reference Architecture

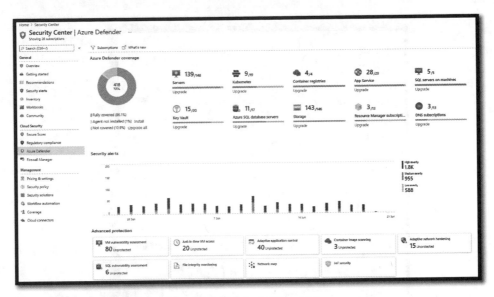

Figure 5.50: Azure Defender (Security Center for IoT Security)

to demonstrate how to think about threat modeling for IoT and how to address the threats identified. See Figure 5.51.

This example identifies four main areas of focus:

- Devices and data sources
- Data transport
- Device and event processing
- Presentation

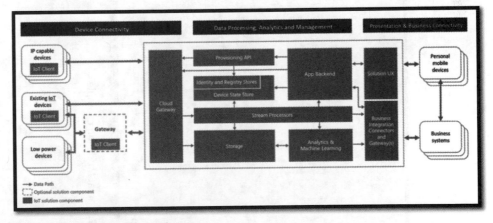

Figure 5.51: IoT Reference Architecture

Figure 5.52 provides a simplified view of Microsoft's IoT Architecture using a Data Flow Diagram model that is used by the Microsoft Threat Modeling Tool.

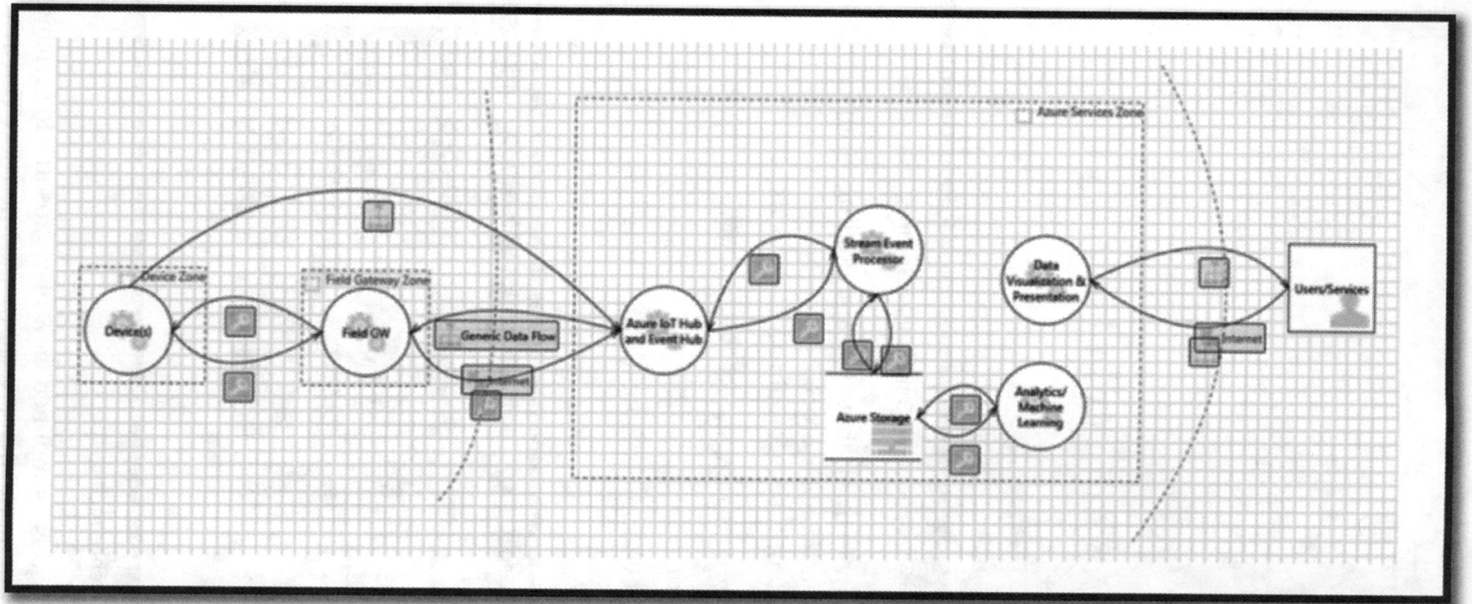

Figure 5.52: Threat Modeling example

It is important to note that the architecture separates the device and gateway capabilities. This approach enables the user to leverage gateway devices that are more secure: they are capable of communicating with the Cloud Gateway using secure protocols, which typically requires greater processing overhead than a native device—such as a thermostat—could provide on its own. In the Azure services zone, you can assume that the Cloud Gateway is represented by the Azure IoT Hub service.

Azure Defender for IoT Architecture (Agentless Solutions)

Defender for IoT connects both to the Azure cloud and to on-premises components. The solution is designed for scalability in large and geographically distributed environments with multiple remote locations. This solution enables a multi-layered distributed architecture by country, region, business unit, or zone. See Figure 5.53.

Azure Defender for IoT includes the following components.

Cloud connected deployments:

- Azure Defender for IoT sensor VM or appliance
- Azure portal for cloud management and integration to Azure Sentinel
- On-premises management console for local-site management
- An embedded security agent (optional)

Air-gapped (offline) deployments:

- Azure Defender for IoT sensor VM or appliance
- On-premises management console for local site management

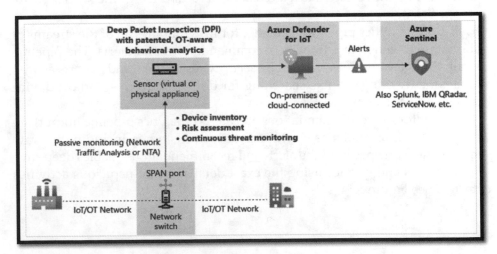

Figure 5.53: IoT Agentless Deployment design

Azure Defender for IoT Architecture (Agent-based solutions)

Defender for IoT is enabled by default in every new IoT Hub that is created. Defender for IoT provides real-time monitoring, recommendations, and alerts, without requiring agent installation on any devices and uses advanced analytics on logged IoT Hub metadata to analyze and protect your field devices and IoT Hubs.

The Defender for IoT micro agents provides in-depth security protection and visibility into device behavior. It collects, aggregates, and analyzes raw security events from your devices. Raw security events can include IP connections, process creation, user logins, and other security-relevant information. Defender for IoT device agents also handle event aggregation to help avoid high network throughput. The agents are highly customizable, allowing you to use them for specific tasks, such as sending only important information at the fastest SLA, or for aggregating extensive security information and context into larger segments, avoiding higher service costs.

Device agents and other applications use the Azure send security message SDK to send security information into Azure IoT Hub. IoT Hub gets this information and forwards it to the Defender for IoT service.

Once the Defender for IoT service is enabled, in addition to the forwarded data, IoT Hub also sends out all of its internal data for analysis by Defender for IoT. This data includes device-cloud operation logs, device identities, and hub configuration. All of this information helps to create the Defender for IoT analytics pipeline.

Defender for IoT analytics pipeline also receives other threat intelligence streams from various sources within Microsoft and Microsoft partners. The Defender for IoT entire analytics pipeline works with every customer configuration made on the service (such as custom alerts and use of the send security message SDK).

Using the analytics pipeline, Defender for IoT combines all of the streams of information to generate actionable recommendations and alerts. The pipeline contains both custom rules created by security researchers and experts as well as machine learning models searching for deviation from standard device behavior and risk analysis.

Defender for IoT recommendations and alerts (analytics pipeline output) are written to the Log Analytics workspace of each customer. Including the raw events in the workspace and the alerts and recommendations enables deep-dive investigations and queries using the exact details of the suspicious activities detected. See Figure 5.54.

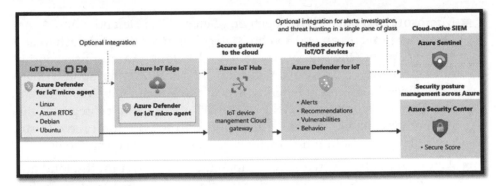

Figure 5.54: IoT Agent-based integration flow

Understanding the Security Operations Solutions

Running and operating a legacy on-premises model of security operation offers many challenges to the SecOps team. Analysts are overloaded with too many false positive signals and alerts. The investigation workflow is very siloed and poor. Integration is mostly manual. On top of that, the security tools and products are constantly evolving, which breaks the integration. Microsoft has solutions to these issues; (see Figure 5.55).

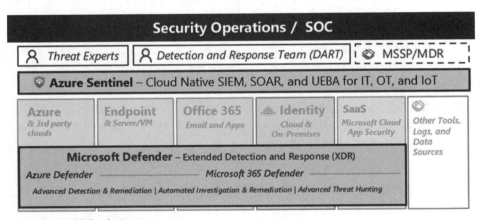

Figure 5.55: SOC solutions

Microsoft provides built-in security capabilities to enable SOCs to secure cloud and on-premises workloads using the cloud's power and its cloud-native SIEM/SOAR service, such as Azure Sentinel. Microsoft also provides other protective and detective tooling and services to manage security threats in an organization.

- **Azure Sentinel, power with AI and build with ML:** Azure Sentinel is Microsoft's cloud-native SIEM and SOAR service. It gives you a bird's-eye view across the enterprise. It put the cloud and large-scale intelligence from decades of Microsoft security experience to work.

- **Microsoft Defender XDR:** Together, Microsoft 365 Defender and Azure Defender provides an end-to-end XDR solution for threat detection and response across the Microsoft estate in the cloud, on-premises, and in other clouds. It provides advanced endpoint detection and response (EDR) capabilities, Web Content Filtering, Threat and Vulnerability Management, and Data Loss Protection (DLP). Like MCAS, Microsoft integrates this with other capabilities across their portfolio so you don't have to run multiple agents/solutions to achieve your endpoint security goals.

- **Azure Defender:** Delivers XDR capabilities to protect multi-cloud and hybrid workloads, including virtual machines, databases, containers, IoT, and more. Azure Defender is an evolution of the Azure Security Center threat protection capabilities and is accessed from within Azure Security Center.

- **Microsoft Threat Experts:** A new managed threat-hunting service in Windows Defender Advanced Threat Protection such as human adversary intrusions, hands-on keyboard attacks, and advanced attacks like cyber espionage. It provides proactive hunting, prioritization, and additional context and insights that further empower Security Operations Centers (SOCs) to identify and respond to threats quickly and accurately.

- **Microsoft Detection and Response Team (DART):** Provides onsite reactive incident response and remote proactive investigations. This team works with customers globally to identify risks and provide reactive incident response and proactive security investigation services to help developers manage their cyber risk, especially in today's dynamic threat environment.

- **MSSP/MDR providers:** Microsoft partners with top experts in the industry to build their expertise on these capabilities so that they can advise and directly support their customers.

Understanding the People Security Solutions

People security is a new domain that was added to MCRA, and it focuses on enabling, educating, and empowering the team to make good security decisions.

It's hard to keep pace with all the changes happening in the world of cybersecurity. It requires continuously learning (and unlearning) to stay ahead of the ever-evolving threat landscape. You must treat your people as valuable and powerful security assets and address security awareness, behavior, and culture in tandem.

Microsoft continues to invest in services with built-in automation, User and Entity Behavior Analytics (UEBA) so that businesses can bring about real and tangible reductions in their human cyber risk. See Figure 5.56.

Figure 5.56: People Security solutions

Attack Simulator

Simulation Training in Microsoft Defender for Office 365 is an intelligent social engineering risk management tool that empowers all employees to be defenders. It uses a real phish to emulate the employees' attacks, and it delivers security training tailored to each employee's behavior in simulations. These simulated attacks can help you identify and find vulnerable users before an actual attack impacts your bottom line. See Figure 5.57.

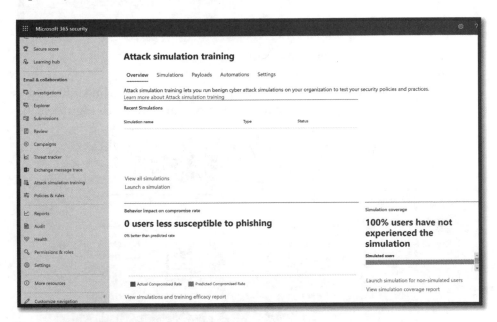

Figure 5.57: Attack Simulator

It also automates the security training program's design and deployment, saving the resource-strapped security teams time and resources.

Insider Risk Management (IRM)

IRM is a compliance solution in Microsoft 365 that helps minimize internal risks by enabling you to detect, investigate, and act on malicious and inadvertent activities in an organization. Insider risk policies allow you to define the types of risks to identify and detect in the organization, including acting on cases and escalating cases to Microsoft Advanced eDiscovery if needed. See Figure 5.58.

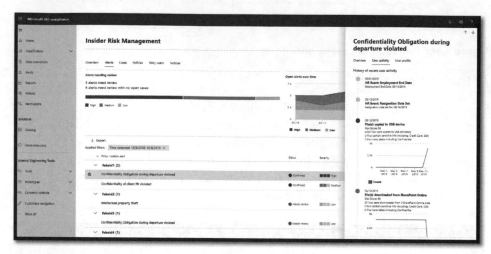

Figure 5.58: Insider Risk Management dashboard

IRM helps the risk analysts quickly take appropriate actions to make sure users are compliant with an organization's compliance standards (see Figure 5.59).

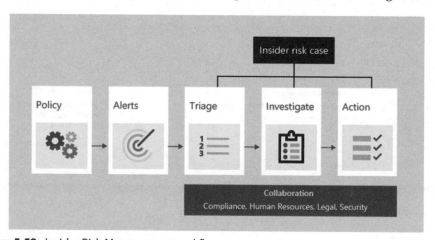

Figure 5.59: Insider Risk Management workflow

IRM is built on the following principles:

- **Transparency:** Allows you to balance user privacy versus organization risk with privacy-by-design architecture.
- **Configurable:** Easily configurable policies based on industry, geographical, and business groups.

- **Integrated:** Highly integrated workflow across Microsoft 365 compliance solutions.

- **Actionable:** Insights to enable reviewer notifications, data investigations, and user investigations.

Communication Compliance

Communication Compliance is another insider risk solution in Microsoft 365 that helps minimize communication risks to detect, capture, and act on inappropriate messages in the organization.

Communication Compliance offers built-in remediation workflows and insights that enable you to act on risks across Microsoft Teams messages, Exchange email, Skype for Business Online, or even third parties such as Instant Bloomberg. See Figure 5.60.

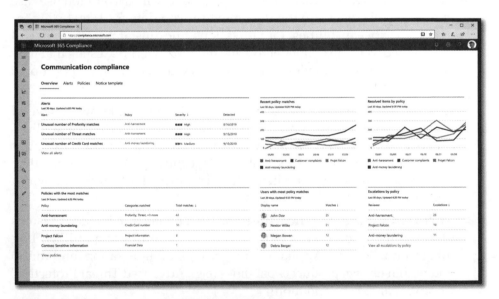

Figure 5.60: Communication Compliance dashboard

This also allows an organization to overcome many modern challenges associated with compliance and internal and external communications, including:

- Scanning increasing types of communication channels

- Scanning the increasing volume of message data

- Dealing with regulatory enforcement and the risk of fines

- Leveraging machine learning classifiers to quickly detect threats (to others or one's self), harassment, and profanities across company communication channels in keeping with corporate policies

- Supporting employee mental health, enabling safe remote learning, and minimizing the impact of internal risk by detecting threatening language in a timely manner.

Summary

Microsoft Cybersecurity Reference Architecture can be used for several purposes (beyond a geeky wall decoration to shock and impress your cubical neighbor), including the following:

- **As a learning tool:** MCRA can be leveraged as a great learning tool for those who are starting their career in cybersecurity and those who want to learn how Microsoft services integrate and work together.

- **Starting template for a security architecture:** The most common use case is that organizations use the document to help define a target state for cybersecurity capabilities. Organizations find this architecture useful because it covers capabilities across the modern enterprise estate that now span on-premises, mobile devices, many clouds, and IoT/Operational Technology.

- **Comparison reference for security capabilities:** We know of several organizations that have marked up a printed copy with what capabilities they already own from various Microsoft license suites (many customers don't know they own quite a bit of this technology), which ones they already have in place (from Microsoft or a partner/third party), and which ones are new and could fill a need.

- **Microsoft's integration investments:** The architecture includes visuals of key integration points with partner capabilities (e.g., SIEM/Log integration, Security Appliances in Azure, DLP integration, and more) and within its own product capabilities (e.g., Advanced Threat Protection, Conditional Access, and more).

Hunting in AWS

In This Part

Chapter 6: AWS Cloud Threat Prevention Framework
Chapter 7: AWS Reference Architecture

AWS Cloud Threat Prevention Framework

What's in This Chapter

- Using the AWS Well-Architected Framework
- Using the Shared Responsibility Model
- Using AWS Services for monitoring, logging, and alerting
- AWS Protect Features
  - How do you use Information Protection and Data Classification?
  - How do you prevent Initial Access?
- AWS Detection Features
  - How do you detect Privilege Escalation?
  - How do you detect credential access?
  - How do you detect lateral movement?
  - How do you detect Command and Control?
  - How do you detect data exfiltration?
- AWS Response and Recover Features
  - How do you create automated response?
  - How do you orchestrate and recover?
- How do you use machine learning and artificial intelligence?

This chapter focuses on using AWS services for various cloud threat protection in alignment with MITRE ATT&CK Framework.

Introduction to AWS Well-Architected Framework

The AWS Well-Architected Framework encapsulates a set of principles, processes, and best practices to follow when designing and running workloads in the cloud. Designing for the cloud is much different than designing for an on-premises architecture, and this framework helps you understand the pros and cons of decisions you make while building systems on AWS. By using the framework, you will learn architectural best practices for designing and operating reliable, secure, efficient, and cost-effective systems in the cloud. The well-architected approach to building systems will highly likely provide substantial benefits and measurable returns on investment.

The AWS Well-Architected Framework consists of a set of foundational questions for you to consistently measure your architectures against best practices and identify areas for improvement. The framework provides a consistent approach to evaluating systems against the qualities you expect from modern cloud-based systems, and the remediation that would be required to achieve those qualities. To help you review your systems against the best practices, AWS offers AWS Well-Architected Tool (AWS WA Tool), a free service in the cloud that provides a consistent process for you to review and measure your architecture using the AWS Well-Architected Framework. In addition, AWS offers AWS Well-Architected Labs to help you apply best practices. The lab provides you with a repository of code and documentation to give you hands-on experience implementing best practices.

Typically, organizations often have central Enterprise Technology Architecture teams to provide strategic context for the evolution and reach of digital capability in response to the constantly changing needs of the business environment. A typical Enterprise Architecture capability includes a set of architecture roles such as Business Architects, Infrastructure Architects, and Security Architects. AWS Well-Architected Framework prefers to distribute technology architecture capabilities into teams rather than having a central team with that capability. Undoubtedly, this approach introduces risks with distribution of the enterprise architecture decision-making authority. The framework mitigates these risks by enabling each team, along with an expert, to raise the bar on technology architecture standards and maintain them. Additionally, it implements automated methods to ensure the technology standards are being met. The approach enables security architects and threat hunters to be embedded in the SOC and security operation team to work closely with vulnerability threat and management. The distributed approach of the framework is supported by Amazon's leadership principles and establishes a culture across all roles that works back from the customer. Customer-obsessed teams build products in response to a customer need.

The framework also provides a set of general guidance and principles to design a robust cloud architecture. With cloud computing there is no need to guess the system capacity needs upfront. You can start with as little capacity as you need, knowing the compute will scale up and down automatically. The cloud provides the ability to test the applications at production-scale for a fraction of the cost of testing on-premises. With the cloud automation to create and replicate the workloads at low cost, the architecture experimentation has never been easier. This allows systems to evolve to meet the ongoing business needs. The cloud provides the ability to drive system architecture using data. The real-time system monitoring can inform the architecture choices and improvements over time. In cloud, there is also the ability to improve through game days by simulating a failure or event to test systems, processes, and team responses.

The Five Pillars of the Well-Architected Framework

If you have ever built a house, you would agree foundation is one of the most critical elements even though it is not visible when the house is built. Software development in cloud is like designing a house. If the foundation is not solid, structural problems can undermine the integrity and function of the building. Speaking in metaphor, a professional residential architect, together with a reputable building contractor, structural engineers, and various others, design a house. Once the design is complete, the same design can be constructed multiple times. When architecting the systems in AWS, incorporating the five pillars of the Well-Architected Framework will help you develop stable and efficient systems.

The five pillars are Operational Excellence, Security, Reliability, Performance Efficiency, and Cost Optimization. Figure 6.1 and the following sections show further details.

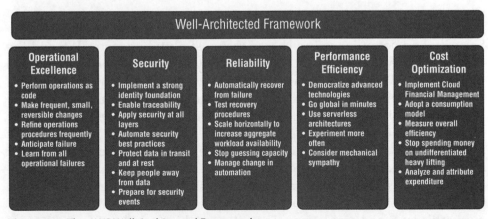

Figure 6.1: The AWS Well-Architected Framework

Operational Excellence

The Operational Excellence pillar includes the ability to support development and run workloads effectively, gain insight into their operations, and to continuously improve supporting processes and procedures to deliver business value.

Security

The Security pillar encompasses the ability to protect data, systems, and assets to take advantage of cloud technologies to improve your security.

Reliability

The Reliability pillar encompasses the ability of a workload to perform its intended function correctly and consistently when it's expected to. This includes the ability to operate and test the workload through its total lifecycle.

Performance Efficiency

The Performance Efficiency pillar includes the ability to use computing resources efficiently to meet system requirements, and to maintain that efficiency as demand changes and technologies evolve.

Cost Optimization

The Cost Optimization pillar includes the ability to run systems to deliver business value at the lowest price point.

The Shared Responsibility Model

Security and compliance is a shared responsibility between AWS and the customer. This shared model can help relieve the customer's operational burden as AWS operates, manages, and controls the components from the host operating system and virtualization layer down to the physical security of the facilities in which the service operates. The customer assumes responsibility and management of the guest operating system (including updates and security patches), other associated application software, as well as the configuration of the AWS-provided security group firewall. Customers should carefully consider the services they choose as their responsibilities vary depending on the services used, the integration of those services into their IT environment, and applicable laws and regulations. The nature of this shared responsibility also provides the flexibility and customer control that permits the deployment. As shown in Figure 6.2, this differentiation of responsibility is commonly referred to as security "of" the cloud versus security "in" the cloud.

- AWS's responsibility is "Security of the Cloud." AWS is responsible for protecting the infrastructure that runs all of the services offered in the AWS Cloud. This infrastructure is composed of the hardware, software, networking, and facilities that run AWS Cloud services.

- The customer responsibility is "Security in the Cloud." Customer responsibility will be determined by the AWS Cloud services that a customer selects. This determines the amount of configuration work the customer must perform as part of their security responsibilities. For example, a service such as Amazon Elastic Compute Cloud (Amazon EC2) is categorized as Infrastructure as a Service (IaaS) and, as such, requires the customer to perform all of the necessary security configuration and management tasks. Customers that deploy an Amazon EC2 instance are responsible for management of the guest operating system (including updates and security patches), any application software or utilities installed by the customer on the instances, and the configuration of the AWS-provided firewall (called a security group) on each instance. For abstracted services, such as Amazon S3 and Amazon DynamoDB, AWS operates the infrastructure layer, the operating system, and platforms, and customers access the endpoints to store and retrieve data. Customers are responsible for managing their data (including encryption options), classifying their assets, and using IAM tools to apply the appropriate permissions.

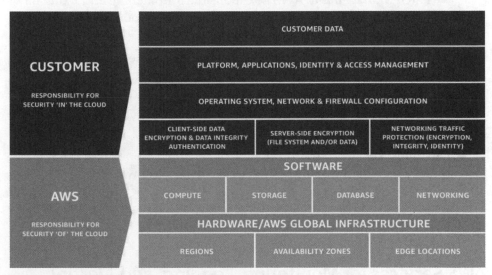

Figure 6.2: The AWS Shared Responsibility Model

This customer/AWS shared responsibility model also extends to IT controls. Just as the responsibility to operate the IT environment is shared between AWS and its customers, so is the management, operation, and verification of IT controls shared. AWS can help relieve customer burden of operating controls by managing those controls associated with the physical infrastructure deployed in the AWS environment that may previously have been managed by the customer. As every customer is deployed differently in AWS, customers can take advantage of shifting management of certain IT controls to AWS, which results in a (new) distributed control environment. Customers can then use the AWS control and compliance documentation available to them to perform their control evaluation and verification procedures as required.

Here are examples of controls that are managed by AWS, AWS customers, and/or both:

- **Inherited controls:** Controls that a customer fully inherits from AWS, such as physical and environmental controls.

- **Shared controls:** Controls that apply to both the infrastructure layer and customer layers, but in completely separate contexts or perspectives. In a shared control, AWS provides the requirements for the infrastructure and the customer must provide their own control implementation within their use of AWS services. Examples include:

  - **Patch Management:** AWS is responsible for patching and fixing flaws within the infrastructure, but customers are responsible for patching their guest OS and applications.

  - **Configuration Management:** AWS maintains the configuration of its infrastructure devices, but a customer is responsible for configuring their own guest operating systems, databases, and applications.

- **Awareness and training:** AWS trains AWS employees, but a customer must train their own employees.

- **Customer specific:** Controls that are solely the responsibility of the customer based on the application they are deploying within AWS services. Examples include service and communications protection or zone security, which may require a customer to route or zone data within specific security environments.

AWS Services for Monitoring, Logging, and Alerting

The monitoring, logging, and alerting polices are an important aspect of the customer responsibility in the AWS Shared Responsibility. These policies enable the customers to improve their chances of detecting malicious behavior on systems and networks. Monitoring is an important part of maintaining the reliability, availability, and performance of AWS solutions. AWS provides tools and features that enable the customers to record and monitor the cyber security-related events on a continual basis within the AWS environment.

Monitoring, logging, and alerting are an important part of maintaining security controls in AWS solutions. Monitoring is also important to maintain the reliability, availability, and performance of AWS solutions. Being able to visualize AWS security alerts, compliance, and detailed information in one location allows for faster threat response times.

This section takes a deep dive into the different AWS services for logging, monitoring, and alerting that are available for AWS hosted applications.

NOTE   Chapter 7 contains more detailed descriptions for following monitoring, logging, and alerting AWS services.

AWS CloudTrail

AWS CloudTrail is a service that enables governance, compliance, operational auditing, and risk auditing of your AWS account. With CloudTrail, you can log, continuously monitor, and retain account activity related to actions across your AWS infrastructure. CloudTrail provides event history of your AWS account activity, including actions taken through the AWS Management Console, AWS SDKs, command-line tools, and other AWS services. This event history simplifies security analysis, resource change tracking, and troubleshooting. In addition, you can use CloudTrail to detect unusual activity in your AWS accounts. These capabilities help simplify operational analysis and troubleshooting.

AWS CloudTrail is one of the most used and effective tools to govern compliance and auditing in the AWS environment. Typically, in a large organization the AWS environment may include hundreds of EC2 servers, databases, load balancers, security groups, route tables, transit gateways, network ACLs, and endpoints. In such a complex environment, it is a nightmare if the network goes down. Analyzing through all networking resources to determine why the traffic is no longer routing correctly is tedious. It might take hours to resolve a simple route table misconfiguration and have the traffic back up and running. Having AWS CloudTrail enabled will allow the organization to troubleshoot and pinpoint the root cause in minutes.

AWS CloudTrail is enabled on your AWS account when you create it. The AWS CloudTrail dashboard shows the CloudTrail insights and event history as shown in Figure 6.3. When activity occurs in your AWS account, that activity is recorded in a CloudTrail event. You can easily view events in the CloudTrail console by going to Event History.

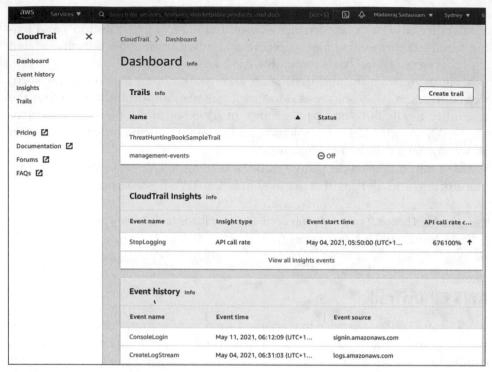

Figure 6.3: The CloudTrail console dashboard page

Event History allows you to view, search, and download the past 90 days of activity in your AWS account. In addition, you can create a CloudTrail trail to archive, analyze, and respond to changes in your AWS resources. A trail is a configuration that enables delivery of events to an Amazon S3 bucket that you specify. You can also deliver and analyze events in a trail with Amazon CloudWatch Logs and Amazon CloudWatch Events. You can create a trail with the CloudTrail console, the AWS CLI, or the CloudTrail API. You can create two types of trails for an AWS account:

- **A trail that applies to all regions:** When you create a trail that applies to all regions, CloudTrail records events in each region and delivers the CloudTrail event log files to an S3 bucket that you specify. If a region is added after you create a trail that applies to all regions, that new region is automatically included, and events in that region are logged. Because creating a trail in all regions is a recommended best practice so you capture activity in all regions in your account, an all-regions trail is the default option when you create a trail in the CloudTrail console. You can only update a single-region trail to log all regions by using the AWS CLI.

- **A trail that applies to one region:** When you create a trail that applies to one region, CloudTrail records the events in that region only. It then delivers the CloudTrail event log files to an Amazon S3 bucket that you specify. You can only create a single-region trail by using the AWS CLI. If you create additional single trails, you can have those trails deliver CloudTrail event log files to the same Amazon S3 bucket or to separate buckets. This is the default option when you create a trail using the AWS CLI or the CloudTrail API.

Amazon CloudWatch Logs

Amazon CloudWatch monitors your Amazon Web Services (AWS) resources and the applications you run on AWS in real time. You can use CloudWatch to collect and track metrics, which are variables you can measure for your resources and applications.

The CloudWatch home page automatically displays metrics about every AWS service you use. You can additionally create custom dashboards to display metrics about your custom applications, and display custom collections of metrics that you choose.

You can create alarms that watch metrics and send notifications or automatically make changes to the resources you are monitoring when a threshold is breached. For example, you can monitor the CPU usage and disk reads and writes of your Amazon EC2 instances and then use this data to determine whether you should launch additional instances to handle increased load. You can also use this data to stop underused instances to save money. With CloudWatch, you gain system-wide visibility into resource utilization, application performance, and operational health.

Amazon CloudWatch dashboards are customizable home pages in the Cloud-Watch console that you can use to monitor your resources in a single view, even those resources that are spread across different regions (see Figure 6.4). You can use CloudWatch dashboards to create customized views of the metrics and alarms for your AWS resources. With dashboards, you can create the following:

- A single view for selected metrics and alarms to help you assess the health of your resources and applications across one or more regions. You can select the color used for each metric on each graph, so that you can easily track the same metric across multiple graphs.

- Dashboards that display graphs and other widgets from multiple AWS accounts and multiple regions.

- An operational playbook that provides guidance for team members during operational events about how to respond to specific incidents.

- A common view of critical resource and application measurements that can be shared by team members for faster communication flow during operational events.

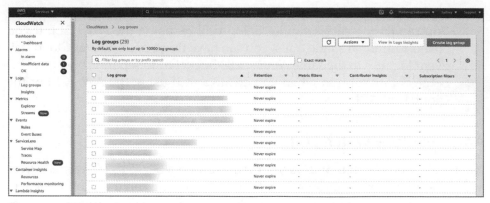

Figure 6.4: The CloudWatch Logs console

The CloudWatch Logs console shows the log groups. The log group details page shows information such as the stored bytes, subscriptions, Amazon Resource Name (ARN), included log streams, and more. The service allows you to inter-actively search and analyze the insights related to your Amazon CloudWatch Logs when a security event occurs.

Amazon VPC Flow Logs

VPC Flow Logs is a feature that enables you to capture information about the IP traffic going to and from network interfaces in your VPC. Flow log data can be published to Amazon CloudWatch Logs or Amazon S3. After you've created a flow log, you can retrieve and view its data in the chosen destination.

Flow logs can help you with a number of tasks, such as:

- Diagnosing overly restrictive security group rules
- Monitoring the traffic that is reaching your instance
- Determining the direction of the traffic to and from the network interfaces

Flow log data is collected outside of the path of your network traffic, and therefore does not affect network throughput or latency. You can create or delete flow logs without any risk of impact to network performance.

You can create a flow log for a VPC, a subnet, or a network interface. If you cre-ate a flow log for a subnet or VPC, each network interface in that subnet or VPC is monitored. Flow log data for a monitored network interface is recorded as flow log records, which are log events consisting of fields that describe the traffic flow.

To create a flow log, you specify:

- The resource for which to create the flow log
- The type of traffic to capture (accepted traffic, rejected traffic, or all traffic)
- The destinations to which you want to publish the flow log data

You can see in Figure 6.5 where the Amazon VPC flow logs can be found.

Figure 6.5: The VPC flow logs console

Amazon GuardDuty

Amazon GuardDuty is a continuous security monitoring service that analyzes and processes the following data sources: VPC Flow Logs, AWS CloudTrail management event logs, CloudTrail S3 data event logs, and DNS logs. It uses threat intelligence feeds, such as lists of malicious IP addresses and domains, and machine learning to identify unexpected and potentially unauthorized and malicious activity within your AWS environment. This can include issues like escalations of privileges, uses of exposed credentials, or communication with malicious IP addresses or domains. For example, GuardDuty can detect compromised EC2 instances serving malware or mining bitcoin. It also monitors AWS account access behavior for signs of compromise, such as unauthorized infrastructure deployments, like instances deployed in a region that has never been used, or unusual API calls, like a password policy change to reduce password strength.

GuardDuty informs you of the status of your AWS environment by producing security findings that you can view in the GuardDuty console or through Amazon CloudWatch events. You can see in Figure 6.6 an example of the Amazon GuardDuty dashboard.

Amazon GuardDuty correlates the system logs to allow for a more intelligent decision by providing more accurate events than other tools.

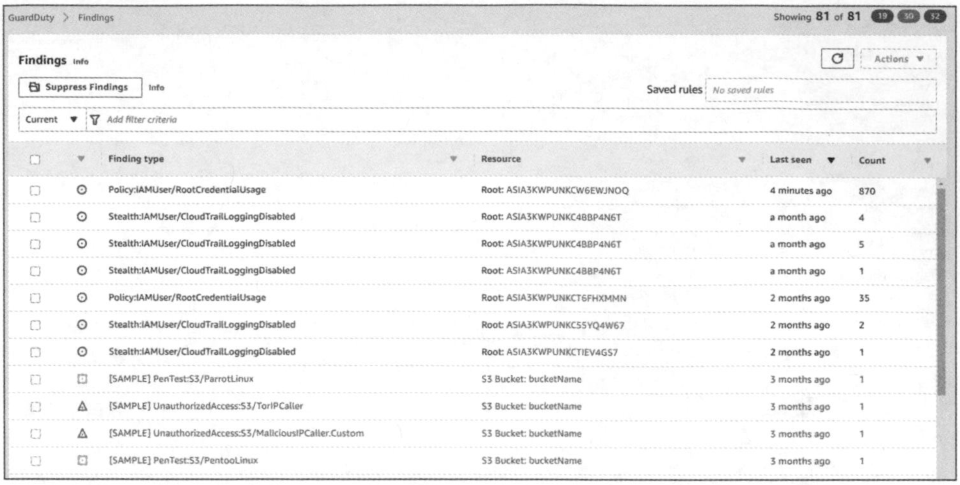

Figure 6.6: View of the GuardDuty dashboard

AWS Security Hub

AWS Security Hub gives you a comprehensive view of your security alerts and security posture across your AWS accounts. There are a range of powerful security tools at your disposal, from firewalls and endpoint protection to vulnerability and compliance scanners. But oftentimes this leaves your team switching back-and-forth between these tools to deal with hundreds, and sometimes thousands, of security alerts every day. With Security Hub, you now have a single place that aggregates, organizes, and prioritizes your security alerts, or findings, from multiple AWS services, such as Amazon GuardDuty, Amazon Inspector, Amazon Macie, AWS Identity and Access Management (IAM) Access Analyzer, AWS Systems Manager, and AWS Firewall Manager, as well as from AWS Partner Network (APN) solutions. AWS Security Hub continuously monitors your environment using automated security checks based on the AWS best practices and industry standards that your organization follows. You can also take action on these security findings by investigating them in Amazon Detective or by using Amazon CloudWatch Event rules to send the findings to ticketing, chat, Security Information and Event Management (SIEM), Security Orchestration Automation and Response (SOAR), and incident management tools or to custom remediation playbooks. Get started with AWS Security Hub in just a few clicks in the Management Console and once enabled, Security Hub will begin aggregating and prioritizing findings and conducting security checks.

As you can see in Figure 6.7, the AWS Security Hub dashboard gives a summary of security insights for small findings. Integrated dashboards bring together your security findings across accounts to show you the current security and compliance status. Now you can easily spot trends, identify potential issues, and take the necessary next steps. For example, you can send findings to ticketing, chat, email, or automated remediation systems using integration with Amazon CloudWatch Events.

Figure 6.7: View of the Security Hub dashboard

AWS Protect Features

Organizations need to develop and implement the necessary security protections to restrict the effect of a possible cybersecurity incident. To comply with this requirement, an organization should track access to digital and physical resources, provide awareness and training, set up processes to secure data, manage network configuration baselines and operations to fix system components on time, and implement protective technologies to ensure cyber resilience.

How Do You Prevent Initial Access?

Adversaries may attempt to take advantage of a weakness in an Internet-facing computer or program using software, data, or commands in order to cause unintended or unanticipated behavior. The weakness in the system can be a bug, a glitch, or a design vulnerability. These applications are often websites, but can include databases, standard services such as SSH, network device administration and management protocols (like SNMP and Smart Install), and any other applications with Internet-accessible open sockets, such as web servers and related services.

SQL injection is one of several different types of code injection techniques used to attack data-driven applications. This is done by the attacker injecting an input in the query not intended by the programmer of the application gaining access of the database, which results in potential reading, modification, or deletion of users' data. The vulnerabilities are due to the lack of input validation, which is the most critical part of software security that is often not properly covered in the design phase of the software development lifecycle.

How Do You Protect APIs from SQL Injection Attacks Using API Gateway and AWS WAF?

When you build web applications, you probably look for a platform where you can build highly scalable, secure, and robust REST APIs. As APIs are publicly exposed, the use of Amazon API Gateway and AWS WAF avoids the malicious codes injected by the attackers. See Figure 6.8.

Amazon API Gateway handles all the tasks involved in accepting and processing up to hundreds of thousands of concurrent API calls, including traffic management, authorization and access control, monitoring, and API version management.

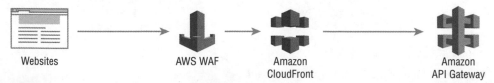

Websites   AWS WAF   Amazon CloudFront   Amazon API Gateway

Figure 6.8: Amazon API Gateway and AWS WAF

AWS WAF is a web application firewall that helps protect your web applications from common web exploits such as SQL injection and cross-site scripting that could affect application availability, compromise security, or consume excessive resources.

The following walkthrough describes how to protect APIs provided by Amazon API Gateway using AWF WAF.

Prerequisites

1. To use AWS WAF, Amazon API Gateway, and other AWS services, you need an AWS account. If you don't have an account, visit `https://aws.amazon.com` and choose Create an AWS Account.

2. As a best practice, you should also create an AWS Identity and Access Management (IAM) user with administrator permissions and use that for all work that does not require root credentials.

3. For an Amazon API Gateway REST API, AWS WAF is available in the regions listed at AWS service endpoints. You can use any of the regions in the list. For this walkthrough, use Asia Pacific (Sydney) region.

Create an API

For this walkthrough, use the example PetStore API provided in Amazon API Gateway by default. See Figure 6.9.

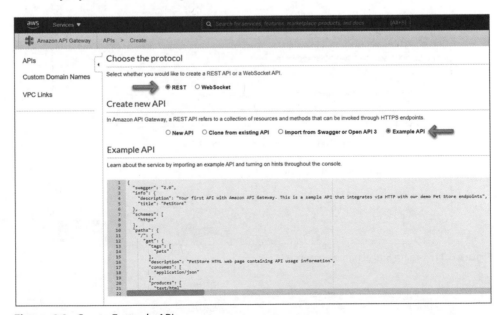

Figure 6.9: Create Example API

After you have created the PetStore API on your account, deploy a stage called "prod" for the PetStore API. On the API Gateway console, select the PetStore API and choose Actions ⇨ Deploy API, as shown in Figure 6.10.

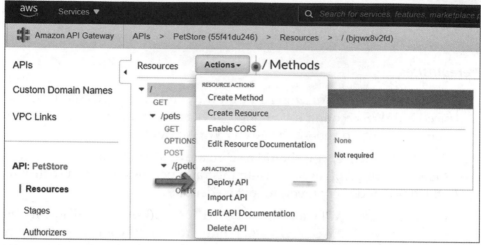

Figure 6.10: Deploy API screen

For Deployment Stage name, select [New Stage] and type **prod** for Stage name. Click Deploy and the new API stage is created. See Figure 6.11.

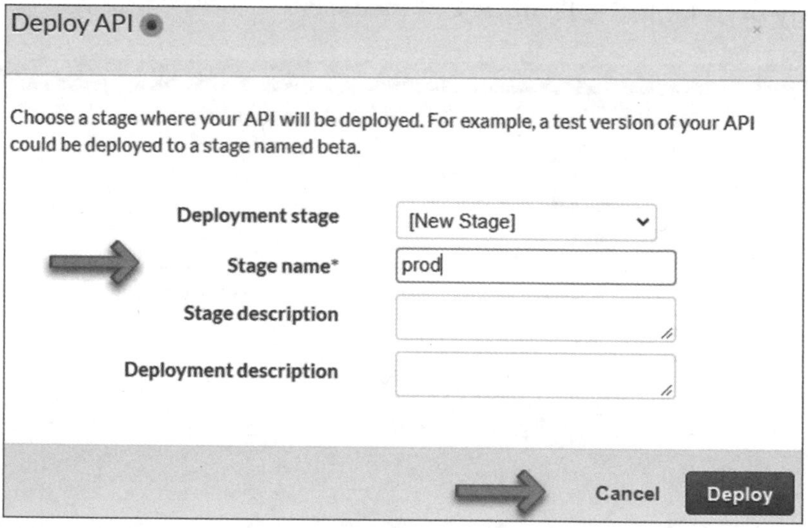

Figure 6.11: Create Stage name screen

Create and Configure an AWS WAF

Log in to AWS WAF and the AWS Shield dashboard. You should see Go to links for AWS WAF, AWS Shield, and AWS Firewall Manager. Currently, AWS WAF, AWS Shield, and AWS Firewall Manager are accessible from the same dashboard. If AWS decides to separate them, go to the dashboard for AWS WAF and continue with this walkthrough.

Next, click Go to AWS WAF. You should see the new AWS WAF landing page, as shown in Figure 6.12.

Figure 6.12: AWS WAF screen

AWS currently provides an option to switch to AWS WAF Classic. We will be using New AWS WAF, which is more flexible than AWS WAF Classic. AWS managed rule groups are only supported by the new WAF. Next, follow these steps:

1. Click on Create Web ACL.

2. In the Web ACL details section, provide a name in the Name field. Optionally, provide a description in the Description field.

3. You can use the auto-populated value for the CloudWatch metric name field.

4. For Resource type, select Regional resources (Application Load Balancer, API Gateway, AWS AppSync). See Figure 6.13.

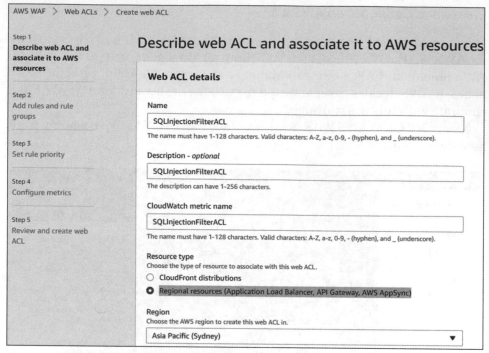

Figure 6.13: Describe Web ACL screen

5. Under the Associated AWS resources section, click Add AWS Resources.

6. On the Add AWS Resources screen, select the PetStore API created for this walkthrough and click Add. See Figure 6.14.

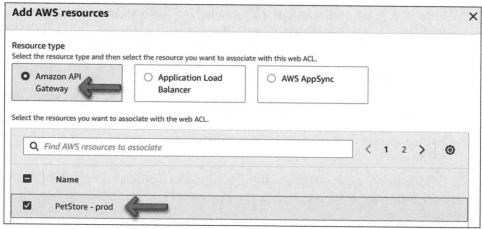

Figure 6.14: Add AWS Resource screen

7. Once you're back at the Associated AWS resources section, select the PetStore – prod, API Gateway and click Next, as shown in Figure 6.15.

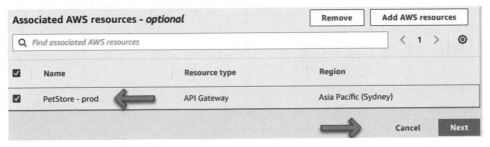

Figure 6.15: Associated AWS Resources screen

8. On the Add Rules and Rule Groups page, expand the Add Rules dropdown and select Add My Own Rules and rule Groups. See Figure 6.16.

Add rules and rule groups Info

A rule defines attack patterns to look for in web requests and the action to take when a request matches the patterns. Rule groups are reusable collections of rules. You can use managed rule groups offered by AWS and AWS Marketplace sellers. You can also write your own rules and use your own rule groups.

Rules

If a request matches a rule, take the corresponding action. The rules are prioritized in order they appear.

Edit	Delete	Add rules ▲
		Add managed rule groups
☐ Name		Add my own rules and rule groups	Action

Figure 6.16: Add Rules and Rule Groups screen

9. Under Rule builder, in the Rule section, provide a name in the Name field and set Type to Regular rule. Under If a Request, choose Matches the Statement. Under Inspect and Match type, in the Rule section, choose All Query Parameters and Contains SQL Injection Attacks, respectively. See Figure 6.17.

10. Under the Then section, add an Action to Block and click Add rule, as shown in Figure 6.18.

11. On the Add Rules and Rule Groups page, select Rule and for Default Web ACL action for requests that don't match any rules, select Allow. Click Next.

12. On the Set Rule Priority page, select Rule as the first one and click Next.

13. On the Configure Metrics page, select Rule. You will use the auto-populated value for the CloudWatch metric name. Click Next.

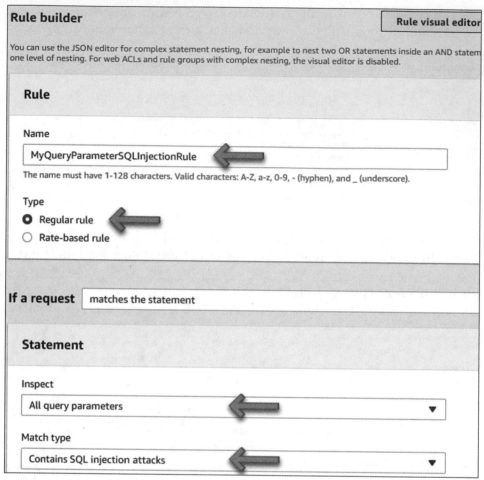

Figure 6.17: Rule Builder screen

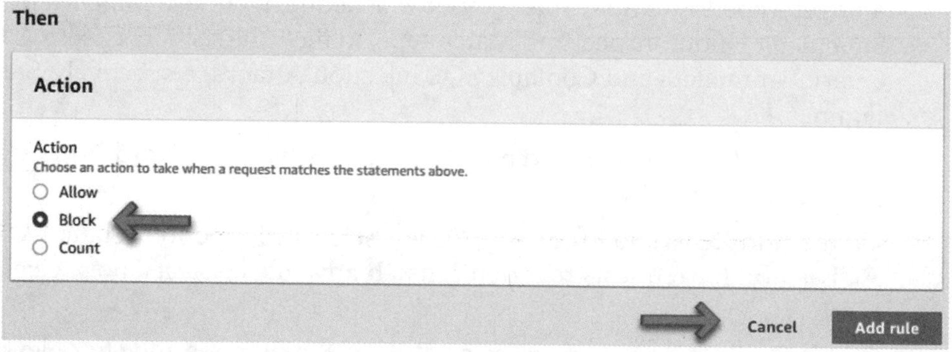

Figure 6.18: Action screen

14. On the Review and Create Web ACL page, review the changes and click Create Web ACL. The ACL will be successfully created. See Figure 6.19.

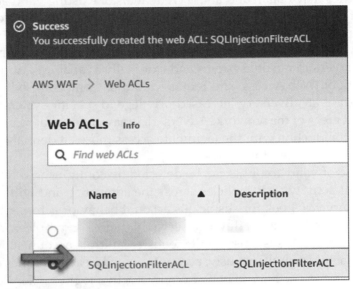

Figure 6.19: Confirmation of Web ACL Creation screen

AWS Detection Features

Organizations need to take appropriate action to detect cybersecurity threat alerts. The continuous monitoring solutions play a key role in detecting anomalous activity and other operational continuity threats. The organization should have network transparency to predict cyber incidents and access the required information to respond to one. Continuous surveillance and tracking security alerts are very effective ways of detecting and avoiding cyberattacks in the networks.

How Do You Detect Privilege Escalation?

Privilege escalation consists of techniques that adversaries use to gain higher-level permissions on a system or network. Adversaries can often enter and explore a network with unprivileged access but require elevated permissions to follow through on their objectives. Common approaches are to take advantage of system weaknesses, misconfigurations, and vulnerabilities. Examples of elevated access include: SYSTEM/root level, local administrator, user account with admin-like access, user accounts with access to a specific system or perform a specific function. These techniques often overlap with Persistence techniques, as OS features that let an adversary persist can execute in an elevated context.

Adversaries may obtain and abuse credentials of existing valid accounts as a means of gaining Initial Access, Persistence, Privilege Escalation, or Defense Evasion. Compromised credentials may be used to bypass access controls placed on various resources on systems within the network and may even be used for persistent access to remote systems and externally available services, such as VPNs, Outlook Web Access, and remote desktop. Compromised credentials may also grant an adversary increased privilege to specific systems or access to restricted areas of the network. Adversaries may choose not to use malware or tools in conjunction with the legitimate access those credentials provide to make it harder to detect their presence.

The abuse of valid accounts can be detected by configuring robust, consistent account activity audit policies across the enterprise and with externally accessible services. Look for suspicious account behavior across systems that share accounts, either user, admin, or service accounts. Examples: one account logged in to multiple systems simultaneously; multiple accounts logged in to the same machine simultaneously; accounts logged in at odd times or outside of business hours. Activity may be from interactive login sessions or process ownership from accounts being used to execute binaries on a remote system as a particular account. Correlate other security systems with login information (e.g., a user has an active login session but has not entered the building or does not have VPN access).

How Do You Detect the Abuse of Valid Account to Obtain High-Level Permissions?

Amazon GuardDuty uses threat intelligence feeds, such as lists of malicious IP addresses and domains, and machine learning to identify unexpected and potentially unauthorized and malicious activity within your AWS environment. This can include issues like escalations of privileges, uses of exposed credentials, or communication with malicious IP addresses or domains.

The following walkthrough describes how to set up and use Amazon Guard-Duty to analyze Privilege Escalation anomaly detection.

Prerequisites

To use AWS GuardDuty services, you need an AWS account. If you don't have an account, visit `https://aws.amazon.com` and choose Create an AWS Account.

As a best practice, you should also create an AWS Identity and Access Management (IAM) user with administrator permissions and use that for all work that does not require root credentials.

Configure GuardDuty to Detect Privilege Escalation

Go to the GuardDuty service in the console. If you are logging in for the first time, you should see a Get Started page. Click Get Started. You should now see the Welcome to GuardDuty screen, as shown in Figure 6.20.

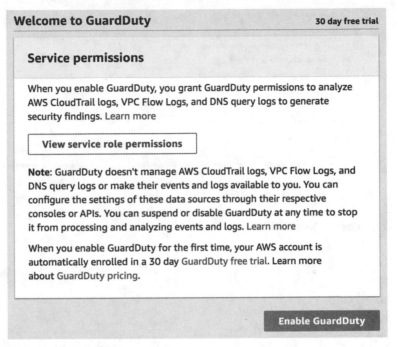

Figure 6.20: GuardDuty Welcome screen

1. Click Enable GuardDuty. You can see GuardDuty in action using the sample events provided by AWS.
2. Click Settings from the left sidebar in the GuardDuty dashboard.
3. Click Generate Sample Findings under Sample Findings. See Figure 6.21.
4. Click Findings on the left sidebar to go to the Findings page. New sample findings will now be generated.
5. Click the `PrivilegeEscalation:IAMUser/AnomalousBehavior` event to see additional information provided about the finding, as shown in Figure 6.22.

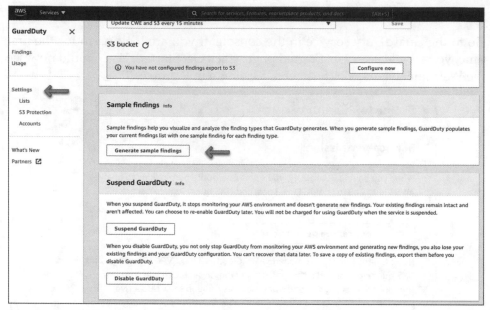

Figure 6.21: Generate Sample Findings screen

Figure 6.22: GuardDuty Findings screen

Reviewing the Findings

In the example shown in Figure 6.23, you see a `PrivilegeEscalation:IAMUser/AnomalousBehavior` finding. This finding informs you that an anomalous API request was observed in your account. This finding may include a single API or a series of related API requests made in proximity by a single user. The API observed is commonly associated with privilege escalation tactics where an adversary is attempting to gain higher-level permissions to an environment. APIs in this category typically involve operations that change IAM policies, roles, and users, such as, AssociateIamInstanceProfile, AddUserToGroup, or PutUserPolicy.

Figure 6.23: Privilege Escalation screen, upper portion

Looking at the information in this finding, you see the severity as MEDIUM, meaning it's something to check but not especially concerning. Now if you see many of these events back to back, there is room for concern, as it could mean a potential bad actor. You can see the region and account ID this event occurred in and the AWS Resource against which this activity took place. Moving down, you see the Anomalous APIs and the Unusual behavior details. The details point to the API name and the error response that triggered the findings. Moving down again, you can see the AWS resource that was targeted by the trigger activity. The information available varies based on resource type and action type. In this example, you can see the access key ID and resource details of the user engaged in the activity that prompted GuardDuty to generate the finding.

Moving down again, you see the action type, API, service name, and time-stamps of when the event was first and last seen. Again, this is especially important if you see this type of event many times back to back. And at the bottom, there is information about the location of where the event occurred. You can see the caller type, IP address, location, and even the ISP information the activity occurred on. These are important when looking into geo-locations of events to determine patterns. See Figure 6.24.

Action		
Action type	AWS_API_CALL	🔍🔍
API	GeneratedFindingAPIName	🔍🔍
Service name	GeneratedFindingAPIServiceName	🔍🔍
Error code	AccessDenied	🔍🔍
User agent	GeneratedFindingUserAgentCategory	
First seen	03-23-2021 06:28:16 (a day ago)	
Last seen	03-23-2021 06:28:16 (a day ago)	
Actor		
Caller type	Remote IP	🔍🔍
IP address	198.51.100.0	🔍🔍
Location		
City	GeneratedFindingCityName	
Country	GeneratedFindingCountryName	
Organization		
Asn	-1	
Asn org	GeneratedFindingASNOrg	
Isp	GeneratedFindingISP	
Org	GeneratedFindingOrg	
Additional information		
Sample	true	
Archived	false	

Figure 6.24: Privilege Escalation screen, lower portion

How Do You Detect Credential Access?

Credential Access consists of techniques for stealing credentials like account names and passwords. Techniques used to get credentials include keylogging or credential dumping. Using legitimate credentials can give adversaries access to systems, make them harder to detect, and provide the opportunity to create more accounts to help achieve their goals.

Adversaries may search compromised systems to find and obtain insecurely stored credentials. These credentials can be stored and/or misplaced in many locations on a system, including plaintext files (e.g., bash history), operating system or application-specific repositories (e.g., credentials in Registry), or other specialized files/artifacts (e.g., private keys).

While detecting adversaries accessing credentials may be difficult without knowing they exist in the environment, it may be possible to detect adversary use of credentials they have obtained. Monitor the command-line arguments of executing processes for suspicious words or regular expressions that may indicate searching for a password (for example: password, pwd, login, secure, or credentials).

Monitor for suspicious file access activity, specifically indications that a process is reading multiple files in a short amount of time and/or using command-line arguments indicative of searching for credential material (such as regex patterns). These may be indicators of automated/scripted credential access behavior.

Monitoring when the user's `.bash_history` is read can help alert to suspicious activity. While users do typically rely on their history of commands, they often access this history through other utilities like "history" instead of commands like `cat ~/.bash_history`.

Additionally, monitor processes for applications that can be used to query the Registry, such as Reg, and collect command parameters that may indicate credentials are being searched. Correlate activity with related suspicious behavior that may indicate an active intrusion to reduce false positives.

How Do You Detect Unsecured Credentials?

Amazon Macie is a fully managed data security and data privacy service that uses machine learning and pattern matching to help you discover, monitor, and protect your sensitive data in AWS.

Macie automates the discovery of sensitive data, such as credentials, personally identifiable information (PII), and financial data, to provide you with a better understanding of the data that your organization stores in Amazon Simple Storage Service (Amazon S3). Macie also provides you with an inventory of your S3 buckets, and it automatically evaluates and monitors those buckets for security and access control. Within minutes, Macie can identify and report overly permissive or unencrypted buckets for your organization.

The following walkthrough describes how to set up and use Amazon Macie to detect unsecured credentials.

Prerequisites

To use Amazon Macie and other AWS services, you need an AWS account. If you don't have an account, visit `http://aws.amazon.com` and choose Create an AWS Account.

As a best practice, you should also create an AWS Identity and Access Management (IAM) user with administrator permissions and use that for all work that does not require root credentials.

You need an S3 bucket. The bucket should be in the same region in which you configure Macie. We created a bucket named `threat-hunting-book-tutorial` in the `sydney` region. See Figure 6.25.

You need to upload an AWS Access key file into the S3 bucket. Follow these steps to download the AWS access key file:

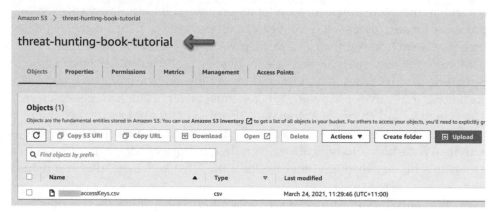

Figure 6.25: S3 bucket

1. Open the IAM console at `https://console.aws.amazon.com/iam/`.

2. On the navigation menu, choose Users.

3. Choose your IAM username (not the check box).

4. Open the Security credentials tab, and then choose Create Access Key.

5. To download the key pair, choose Download .csv File. Store the .csv file with keys in a secure location.

6. Configure Macie to discover and classify risks in an S3 bucket.

7. Go to the Macie service in the console.

8. By using the AWS Region selector in the upper-right corner of the page, select the region in which you want to enable Macie.

9. If you are logging in for the first time, you should see a Get Started page, as shown in Figure 6.26. Click Get Started.

Figure 6.26: Macie screen

You should now see the Welcome to Macie screen with an option to enable it, as shown in Figure 6.27.

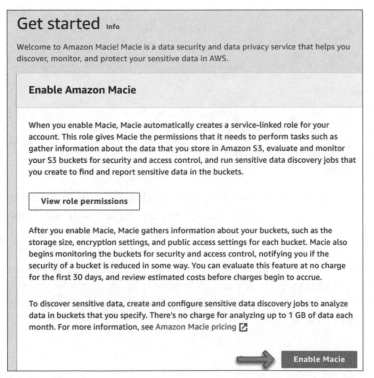

Figure 6.27: Enable Macie screen

Next, click Enable Macie. Within minutes, Macie generates an inventory of the Amazon Simple Storage Service (Amazon S3) buckets for your account in the current AWS region. Macie also begins monitoring the buckets for potential policy violations.

Macie stores your sensitive data discovery results for 90 days. To access the results and enable long-term storage and retention of them, configure Macie to store the results in an S3 bucket. Although this is optional, you must do this within 30 days of enabling Macie. After you do this, the S3 bucket can serve as a definitive, long-term repository for all of your discovery results. Specify the S3 bucket to use by navigating to the Settings | Discovery results on the sidebar menu, as shown in Figure 6.28.

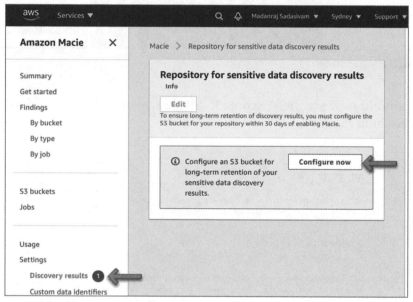

Figure 6.28: Configure S3 Bucket screen

In Macie, sensitive data discovery jobs analyze objects in S3 buckets to discover and report sensitive data. Click Jobs on the left sidebar. This will show you the list of discovery jobs currently created in Macie, as shown in Figure 6.29.

Click Create Job. This will show you an inventory of all S3 buckets for your account. The S3 bucket called `threat-hunting-book-tutorial` that we created in the Prerequisites steps is shown in Figure 6.30.

For the Select S3 buckets step, select the check box of the threat-hunting-book-tutorial bucket to analyze. Then click Next.

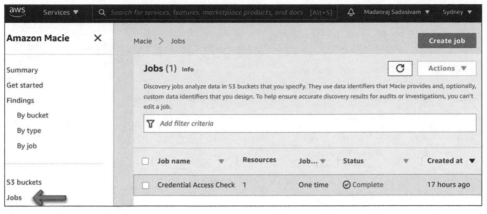

Figure 6.29: Macie Jobs screen

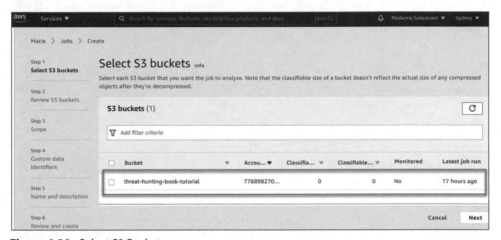

Figure 6.30: Select S3 Buckets screen

For the Review S3 buckets step, review and verify your bucket selections. You can also review the total estimated cost (in US dollars) of analyzing the data in each bucket and change your bucket selections as necessary. When you finish, click Next.

For the Scope step, select one-time job for Sensitive Data Discovery options. Then click Next, as shown in Figure 6.31.

For the Custom Data Identifiers step, click Next. For the Name and Description step, enter **Unsecured Credentials Check** for the name and, optionally, a description of the job. Then click Next. See Figure 6.32.

For the Review and create step, review the configuration settings for the job and verify that they're correct. You can also review the total estimated cost (in US dollars) of running the job once based on your bucket selections.

When you finish reviewing and verifying the settings, click Submit.

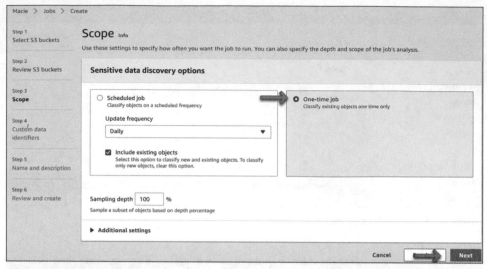

Figure 6.31: Scope screen

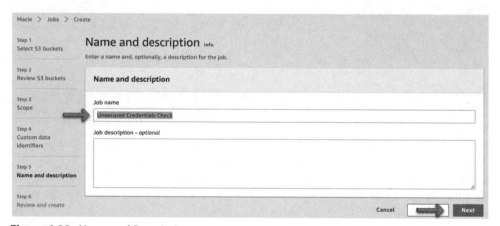

Figure 6.32: Name and Description screen

Reviewing the Findings

Macie monitors your S3 buckets and reports any potential policy violations as policy findings. If you create and run a sensitive data discovery job, Macie reports any sensitive data that it discovers as sensitive data findings. Use the following procedure to view detailed information for your findings:

1. Open the Macie console at `https://console.aws.amazon.com/macie`.

2. In the navigation pane, choose Findings. Optionally, to filter the findings by specific criteria, use the filter bar above the table to enter the criteria. See Figure 6.33.

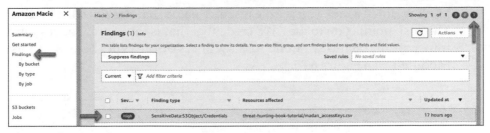

Figure 6.33: Findings screen

3. To view the details of a specific finding, choose any field other than the check box for the finding. The details panel displays information for the finding.

4. In the example shown in Figure 6.33, you see a `SensitiveData:S3Object/Credentials` finding. This finding informs you that the object contains credentials such as access keys, account IDs, or private keys. In this example, the credential is the AWS secret key stored in the S3 bucket.

5. Findings for Macie are similar to GuardDuty. Looking at the information in this finding, you see the severity as HIGH, meaning it's concerning and needs immediately. You have information as to when the event occurred, and the region of the finding. See Figure 6.34.

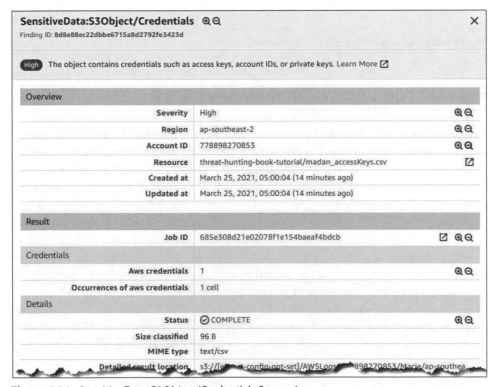

Figure 6.34: SensitiveData:S3Object/Credentials Screen 1

6. Moving down again, you see the resource name that triggered the finding. This also points you to the AWS credential that is unsecure. The resource information includes Public Access, Encryption Type, Size, and Last Modified. See Figure 6.35.

Resources affected (S3 bucket)		
Bucket name	threat-hunting-book-tutorial	🔍🔍
Public access	NOT_PUBLIC	🔍🔍
Encryption type	NONE	🔍🔍
Created at	March 24, 2021, 11:28:57 (18 hours ago)	
Owner	madan	🔍🔍

Resources affected (S3 object)		
Key	madan_accessKeys.csv	🔍🔍
Public access	false	🔍🔍
Encryption type	NONE	🔍🔍
Size	96 B	
Last modified	March 24, 2021, 11:29:46 (18 hours ago)	

Additional information		
Archived	false	
Sample	false	
Count	1	

Figure 6.35: SensitiveData:S3Object/Credentials Screen 2

How Do You Detect Lateral Movement?

Lateral movement consists of techniques that adversaries use to enter and control remote systems on a network. Following through on their primary objective often requires exploring the network to find their target and subsequently gaining access to it. Reaching their objective often involves pivoting through multiple systems and accounts to own. Adversaries might install their own remote access tools to accomplish lateral movement or use legitimate credentials with native network and operating system tools, which may be stealthier.

Adversaries may use alternate authentication material, such as password hashes, Kerberos tickets, and application access tokens, in order to move laterally within an environment and bypass normal system access controls.

Authentication processes generally require a valid identity (e.g., username) along with one or more authentication factors (e.g., password, PIN, physical smart card, token generator, etc.). Alternate authentication material is legitimately generated by systems after a user or application successfully authenticates by providing a valid identity and the required authentication factors. Alternate authentication material may also be generated during the identity creation process.

Caching alternate authentication material allows the system to verify an identity has successfully authenticated without asking the user to reenter authentication factors. Because the alternate authentication must be maintained by the system—either in memory or on disk—it may be at risk of being stolen through Credential Access techniques. By stealing alternate authentication material, adversaries are able to bypass system access controls and authenticate to systems without knowing the plaintext password or any additional authentication factors.

The abuse of stolen alternate authentication material can be detected by configuring robust, consistent account activity audit policies across the enterprise and with externally accessible services. Look for suspicious account behavior across systems that share accounts, either user, admin, or service accounts. Examples: one account logged in to multiple systems simultaneously; multiple accounts logged in to the same machine simultaneously; accounts logged in at odd times or outside of business hours. Activity may be from interactive login sessions or process ownership from accounts being used to execute binaries on a remote system as a particular account. Correlate other security systems with login information (e.g., a user has an active login session but has not entered the building or does not have VPN access).

How Do You Detect the Use of Stolen Alternate Authentication Material?

The following walkthrough describes how to set up and use Amazon GuardDuty to analyze unauthorized access with stolen alternate authentication material.

Prerequisites

To use Amazon GuardDuty and other AWS services, you need an AWS account. If you don't have an account, visit https://aws.amazon.com and choose Create an AWS Account. As a best practice, you should also create an AWS Identity and Access Management (IAM) user with administrator permissions and use that for all work that does not require root credentials.

Configure and enable GuardDuty and generate sample findings and explore the basic operations. Refer to the section entitled "How Do You Detect Privilege Escalation?" earlier in this chapter for further details.

How Do You Detect Potential Unauthorized Access to Your AWS Resources?

Click Findings from the left sidebar to go to the Findings page. See Figure 6.36.

Figure 6.36: GuardDuty Findings menu

Click the `UnauthorizedAccess:IAMUser/ConsoleLoginSuccess.B` event to see additional information provided about the finding. See Figure 6.37.

Figure 6.37: GuardDuty Findings screen

Reviewing the Findings

In the examples shown in Figures 6.38–6.40, you see an `UnauthorizedAccess:IAMUser/ConsoleLoginSuccess.B` finding. This finding informs you that successful logins to the AWS console were seen from multiple countries recently, using the credentials of principal `GeneratedFindingUserName`. This could be an indication of the unauthorized use of this user's password.

Looking at the information in this finding, you see the severity as MEDIUM, meaning it's something to check but not especially concerning. Now if you see many of these events back to back, there is room for concern, as it could mean a potential bad actor. You can see the region and account ID this event occurred in and the AWS Resource against which this activity took place. Moving down, you see the Action details. The details point to the Service name and the error code that triggered the findings. Moving down again, you can see Actor details including the Caller type, IP Address, and the geo-location.

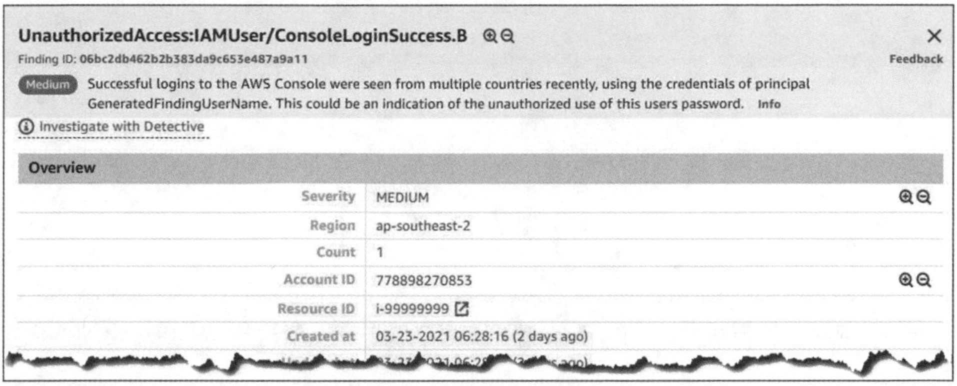

UnauthorizedAccess:IAMUser/ConsoleLoginSuccess.B	⊕ ⊖	✕
Finding ID: 06bc2db462b2b383da9c653e487a9a11		Feedback

Medium   Successful logins to the AWS Console were seen from multiple countries recently, using the credentials of principal GeneratedFindingUserName. This could be an indication of the unauthorized use of this users password.   Info

ⓘ Investigate with Detective

Overview

Severity	MEDIUM
Region	ap-southeast-2
Count	1
Account ID	778898270853
Resource ID	i-99999999 ↗
Created at	03-23-2021 06:28:16 (2 days ago)

Figure 6.38: UnauthorizedAccess:IAMUser overview screen

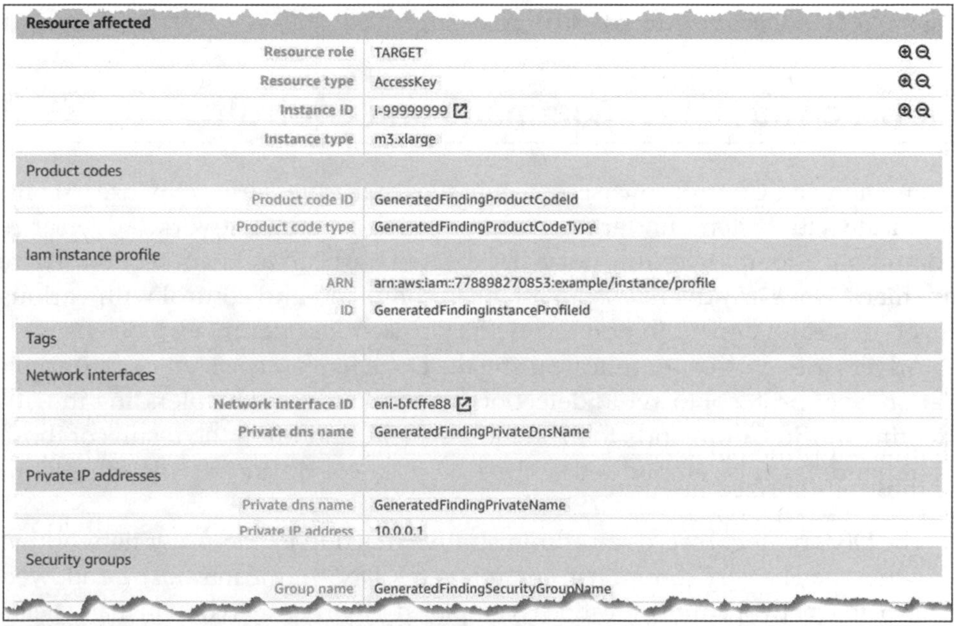

Resource affected

Resource role	TARGET
Resource type	AccessKey
Instance ID	i-99999999 ↗
Instance type	m3.xlarge

Product codes

Product code ID	GeneratedFindingProductCodeId
Product code type	GeneratedFindingProductCodeType

Iam instance profile

ARN	arn:aws:iam::778898270853:example/instance/profile
ID	GeneratedFindingInstanceProfileId

Tags

Network interfaces

Network interface ID	eni-bfcffe88 ↗
Private dns name	GeneratedFindingPrivateDnsName

Private IP addresses

Private dns name	GeneratedFindingPrivateName
Private IP address	10.0.0.1

Security groups

Group name	GeneratedFindingSecurityGroupName

Figure 6.39: UnauthorizedAccess:IAMUser resources screen

Action			
Action type	AWS_API_CALL		🔍🔍
API	GeneratedFindingAPIName		🔍🔍
Service name	GeneratedFindingAPIServiceName		🔍🔍
Error code	AccessDenied		🔍🔍
First seen	03-23-2021 06:28:16 (2 days ago)		
Last seen	03-23-2021 06:28:16 (2 days ago)		
Actor			
Caller type	Remote IP		🔍🔍
IP address	198.51.100.0		🔍🔍
Location			
City	GeneratedFindingCityName		
Country	GeneratedFindingCountryName		
Organization			
Asn	-1		
Asn org	GeneratedFindingASNOrg		
Additional information			
Sample	true		
Archived	false		
Unusual			
Countries	GeneratedFindingUnusualCountryName1GeneratedFindingUnusualCountryName2Ge...		

Figure 6.40: UnauthorizedAccess:IAMUser action screen

How Do You Detect Command and Control?

Command and Control consists of techniques that adversaries may use to communicate with systems under their control within a victim network. Adversaries commonly attempt to mimic normal, expected traffic to avoid detection. There are many ways an adversary can establish command and control with various levels of stealth depending on the victim's network structure and defenses.

Adversaries may communicate using the Domain Name System (DNS) application layer protocol to avoid detection/network filtering by blending in with existing traffic. Commands to the remote system, and often the results of those commands, will be embedded within the protocol traffic between the client and server.

The DNS protocol serves an administrative function in computer networking and thus may be very common in environments. DNS traffic may also be allowed even before network authentication is completed. DNS packets contain many fields and headers in which data can be concealed. Often known as DNS tunneling, adversaries may abuse DNS to communicate with systems under their control within a victim network while also mimicking normal, expected traffic.

The use of DNS for command and control can be detected by analyzing network data for uncommon data flows (e.g., a client sending significantly more data than it receives from a server). Processes utilizing the network that do not normally have network communication or have never been seen before are suspicious. Analyze packet contents to detect application layer protocols that do not follow the expected protocol standards regarding syntax, structure, or any other variable adversaries could leverage to conceal data.

How Do You Detect the Communications to a Command and Control Server Using the Domain Name System (DNS)?

The following walkthrough describes how to set up and use Amazon GuardDuty to determine if the EC2 instances within your AWS environment are querying a domain name associated with a known command and control (C&C) server.

Prerequisites

To use Amazon GuardDuty and other AWS services, you need an AWS account. If you don't have an account, visit https://aws.amazon.com and choose Create an AWS Account.

As a best practice, you should also create an AWS Identity and Access Management (IAM) user with administrator permissions and use that for all work that does not require root credentials.

Configure and enable GuardDuty, then generate sample findings and explore the basic operations. Refer to the "How Do You Detect Privilege Escalation?" section in this chapter for details.

How Do You Detect EC2 Instance Communication with a Command and Control (C&C) Server Using DNS

Click Findings from the left sidebar to go to the Findings page. See Figure 6.41.

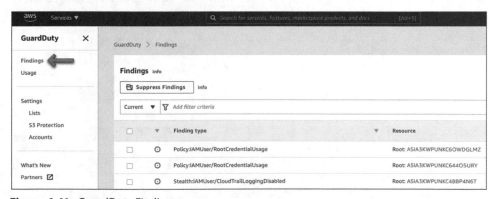

Figure 6.41: GuardDuty Findings screen

Click the `Backdoor:EC2/C&CActivity.B!DNS` event to see additional information provided about the finding. See Figure 6.42.

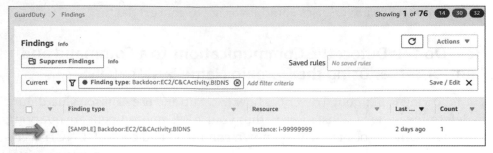

Figure 6.42: Findings screen

Reviewing the Findings

In the example shown in Figure 6.42, you see a `Backdoor:EC2/C&CActivity.B!DNS` finding. This finding informs you that the listed instance within your AWS environment is querying a domain name associated with a known command and control (C&C) server. The listed instance might be compromised. Command and control servers are computers that issue commands to members of a botnet. A botnet is a collection of Internet-connected devices, which might include PCs, servers, mobile devices, and Internet of Things devices, that are infected and controlled by a common type of malware. Botnets are often used to distribute malware and gather misappropriated information, such as credit card numbers. Depending on the purpose and structure of the botnet, the C&C server might also issue commands to begin a distributed denial-of-service (DDoS) attack.

Looking at the information in this finding, you see the severity as HIGH, as shown in Figure 6.43, meaning it's concerning and requires action immediately. You can see the region and account ID this event occurred in.

Backdoor:EC2/C&CActivity.B!DNS ⊕ ⊖
Finding ID: fcbc2db462b35eea04f0c62cfdd9091d   Feedback

[High] EC2 instance i-99999999 is querying a domain name associated with a known Command & Control server.   Info

ⓘ Investigate with Detective

Overview

Severity	HIGH
Region	ap-southeast-2
Count	1
Account ID	778898270853
Resource ID	i-99999999
Created at	03-23-2021 06:28:16 (2 days ago)

Figure 6.43: Backdoor:EC2/C&CActivity.B!DNS screen

Moving down, you see the AWS Resource against which this activity took place. See Figure 6.44.

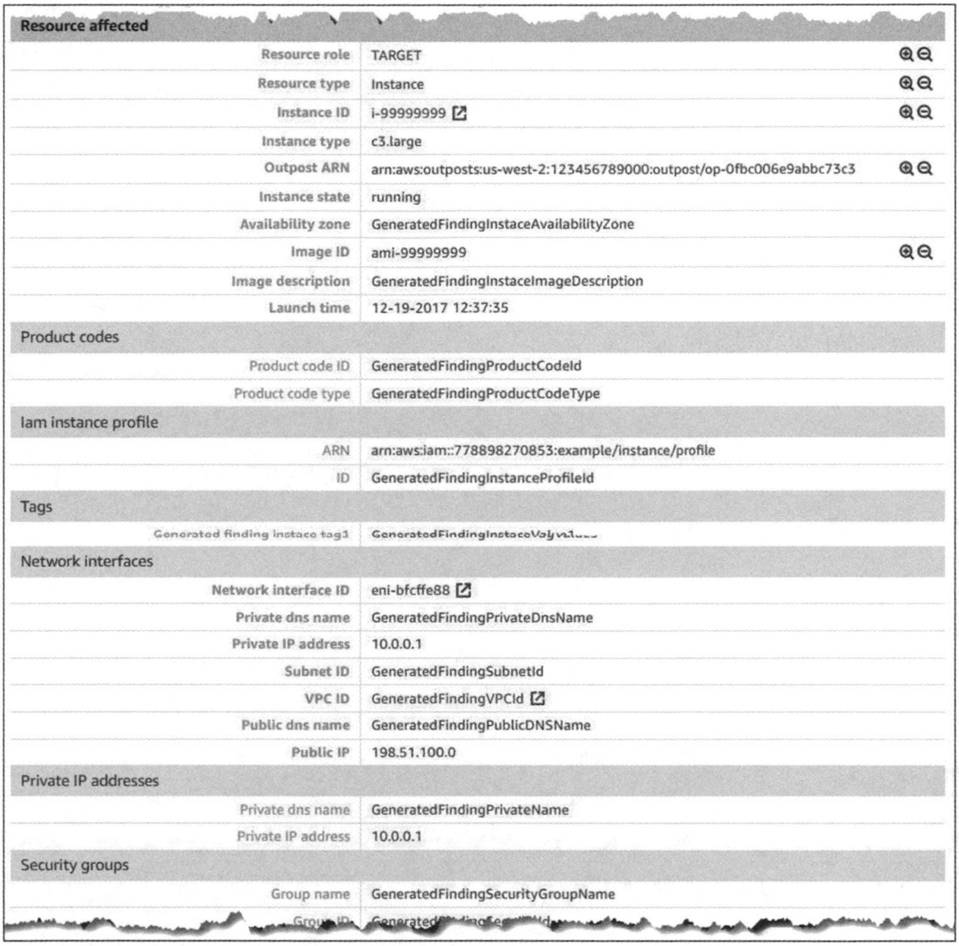

Resource affected		
Resource role	TARGET	🔍🔍
Resource type	Instance	🔍🔍
Instance ID	i-99999999 ↗	🔍🔍
Instance type	c3.large	
Outpost ARN	arn:aws:outposts:us-west-2:123456789000:outpost/op-0fbc006e9abbc73c3	🔍🔍
Instance state	running	
Availability zone	GeneratedFindingInstaceAvailabilityZone	
Image ID	ami-99999999	🔍🔍
Image description	GeneratedFindingInstaceImageDescription	
Launch time	12-19-2017 12:37:35	
Product codes		
Product code ID	GeneratedFindingProductCodeId	
Product code type	GeneratedFindingProductCodeType	
Iam instance profile		
ARN	arn:aws:iam::778898270853:example/instance/profile	
ID	GeneratedFindingInstanceProfileId	
Tags		
Generated finding instace tag1	GeneratedFindingInstaceValyn1...	
Network interfaces		
Network interface ID	eni-bfcffe88 ↗	
Private dns name	GeneratedFindingPrivateDnsName	
Private IP address	10.0.0.1	
Subnet ID	GeneratedFindingSubnetId	
VPC ID	GeneratedFindingVPCId ↗	
Public dns name	GeneratedFindingPublicDNSName	
Public IP	198.51.100.0	
Private IP addresses		
Private dns name	GeneratedFindingPrivateName	
Private IP address	10.0.0.1	
Security groups		
Group name	GeneratedFindingSecurityGroupName	
Group ID	GeneratedFindingSec...Id	

Figure 6.44: Backdoor:EC2/C&CActivity.B!DNS screen

Moving down, you see the Action details. The details point to the protocol and action status that triggered the findings. Moving down again, you can see Actor details, including the domain name. See Figure 6.45.

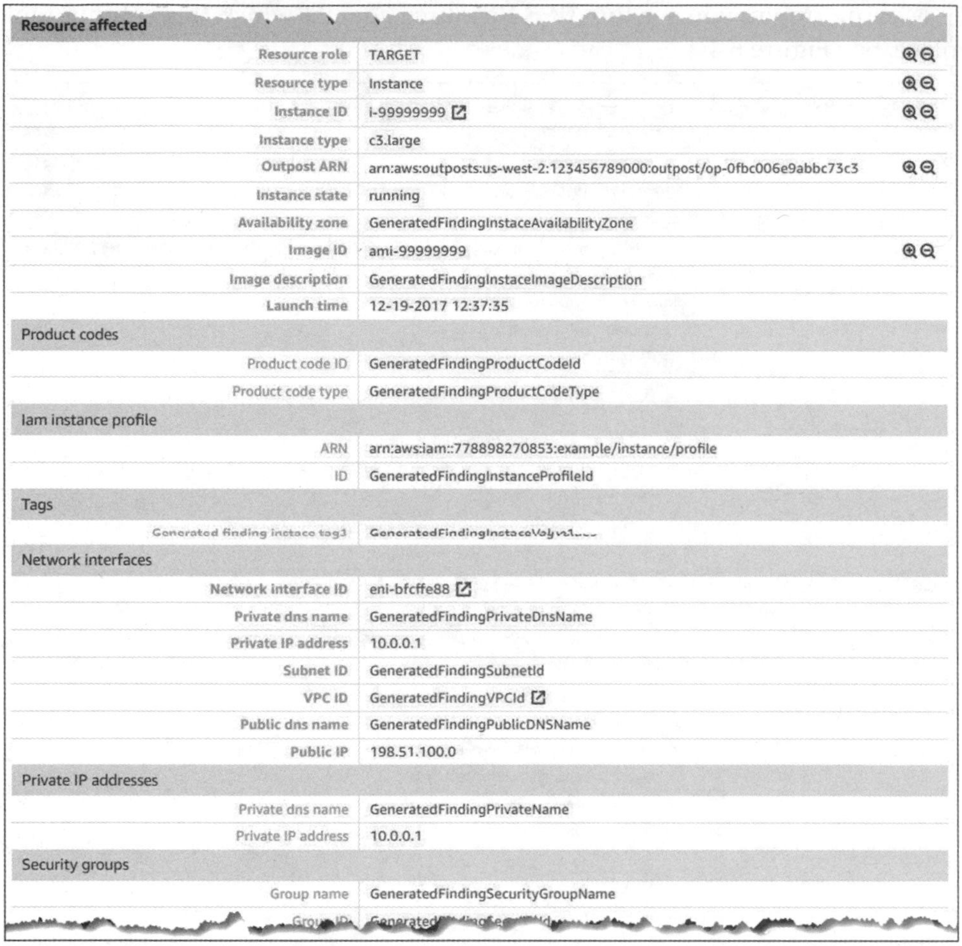

Resource affected		
Resource role	TARGET	🔍🔍
Resource type	Instance	🔍🔍
Instance ID	i-99999999 ↗	🔍🔍
Instance type	c3.large	
Outpost ARN	arn:aws:outposts:us-west-2:123456789000:outpost/op-0fbc006e9abbc73c3	🔍🔍
Instance state	running	
Availability zone	GeneratedFindingInstanceAvailabilityZone	
Image ID	ami-99999999	🔍🔍
Image description	GeneratedFindingInstaceImageDescription	
Launch time	12-19-2017 12:37:35	
Product codes		
Product code ID	GeneratedFindingProductCodeId	
Product code type	GeneratedFindingProductCodeType	
Iam instance profile		
ARN	arn:aws:iam::778898270853:example/instance/profile	
ID	GeneratedFindingInstanceProfileId	
Tags		
Generated finding instace tag3	GeneratedFindingInstaceValvic1....	
Network interfaces		
Network interface ID	eni-bfcffe88 ↗	
Private dns name	GeneratedFindingPrivateDnsName	
Private IP address	10.0.0.1	
Subnet ID	GeneratedFindingSubnetId	
VPC ID	GeneratedFindingVPCId ↗	
Public dns name	GeneratedFindingPublicDNSName	
Public IP	198.51.100.0	
Private IP addresses		
Private dns name	GeneratedFindingPrivateName	
Private IP address	10.0.0.1	
Security groups		
Group name	GeneratedFindingSecurityGroupName	
Group ID	GeneratedFindingSec...Id	

Figure 6.45: Backdoor:EC2/C&CActivity.B!DNS screen

How Do You Detect Data Exfiltration?

Once an attacker has gained initial access to a network, they will be looking for ways to extract data from a system. Exfiltration consists of techniques that adversaries may use to steal data from your network. Once they've collected data, adversaries often package it to avoid detection while removing it. This can include compression and encryption. Techniques for getting data out of a target network typically include transferring it over their command and control channel or an alternate channel and may also include putting size limits on the transmission.

Adversaries may steal data by exfiltrating it over a different protocol than that of the existing command and control channel. The data may also be sent to an alternate network location from the main command and control server.

Alternate protocols include FTP, SMTP, HTTP/S, DNS, SMB, or any other network protocol not being used as the main command and control channel. Different protocol channels could also include web services such as cloud storage. Adversaries may also opt to encrypt and/or obfuscate these alternate channels.

The Data Exfiltration can be detected by analyzing network data for uncommon data flows (e.g., a client sending significantly more data than it receives from a server). Processes utilizing the network that do not normally have network communication or have never been seen before are suspicious. Analyze packet contents to detect communications that do not follow the expected protocol behavior for the port that is being used.

The following walkthrough describes how to set up and use Amazon Guard-Duty to find an anomalous API commonly used to collect data from an AWS environment.

Prerequisites

If you don't have an account, visit `https://aws.amazon.com` and choose Create an AWS Account. As a best practice, you should also create an AWS Identity and Access Management (IAM) user with administrator permissions and use that for all work that does not require root credentials.

Configure and enable GuardDuty and generate sample findings and explore basic operations. Refer to the "How Do You Detect Privilege Escalation" section in this chapter for details.

How Do You Detect the Exfiltration Using an Anomalous API Request?

Click Findings from the left sidebar to go to the Findings page. See Figure 6.46.

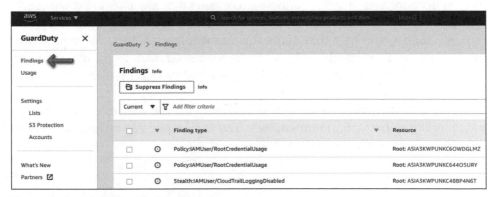

Figure 6.46: GuardDuty Findings screen

Click the `Exfiltration:IAMUser/AnomalousBehavior` event to see additional information provided about the finding. See Figure 6.47.

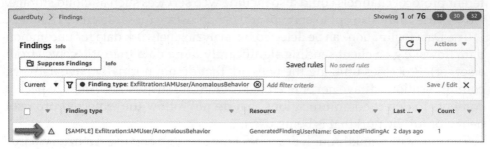

Figure 6.47: Findings screen

Reviewing the Findings

In the example shown in Figure 6.47, you see an `Exfiltration:IAMUser/AnomalousBehavior` finding. This finding informs you that an anomalous API request was observed in your account. This finding may include a single API or a series of related API requests made in proximity by a single CloudTrail user identity. The API observed is commonly associated with exfiltration tactics where an adversary is trying to collect data from your network using packaging and encryption to avoid detection. APIs for this finding type are CloudTrail management (control-plane) operations only and are typically related to S3, snapshots, and databases, such as PutBucketReplication, CreateSnapshot, or RestoreDBInstanceFromDBSnapshot.

This API request was identified as anomalous by GuardDuty's anomaly detection machine learning (ML) model. The ML model evaluates all API requests in your account and identifies anomalous events that are associated with techniques used by adversaries. The ML model tracks various factors of the API request, such as the user that made the request, the location the request was made from, and the specific API that was requested. Details on which factors of the API request are unusual for the user identity that invoked the request can be found in the finding details.

Looking at the information in this finding, you see the severity as HIGH, meaning it requires action immediately. You can see the region and account ID this event occurred in. See Figure 6.48.

Figure 6.48: Exfiltration:IAMUser/AnomalousBehavior screen

Moving down, in Figure 6.49, you see the Anomalous APIs that took place. The unusual behavior Account and the User Identity are also shown in the finding.

Anomalous APIs (4)	Usual APIs
Successfully called	
Generated finding API service name three	GeneratedFindingAPINameThree
Generated finding API service name four	GeneratedFindingAPINameFour
Error Response: AccessDenied	
Generated finding API service name	GeneratedFindingAPIName
	GeneratedFindingAPINameTwo

Unusual behavior (Account)	Usual behavior
API	GeneratedFindingAPIName
ASN org	GeneratedFindingASNOrg (-1)
User agent	GeneratedFindingUserAgentCategory

Unusual behavior (User Identity)	Usual behavior
API	GeneratedFindingAPIName
ASN org	GeneratedFindingASNOrg (-1)
User agent	GeneratedFindingUserAgentCategory

Figure 6.49: Exfiltration:IAMUser/AnomalousBehavior screen

Moving down, in Figure 6.50, you see the AWS Resource against which this activity took place.

Resource affected	
Resource role	TARGET
Resource type	AccessKey
Instance ID	i-99999999
Instance type	m3.xlarge
Outpost ARN	arn:aws:outposts:us-west-2:123456789000:outpost/op-0fbc006e9abbc73c3
Instance state	running
Availability zone	GeneratedFindingInstanceAvailabilityZone
Image ID	ami-99999999
Image description	GeneratedFindingInstanceImageDescription
Launch time	08-02-2016 12:05:06
Product codes	
Product code ID	GeneratedFindingProductCodeId
Product code type	GeneratedFindingProductCodeType
Iam instance profile	
ARN	arn:aws:iam::778898270853:example/instance/profile
ID	GeneratedFindingInstanceProfileId
Tags	
Generated finding instance tag9	GeneratedFindingInstanceTagValue9
Network interfaces	
Network interface ID	eni-bfcffe88
Private dns name	GeneratedFindingPrivateDnsName
Private IP address	10.0.0.1
Subnet ID	GeneratedFindingSubnetId
VPC ID	GeneratedFindingVPCId
Public dns name	GeneratedFindingPublicDNSName
Public IP	198.51.100.0
Private IP addresses	
Private dns name	GeneratedFindingPrivateName
Private IP address	10.0.0.1
Security groups	
Group name	GeneratedFindingSecurityGroupName
Group ID	GeneratedFindingSecurityId

Figure 6.50: Exfiltration:IAMUser/AnomalousBehavior screen

Moving down, in Figure 6.51, you see the Action details. The details point to the Service Name and Error Code that triggered the findings. Moving down again, you can see Actor details, including the caller type, IP address, and the geo-location.

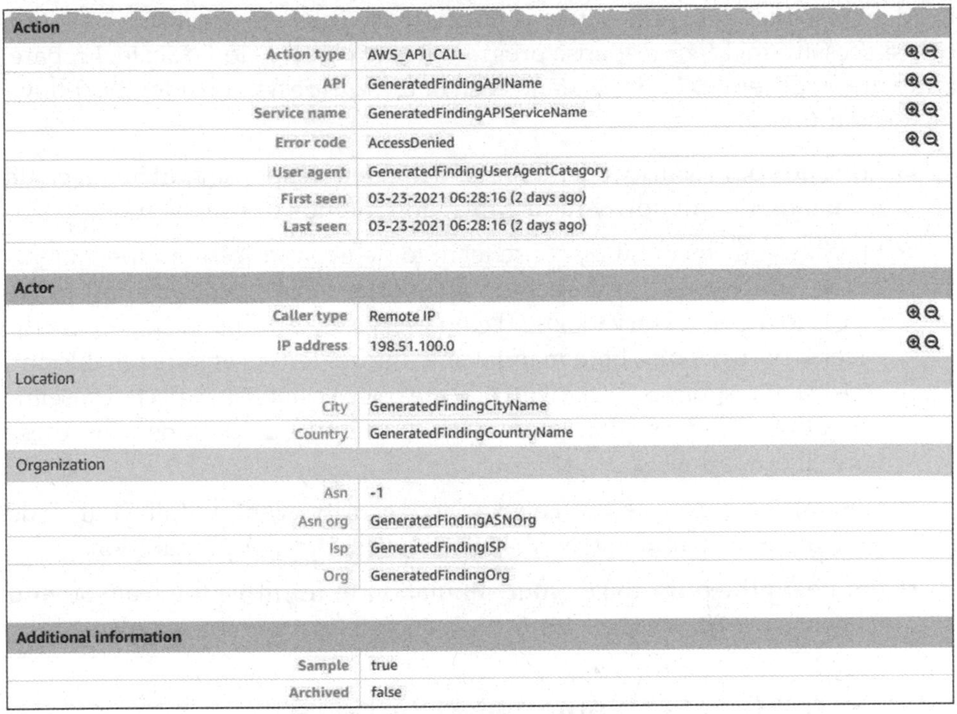

Action		
Action type	AWS_API_CALL	🔍 🔍
API	GeneratedFindingAPIName	🔍 🔍
Service name	GeneratedFindingAPIServiceName	🔍 🔍
Error code	AccessDenied	🔍 🔍
User agent	GeneratedFindingUserAgentCategory	
First seen	03-23-2021 06:28:16 (2 days ago)	
Last seen	03-23-2021 06:28:16 (2 days ago)	

Actor		
Caller type	Remote IP	🔍 🔍
IP address	198.51.100.0	🔍 🔍
Location		
City	GeneratedFindingCityName	
Country	GeneratedFindingCountryName	
Organization		
Asn	-1	
Asn org	GeneratedFindingASNOrg	
Isp	GeneratedFindingISP	
Org	GeneratedFindingOrg	

Additional information		
Sample	true	
Archived	false	

Figure 6.51: Exfiltration:IAMUser/AnomalousBehavior screen

How Do You Handle Response and Recover?

For the Response domain, if a cyber incident occurs, the effects must be managed by organizations. To comply with this requirement, the company should create a response plan, identify communication lines among the relevant parties, collect and analyze information about the case, conduct all the activities necessary to eliminate the incident, and integrate lessons learned into revised response strategies.

Organizations need to develop and implement effective activities to restore any capabilities or services that a cybersecurity event has impaired for the Recover domain. Your organization needs to have a recovery plan in place, coordinate recovery activities with outside parties, and incorporate lessons learned into your updated recovery strategy.

Foundation of Incident Response

All AWS users within an organization should have a basic understanding of security incident response processes, and security staff must deeply understand how to react to security issues. Experience and education are vital to a cloud incident response program, before you handle a security event. The foundation of a successful incident response program in the cloud is to Educate, Prepare, Simulate, and Iterate. To understand each of these aspects, consider the following descriptions:

- Educate your security operations and incident response staff about cloud technologies and how your organization intends to use them.

- Prepare your incident response team to detect and respond to incidents in the cloud, enabling detective capabilities, and ensuring appropriate access to the necessary tools and cloud services. Additionally, prepare the necessary runbooks, both manual and automated, to ensure reliable and consistent responses. Work with other teams to establish expected baseline operations, and use that knowledge to identify deviations from those normal operations.

- Simulate both expected and unexpected security events within your cloud environment to understand the effectiveness of your preparation.

- Iterate on the outcome of your simulation to improve the scale of your response posture, reduce time to value, and further reduce risk.

How Do You Create an Automated Response?

Automation is a force multiplier, which means it scales the efforts of your responders to match the speed of the organization. Moving from manual processes to automated processes enables you to spend more time increasing the security of your AWS Cloud environment.

Automating Incident Responses

To automate security engineering and operations functions, you can use a comprehensive set of APIs and tools from AWS. You can fully automate identity management, network security, data protection, and monitoring capabilities and deliver them using popular software development methods that you already have in place. When you build security automation, your system can monitor, review, and initiate a response, rather than having people monitor your security posture and manually react to events. If your incident response teams continue to respond to alerts in the same way, they risk alert fatigue. Over time, the team can become desensitized to alerts and can either make mistakes handling ordinary situations or miss unusual alerts.

Automation helps avoid alert fatigue by using functions that process the repetitive and ordinary alerts, leaving humans to handle the sensitive and unique incidents. You can improve manual processes by programmatically automating steps in the process. After you define the remediation pattern to an event, you can decompose that pattern into actionable logic, and write the code to perform the logic. Responders can then execute that code to remediate the issue. Over time, you can automate more and more steps, and ultimately automatically handle whole classes of common incidents. However, your objective should be to further reduce the time gap between detective mechanisms and responsive mechanisms. Historically, this time gap can take hours, days, or even months. An Incident Response survey by SANS in 2016 found that 21% of respondents stated their time to detection took two to seven days, and only 29% of respondents were able to remediate events within the same time frame. In the cloud, you can reduce that response time gap to seconds by building event-driven response capabilities.

Options for Automating Responses

It is important to make sure that you balance the enterprise implementation and organization structure. Figure 6.52 illustrates the differences in technical attributes for each automated response option in your AWS implementation. In the radar chart, the further the technical attribute moves from the center of the chart, the greater the strength of that technical attribute for the corresponding automation response. For example, AWS Lambda offers more speed and requires a less technical skillset. AWS Fargate offers more flexibility and requires less maintenance and a less technical skillset. Table 6.1 provides an overview of these automation options and a summary of the technical attributes of each.

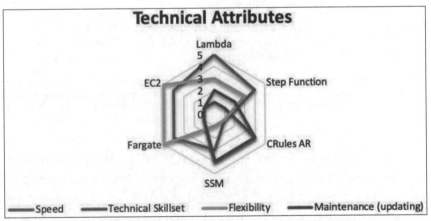

Figure 6.52: Differences in technical attributes across automated response approaches

Table 6.1: Options for Automated Responses

AWS SERVICE OR FEATURE	DESCRIPTION	ATTRIBUTES SUMMARY*
AWS Lambda	System using AWS Lambda only, using your organization's enterprise language.	Speed Flexibility Maintenance Skillset
AWS Step Functions	System using AWS Step Functions, Lambda, and SSM Agent.	Speed Flexibility Maintenance Skillset
Auto Remediation with AWS Config Rules	Set of AWS Config Rules and auto remediation that evaluate the environment and push it back into the approved specification.	Maintenance & Skillset Speed & Flexibility
SSM Agent	Set of automation rules and documents reviewing many pieces of the environments and internal systems and making corrections.	Maintenance & Skillset Speed Flexibility
AWS Fargate	AWS Fargate system using open source step function code and the events from Amazon CloudWatch, and other systems to drive detection and remediation.	Flexibility Speed Maintenance & Skillset
Amazon EC2	A system running on a full instance, similar to the AWS Fargate option.	Flexibility Speed Maintenance Skillset

* Attributes are listed in descending order for each service or feature. For example, AWS Lambda offers more speed and requires a less technical skillset. AWS Fargate offers more flexibility and requires less maintenance and less technical skillset.

As you consider these automation options in your AWS environment, you also need to consider centralization and scan period (events per second [EPS]). Centralization refers to a central account that drives all of the detection and remediation for an organization. This approach may seem like the best choice out-of-the-box, and it is the current best practice. However, some circumstances require that you deviate from this approach, and understanding when depends on how you handle your subordinate accounts. If you have a red team or regulatory difference in your enterprise, you may need to implement differently for that portion of the organization. In that case, your security team should set up a separate security account, similar to the Security Tools account in the Multi-Account Framework in AWS Organizations or AWS Control Tower. The following table addresses pros and cons of centralization and decentralization.

	CENTRALIZATION	**DECENTRALIZATION**
Pros	Simple configuration management Unable to cancel or modify response	Simple architecture Faster initial setup
Cons	Increased complexity in architecture Onboarding offboarding accounts and resources	More resources to manage Difficulty maintaining a software baseline

A cost comparison for these implementations may also drive your enterprise decision in determining the best option. Events per second (EPS) is the metric that you use to best estimate cost. In the end, it may be far easier and cheaper to use centralized or decentralized approaches, but it is impossible for us to review how you will evaluate that cost specifically in your account. Make sure to consider EPS when sending those events to a central account to be responded to. The more EPS, the higher the cost of sending those events to a centralized account.

Cost Comparisons in Scanning Methods

Costs are further determined by the scanning method by which an anomaly is detected and the time frame between validations. For scanning methods, you can choose between event based or periodic scan review. The following table shows the pros and cons of both approaches.

	EVENT-BASED	**PERIODIC SCAN**
Pros	Less time from event to response Limited need to query additional API calls	Full picture at a given point in time
Cons	Limited state context around the resource Events triggered may be for a resource not readily available	Service limits against large accounts Can potentially run into throttling due to high volume of API calls

In many cases, a combination of both scanning approaches is most likely the best choice in a fully mature organization. The AWS Security Hub and AWS Foundational Security Best Practices standard provide a combination of both scanning methods. Figure 6.53 provides a radar chart illustrating the cost comparison of events per second (EPS) for each of the automation approaches.

For example, Amazon EC2 and AWS Fargate have the highest costs for running 0–10 EPS, whereas AWS Lambda and AWS Step Functions have the highest costs for running 76+ EPS.

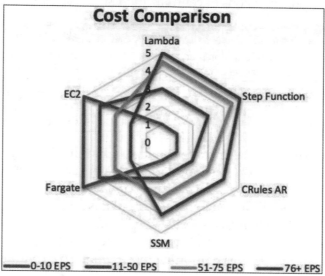

Figure 6.53: Cost comparison of automation options scanning methods (events per second [EPS])

Event-Driven Responses

With an event-driven response system, a detective mechanism triggers a responsive mechanism to automatically remediate the event. You can use event-driven response capabilities to reduce the time-to-value between detective mechanisms and responsive mechanisms. To create this event-driven architecture, you can use AWS Lambda, which is a serverless compute service that runs your code in response to events and automatically manages the underlying compute resources for you.

For example, assume that you have an AWS account with the AWS CloudTrail service enabled. If AWS CloudTrail is ever disabled (through the cloudtrail:StopLogging API), the response procedure is to enable the service again and investigate the user that disabled the AWS CloudTrail logging. Instead of performing these steps manually in the AWS Management Console, you can programmatically enable the logging again (through the cloudtrail:StartLogging API). If you implement this with code, your response objective is to perform this task as quickly as possible and notify the responders that the response was performed. You can decompose the logic into simple code to run in an AWS Lambda function to perform these tasks. You can then use Amazon CloudWatch Events to monitor for the specific cloudtrail:StopLogging event, and invoke the function if it occurs. When this AWS Lambda responder function is invoked by Amazon CloudWatch Events, you can pass it the details of the specific event with the information of the principal that disabled AWS CloudTrail, when it was disabled, the specific resource that was affected, and other relevant information.

You can use this information to enrich the finding from logs, and then generate a notification or alert with only the specific values that a response analyst would require. Ideally, the goal of event-driven response is for the Lambda responder function to perform the response tasks and then notify the responder that the anomaly has been successfully resolved with any pertinent contextual information. It is then up to the human responder to decide how to determine why it occurred and how future reoccurrences might be prevented.

This feedback loop drives further security improvement into your cloud environments. To achieve this objective, you must have a culture that enables your security team to work closer with your development and operations teams.

How Do You Automatically Respond to Unintended Disabling of CloudTrail Logging?

The following walkthrough describes an automated response for a simulated event that indicates potential unauthorized activity—the unintended disabling of CloudTrail logging. Outside parties might want to disable logging to prevent detection and recording of their unauthorized activity. The standard response is to immediately notify the security contact.

Amazon GuardDuty generates the finding `Stealth:IAMUser/CloudTrail-LoggingDisabled` when CloudTrail logging is disabled, and AWS Security Hub collects findings from GuardDuty using the standardized finding format mentioned earlier. See Figure 6.54.

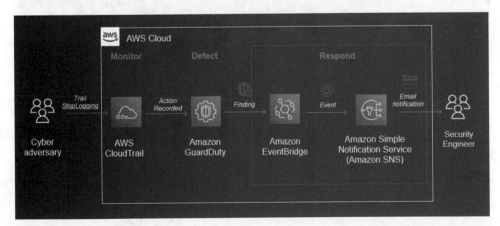

Figure 6.54: CloudTrail screen

CloudTrail logs are monitored for undesired activities. For example, if a trail is stopped, there will be a corresponding log record. GuardDuty detects this activity and retrieves additional data points about the source IP that executed the API call. Two common examples of those additional data points in GuardDuty findings include whether the API call came from an IP address on a threat list, or whether it came from a network not commonly used in your AWS account. Using EventBridge and SNS, you can configure GuardDuty to notify the security contact.

Prerequisites

To use AWS Event Bridge and other AWS services, you need an AWS account. If you don't have an account, visit https://aws.amazon.com and choose Create an AWS Account. As a best practice, you should also create an AWS Identity and Access Management (IAM) user with administrator permissions and use that for all work that does not require root credentials.

Configure and enable GuardDuty. Refer to the "How Do You Detect Privilege Escalation" section in this chapter for details.

Creating a Trail in CloudTrail

Go to the CloudTrail service in the console and then follow these steps:

1. Click Create a Trail in the dashboard. See Figure 6.55.

Figure 6.55: Create a Trail screen

2. Set a meaningful name for the Trail and optionally choose Enable for all accounts in my organization if appropriate. See Figure 6.56.

Choose trail attributes

General details

A trail created in the console is a multi-region trail. **Learn more** 🔗

Trail name
Enter a display name for your trail.

| ThreatHuntingBookSampleTrail |

3-128 characters. Only letters, numbers, periods, underscores, and dashes are allowed.

☐ Enable for all accounts in my organization

To review accounts in your organization, open AWS Organizations. **See all accounts** 🔗

Figure 6.56: Trail Attributes screen

3. Under the Storage Location, select Create New S3 Bucket. Note that the S3 bucket name is auto-generated. See Figure 6.57.

Figure 6.57: Create S3 Bucket screen

4. Enable the Log File SSE-KMS Encryption.

5. Under AWS KMS Customer Managed CMK, select New and provide a meaningful AWS KMS alias name. See Figure 6.58.

Figure 6.58: Enable Encryption screen

6. Expand the Advanced option to verify the additional settings. Leave them with their default values, as shown in Figure 6.59.

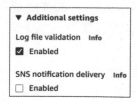

Figure 6.59: Enable Advanced Option screen

7. Scroll to the bottom of the page and click Next. You should now see the Choose Log Events screen.

8. Under Events, choose all event types—Management events, Data events, and Insight events. See Figure 6.60.

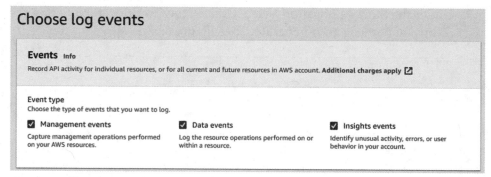

Figure 6.60: Events screen

9. Accept the default options for the Management events and scroll to the bottom of the page. Click Next. You should now see the Management Events screen. See Figure 6.61.

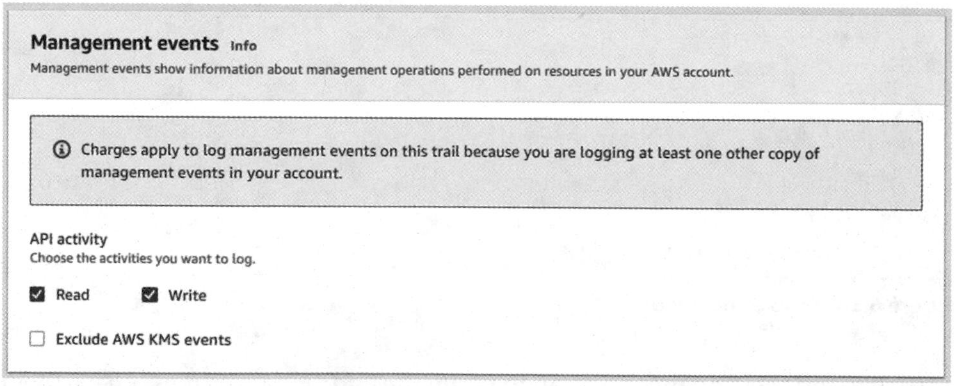

Figure 6.61: Management Events screen

10. Scroll to the bottom of the page and click Create. You can click Trails from the left sidebar of the CloudTrail dashboard and verify that the trail's status is a success.

11. Click the trail's name to go to the trail's details page. You can change any settings from this page. You can also stop logging for this trail using the Stop Logging button. See Figure 6.62.

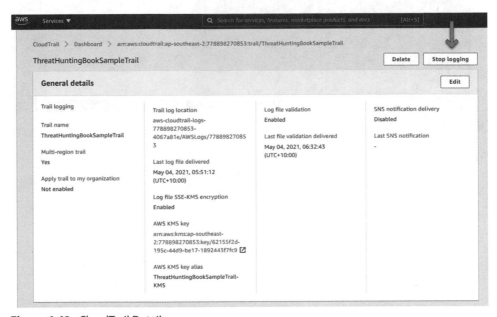

Figure 6.62: CloudTrail Details screen

Creating an SNS Topic to Send Emails

We will walk through how to create an SNS topic for sending emails. SNS is a managed publish/subscribe messaging service and can be used with many endpoints, such as email, Lambda, and more.

1. Go to the Amazon Simple Notification Service in the console.

2. Provide a meaningful name for the topic and click Next Step. See Figure 6.63.

3. Leave the other options as they are and scroll down to the bottom of the page. Click Create Topic. See Figure 6.64.

4. Go to Topic and select the Subscriptions tab.

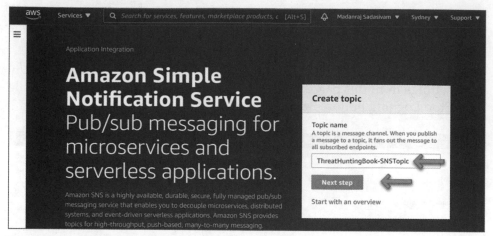

Figure 6.63: Simple Notification Service screen

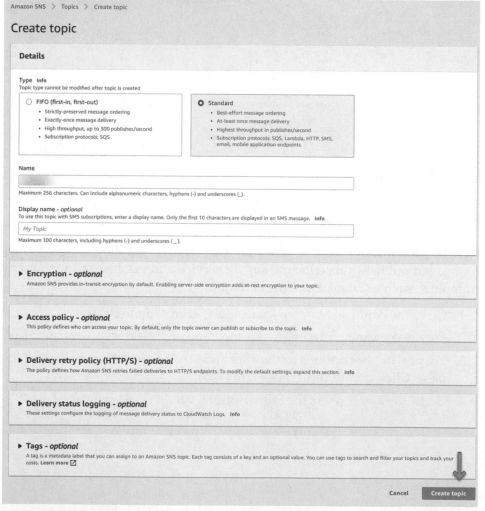

Figure 6.64: Create Topic screen

5. Click Create Subscription. See Figure 6.65.

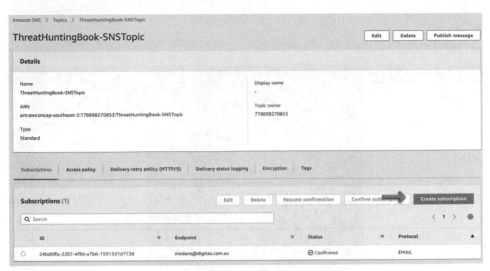

Figure 6.65: Create SNS Subscription screen

6. Set the Protocol to Email and provide an email address for Endpoint. See Figure 6.66.

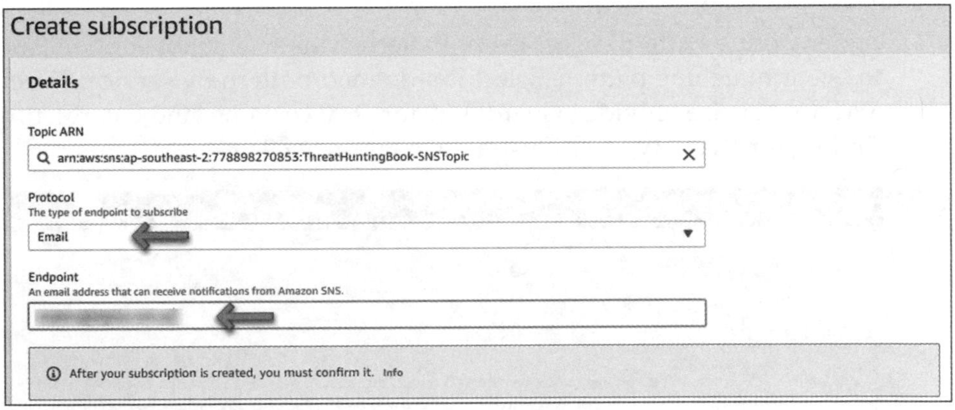

Figure 6.66: Create Subscription screen

7. Scroll down and click Create Subscription. The status of the subscription will be Pending Confirmation.

8. Log in to your email and click the Confirm Subscription hyperlink. You should get a success message. If you go back to the subscription in the AWS console, the status should be Confirmed.

Creating Rules in Amazon EventBridge

1. Go to the EventBridge service in the console.
2. Click Create rule in the dashboard. See Figure 6.67.

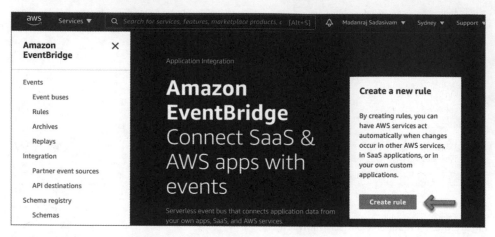

Figure 6.67: EventBridge screen

3. Set a meaningful name for the rule name and optionally provide a description. See Figure 6.68.
4. Under Define Pattern, select Event Pattern. This will enable options for an event matching pattern. Select Pre-defined pattern by service. Select AWS for Service provider, GuardDuty for Service name, and GuardDuty Finding for Event type, as illustrated in Figure 6.69.

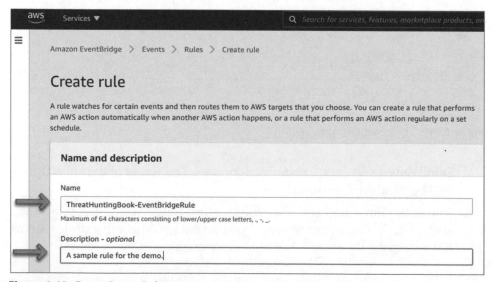

Figure 6.68: Event Create Rule screen

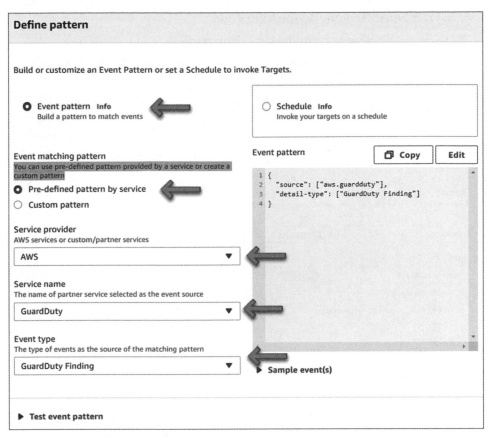

Figure 6.69: GuardDuty Settings screen

5. Under Select Event Bus, select AWS Default Event Bus and Enable the Rule on the Selected Event Bus. See Figure 6.70.

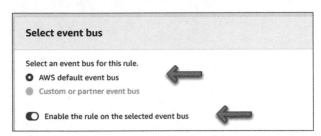

Figure 6.70: Select Event Bus screen

6. Under Select Targets, do the following:

   a. Select SNS topic from the drop-down.

   b. Select the SNS topic you created in the previous SNS topic section, as shown in Figure 6.71.

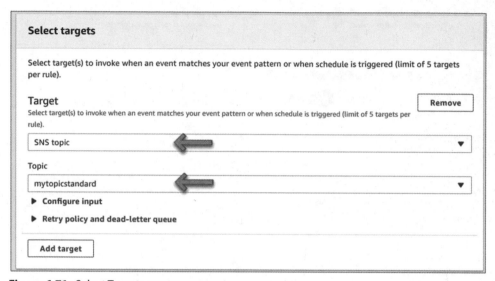

Figure 6.71: Select Targets screen

7. Scroll down and click Create Rule. The rule should now appear on the Rules page. See Figure 6.72.

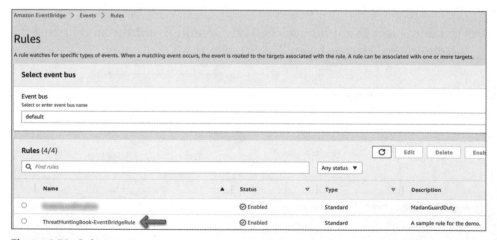

Figure 6.72: Rules screen

How Do You Orchestrate and Recover?

Once appropriate access has been provisioned and tested, your incident response team must define and prepare the related processes necessary for investigation and remediation. This stage is effort intensive, because you must sufficiently plan the appropriate response to security events within your cloud environments. Work closely with your internal cloud services teams and partners to identify the tasks required to ensure that these processes are possible. Collaborate or assign each other response activity task and ensure necessary account configurations are in place. We recommend preparing processes and prerequisite configurations in advance to give your organization the following response capabilities.

Decision Trees

Sometimes, different conditions can require different actions or steps. For example, you might take different actions based on the type of AWS account (development versus production), the tags of the resources, the AWS Config rules compliance status of those resources, or other inputs. To support you in the creation and documentation of these decisions, we recommend you draft a decision tree with your other teams and stakeholders. Similar to a flow chart, a decision tree is a tool that can be leveraged to support decision making, helping to guide you to determine the optimal actions and outcomes based on potential conditions and inputs, including probabilities.

Use Alternative Accounts

Although responding to an event in the impacted account might be required, it is ideal to investigate data outside of the affected account. Some customers have a process for creating separate, isolated AWS account environments, using templates that preconfigure the resources they must provision. These templates are deployed through a service, such as AWS CloudFormation or Terraform, which provides an easy method to create a collection of related AWS resources and provision them in an orderly and predictable fashion.

Preconfiguring these accounts using templated mechanisms helps to remove human interactions during the initial stages of an incident and ensure the environment and resources are prepared in a repeatable and predictable manner, which can be verified by an audit. In addition, this mechanism also increases the ability to maintain security and containment of data in the forensics environment. This approach requires you to work with your cloud services and architect teams to determine an appropriate AWS account process that can be used for investigations. For example, your cloud services teams could use AWS Organizations to generate new accounts and assist you in preconfiguring those accounts using a templated or scripted method. This method of segmentation is best when you need to keep a larger organization removed from a potential threat. This segmentation, of a new and largely unconnected AWS account, means that a user from the organization, labeled in multi-account documentation as the security Organizational Unit (OU), is able to move into the account, perform the needed forensics activities, and potentially hand off the account as a whole to a legal entity, if needed. This method of forensics and attribution requires significant review and planning and should match with the enterprise's GRC policies. Although this work is not easy, it is far easier to do this work prior to building a large account base.

View or Copy Data

Responders require access to logs or other evidence to analyze and must ensure that they have the ability to view or copy data. At a minimum, the IAM permission policy for the responders should provide read-only access so that they can investigate. To enable appropriate access, you might consider some pre-built AWS Managed Policies, such as SecurityAudit or ViewOnlyAccess. For example, responders might want to make a point-in-time copy of data, such as the AWS CloudTrail logs, from an Amazon S3 bucket in one account to an Amazon S3 bucket in another account. The permissions provided by the ReadOnlyAccess managed policy, for example, enable the responder to perform these actions.

Sharing Amazon EBS Snapshots

Many customers use Amazon Elastic Block Store (Amazon EBS) snapshots as part of their investigation for security events that involve their Amazon EC2 instances. Snapshots of Amazon EBS volumes are incremental backups. To perform an investigation of an Amazon EBS volume in a separate, isolated account, you must modify the permissions of the snapshot to share it with the AWS accounts that you specify. Users that you have authorized can use the snapshots you share as the basis to create their own EBS volumes, while your original snapshot remains unaffected. If your snapshot is encrypted, you must also share the custom KMS Customer Managed Key (CMK) used to encrypt the snapshot. You can apply cross-account permissions to a custom CMK either when it is created or at a later time. Snapshots are constrained to the region in which they were created, but you can share a snapshot with another region by copying the snapshot to that region.

Sharing Amazon CloudWatch Logs

Logs that are recorded within Amazon CloudWatch Logs, such as Amazon VPC flow logs, can be shared with another account (such as your centralized security account) through a CloudWatch Logs subscription. For example, the log event data can be read from a centralized Amazon Kinesis stream to perform custom processing and analysis. Custom processing is especially useful when you collect logging data from across many accounts. Ideally, create this configuration early in your cloud journey, before a security-related event occurs.

Use Immutable Storage

When copying logs and other evidence to an alternative account, make sure that the replicated data is protected. However, in addition to protecting the secondary evidence, you must protect the integrity of the data at the source. Known as immutable storage, these mechanisms protect the integrity of your data by preventing the data from being tampered with or deleted. Using the native features of Amazon S3, you can configure an Amazon S3 bucket to protect the integrity of your data, S3 Object Lock. By managing access permissions with S3 bucket policies, configuring S3 versioning, and enabling MFA Delete, you can restrict how data can be written or read. This type of configuration is useful for storing investigation logs and evidence, and is often referred to as write once, read many (WORM).

You can also protect the data by using server-side encryption with AWS Key Management Service (KMS) and verifying that only appropriate IAM principals are authorized to decrypt the data. Additionally, if you want to securely keep data in a long-term storage after the investigation is completed, consider moving the data from Amazon S3 to Amazon S3 Glacier using object lifecycle policies. Amazon S3 Glacier is a secure, durable, and extremely low-cost cloud storage service for data archiving and long-term backup. It is designed to deliver 99.999999999% durability, and provides comprehensive security designed to meet your regulatory requirements. Moreover, you can protect the data in Amazon S3 Glacier by using the Amazon S3 Glacier Vault Lock, which allows you to easily deploy and enforce compliance controls for individual Amazon S3 Glacier vaults with a vault lock policy.

You can specify security controls, such as WORM, in a vault lock policy and lock the policy from future edits. Once locked, the policy can no longer be changed. Amazon S3 Glacier enforces the controls set in the vault lock policy to help achieve your compliance objectives, such as for data retention. You can deploy a variety of compliance controls in a vault lock policy using the AWS Identity and Access Management (IAM) policy language.

Launch Resources Near the Event

For responders who are new to the cloud, it can be tempting to try to conduct cloud investigations on-premises where your existing tools are located. In our experience, AWS customers who respond to incidents using cloud technologies achieve better results—isolations can be automated, copies can be made more easily, evidence is ready for analysis sooner, and the analysis can be completed faster. The best practice is to perform investigations and forensics in the cloud, where the data is, rather than attempting to transfer the data to a datacenter before you investigate. You can use the secure compute and storage capabilities of the cloud practically anywhere in the world to perform the secure response operations. Many customers choose to pre-build a separate AWS account that is ready to perform an investigation, though there might be cases where you choose to operate your analysis in the same AWS account. If your organization is expected to retain records for compliance and legal reasons, it might be prudent to maintain separate accounts for long-term storage and legal activities.

It is also a best practice to perform the investigation in the same AWS Region where the event occurred, rather than replicating the data to another AWS Region. We recommend this practice primarily because of the additional time required to transfer the data between regions. For each AWS Region you choose to operate in, make sure that both your incident response process and the responders abide by the relevant data privacy laws. If you do need to move data between AWS Regions, consider the legal implications of moving data between jurisdictions. It is generally a best practice to keep the data within the same national jurisdiction. If you believe a security event is impacting your security, identity, or communication systems, you might need to seek alternative mechanisms and access to investigate and remediate the impact. AWS offers you the ability to quickly launch new infrastructure that can be used for secure, alternate work environments.

For example, while you investigate the potential severity of the situation, you might want to create a new AWS account with the secure tools for your legal counsel, public relations, and security teams to communicate and continue working. Services such as AWS WorkSpaces (for virtual desktops), AWS WorkMail (for email), and AWS Chime (for communication) can provide your response teams, leadership, and other participants with the capabilities and connectivity they need to communicate, investigate, and remediate an issue.

Isolate Resources

In the course of your investigation, you might need to isolate resources as part of your response to a security anomaly. The intention behind isolating resources is to limit the potential impact, prevent further propagation of affected resources, limit the unintended exposure of data, and prevent further unauthorized access. As with any response, other business, regulatory, legal, or other considerations can apply. Make sure to weigh your intended actions against expected and unexpected consequences. If your cloud teams use resource tags, these tags can help you identify the criticality of the resource or the owner to contact.

Launch Forensic Workstations

Some of your incident response activities might include analyzing disk images, file systems, RAM dumps, or other artifacts that are involved in an incident. Many customers build a customized forensic workstation that they can use to mount copies of any affected data volumes (known as EBS snapshots). To do so, follow these basic steps:

1. Choose a base Amazon Machine Image (AMI) (such as Linux or Windows) that can be used as a forensic workstation.

2. Launch an Amazon EC2 instance from that base AMI.

3. Harden the operating system, remove unnecessary software packages, and configure relevant auditing and logging mechanisms.

4. Install your preferred suite of open source or private toolkits, as well as any vendor software and packages you need.

5. Stop the Amazon EC2 instance and create a new AMI from the stopped instance.

6. Create a weekly or monthly process to update and rebuild the AMI with the latest software patches.

After the forensic system is provisioned using an AMI, your incident response team can use this template to create a new AMI to launch a new forensic workstation for each investigation. The process for launching the AMI as an Amazon EC2 instance can be preconfigured to simplify the deployment process. For example, you can create a template of the forensic infrastructure resources you need within a text file and deploy it into your AWS account utilizing AWS CloudFormation. When your resources are available to be deployed quickly from a template, your well-trained forensic experts are able to use new forensic workstations for each investigation, instead of reusing infrastructure. With this process, you can make sure that there is no cross-contamination from other forensic examinations.

Instance Types and Locations

Amazon EC2 provides a wide selection of instance types that are optimized for different use cases. Instance types comprise varying combinations of CPU, memory, storage, and networking capacity, and give you the flexibility to choose the appropriate mix of resources for your applications. Each instance type includes one or more instance sizes, which enables you to scale your resources to the requirements of your target workload. For incident response instances, follow your company's GRC policies for location and segmentation from the network that runs production instances. AWS enhanced networking uses single root I/O virtualization (SR-IOV) to provide high-performance networking capabilities on supported instance types. SR-IOV is a method of device virtualization that provides higher I/O performance and lower CPU utilization when compared to traditional virtualized network interfaces. Enhanced networking provides higher bandwidth, higher packet per second (PPS) performance, and consistently lower inter-instance latencies. There is no additional charge for using enhanced networking.

How Do You Automatically Recover from Unintended Disabling of CloudTrail Logging?

Figure 6.73 and the following walkthrough describe an automated remediation for a simulated event that indicates potential unauthorized activity—the unintended disabling of CloudTrail logging. Outside parties might want to disable logging to prevent detection and recording of their unauthorized activity. The standard response is to immediately notify the security contact.

Amazon GuardDuty generates the finding `Stealth:IAMUser/CloudTrail-LoggingDisabled` when CloudTrail logging is disabled, and AWS Security Hub collects findings from GuardDuty using the standardized finding format mentioned earlier.

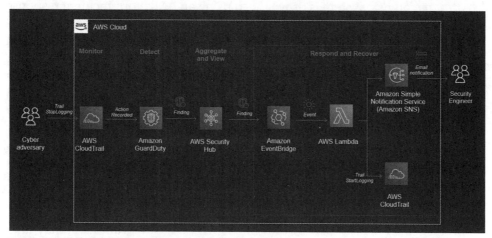

Figure 6.73: GuardDuty screen

CloudTrail logs are monitored for undesired activities. For example, if a trail is stopped, there will be a corresponding log record. GuardDuty detects this activity and retrieves additional data points about the source IP that executed the API call. Two common examples of those additional data points in GuardDuty findings include whether the API call came from an IP address on a threat list, or whether it came from a network not commonly used in your AWS account.

The finding is imported into AWS Security Hub, where it's aggregated with other findings for analyst viewing. Using EventBridge and SNS, you can configure AWS Security Hub to notify the security engineer.

Prerequisites

To use AWS Security Hub, you need an AWS account. If you don't have an account, visit https://aws.amazon.com and choose Create an AWS Account.

As a best practice, you should also create an AWS Identity and Access Management (IAM) user with administrator permissions and use that for all work that does not require root credentials.

Configure and enable GuardDuty. Refer to the section entitled "How Do You Detect Privilege Escalation" earlier in this chapter for further details.

Create a trail in CloudTrail and an SNS topic to send emails. Refer to the section entitled "How Do You Create an Automated Response?" in this chapter for details.

Aggregate and View Security Status in AWS Security Hub

In the following walkthrough you will learn to set up and use AWS Security Hub. Security Hub makes use of findings from services such as Config, GuardDuty, Macie, and Inspector to provide a central view from which to manage security alerts and automate compliance checks.

1. Go to the Security Hub service in the console. If you are using Security Hub for the first time, you should see a Getting started landing page with a Go to Security Hub button.

2. Click Go to Security Hub. You should see the Welcome to AWS Security Hub page with the Enable Security Hub option, and a list of services with Service Linked Roles (SLRs) for conducting compliance checks and permissions for importing findings.

3. Click Enable Security Hub. You should see a screen with sections for Summary, Compliance standards, and Insights. The Summary section has tabs for Insights and Latest findings from AWS integrations. It may take some time for the findings to get updated. See Figure 6.74.

4. Click Findings from the left sidebar to go to the Findings page, where you can see the list of findings across service integrations. You can filter the list based on various criteria, such as the service that exported the finding or the severity of the finding. See Figure 6.75.

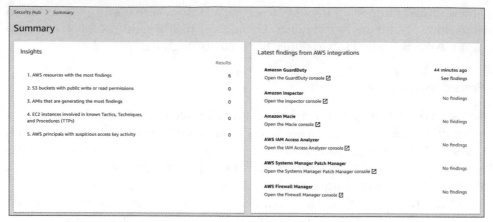

Figure 6.74: Summary screen

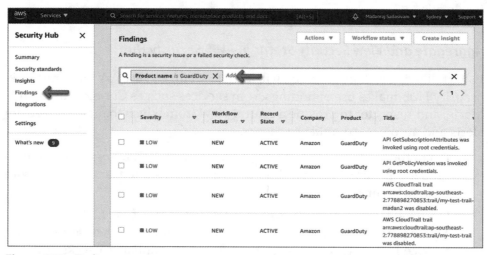

Figure 6.75: Findings screen

Reviewing the Findings

In the example shown in Figure 6.76, you see a `Stealth:IAMUser/` `CloudTrailLoggingDisabled` finding. This finding informs you that a CloudTrail trail within your AWS environment was disabled. This can be an attacker's attempt to disable logging to cover their tracks by eliminating any trace of their activity while gaining access to your AWS resources for malicious purposes. This finding can be triggered by a successful deletion or update of a trail. This finding can also be triggered by a successful deletion of an S3 bucket that stores the logs from a trail that is associated with GuardDuty.

Looking at the information in this finding, you see the severity as LOW, meaning it's something to check but not especially concerning. Now if you see many of these events back to back, there is room for concern, as it could mean a potential bad actor. You can see the account ID this event occurred in and the AWS Resource against which this activity took place. Moving down, you see the Types and Related Findings. Moving down again, you can see AWS resource that was targeted by the trigger activity.

Moving down again, you see the option to investigate in Amazon Detective.

Figure 6.76: CloudTrailLoggingDisabled screen

Create Lambda Function to Orchestrate and Recover

1. Go to the Lambda service in the console and click Create Function. See Figure 6.77.

Figure 6.77: Lambda screen

2. Enter a meaningful function name and choose the Python 3.7 runtime. See Figure 6.78.

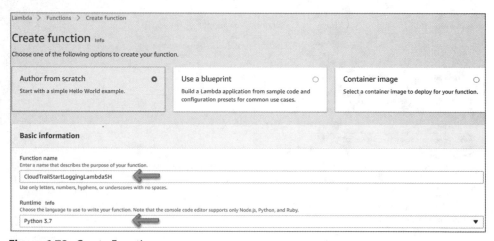

Figure 6.78: Create Function screen

3. Scroll down, accept the defaults for Permissions, and then click Create Function.

4. In the Lambda console, paste the following code in the Function code and select Deploy:

```python
import boto3
import logging
import os
import botocore.session
from botocore.exceptions import ClientError
session = botocore.session.get_session()

logger=logging.getLogger(__name__)
logger.setLevel(logging.INFO)

snsARN = os.environ['SNSTOPIC']


def get_cloudtrail_status(trailname):
    client = boto3.client('cloudtrail')
    response = client.get_trail_status(Name=trailname)

    if response['ResponseMetadata']['HTTPStatusCode'] == 200:
        response = response['IsLogging']
        logger.info("Status of CloudTrail logging for %s - %s" %
(trailname, response))
        else:
            logger.error("Error gettingCloudTrail logging status for
%s - %s" % (trailname, response))

    return response


def enable_cloudtrail(trailname):
    client = boto3.client('cloudtrail')
    response = client.start_logging(Name=trailname)

    if response['ResponseMetadata']['HTTPStatusCode'] == 200:
        logger.info("Response on enable CloudTrail logging for %s -
%s" % (trailname, response))
        else:
            logger.error("Error enabling CloudTrail logging for %s -
%s" % (trailname, response))

    return response


def notify_admin(topic, description):
    snsclient = boto3.client('sns')
    response = snsclient.publish(
        TargetArn = topic,
        Message = "CloudTrail logging state change detected. Event
description: \"%s\" " %description,
        Subject = 'CloudTrail Logging Alert'

    )
```

```
            if response['ResponseMetadata']['HTTPStatusCode'] == 200:
                logger.info("SNS notification sent successfully - %s"
%response)

            else:
                logger.error("Error sending SNS notification - %s"
%response)


            return response


        # Lambda entry point
        def handler(event, context):

            logger.setLevel(logging.INFO)

            logger.info("Starting automatic CloudTrail remediation
response")

            trailARN =
event['detail']['findings'][0]['ProductFields']['action/awsApiCallAction/aff
ectedResources/AWS::CloudTrail::Trail']

            description = event['detail']['findings'][0]['Description']
            region =
event['detail']['findings'][0]['Resources'][0]['Region']

            logger.debug("Event is-- %s" %event)
            logger.debug("trailARN is--- %s" %trailARN)
            logger.debug("snsARN is-- %s" %snsARN)

            try:
                response = enable_cloudtrail(trailARN)
                status = get_cloudtrail_status(trailARN)
                if response['ResponseMetadata']['HTTPStatusCode'] == 200:
                    message = "CloudTrail logging status for trail - " +
trailARN + ": " + str(status) + "\n \n" + str(description) + "\n \n" + \
                            "Review additional information in Security Hub
- https://console.aws.amazon.com/securityhub/home?region=" + region +
"#/findings"
                    notify_admin(snsARN, message)
                    logger.info("Completed automatic CloudTrail
remediation response for %s - %s" % (trailARN, response))

                else:
                    logger.error("Something went wrong - %s, %s" %
(trailARN, event))

            except ClientError as e:
                message = "%s \n \n %s" % (e, event)
                logger.error("%s, %s" % (e, event))
                notify_admin(snsARN, message)
```

5. From the Add Trigger screen, select the EventBridge and then select the existing rule that was created in the previous section. See Figure 6.79.

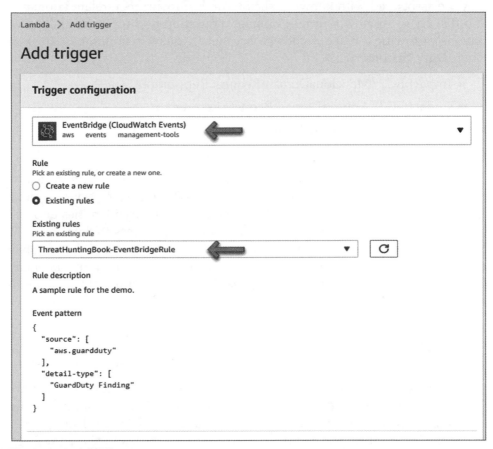

Figure 6.79: Add Trigger screen

6. Go back to EventBridge Rule to confirm that the new target of Lambda is added.

How Are Machine Learning and Artificial Intelligence Used?

Amazon GuardDuty introduces a new machine learning domain reputation model that can categorize previously unseen domains as highly likely to be malicious or benign based on their behavioral characteristics. GuardDuty uses this new capability to alert customers when an EC2 instance in their AWS environment is communicating with a domain identified as malicious and to improve the accuracy of existing domain-based threat detections.

The machine learning domain reputation model analyzes domain requests based on behavioral characteristics, such as popularity, history, and whether they are associated with known malicious or cryptocurrency-related domains and IPs. There are now four new domain reputation finding types in the continuously growing threat detection library that are on by default for all Amazon GuardDuty customers:

- Impact:EC2/MaliciousDomainRequest.Reputation
- Impact:EC2/AbusedDomainRequest.Reputation
- Impact:EC2/SuspiciousDomainRequest.Reputation
- Impact:EC2/BitcoinDomainRequest.Reputation

Available globally, Amazon GuardDuty continuously monitors for malicious or unauthorized behavior to help protect your AWS resources, including your AWS accounts, access keys, and EC2 instances. GuardDuty identifies unusual or unauthorized activity, like cryptocurrency mining, access to data stored in S3 from unusual locations, or infrastructure deployments in a region that has never been used. Powered by threat intelligence, machine learning, and anomaly detection techniques to detect threats, GuardDuty is continuously evolving to help you protect your AWS environment.

Summary

- AWS leverages the five pillar Well-Architected Framework architecture and Shared Security Model concepts extensively. AWS also addresses the industry standard shared responsibility model in detail to clearly articulate customer responsibilities, AWS responsibilities, and shared responsibilities between the customers and AWS.

- Monitoring, logging, and alerting is utilized by a number of services such as CloudTrail, CloudWatch Logs, VPC Flow logs, GuardDuty, and Security Hub.

- There are multiple AWS services to facilitate credential access, lateral movement, command and control, and data exfiltration.

- Privilege escalation is primarily addressed by the AWS GuardDuty service and its configuration settings.

- GuardDuty also addresses lateral movement scenarios and how to prevent malicious activity.

- EC2 configuration and GuardDuty address command and control TTP prevention activities.

- Data exfiltration is addressed by the GuardDuty configuration settings.
- AWS provides mechanisms for automatic response and recovery.
- Machine learning and artificial intelligence are used to combat threats using the AWS ecosystem. This is achieved by key services such as GuardDuty.

References

AWS Well-Architected Framework Whitepaper (`https://aws.amazon.com/architecture/well-architected/?wa-lens-whitepapers.sort-by=item.additionalFields.sortDate&wa-lens-whitepapers.sort-order=desc`)

AWS Shared Responsibility Model (`https://aws.amazon.com/compliance/shared-responsibility-model/`)

AWS Security Incident Response Guide (`https://d1.awsstatic.com/whitepapers/aws_security_incident_response.pdf`)

Amazon GuardDuty introduces machine learning domain reputation model to expand threat detection and improve accuracy (`https://aws.amazon.com/about-aws/whats-new/2021/01/amazon-guardduty-introduces-machine-learning-domain-reputation-model/`)

AWS Reference Architecture

What's in This Chapter

- Understanding how AWS Security architecture aligns with NIST Cybersecurity Framework (CSF)
- Exploring the Identify, Protect, Detect, Respond, and Recover functions attributed to AWS Security
- Learning about the reference architecture for AWS services aligned with the MITRE ATT&CK Threat Hunting Framework
- Exploring the key elements of the AWS threat-hunting capability (i.e., specific services) across Identify, Protect, Detect, Respond, and Recover

As mentioned in Chapter 5, the NIST Cybersecurity Framework (CSF) was originally published in February 2014 in response to Presidential Executive Order 13636, "Improving Critical Infrastructure Cybersecurity," which called for the development of a voluntary framework to help organizations improve the cybersecurity, risk management, and resilience of their systems.

NIST conferred with a broad range of partners from government, industry, and academia for over a year to build a consensus-based set of sound guidelines and practices. While intended for adoption by the critical infrastructure sector, the foundational set of cybersecurity disciplines comprising the CSF have been supported by government and industry as a recommended baseline for use by any organization, regardless of its sector or size. Industry is increasingly referencing the CSF as a de facto cybersecurity standard.

AWS Security Framework Overview

The Amazon NIST Cybersecurity Framework report articulates that the NIST CSF offers a simple construct consisting of three elements—core, tiers, and profiles. See Figure 7.1.

- The *core* represents a set of cybersecurity practices and outcomes, and technical, operational, and managerial security controls (referred to as *informative references*) that support the five risk management functions– Identify, Protect, Detect, Respond, and Recover.

- The *tiers* characterize an organization's aptitude and maturity for managing the CSF functions and controls.

- *Profiles* are intended to convey the organization's "as is" and "to be" cybersecurity postures.

These three elements enable organizations to prioritize and address cybersecurity risks consistent with their business and mission needs. It is important to note that implementation of the core, tiers, and profiles are the responsibility of the organization adopting the CSF (e.g., government agency, financial institution, commercial startup, etc.).

This chapter focuses on AWS solutions and capabilities supporting the core that can enable you to achieve the security outcomes (i.e., subcategories) in the CSF. It also describes how AWS services that have been accredited under FedRAMP Moderate and ISO 9001/27001/27017/27018 align to the CSF. The core references security controls from widely adopted, internationally recognized standards such as ISO/IEC 27001, NIST 800-53, and Control Objectives for Information and Related Technology (COBIT).

> **NOTE**   The CSF encourages organizations to use any controls catalogue to best meet their organizational needs. The CSF was also designed to be size-, sector-, and country-agnostic; therefore, public and private sector organizations should have assurance in the applicability of the CSF regardless of the type of entity or nation state location.
>
> AWS also provides other best practices and frameworks for customers moving their organizations into the cloud (AWS Cloud Adoption Framework) and customers designing, building, or optimizing solutions on AWS (Well-Architected Framework). These frameworks supply complementary tools to support an organization in building and maturing their cybersecurity risk management programs, processes, and practices

in the cloud. More specifically, the NIST CSF can be used in parallel with either of these AWS best practices frameworks, serving as the foundation for your security program with Cloud Adoption Framework or Well-Architected Framework as an overlay for operationalizing the CSF security outcomes in the cloud.

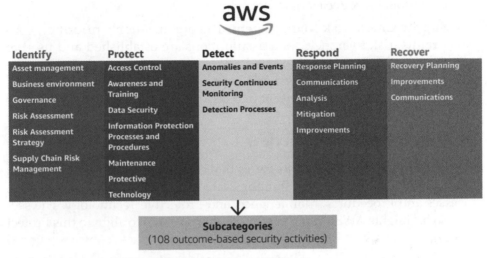

Figure 7.1: Amazon NIST Cybersecurity Framework (CSF)

The Identify Function Overview

This section addresses the six categories that comprise the "Identify" function: Asset Management, Business Environment, Governance, Risk Assessment, Risk Management Strategy, and Supply Chain Risk Management. They "develop an organizational understanding to manage cybersecurity risk to systems, people, assets, data, and capabilities."

- **Asset Management:** The data, personnel, devices, systems, and facilities that enable the organization to achieve business purposes are identified and managed consistent with their relative importance to business objectives and the organization's risk strategy.

- **Business Environment:** The organization's mission, objectives, stakeholders, and activities are understood and prioritized; this information is used to inform cybersecurity roles, responsibilities, and risk management decisions.

- **Governance:** The policies, procedures, and processes to manage and monitor the organization's regulatory, legal, risk, environmental, and operational requirements are understood and inform the management of cybersecurity risk.

- **Risk Assessment:** The organization understands the cybersecurity risk to organizational operations (including mission, functions, image, or reputation), organizational assets, and individuals.

- **Risk Management Strategy:** The organization's priorities, constraints, risk tolerances, and assumptions are established and used to support operational risk decisions.

- **Supply Chain Risk Management:** The organization's priorities, constraints, risk tolerances, and assumptions are established and used to support risk decisions associated with managing supply chain risk. The organization has established and implemented the processes to identify, assess, and manage supply chain risks.

The Protect Function Overview

This section addresses the six categories that comprise the "Protect" function: Access Control, Awareness and Training, Data Security, Information Protection Processes and Procedures, Maintenance, and Protective Technology. The section also highlights AWS solutions that you can leverage to align to this Protect function.

- **Identity Management, Authentication, and Access Control:** Access to physical and logical assets and associated facilities is limited to authorized users, processes, and devices and is managed consistent with the assessed risk of unauthorized access to authorized activities and transactions.

- **Awareness and Training:** The organization's personnel and partners are provided cybersecurity awareness education and are trained to perform their cybersecurity-related duties and responsibilities consistent with related policies, procedures, and agreements.

- **Data Security:** Information and records (data) are managed consistent with the organization's risk strategy to protect the confidentiality, integrity, and availability of information.

- **Information Protection Processes and Procedures:** Security policies (that address purpose, scope, roles, responsibilities, management commitment, and coordination among organizational entities), processes, and procedures are maintained and used to manage protection of information systems and assets.

- **Maintenance:** Maintenance and repairs of industrial control and information system components is performed consistent with policies and procedures.

- **Protective Technology:** Technical security solutions are managed to ensure the security and resilience of systems and assets, consistent with related policies, procedures, and agreements.

The Detect Function Overview

This section addresses the three categories that comprise the "Detect" function: Anomalies and Events, Security Continuous Monitoring, and Detection Processes. We summarize the key AWS solutions that you can leverage to align to this function.

- **Anomalies and Events:** Anomalous activity is detected in a timely manner and the potential impact of events is understood.

- **Security Continuous Monitoring:** The information system and assets are monitored at discrete intervals to identify cybersecurity events and verify the effectiveness of protective measures.

- **Detection Processes:** Detection processes and procedures are maintained and tested to ensure timely and adequate awareness of anomalous events.

The Respond Function Overview

This section addresses the five categories that comprise the "Respond" function: Response Planning, Communications, Analysis, Mitigations, and Improvements. We also summarize the key AWS solutions that you can leverage to align to this function.

- **Response Planning:** Response processes and procedures are executed and maintained to ensure timely response to detected cybersecurity events.

- **Communications:** Response activities are coordinated with internal and external stakeholders, as appropriate, to include external support from law enforcement agencies.

- **Analysis:** Analysis is conducted to ensure adequate response and support recovery activities.

- **Mitigation:** Activities are performed to prevent expansion of an event, mitigate its effects, and eradicate the incident.

- **Improvements:** Organizational response activities are improved by incorporating lessons learned from current and previous detection/response activities.

The Recover Function Overview

This section addresses the three categories that comprise the "Recover" function: Recovery Planning, Improvements, and Communications. We also summarize the key AWS solutions that you can leverage to align to this function.

- **Recovery Planning:** Recovery processes and procedures are executed and maintained to ensure timely restoration of systems or assets affected by cybersecurity events.

- **Improvements:** Recovery planning and processes are improved by incorporating lessons learned into future activities.
- **Communications:** Restoration activities are coordinated with internal and external parties, such as coordinating centers, Internet service providers, owners of attacking systems, victims, other CSIRTs, and vendors.

AWS solutions validated by third-party assessors are available today for public and commercial sector alignment with the NIST CSF. Each of these services maintains a current accreditation under FedRAMP Moderate and/or ISO 27001. When deploying AWS solutions, organizations can have the assurance that AWS services uphold risk management best practices defined in the CSF and can leverage these solutions for their own alignment to the CSF.

TIP Further information about NIST compliance capability and AWS Security strategy is available at `https://aws.amazon.com/products/security/`.

Let's investigate these capabilities in detail. The next section refers to an AWS capability reference architecture that can be aligned to the MITRE ATT&CK Framework.

AWS Reference Architecture

Figure 7.2 illustrates an AWS Reference Architecture that was introduced at the AWS re-Invent conference and is slowly gaining traction in the industry. We discuss each of these capabilities in detail in the following sections.

NOTE We have attempted to provide a concise summary of key AWS Services related to the AWS Reference Architecture. Note that we are not attempting to discuss the details of each AWS Service and its architecture. Our objective is to position the key attributes of each service and cover how they address the TTPs. We have used extracts from AWS knowledge repositories to achieve this. Note the scope of these services also changes regularly due to frequent cloud update cadence. Hence, we advise readers to refer to www.amazon.com for the latest information about each of these services.

The Identify Function

This section discusses the Identify capability addressed by the AWS service shown in Figure 7.3. We discuss each of the key services in detail in the subsequent sections.

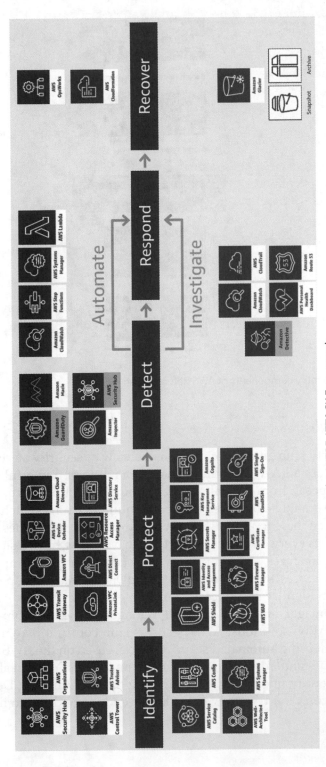

Figure 7.2: AWS Reference Architecture aligned to the MITRE ATT&CK Framework

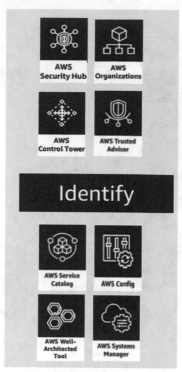

Figure 7.3: Identify components of AWS Reference Architecture

Security Hub

AWS Security Hub gives a comprehensive view of security alerts and security posture across all AWS accounts. There is a range of powerful security tools at your disposal, from firewalls and endpoint protection to vulnerability and compliance scanners. But often this leaves hunting teams switching back-and-forth between these tools to deal with hundreds, and sometimes thousands, of security alerts every day. With Security Hub, you now have a single place that aggregates, organizes, and prioritizes your security alerts, or findings, from multiple AWS services, such as Amazon GuardDuty, Amazon Inspector, Amazon Macie, AWS Identity and Access Management (IAM) Access Analyzer, AWS Systems Manager, and AWS Firewall Manager, as well as from AWS Partner Network (APN) solutions. AWS Security Hub continuously monitors your environment using automated security checks based on the AWS best practices and industry standards that your organization follows. You can also take action on these security findings by investigating them in Amazon Detective or by using Amazon CloudWatch Event rules to send the findings to ticketing, chat,

Security Information and Event Management (SIEM), Security Orchestration Automation and Response (SOAR), and incident management tools or to custom remediation playbooks. Figure 7.4 articulates its components and architecture.

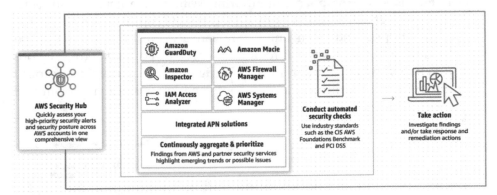

Figure 7.4: Security Hub architecture

AWS Config

AWS Config is a service that enables organizations to assess, audit, and evaluate the configurations of their AWS resources (see Figure 7.5). Config continuously monitors and records their AWS resource configurations and allows them to automate the evaluation of recorded configurations against desired configurations. With Config, your company can review changes in configurations and relationships between AWS resources, dive into detailed resource configuration histories, and determine your overall compliance against the configurations specified in your internal guidelines. This enables you to simplify compliance auditing, security analysis, change management, and operational troubleshooting. The key benefits are as follows:

- **Continuous monitoring:** With AWS Config, you are able to continuously monitor and record configuration changes of your AWS resources. Config also enables you to inventory your AWS resources, the configurations of your AWS resources, as well as software configurations within EC2 instances at any point in time. Once change from a previous state is detected, an Amazon Simple Notification Service (SNS) notification can be delivered for you to review and take action.

- **Change management:** With AWS Config, you can track the relationships among resources and review resource dependencies prior to making changes. Once a change occurs, you are able to quickly review the history of the resource's configuration and determine what the resource's configuration looked like at any point in the past. Config provides you with information to assess how a change to a resource configuration would affect your other resources, which minimizes the impact of change-related incidents.

- **Enterprise-wide compliance monitoring:** With multi-account, multi-region data aggregation in AWS Config, you can view compliance status across your enterprise and identify non-compliant accounts. You can dive deeper to view status for a specific region or a specific account across regions. You can view this data from the Config console in a central account, removing the need to retrieve this information individually from each account and each region.

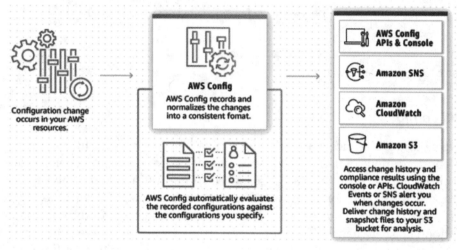

Figure 7.5: AWS Config components

AWS Organizations

AWS Organizations helps centrally manage and govern environment as you grow and scale your AWS resources (see Figure 7.6). Using AWS Organizations, you can programmatically create new AWS accounts and allocate resources, group accounts to organize your workflows, apply policies to accounts or groups for governance, and simplify billing by using a single payment method for all of your accounts.

In addition, AWS Organizations is integrated with other AWS services so you can define central configurations, security mechanisms, audit requirements, and resource sharing across accounts in your organization. AWS Organizations is available to all AWS customers at no additional charge. The key benefits are:

- **Centrally secure and audit your environment across accounts:** Manage auditing at scale using AWS CloudTrail to create an immutable log of all events from accounts. You can enforce and monitor backup requirements with AWS Backup, or centrally define your recommended configuration criteria across resources, AWS Regions, and accounts with AWS Config. You can also use AWS Control Tower to establish cross-account security audits, or manage and view policies applied across accounts. In addition, you can protect your resources by centrally managing security services, such as detecting threats with Amazon GuardDuty, or reviewing unintended access with AWS IAM Access Analyzer.

■ **Efficiently provision resources across accounts:** You can reduce resource duplication by sharing critical resources within your organization using AWS Resource Access Manager (RAM). Organizations also helps you meet your software license agreements with AWS License Manager, and maintain a catalog of IT services and custom products with AWS Service Catalog.

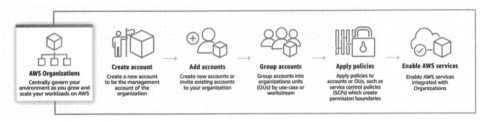

Figure 7.6: AWS Organizations components

AWS Control Tower

If you have multiple AWS accounts and teams, cloud setup and governance can be complex and time-consuming. AWS Control Tower provides the easiest way to set up and govern a secure, multi-account AWS environment, called a landing zone (see Figure 7.7). AWS Control Tower creates a landing zone using AWS Organizations, bringing ongoing account management and governance as well as implementation best practices based on AWS's experience. With AWS Control Tower, builders can provision new AWS accounts in a few clicks, while you have peace of mind knowing that your accounts conform to company-wide policies. AWS customers can implement AWS Control Tower, extend governance into new or existing accounts, and gain visibility into their compliance status quickly. If you are building a new AWS environment, starting out on your journey to AWS, or starting a new cloud initiative, Control Tower will help you get started quickly with built-in governance and best practices. The key features are as follows:

■ **Automate ongoing policy management:** Control Tower provides mandatory and strongly recommended high-level rules, called guardrails, that help enforce your policies using service control policies (SCPs), or detect policy violations using AWS Config rules. These rules remain in effect as you create new accounts or make changes to your existing accounts, and Control Tower provides a summary report of how each account conforms to your enabled policies.

- **View policy-level summaries of your AWS environment:** Control Tower provides you with an integrated dashboard so you can see a top-level summary of policies applied to your AWS environment. You can view details on the accounts provisioned, the guardrails enabled across your accounts, and account-level status for compliance with your guardrails.

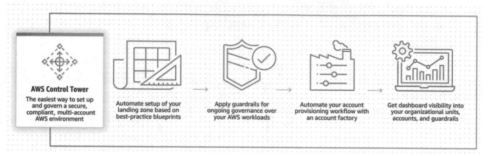

Figure 7.7: AWS Control Tower components

AWS Trusted Advisor

AWS Trusted Advisor is an online tool that provides real-time guidance to help provision your resources following AWS best practices (see Figure 7.8). Trusted Advisor checks help optimize AWS infrastructure, improve security and performance, reduce your overall costs, and monitor service limits. Whether establishing new workflows, developing applications, or as part of ongoing improvement, take advantage of the recommendations provided by Trusted Advisor on a regular basis to help keep your solutions provisioned optimally.

AWS Basic Support and AWS Developer Support customers get access to six security checks (S3 Bucket Permissions, Security Groups - Specific Ports Unrestricted, IAM Use, MFA on Root Account, EBS Public Snapshots, RDS Public Snapshots) and 50 service limit checks. AWS Business Support and AWS Enterprise Support customers get access to all 115 Trusted Advisor checks (14 cost optimization, 17 security, 24 fault tolerance, 10 performance, and 50 service limits) and recommendations. The key features are as follows:

- **Cost optimization:** AWS Trusted Advisor can save you money on AWS by eliminating unused and idle resources or by making commitments to reserved capacity.

- **Security:** AWS Trusted Advisor can improve the security of your application by closing gaps, enabling various AWS security features, and examining your permissions.

- **Fault tolerance:** AWS Trusted Advisor can increase the availability and redundancy of your AWS application by taking advantage of auto scaling, health checks, multi AZ, and backup capabilities.

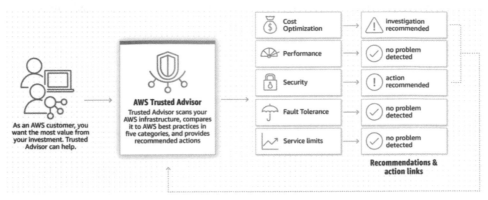

Figure 7.8: AWS Trusted Advisor components

AWS Well-Architected Tool

The AWS Well-Architected Tool helps to review the state of workloads and compares them to the latest AWS architectural best practices (see Figure 7.9). The tool is based on the AWS Well-Architected Framework, developed to help cloud architects build secure, high-performing, resilient, and efficient application infrastructure. This framework provides a consistent approach for customers and partners to evaluate architectures, has been used in tens of thousands of workload reviews conducted by the AWS solutions architecture team, and provides guidance to help implement designs that scale with application needs over time.

To use this free tool, available in the AWS Management Console, just define your workload and answer a set of questions regarding operational excellence, security, reliability, performance efficiency, and cost optimization. The AWS Well-Architected Tool then provides a plan for how to architect for the cloud using established best practices. The key features are as follows:

- **Review your workloads consistently:** The AWS Well-Architected Tool offers your organization a single tool and consistent process to help you review and measure your cloud architectures. When you are responsible for multiple workloads across your organization, the tool enables you to monitor their overall status and helps you to understand potential risks.

Use the results that the tool provides to identify next steps for improvement, drive architectural decisions, and bring architecture considerations into your corporate governance process.

- **Identify and implement improvements:** Use the AWS Well-Architected Tool to support continuous improvement throughout the workload lifecycle. The tool makes it easy to save point-in-time milestones and track changes to your workload. Whenever you want, initiate a new review process to help ensure your architecture continues to improve over time.

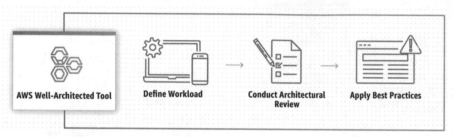

Figure 7.9: AWS Well-Architected Tool components

AWS Service Catalog

AWS Service Catalog allows organizations to create and manage catalogs of IT services that are approved for use on AWS. These IT services can include everything from virtual machine images, servers, software, and databases to complete multi-tier application architectures. AWS Service Catalog allows you to centrally manage deployed IT services and your applications, resources, and metadata. This helps you achieve consistent governance and meet your compliance requirements, while enabling users to quickly deploy only the approved IT services they need. With AWS Service Catalog AppRegistry, organizations can understand the application context of their AWS resources. You can define and manage your applications and their metadata, to keep track of cost, performance, security, compliance, and operational status at the application level. The key features are as follows:

- **Manage all of your application information on AWS:** AWS Service Catalog AppRegistry provides a single repository for collecting and managing your application resources on AWS. You define your application metadata, which may include information from your internal systems, other AWS services, and software vendors. Builders can include a reference to their application within the infrastructure code, and business stakeholders have up-to-date information on application contents and metadata, such as organizational ownership, data sensitivity, and cost center.

- **Ensure compliance with corporate standards:** AWS Service Catalog provides a single location where organizations can centrally manage catalogs of IT services. With AWS Service Catalog you can control which IT services and versions are available, what is configured in each of the available services, and who gets permission access by individual, group, department, or cost center.

- **Connect with ITSM/ITOM software:** The AWS Service Management Connector helps IT Service Management (ITSM) administrators improve governance over provisioned AWS and third-party products. ITSM tools, such as ServiceNow and Jira Service Desk, connect with the AWS Management and Governance services AWS Service Catalog, AWS Config, and AWS Systems Manager. ITSM users can connect to AWS Service Catalog to request, provision, and manage AWS and third-party services and resources.

AWS Systems Manager

AWS Systems Manager gives visibility and control of your infrastructure on AWS. Systems Manager provides a unified user interface so you can view operational data from multiple AWS services and allows you to automate operational tasks across your AWS resources. With Systems Manager, you can group resources, like Amazon EC2 instances, Amazon EKS clusters, Amazon S3 buckets, or Amazon RDS instances, by application, view operational data for monitoring and troubleshooting, implement pre-approved change work flows, and audit operational changes for your groups of resources. Systems Manager simplifies resource and application management, shortens the time to detect and resolve operational problems, and makes it easy to operate and manage your infrastructure securely at scale (see Figure 7.10). The key features are as follows:

- **Shorten the time to detect problems:** AWS Systems Manager helps you quickly view operational data for groups of resources, so you can quickly identify any issues that might impact applications that use those resources. You can group your resources by applications, application layers, production versus development environments, or anything else you choose. Systems Manager presents the operational data for your resource groups in a single, easy-to-read dashboard so you don't have to navigate to other AWS consoles. For example, if you have an application that uses Amazon EC2, Amazon EKS, Amazon S3, and Amazon RDS, you can use Systems Manager to create a resource group for the application and easily see the software installed on your Amazon EC2 instances, any changes in your Amazon S3 objects, or database instances that have stopped.

- **Improve visibility and control:** Using AWS Systems Manager, you can discover applications, view operations data (e.g., deployment status, Amazon CloudWatch alarms, resource configurations, and operational issues), and perform remedial actions in the context of an application. You can request operational changes using predefined approval workflows and audit each change after it has been completed. You can then view detailed system configurations, operating system patch levels, software installations, application configurations, and other details about your environment through the Systems Manager Explorer and Inventory dashboards. Systems Manager is integrated with AWS Config so you can easily view changes across your resources as they occur over time.

- **Manage hybrid environments:** With AWS Systems Manager, you can manage servers running on AWS and in your on-premises datacenter through a single interface. Systems Manager securely communicates with a lightweight agent installed on your servers to run management tasks. This helps you manage resources for Windows, Linux, and Mac operating systems running on Amazon EC2 or on-premises. Systems Manager offers you a consistent administrator experience across your fleet of servers, making it easier to configure and audit logs, manipulate registry keys, navigate file systems, update user access permissions, and monitor critical metrics.

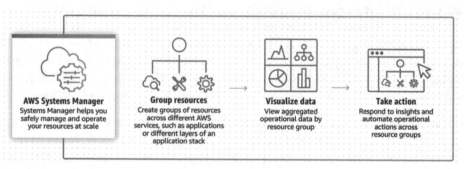

Figure 7.10: AWS Systems Manager components

Let's now discuss the Protect capability of the AWS Reference Architecture (see Figure 7.11). AWS presents a number of key services to augment an organization's Protect capability posture. We dive into all these key services in the subsequent sections.

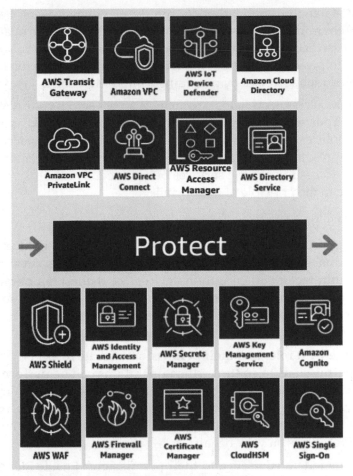

Figure 7.11: Protect components of AWS Reference Architecture

AWS Identity and Access Management (IAM)

AWS Identity and Access Management (IAM) enables organizations to manage access to AWS services and resources securely. Using IAM, you can create and manage AWS users and groups, and use permissions to allow and deny their access to AWS resources. IAM is a feature of your AWS account offered at no additional charge. You will be charged only for use of other AWS services by your users. The key features are as follows:

■ **Fine-grained access control to AWS resources:** IAM enables your users to control access to AWS service APIs and to specific resources. IAM also enables you to add specific conditions such as time of day to control how a user can use AWS, their originating IP address, whether they are using SSL, or whether they have authenticated with a multi-factor authentication device.

- **Multi-factor authentication for highly privileged users:** Protect your AWS environment by using AWS MFA, a security feature available at no extra cost that augments user name and password credentials. MFA requires users to prove physical possession of a hardware MFA token or MFA-enabled mobile device by providing a valid MFA code.

- **Analyze access:** IAM helps you analyze access across your AWS environment. Your security teams and administrators can quickly validate that your policies only provide the intended public and cross-account access to your resources. You can also easily identify and refine your policies to allow access to only the services being used. This helps you to better adhere to the principle of least privilege.

AWS IAM allows you to:

- **Manage IAM users and their access:** Create users in IAM, assign them individual security credentials (in other words, access keys, passwords, and multi-factor authentication devices), or request temporary security credentials to provide users access to AWS services and resources. You can manage permissions in order to control which operations a user can perform.

- **Manage IAM roles and their permissions:** Create roles in IAM and manage permissions to control which operations can be performed by the entity, or AWS service, that assumes the role. You can also define which entity is allowed to assume the role. In addition, you can use service-linked roles to delegate permissions to AWS services that create and manage AWS resources on your behalf.

- **Manage federated users and their permissions:** Enable identity federation to allow existing identities (users, groups, and roles) in your enterprise to access the AWS Management Console, call AWS APIs, and access resources, without the need to create an IAM user for each identity. Use any identity management solution that supports SAML 2.0, or use one of our federation samples (AWS Console SSO or API federation).

AWS Single Sign-On (SSO)

AWS Single Sign-On (SSO) makes it easy to centrally manage access to multiple AWS accounts and business applications and provide users with single sign-on access to all their assigned accounts and applications from one place. With AWS SSO, you can easily manage access and user permissions to all of your accounts in AWS Organizations centrally. AWS SSO configures and maintains all the necessary permissions for your accounts automatically, without requiring any additional setup in the individual accounts. You can assign user permissions based on common job functions and customize these permissions to meet your specific security requirements. AWS SSO also includes built-in integrations to many business applications, such as Salesforce, Box, and Microsoft 365. See Figure 7.12.

With AWS SSO, you can create and manage user identities in AWS SSO's identity store, or easily connect to your existing identity source, including Microsoft Active Directory, Okta Universal Directory, and Azure Active Directory (Azure AD). AWS SSO allows you to select user attributes, such as cost center, title, or locale, from your identity source, and then use them for attribute-based access control in AWS. The key features are as follows:

- **Access accounts and applications from one place:** AWS SSO provides a user portal so users can find and access the roles they can assume in their assigned AWS accounts and business applications in one place. AWS SSO offers pre-configured SAML integrations to many business applications, including Salesforce, Box, and Microsoft 365. AWS monitors these integrations for changes and updates the integration on your behalf automatically. The AWS SSO application configuration wizard helps you extend SSO access to any application that supports Security Assertion Markup Language (SAML) 2.0.

- **Create users in AWS SSO or connect to your existing identities:** AWS SSO gives you the option to create your user identities and groups in AWS SSO. And, if you already use Microsoft Active Directory Domain Services, Okta Universal Directory, Azure AD, or another supported identity provider, your users can access AWS with their existing corporate credentials, and your administrators can continue to manage users and groups in your existing identity source. With AWS SSO, you can enable standards-based strong authentication capabilities for all your users across all identity sources.

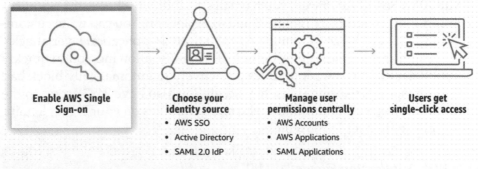

Figure 7.12: AWS Single Sign-On components

AWS Shield

AWS Shield is a managed Distributed Denial of Service (DDoS) protection service that safeguards applications running on AWS. AWS Shield provides always-on detection and automatic inline mitigations that minimize application downtime and latency, so there is no need to engage AWS Support to benefit from DDoS protection. There are two tiers of AWS Shield: Standard and Advanced.

All AWS customers benefit from the automatic protections of AWS Shield Standard, at no additional charge. AWS Shield Standard defends against most common, frequently occurring network and transport layer DDoS attacks that target your website or applications. When you use AWS Shield Standard with Amazon CloudFront and Amazon Route 53, you receive comprehensive availability protection against all known infrastructure (Layers 3 and 4) attacks.

For higher levels of protection against attacks targeting your applications running on Amazon Elastic Compute Cloud (EC2), Elastic Load Balancing (ELB), Amazon CloudFront, AWS Global Accelerator, and Amazon Route 53 resources, you can subscribe to AWS Shield Advanced. In addition to the network and transport layer protections that come with Standard, AWS Shield Advanced provides additional detection and mitigation against large and sophisticated DDoS attacks, near real-time visibility into attacks, and integration with AWS WAF, a web application firewall. AWS Shield Advanced also gives you 24x7 access to the AWS DDoS Response Team (DRT) and protection against DDoS-related spikes in your Amazon Elastic Compute Cloud (EC2), Elastic Load Balancing (ELB), Amazon CloudFront, AWS Global Accelerator, and Amazon Route 53 charges.

AWS Shield Advanced is available globally on all Amazon CloudFront, AWS Global Accelerator, and Amazon Route 53 edge locations. You can protect your web applications hosted anywhere in the world by deploying Amazon CloudFront in front of your application. Your origin servers can be Amazon S3, Amazon Elastic Compute Cloud (EC2), Elastic Load Balancing (ELB), or a custom server outside of AWS.

With AWS Shield Advanced, you have the flexibility to choose the resources to protect for infrastructure (Layers 3 and 4) protection. You can write customized rules with AWS WAF to mitigate sophisticated application layer attacks. These customizable rules can be deployed instantly, allowing you to quickly mitigate attacks. You can set up rules proactively to automatically block bad traffic, or respond to incidents as they occur. You also have 24x7 access to the AWS DDoS Response Team (DRT), who can write rules on your behalf to mitigate application layer DDoS attacks.

AWS Web Application Firewall (WAF)

AWS WAF is a web application firewall that helps protect web applications or APIs against common web exploits and web bots (i.e., web robots) that may affect availability, compromise security, or consume excessive resources. AWS WAF gives you control over how traffic reaches your applications by enabling you to create security rules that control web bot traffic and block common attack patterns, such as SQL injection or cross-site scripting. You can also customize rules that filter out specific traffic patterns. You can get started quickly using Managed Rules for AWS WAF, a pre-configured set of rules managed by AWS or AWS Marketplace Sellers to address issues like the OWASP Top 10 security risks and automated bots that consume excess resources, skew metrics, or can cause downtime. These rules are regularly updated as new issues emerge. AWS WAF includes a full-featured API that you can use to automate the creation, deployment, and maintenance of security rules.

You can deploy AWS WAF on Amazon CloudFront as part of your CDN solution, the Application Load Balancer that fronts your web servers or origin servers running on EC2, Amazon API Gateway for your REST APIs, or AWS AppSync for your GraphQL APIs. With AWS WAF, you pay only for what you use and the pricing is based on how many rules you deploy and how many web requests your application receives.

With Managed Rules for AWS WAF, you can quickly get started and protect your web application or APIs against common threats. You can select from many rule types, such as ones that address issues like the Open Web Application Security Project (OWASP) Top 10 security risks, threats specific to Content Management Systems (CMS), or emerging Common Vulnerabilities and Exposures (CVE). Managed rules are automatically updated as new issues emerge, so that you can spend more time building applications.

With AWS WAF Bot Control, you get visibility and control over common and pervasive bot traffic to your applications. Within the AWS WAF console, you can monitor common bots, such as status monitors and search engines, and get detailed, real-time visibility into the category, identity, and other details of web bot traffic. You can also block, or rate-limit, traffic from pervasive bots, such as scrapers, scanners, and crawlers. Using AWS Firewall Manager, you can deploy the Bot Control managed rule group across multiple accounts in your AWS Organization. See Figure 7.13.

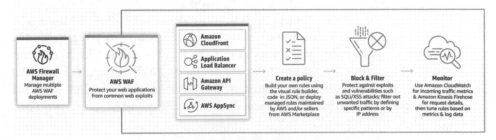

Figure 7.13: AWS Web Application Firewall components

AWS Firewall Manager

AWS Firewall Manager is a security management service that allows organizations to centrally configure and manage firewall rules across all accounts and applications in AWS Organizations. As new applications are created, Firewall Manager makes it easy to bring new applications and resources into compliance by enforcing a common set of security rules. Now you have a single service to build firewall rules, create security policies, and enforce them in a consistent, hierarchical manner across your entire infrastructure, from a central administrator account.

Using AWS Firewall Manager, you can easily roll out AWS WAF rules for your Application Load Balancers, API Gateways, and Amazon CloudFront distributions. You can create AWS Shield Advanced protections for your Application Load Balancers, ELB Classic Load Balancers, Elastic IP Addresses, and CloudFront distributions. You can also configure new Amazon Virtual Private Cloud (VPC) security groups and audit any existing VPC security groups for your Amazon EC2, Application Load Balancer (ALB), and ENI resource types. You can deploy AWS Network Firewalls across accounts and VPCs in your organization. Finally, with AWS Firewall Manager, you can also associate your VPCs with Amazon Route 53 Resolvers DNS Firewall rules. The key features are as follows:

- **Simplify management of firewall rules across your accounts:** AWS Firewall Manager is integrated with AWS Organizations so you can enable AWS WAF rules, AWS Shield Advanced protections, security groups, AWS Network Firewall rules, and Amazon Route 53 Resolver DNS Firewall rules for your Amazon VPC across multiple AWS accounts and resources from a single place. You can group rules, build policies, and centrally apply those policies across your entire infrastructure. For example, you can delegate the creation of application-specific rules within an account while retaining the ability to enforce global security policies across accounts.

- **Centrally deploy protections for your VPCs:** With Firewall Manager, your security administrator can deploy a baseline set of VPC security group rules for EC2 instances, Application Load Balancers (ALBs), and Elastic Network Interfaces (ENIs) in your Amazon VPCs. At the same time, you can also audit any existing security groups in your VPCs for over-permissive rules and remediate them from a single place. You can leverage Firewall Manager to deploy rules for AWS Network Firewalls across your VPCs in your organization, to control traffic leaving and entering your network. At the same time, with Firewall Manager, you can also associate your VPCs with Route 53 Resolver DNS Firewall rules to block DNS queries made for known malicious domains and to allow queries for trusted domains.

- **Ensure compliance of existing and new applications:** AWS Firewall Manager automatically enforces mandatory security policies that you define across existing and newly created resources. The service discovers new resources as they are created across accounts. For example, if you are required to meet U.S. Department of Treasury's Office of Foreign Assets Control (OFAC) regulations, you can use Firewall Manager to deploy an AWS WAF rule to block traffic from embargoed countries across your Application Load Balancer, API Gateway, and Amazon CloudFront accounts. As new resources are created, they will automatically be brought under the policy scope.

AWS Cloud HSM

AWS CloudHSM is a cloud-based hardware security module (HSM) that enables you to easily generate and use your own encryption keys on the AWS Cloud. With CloudHSM, you can manage your own encryption keys using FIPS 140-2 Level 3 validated HSMs. CloudHSM offers you the flexibility to integrate with your applications using industry-standard APIs, such as PKCS#11, Java Cryptography Extensions (JCE), and Microsoft CryptoNG (CNG) libraries. See Figure 7.14.

CloudHSM is standards-compliant and enables you to export all of your keys to most other commercially available HSMs, subject to your configurations. It is a fully managed service that automates time-consuming administrative tasks for you, such as hardware provisioning, software patching, high-availability, and backups. CloudHSM also enables you to scale quickly by adding and removing HSM capacity on-demand, with no up-front costs.

AWS CloudHSM enables you to generate and use your encryption keys on a FIPS 140-2 Level 3 validated hardware. CloudHSM protects your keys with exclusive, single-tenant access to tamper-resistant HSM instances in your own Amazon Virtual Private Cloud (VPC).

You can configure AWS Key Management Service (KMS) to use your AWS CloudHSM cluster as a custom key store rather than the default KMS key store. With a KMS custom key store you benefit from the integration between KMS and AWS services that encrypt data while retaining control of the HSMs that protect your KMS master keys. KMS custom key store gives you the best of both worlds, combining single-tenant HSMs under your control with the ease of use and integration of AWS KMS.

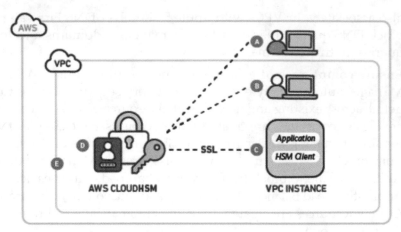

Figure 7.14: AWS Cloud HSM components

AWS CloudHSM runs in your own Amazon Virtual Private Cloud (VPC), enabling you to easily use your HSMs with applications running on your Amazon EC2 instances. With CloudHSM, you can use standard VPC security controls to manage access to your HSMs. Your applications connect to your HSMs using mutually authenticated SSL channels established by your HSM client software. Since your HSMs are located in Amazon datacenters near your EC2 instances, you can reduce the network latency between your applications and HSMs versus an on-premises HSM. The following components are illustrated in Figure 7.14.

- **A:** AWS manages the hardware security module (HSM) appliance, but does not have access to your keys
- **B:** You control and manage your own keys
- **C:** Application performance improves (due to close proximity with AWS workloads)
- **D:** Secure key storage in tamper-resistant hardware available in multiple Availability Zones (AZs)
- **E:** Your HSMs are in your Virtual Private Cloud (VPC) and isolated from other AWS networks

Separation of duties and role-based access control is inherent in the design of the AWS CloudHSM. AWS monitors the health and network availability of your HSMs but is not involved in the creation and management of the key material stored within your HSMs. You control the HSMs and the generation and use of your encryption keys.

AWS Secrets Manager

AWS Secrets Manager helps to protect secrets needed to access your applications, services, and IT resources. The service enables you to easily rotate, manage, and retrieve database credentials, API keys, and other secrets throughout their lifecycle. Users and applications retrieve secrets with a call to Secrets Manager APIs, eliminating the need to hardcode sensitive information in plain text. Secrets Manager offers secret rotation with built-in integration for Amazon RDS, Amazon Redshift, and Amazon DocumentDB. Also, the service is extensible to other types of secrets, including API keys and OAuth tokens. In addition, Secrets Manager enables you to control access to secrets using fine-grained permissions and audit secret rotation centrally for resources in the AWS Cloud, third-party services, and on-premises.

AWS Secrets Manager helps you meet your security and compliance requirements by enabling you to rotate secrets safely without the need for code deployments. For example, Secrets Manager offers built-in integration for Amazon RDS, Amazon Redshift, and Amazon DocumentDB and rotates these database credentials on your behalf automatically. You can customize Lambda functions to extend Secrets Manager rotation to other secret types, such as API keys and OAuth tokens. Retrieving the secret from Secrets Manager ensures that developers and applications are using the latest version of your secrets.

AWS Secrets Manager enables you to easily replicate secrets in multiple AWS regions to support your multi-region applications and disaster recovery scenarios. The multi-Region secrets feature abstracts the complexity of replicating and managing secrets across multiple regions, enabling you to simply access and read secrets where you need them.

AWS Key Management Service (KMS)

AWS Key Management Service (KMS) makes it easy to create and manage cryptographic keys and control their use across a wide range of AWS services and applications. AWS KMS is a secure and resilient service that uses hardware security modules that have been validated under FIPS 140-2, or are in the process of being validated, to protect your keys. AWS KMS is integrated with AWS CloudTrail to provide you with logs of all key usage to help meet your regulatory and compliance needs. The key features are as follows:

- **Encrypt data in your applications:** AWS KMS is integrated with the AWS Encryption SDK to enable you to use KMS-protected data encryption keys to encrypt locally within your applications. Using simple APIs, you can also build encryption and key management into your own applications wherever they run.

- **Digitally sign data:** AWS KMS enables you to perform digital signing operations using asymmetric key pairs to ensure the integrity of your data. Recipients of digitally signed data can verify the signatures whether they have an AWS account or not.

- **Centralized key management:** AWS KMS presents a single control point to manage keys and define policies consistently across integrated AWS services and your own applications. You can easily create, import, rotate, delete, and manage permissions on keys from the AWS Management Console or by using the AWS SDK or CLI.

- **Manage encryption for AWS services:** AWS KMS is integrated with AWS services to simplify using your keys to encrypt data across your AWS workloads. You choose the level of access control that you need, including the ability to share encrypted resources between accounts and services. KMS logs all use keys to AWS CloudTrail to give you an independent view of who accessed your encrypted data, including AWS services using them on your behalf.

AWS Certificate Manager

AWS Certificate Manager is a service that lets organizations easily provision, manage, and deploy public and private Secure Sockets Layer/Transport Layer Security (SSL/TLS) certificates for use with AWS services and your internal connected resources. SSL/TLS certificates are used to secure network communications and establish the identity of websites over the Internet as well as resources on private networks. AWS Certificate Manager removes the time-consuming manual process of purchasing, uploading, and renewing SSL/TLS certificates.

With AWS Certificate Manager, you can quickly request a certificate, deploy it on ACM-integrated AWS resources, such as Elastic Load Balancers, Amazon CloudFront distributions, and APIs on API Gateway, and let AWS Certificate Manager handle certificate renewals. It also enables you to create private certificates for your internal resources and manage the certificate lifecycle centrally. Public and private certificates provisioned through AWS Certificate Manager for use with ACM-integrated services are free. You pay only for the AWS resources you create to run your application. With AWS Certificate Manager Private Certificate Authority, you pay monthly for the operation of the private CA and for the private certificates you issue.

AWS Certificate Manager manages the renewal process for the certificates managed in ACM and used with ACM-integrated services, such as Elastic Load Balancing and API Gateway. ACM can automate renewal and deployment of these certificates. With ACM Private CA APIs, ACM enables you to automate creation and renewal of private certificates for on-premises resources, EC2 instances, and IoT devices.

AWS IoT Device Defender

AWS IoT Device Defender is a fully managed service that helps you secure your fleet of IoT devices. AWS IoT Device Defender continuously audits your IoT configurations to make sure that they aren't deviating from security best practices. A configuration is a set of technical controls you set to help keep information secure when devices are communicating with each other and the cloud. AWS IoT Device Defender makes it easy to maintain and enforce IoT configurations, such as ensuring device identity, authenticating and authorizing devices, and encrypting device data. AWS IoT Device Defender continuously audits the IoT configurations on your devices against a set of predefined security best practices. AWS IoT Device Defender sends an alert if there are any gaps in your IoT configuration that might create a security risk, such as identity certificates being shared across multiple devices or a device with a revoked identity certificate trying to connect to AWS IoT Core.

AWS IoT Device Defender also lets you continuously monitor security metrics from devices and AWS IoT Core for deviations from the expected behaviors for each device. You can define the appropriate behavior for your devices or use machine learning to model the regular device behavior based on historical data. If something doesn't look right according to defined behaviors or ML models, AWS IoT Device Defender pushes an alarm so you can take action to mitigate the issue. For example, traffic spikes in outbound traffic might indicate that a device is participating in a DDoS attack. AWS IoT Greengrass automatically integrates with AWS IoT Device Defender to provide security metrics from the devices for evaluation.

AWS IoT Device Defender can send alarms to the AWS IoT Console, Amazon CloudWatch, and Amazon SNS. If you determine that you need to take an action based on an alarm, you can use AWS IoT Device Defender built-in mitigation actions such as adding them to a group (for example, quarantine) or AWS IoT Device Management to take additional mitigation steps such as pushing security fixes.

Amazon Virtual Private Cloud

Amazon Virtual Private Cloud (Amazon VPC) is a service enabling the launch of AWS resources in a logically isolated virtual network that you define. You have complete control over your virtual networking environment, including selection of your own IP address range, creation of subnets, and configuration of route tables and network gateways. You can use both IPv4 and IPv6 for most resources in your virtual private cloud, helping to ensure secure and easy access to resources and applications.

As one of AWS's foundational services, Amazon VPC makes it easy to customize your VPC's network configuration. You can create a public-facing subnet for your web servers that have access to the Internet. It also lets you place your backend systems, such as databases or application servers, in a private-facing subnet with no Internet access. Amazon VPC lets you use multiple layers of security, including security groups and network access control lists, to help control access to Amazon EC2 instances in each subnet. The key features are as follows:

- **Secure and monitored network connections:** Amazon VPC provides advanced security features that allow you to perform inbound and outbound filtering at the instance and subnet level. Additionally, you can store data in Amazon S3 and restrict access so that it's only accessible from instances inside your VPC. Amazon VPC also has monitoring features that let you perform functions like out-of-band monitoring and inline traffic inspection, which help you screen and secure traffic.

- **Customizable virtual network:** Amazon VPC helps you control your virtual networking environment by letting you choose your own IP Address range, create your own subnets, and configure route tables to any available gateways. You can customize the network configuration by creating a public-facing subnet for your web servers that has access to the Internet. Place your backend systems, such as databases or application servers, in a private-facing subnet. With Amazon VPC, you can ensure that your virtual private cloud is configured to fit your specific business needs.

- **Host multi-tier web applications:** Host multi-tier web applications and strictly enforce access and security restrictions between your web servers, application servers, and databases. Launch web servers in a publicly accessible subnet while running your application servers and databases in private subnets. This will ensure that application servers and databases cannot be directly accessed from the Internet. You control access between the servers and subnets using inbound and outbound packet filtering provided by network access control lists and security groups. To create a VPC that supports this use case, you can select "VPC with Public and Private Subnets" in the Amazon VPC console wizard.

- **Back up and recover your data after a disaster:** By using Amazon VPC for disaster recovery, you receive all the benefits of a disaster recovery site at a fraction of the cost. You can periodically back up critical data from your datacenter to a small number of Amazon EC2 instances with Amazon Elastic Block Store (EBS) volumes, or import your virtual machine images to Amazon EC2. To ensure business continuity, Amazon VPC allows you to quickly launch replacement compute capacity in AWS. When the disaster is over, you can send your mission-critical data back to your datacenter and terminate the Amazon EC2 instances that you no longer need.

AWS PrivateLink

AWS PrivateLink provides private connectivity between VPCs, AWS services, and your on-premises networks, without exposing your traffic to the public Internet. AWS PrivateLink makes it easy to connect services across different accounts and VPCs to significantly simplify your network architecture.

Interface VPC endpoints, powered by AWS PrivateLink, connect you to services hosted by AWS Partners and supported solutions available in AWS Marketplace. By powering Gateway Load Balancer endpoints, AWS PrivateLink brings the same level of security and performance to your virtual network appliances or custom traffic inspection logic. The key features are as follows:

- **Simplify network management:** You can connect services across different accounts and Amazon VPCs, with no need for firewall rules, path definitions, or route tables. There is no need to configure an Internet gateway, VPC peering connection, or manage VPC Classless Inter-Domain Routing (CIDRs). Because AWS PrivateLink simplifies your network architecture, it is easier for you to manage your global network.

- **Accelerate your cloud migration:** More easily migrate traditional on-premises applications to SaaS offerings hosted in the cloud with AWS PrivateLink. Since your data does not get exposed to the Internet where it can be compromised, you can migrate and use more cloud services with the confidence that your traffic remains secure. You no longer have to choose between using a service and exposing your critical data to the Internet. You can find the latest controls in place to help customers stay complaint on our AWS Compliance Programs page. See Figure 7.15.

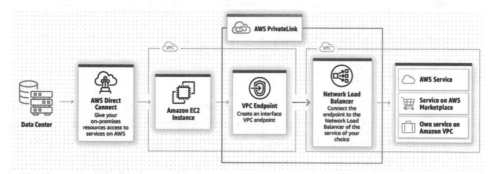

Figure 7.15: AWS PrivateLink components

AWS Direct Connect

AWS Direct Connect is a cloud service solution that makes it easy to establish a dedicated network connection from your premises to AWS. Using AWS Direct

Connect, you establish a private connection between AWS and your datacenter, office, or colocation environment. This can increase bandwidth throughput and provide a more consistent network experience than Internet-based connections.

AWS Direct Connect is compatible with all AWS services accessible over the Internet, and is available in speeds starting at 50 Mbps and scaling up to 100 Gbps. The key features are illustrated in Figure 7.16.

- **Protect data in transit:** Ensure communication between your datacenter, branch office, or colocation facility is protected by taking advantage of Direct Connect encryption options. 10 Gbps and 100 Gbps connections offer native IEEE 802.1AE (MACsec) point-to-point encryption at select locations. AWS Site-to-Site VPN connections using IPsec (IP security) are also available and can be used with any AWS Direct Connect connection.

- **Consistent network performance:** AWS Direct Connect links to all your AWS resources, transferring data directly from your datacenter, office, or colocation environment into and from AWS. With AWS Direct Connect, you choose the data that utilizes the private connection and how that data is routed, which can provide a more consistent network experience than Internet-based connections.

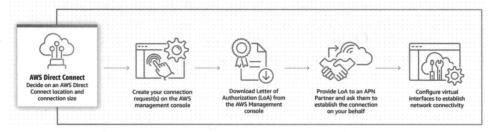

Figure 7.16: AWS Direct Connect components

AWS Transit Gateway

AWS Transit Gateway connects VPCs and on-premises networks through a central hub. This simplifies your network and puts an end to complex peering relationships. It acts as a cloud router, as each new connection is only made once. See Figure 7.17.

As you expand globally, inter-Region peering connects AWS Transit Gateways together using the AWS global network. Your data is automatically encrypted, and never travels over the public Internet. And, because of its central position,

AWS Transit Gateway Network Manager has a unique view over your entire network, even connecting to Software-Defined Wide Area Network (SD-WAN) devices. The key features are as follows:

- **Better visibility and control:** With AWS Transit Gateway Network Manager, you can easily monitor your Amazon VPCs and edge connections from a central console. Integrated with popular SD-WAN devices, AWS Transit Gateway Network Manager helps you quickly identify issues and react to events on your global network.

- **Flexible multicast:** AWS Transit Gateway multicast support distributes the same content to multiple specific destinations. This eliminates the need for expensive on-premises multicast networks and reduces the bandwidth needed for high-throughput applications such as video conferencing, media, or teleconferencing.

AWS Resource Access Manager

AWS Resource Access Manager (RAM) is a service that enables easy and secure sharing of AWS resources with any AWS account or within the AWS Organization. You can share AWS Transit Gateways, Subnets, AWS License Manager configurations, and Amazon Route 53 Resolver rules resources with RAM. See Figure 7.18.

Many organizations use multiple accounts to create administrative or billing isolation, and to limit the impact of errors. RAM eliminates the need to create duplicate resources in multiple accounts, reducing the operational overhead of managing those resources in every single account you own. You can create resources centrally in a multi-account environment, and use RAM to share those resources across accounts in three simple steps: create a Resource Share, specify resources, and specify accounts. RAM is available to you at no additional charge. The key features are as follows:

- **Reduce operational overhead:** Procure AWS resources centrally, and use RAM to share resources such as subnets or License Manager configurations with other accounts. This eliminates the need to provision duplicate resources in every account in a multi-account environment, reducing the operational overhead of managing those resources in every account.

- **Improve security and visibility:** RAM leverages existing policies and permissions set in AWS Identity and Access Management (IAM) to govern the consumption of shared resources. RAM also provides comprehensive visibility into shared resources to set alarms and visualize logs through integration with Amazon CloudWatch and AWS CloudTrail.

With AWS Transit Gateway

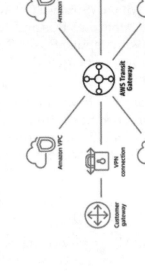

Without AWS Transit Gateway

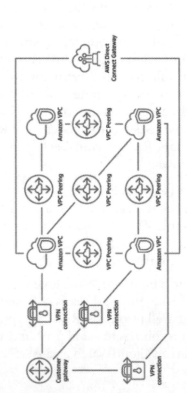

Figure 7.17: AWS Transit Gateway components

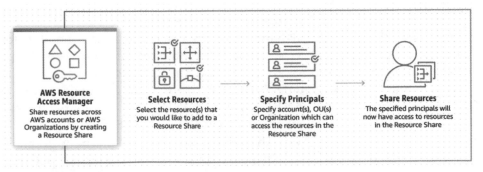

Figure 7.18: AWS Resource Access Manager components

The Detect and Respond Functions

Figure 7.19 shows the specific Detect and Respond capabilities available in the AWS Reference Architecture. Note that Amazon has aggregated the Detect and Respond capabilities under one heading due to the close alignment of their services.

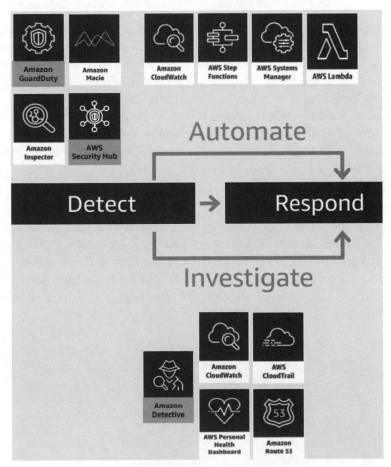

Figure 7.19: Detect components of the AWS Reference Architecture

GuardDuty

Amazon GuardDuty is a threat detection service that continuously monitors for malicious activity and unauthorized behavior to protect AWS accounts, workloads, and data stored in Amazon S3. With the cloud, the collection and aggregation of account and network activities is simplified, but it can be time-consuming for security teams to continuously analyze event log data for potential threats. With GuardDuty, you now have an intelligent and cost-effective option for continuous threat detection in AWS. The service uses machine learning, anomaly detection, and integrated threat intelligence to identify and prioritize potential threats. See Figure 7.20.

GuardDuty analyzes tens of billions of events across multiple AWS data sources, such as AWS CloudTrail event logs, Amazon VPC Flow Logs, and DNS logs. With a few clicks in the AWS Management Console, GuardDuty can be enabled with no software or hardware to deploy or maintain. By integrating with Amazon CloudWatch Events, GuardDuty alerts are actionable, easy to aggregate across multiple accounts, and straightforward to push into existing event management and workflow systems. The key features are as follows:

- **Comprehensive threat identification:** Amazon GuardDuty identifies threats by continuously monitoring the network activity, data access patterns, and account behavior within the AWS environment. GuardDuty comes integrated with up-to-date threat intelligence feeds from AWS, CrowdStrike, and Proofpoint. Threat intelligence coupled with machine learning and behavior models help you detect activity such as cryptocurrency mining, credential compromise behavior, unauthorized and unusual data access, communication with known command-and-control servers, or API calls from known malicious IPs.

- **Strengthens security through automation:** In addition to detecting threats, Amazon GuardDuty also makes it easy to automate how you respond to threats, reducing your remediation and recovery time. GuardDuty can perform automated remediation actions by leveraging Amazon CloudWatch events and AWS Lambda. GuardDuty security findings are informative and actionable for security operations. The findings include the affected resource's details and attacker information, such as IP address and geolocation.

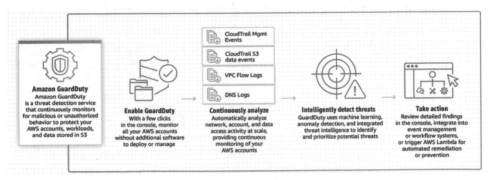

Figure 7.20: AWS GuardDuty components and architecture

Amazon GuardDuty gives you access to built-in detection techniques that are developed and optimized for the cloud. The detection algorithms are maintained and continuously improved on by AWS Security. The primary detection categories include:

- **Reconnaissance:** Activity suggesting reconnaissance by an attacker, such as unusual API activity, intra-VPC port scanning, unusual patterns of failed login requests, or unblocked port probing from a known bad IP.

- **Instance compromise:** Activity indicating an instance compromise, such as cryptocurrency mining, backdoor command and control (C&C) activity, malware using domain generation algorithms (DGA), outbound denial of service activity, unusually high volume of network traffic, unusual network protocols, outbound instance communication with a known malicious IP, temporary Amazon EC2 credentials used by an external IP address, and data exfiltration using DNS.

- **Account compromise:** Common patterns indicative of account compromise include API calls from an unusual geolocation or anonymizing proxy, attempts to disable AWS CloudTrail logging, changes that weaken the account password policy, unusual instance or infrastructure launches, infrastructure deployments in an unusual region, and API calls from known malicious IP addresses.

- **Bucket compromise:** Activity indicating a bucket compromise, such as suspicious data access patterns indicating credential misuse, unusual S3 API activity from a remote host, unauthorized S3 access from known malicious IP addresses, and API calls to retrieve data in S3 buckets from users that had no prior history of accessing the bucket or invoked from an unusual location. Amazon GuardDuty continuously monitors and analyzes AWS CloudTrail S3 data events (e.g., GetObject, ListObjects, and DeleteObject) to detect suspicious activity across all of your Amazon S3 buckets.

Amazon Detective

Amazon Detective makes it easy to analyze, investigate, and quickly identify the root cause of potential security issues or suspicious activities. Amazon Detective automatically collects log data from your AWS resources and uses machine learning, statistical analysis, and graph theory to build a linked set of data that enables you to easily conduct faster and more efficient security investigations.

AWS security services like Amazon GuardDuty, Amazon Macie, and AWS Security Hub as well as partner security products can be used to identify potential security issues, or findings. These services are really helpful in alerting you when something is wrong and pointing out where to go to fix it. But sometimes there might be a security finding where you need to dig a lot deeper and analyze more information to isolate the root cause and take action. Determining the root cause of security findings can be a complex process that often involves collecting and combining logs from many separate data sources, using extract, transform, and load (ETL) tools or custom scripting to organize the data, and then security analysts having to analyze the data and conduct lengthy investigations.

Amazon Detective simplifies this process by enabling your security teams to easily investigate and quickly get to the root cause of a finding. Amazon Detective can analyze trillions of events from multiple data sources such as Virtual Private Cloud (VPC) Flow Logs, AWS CloudTrail, and Amazon Guard-Duty, and automatically creates a unified, interactive view of your resources, users, and the interactions between them over time. With this unified view, you can visualize all the details and context in one place to identify the underlying reasons for the findings, drill down into relevant historical activities, and quickly determine the root cause.

Amazon Detective produces visualizations with the information you need to investigate and respond to security findings. It helps you answer questions like "is this normal for this role to have so many failed API calls?" or "is this spike in traffic from this instance expected?" without having to organize any data or develop, configure, or tune your own queries and algorithms. Amazon Detective maintains up to a year of aggregated data that shows changes in the type and volume of activity over a selected time window, and links those changes to security findings. See Figure 7.21.

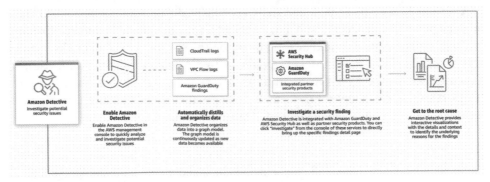

Figure 7.21: AWS Amazon Detective components

Amazon Macie

Amazon Macie is a fully managed data security and data privacy service that uses machine learning and pattern matching to discover and protect your sensitive data in AWS.

As organizations manage growing volumes of data, identifying and protecting their sensitive data at scale can become increasingly complex, expensive, and time-consuming. Amazon Macie automates the discovery of sensitive data at scale and lowers the cost of protecting your data. Macie automatically provides an inventory of Amazon S3 buckets including a list of unencrypted buckets, publicly accessible buckets, and buckets shared with AWS accounts outside those you have defined in AWS Organizations. Then, Macie applies machine learning and pattern matching techniques to the buckets you select to identify and alert you to sensitive data, such as personally identifiable information (PII). See Figure 7.22.

Macie's alerts, or findings, can be searched and filtered in the AWS Management Console and sent to Amazon EventBridge, formerly called Amazon CloudWatch Events, for easy integration with existing workflow or event management systems, or to be used in combination with AWS services, such as AWS Step Functions to take automated remediation actions. This can help you meet regulations, such as the Health Insurance Portability and Accountability Act (HIPAA) and General Data Privacy Regulation (GDPR). You can get started with Amazon Macie by leveraging the 30-day free trial for bucket evaluation.

Amazon Macie uses machine learning and pattern matching to cost efficiently discover sensitive data at scale. Macie automatically detects a large and growing list of sensitive data types, including personal identifiable information (PII) such as names, addresses, and credit card numbers. The service also allows you to define your own custom sensitive data types so you can discover and protect the sensitive data that may be unique to your business or use case.

Amazon Macie gives you constant visibility of the data security and data privacy of your data stored in Amazon S3. Macie automatically and continually evaluates all of your S3 buckets and alerts you to any unencrypted buckets, publicly accessible buckets, or buckets shared with AWS accounts outside those you have defined in the AWS Organizations. Macie provides native multi-account support so you can view your data security posture across your entire S3 environment from a single Macie administrator account.

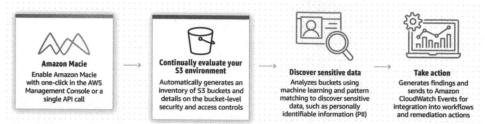

Figure 7.22: Amazon Macie components

Amazon Inspector

Amazon Inspector is an automated security assessment service that helps improve the security and compliance of applications deployed on AWS. Amazon Inspector automatically assesses applications for exposure, vulnerabilities, and deviations from best practices. After performing an assessment, Amazon Inspector produces a detailed list of security findings prioritized by level of severity. These findings can be reviewed directly or as part of detailed assessment reports that are available via the Amazon Inspector console or API.

Amazon Inspector security assessments help you check for unintended network accessibility of your Amazon EC2 instances and for vulnerabilities on those EC2 instances. Amazon Inspector assessments are offered to you as predefined rules packages mapped to common security best practices and vulnerability definitions. Examples of built-in rules include checking for access to your EC2 instances from the Internet, remote root login being enabled, or vulnerable software versions installed. These rules are regularly updated by AWS security researchers. The key features are as follows:

- Amazon Inspector helps you to identify security vulnerabilities as well as deviations from security best practices in applications, both before they are deployed, and while they are running in a production environment. This helps improve the overall security posture of your applications deployed on AWS.

- Amazon Inspector is an API-driven service that analyzes network configurations in your AWS account and uses an optional agent for visibility into your Amazon EC2 instances. This makes it easy for you to build Inspector assessments right into your existing DevOps process, decentralizing and automating vulnerability assessments, and empowering your development and operations teams to make security assessments an integral part of the deployment process.

■ Amazon Inspector allows you to define standards and best practices for your applications and validate adherence to these standards. This simplifies enforcement of your organization's security standards and best practices, and helps to proactively manage security issues before they impact your production application.

Amazon CloudTrail

AWS CloudTrail is a service that enables governance, compliance, operational auditing, and risk auditing of your AWS account. With CloudTrail, you can log, continuously monitor, and retain account activity related to actions across your AWS infrastructure. CloudTrail provides event history of your AWS account activity, including actions taken through the AWS Management Console, AWS SDKs, command-line tools, and other AWS services. This event history simplifies security analysis, resource change tracking, and troubleshooting. See Figure 7.23.

In addition, you can use CloudTrail to detect unusual activity in your AWS accounts. These capabilities help simplify operational analysis and troubleshooting. The key features are as follows:

■ **Visibility into user and resource activity:** AWS CloudTrail increases visibility into your user and resource activity by recording AWS Management Console actions and API calls. You can identify which users and accounts called AWS, the source IP address from which the calls were made, and when the calls occurred.

■ **Security analysis and troubleshooting:** With AWS CloudTrail, you can discover and troubleshoot security and operational issues by capturing a comprehensive history of changes that occurred in your AWS account within a specified period of time.

■ **Security automation:** AWS CloudTrail allows you to track and automatically respond to account activity threatening the security of your AWS resources. With Amazon CloudWatch Events integration, you can define workflows that execute when events that can result in security vulnerabilities are detected. For example, you can create a workflow to add a specific policy to an Amazon S3 bucket when CloudTrail logs an API call that makes that bucket public.

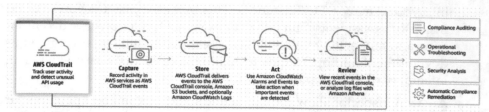

Figure 7.23: AWS CloudTrail components

Amazon CloudWatch

Amazon CloudWatch is a monitoring and observability service built for DevOps engineers, developers, site reliability engineers (SREs), and IT managers. CloudWatch provides you with data and actionable insights to monitor your applications, respond to system-wide performance changes, optimize resource utilization, and get a unified view of operational health. CloudWatch collects monitoring and operational data in the form of logs, metrics, and events, providing you with a unified view of AWS resources, applications, and services that run on AWS and on-premises servers. You can use CloudWatch to detect anomalous behavior in your environments, set alarms, visualize logs and metrics side by side, take automated actions, troubleshoot issues, and discover insights to keep your applications running smoothly. See Figure 7.24.

The key features are as follows:

- **Observability on a single platform across applications and infrastructure:** Modern applications such as those running on microservices architectures generate large volumes of data in the form of metrics, logs, and events. Amazon CloudWatch enables you to collect, access, and correlate this data on a single platform from across all your AWS resources, applications, and services that run on AWS and on-premises servers, helping you break down data silos so you can easily gain system-wide visibility and quickly resolve issues.

- **Improve operational performance and resource optimization:** Amazon CloudWatch enables you to set alarms and automate actions based on either predefined thresholds, or on machine learning algorithms that identify anomalous behavior in your metrics. For example, it can start Amazon EC2 Auto Scaling automatically, or stop an instance to reduce billing overages. You can also use CloudWatch Events for serverless to trigger workflows with services like AWS Lambda, Amazon SNS, and AWS CloudFormation.

- **Get operational visibility and insight:** To optimize performance and resource utilization, you need a unified operational view, real-time granular data, and historical reference. CloudWatch provides automatic dashboards, data with 1-second granularity, and up to 15 months of metrics storage and retention. You can also perform metric math on your data to derive operational and utilization insights; for example, you can aggregate usage across an entire fleet of EC2 instances.

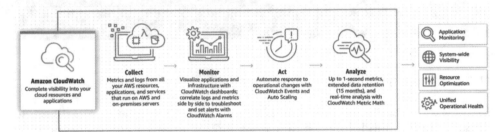

Figure 7.24: Amazon CloudWatch components and architecture

Amazon Lambda

AWS Lambda is a serverless compute service that lets you run code without provisioning or managing servers, creating workload-aware cluster scaling logic, maintaining event integrations, or managing runtimes. With Lambda, you can run code for virtually any type of application or backend service—all with zero administration. Just upload your code as a ZIP file or container image, and Lambda automatically and precisely allocates compute execution power and runs your code based on the incoming request or event, for any scale of traffic. You can set up your code to automatically trigger from 140 AWS services or call it directly from any web or mobile app. You can write Lambda functions in your favorite language (Node.js, Python, Go, Java, and more) and use both serverless and container tools, such as AWS SAM or Docker CLI, to build, test, and deploy your functions. See Figure 7.25.

The key features are as follows:

- **No servers to manage:** AWS Lambda automatically runs your code without requiring you to provision or manage infrastructure. Just write the code and upload it to Lambda either as a ZIP file or container image.

- **Continuous scaling:** AWS Lambda automatically scales your application by running code in response to each event. Your code runs in parallel and processes each trigger individually, scaling precisely with the size of the workload, from a few requests per day, to hundreds of thousands per second.

- **Consistent performance at any scale:** With AWS Lambda, you can optimize your code execution time by choosing the right memory size for your function. You can also keep your functions initialized and hyper-ready to respond within double-digit milliseconds by enabling provisioned concurrency.

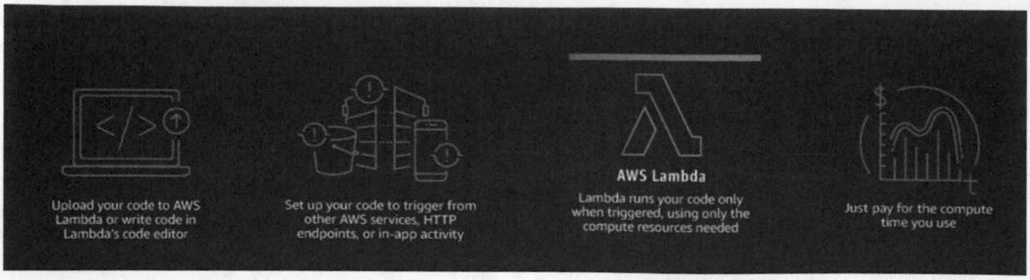

Figure 7.25: AWS Lambda components

AWS Step Functions

AWS Step Functions is a serverless function orchestrator that makes it easy to sequence AWS Lambda functions and multiple AWS services into business-critical applications. Through its visual interface, you can create and run a series of check-pointed and event-driven workflows that maintain the application state. The output of one step acts as an input to the next. Each step in your application executes in order, as defined by your business logic. See Figure 7.26.

Orchestrating a series of individual serverless applications, managing retries, and debugging failures can be challenging. As your distributed applications become more complex, the complexity of managing them also grows. With its built-in operational controls, Step Functions manages sequencing, error handling, retry logic, and state, removing a significant operational burden from your team. The key features are as follows:

- **Build and update apps quickly:** Lets you build visual workflows that enable fast translation of business requirements into technical requirements. You can build applications in a matter of minutes, and when needs change, you can swap or reorganize components without customizing any code.

- **Improve resiliency:** Manages state, checkpoints, and restarts for you to make sure that your application executes in order and as expected. Built-in try/catch, retry, and rollback capabilities deal with errors and exceptions automatically.

- **Write less code:** Manages the logic of your application for you, and implements basic primitives such as branching, parallel execution, and timeouts. This removes extra code that may be repeated in your microservices and functions.

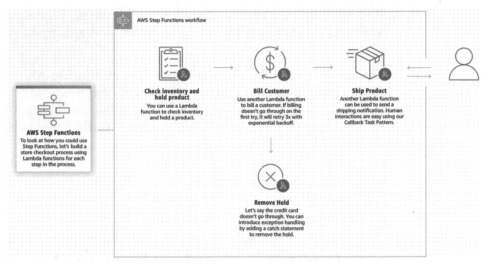

Figure 7.26: AWS Step Functions components and architecture

Amazon Route 53

Amazon Route 53 is a highly available and scalable cloud Domain Name System (DNS) web service. It is designed to give developers and businesses an extremely reliable and cost-effective way to route end users to Internet applications by translating names like `www.example.com` into the numeric IP addresses like 192.0.2.1 that computers use to connect to each other. Amazon Route 53 is fully compliant with IPv6 as well.

Amazon Route 53 effectively connects user requests to infrastructure running in AWS—such as Amazon EC2 instances, Elastic Load Balancing load balancers, or Amazon S3 buckets—and can also be used to route users to infrastructure outside of AWS. You can use Amazon Route 53 to configure DNS health checks to route traffic to healthy endpoints or to independently monitor the health of your application and its endpoints. Amazon Route 53 Traffic Flow makes it easy for you to manage traffic globally through a variety of routing types, including Latency Based Routing, Geo DNS, Geoproximity, and Weighted Round Robin—all of which can be combined with DNS Failover in order to enable a variety of low-latency, fault-tolerant architectures. Using Amazon Route 53 Traffic Flow's simple visual editor, you can easily manage how your end users are routed to your application's endpoints—whether in a single AWS region or distributed around the globe. Amazon Route 53 also offers Domain Name Registration—you can purchase and manage domain names such as example.com and Amazon Route 53 will automatically configure DNS settings for your domains. The key features are as follows:

- **Highly available and reliable:** Amazon Route 53 is built using AWS's highly available and reliable infrastructure. The distributed nature of our DNS servers helps ensure a consistent ability to route your end users to your application. Features such as Amazon Route 53 Traffic Flow help you improve reliability with easy configuration of failover to re-route your users to an alternate location if your primary application endpoint becomes unavailable. Amazon Route 53 is designed to provide the level of dependability required by important applications. Amazon Route 53 is backed by the Amazon Route 53 Service Level Agreement.

- **Flexible:** Amazon Route 53 Traffic Flow routes traffic based on multiple criteria, such as endpoint health, geographic location, and latency. You can configure multiple traffic policies and decide which policies are active at any given time. You can create and edit traffic policies using the simple visual editor in the Route 53 console, AWS SDKs, or the Route 53 API. Traffic Flow's versioning feature maintains a history of changes to your traffic policies, so you can easily roll back to a previous version using the console or API.

- **Simplifies the hybrid cloud:** Amazon Route 53 Resolver provides recursive DNS for your Amazon VPC and on-premises networks over AWS Direct Connect or AWS Managed VPN.

AWS Personal Health Dashboard

AWS Personal Health Dashboard provides alerts and remediation guidance when AWS is experiencing events that may impact you. While the Service Health Dashboard displays the general status of AWS services, Personal Health Dashboard gives you a personalized view into the performance and availability of the AWS services underlying your AWS resources.

The dashboard displays relevant and timely information to help you manage events in progress, and provides proactive notification to help you plan for scheduled activities. With Personal Health Dashboard, alerts are triggered by changes in the health of AWS resources, giving you event visibility and guidance to help quickly diagnose and resolve issues. The key features are as follows:

- **Personalized view of service health:** Gives you a personalized view of the status of the AWS services that power your applications, enabling you to quickly see when AWS is experiencing issues that may impact you. For example, in the event of a lost Amazon Elastic Block Store (EBS) volume associated with one of your Amazon EC2 instances, you would gain quick visibility into the status of the specific service you are using, helping save precious time troubleshooting to determine root cause.

- **Proactive notifications:** Provides forward-looking notifications, and you can set up alerts across multiple channels, including email and mobile notifications, so you receive timely and relevant information to help plan for scheduled changes that may affect you. In the event of AWS hardware maintenance activities that may impact one of your Amazon EC2 instances, for example, you would receive an alert with information to help you plan for, and proactively address any issues associated with the upcoming change.

- **Aggregates health events across AWS Organizations:** If you use AWS Organizations, AWS Health allows you to aggregate notifications from all accounts in your organization. This provides centralized and real-time access to all AWS Health events posted to individual accounts in your organization, including operational issues, scheduled maintenance, and account notifications.

The Recover Functions

This section discusses the Recover capability of the AWS Reference Architecture, as illustrated in Figure 7.27.

Figure 7.27: Recover components of the AWS Reference Architecture

Amazon Glacier

Amazon S3 Glacier and S3 Glacier Deep Archive are secure, durable, and extremely low-cost Amazon S3 cloud storage classes for data archiving and long-term backup. They are designed to deliver 99.999999999% durability, and provide comprehensive security and compliance capabilities that can help meet even the most stringent regulatory requirements. To keep costs low yet suitable for varying retrieval needs, Amazon S3 Glacier provides three options for access to archives, from a few minutes to several hours, and S3 Glacier Deep Archive provides two access options ranging from 12 to 48 hours.

The Amazon S3 Glacier storage class provides three retrieval options to fit your use case. Expedited retrievals typically return data in 1–5 minutes, and are great for Active Archive use cases. Standard retrievals typically complete within 3–5 hours, and work well for less time-sensitive needs like backup data, media editing, or long-term analytics. Bulk retrievals are the lowest-cost retrieval option, returning large amounts of data within 5–12 hours. The Amazon S3 Glacier Deep Archive storage class provides two retrieval options ranging from 12–48 hours.

In addition to integration with most AWS services, Amazon S3 object storage services include tens of thousands of consulting, systems integrator, and independent software vendor partners, with more joining every month. AWS Partner Network partners have adapted their services and software to work with Amazon S3 storage classes for solutions like Backup & Recovery, Archiving, and Disaster Recovery. No other cloud provider has more partners with solutions that are pre-integrated to work with their service.

AWS CloudFormation

AWS CloudFormation gives you an easy way to model a collection of related AWS and third-party resources, provision them quickly and consistently, and manage them throughout their lifecycles, by treating infrastructure as code. A CloudFormation template describes your desired resources and their dependencies so you can launch and configure them together as a stack. You can use a template to create, update, and delete an entire stack as a single unit, as often as you need to, instead of managing resources individually. You can manage and provision stacks across multiple AWS accounts and AWS Regions (see Figure 7.28). The key features are as follows:

- **Automate best practices:** With CloudFormation, you can apply DevOps and GitOps best practices using widely adopted processes such as starting with a Git repository and deploying through a CI/CD pipeline. You can also simplify auditing changes and trigger automated deployments with pipeline integrations such as GitHub Actions and AWS CodePipeline.

- **Scale your infrastructure worldwide:** Manage resource scaling by sharing CloudFormation templates to be used across your organization, to meet safety, compliance, and configuration standards across all AWS accounts and regions. Templates and parameters enable easy scaling so you can share best practices and company policies. Additionally, CloudFormation StackSets enables you to create, update, or delete stacks across multiple AWS accounts and Regions, with a single operation.

- **Manage third-party and private resources:** Model, provision, and manage third-party application resources (such as monitoring, team productivity, incident management, CI/CD, and version control applications) alongside your AWS resources. Use the open source CloudFormation CLI to build your own CloudFormation resource providers—native AWS types published as open source.

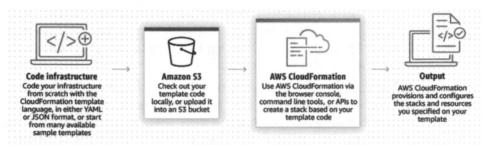

Figure 7.28: AWS CloudFormation components

CloudEndure Disaster Recovery

IT disasters such as datacenter failures, server corruptions, or cyber-attacks can not only disrupt businesses, but also cause data loss, impact your revenue, and damage your reputation. CloudEndure Disaster Recovery minimizes downtime and data loss by providing fast, reliable recovery of physical, virtual, and cloud-based servers into AWS Cloud, including public regions, AWS GovCloud (US), and AWS Outposts.

You can use CloudEndure Disaster Recovery to protect your most critical databases, including Oracle, MySQL, and SQL Server, as well as enterprise applications such as SAP.

CloudEndure Disaster Recovery continuously replicates your machines (including operating system, system state configuration, databases, applications, and files) into a low-cost staging area in your target AWS account and preferred Region. In the case of a disaster, you can instruct CloudEndure Disaster Recovery to automatically launch thousands of your machines in their fully provisioned state in minutes.

By replicating your machines into a low-cost staging area while still being able to launch fully provisioned machines within minutes, CloudEndure Disaster Recovery can significantly reduce the cost of your disaster recovery infrastructure. The key features are as follows:

- **Reduce downtime and protect against data loss:** Unlike snapshot-based solutions that update target locations at distinct, infrequent intervals, CloudEndure Disaster Recovery provides asynchronous, continuous replication. This enables Recovery Point Objectives (RPOs) of seconds. Automated machine conversion and orchestration enable Recovery Time Objectives (RTOs) of minutes. You can meet these stringent recovery objectives even for your largest write-intensive workloads.

- **Protect enterprise applications and databases with a single tool:** CloudEndure Disaster Recovery allows you to achieve business continuity for your most critical databases, including Oracle, MySQL, and SQL Server, as well as enterprise applications such as SAP. This means that you don't need to purchase multiple application-specific replication tools because CloudEndure Disaster Recovery replicates all applications and databases that run on supported operating systems.

- **Protect your data from ransomware attacks:** In the event of a ransomware attack, use CloudEndure Disaster Recovery to launch an unencrypted, uncorrupted version of your servers on your target AWS Region. CloudEndure Disaster Recovery provides point-in-time recovery, which enables failback to a recovery point from before the attack. This minimizes data loss and enables the quick return to normal operations.

AWS OpsWorks

AWS OpsWorks is a configuration management service that provides managed instances of Chef and Puppet. Chef and Puppet are automation platforms that allow you to use code to automate the configurations of your servers. OpsWorks lets you use Chef and Puppet to automate how servers are configured, deployed, and managed across your Amazon EC2 instances or on-premises compute environments. OpsWorks has three offerings—AWS OpsWorks for Chef Automate, AWS OpsWorks for Puppet Enterprise, and AWS OpsWorks Stacks. The key features are as follows:

- **AWS OpsWorks for Chef Automate:** AWS OpsWorks for Chef Automate is a fully managed configuration management service that hosts Chef Automate, a suite of automation tools from Chef for configuration management, compliance and security, and continuous deployment. OpsWorks also maintains your Chef server by automatically patching, updating, and backing up your server. OpsWorks eliminates the need to operate your own configuration management systems or worry about maintaining its infrastructure. OpsWorks gives you access to all of the Chef Automate features, such as configuration and compliance management, which you manage through the Chef console or command-line tools like Knife. It also works seamlessly with your existing Chef cookbooks.

■ **AWS OpsWorks for Puppet Enterprise:** AWS OpsWorks for Puppet Enterprise is a fully managed configuration management service that hosts Puppet Enterprise, a set of automation tools from Puppet for infrastructure and application management. OpsWorks also maintains your Puppet master server by automatically patching, updating, and backing up your server. OpsWorks eliminates the need to operate your own configuration management systems or worry about maintaining its infrastructure. OpsWorks gives you access to all of the Puppet Enterprise features, which you manage through the Puppet console. It also works seamlessly with your existing Puppet code.

Summary

■ AWS aligns its threat-hunting capabilities to simulate the majority of the MITRE ATT&CK Framework TTPs.

■ The Identify function is addressed by services such as security hub, AWS config, AWS organization, AWS Control Tower, AWS Trusted Advisor, AWS Well-Architected Tool, AWS Services Catalog, and AWS Systems Manager.

■ The Protect function is addressed by key services such as AWS Identity & Access Management, AWS Single Sign-On, AWS Shield, AWS Web Application Firewall, AWS Cloud HSM, AWS Secrets Manager, AWS Certificate Manager, AWS IoT Device Defender, and AWS Virtual Private Cloud.

■ The Detect and Respond functions are addressed by GuardDuty, Amazon Detective, Amazon Macie, Amazon Inspector, Amazon CloudTrail, Amazon CloudWatch, Amazon Lambda, and AWS Route 53.

■ Amazon GuardDuty and Inspector are key detection services that leverage machine learning and artificial intelligence. They are very beneficial to organizations' threat-hunting capability.

■ Amazon Macie provides a key data classification capability that prevents many threats to organizations. It can be configured to have automatic detection or manual detection capability.

■ The Recovery function is addressed by Amazon Glacier, AWS CloudFormation, CloudEndure Disaster Recovery, and AWS OpsWorks.

The Future

In This Part

Chapter 8: Threat Hunting in Other Cloud Providers
Chapter 9: The Future of Threat Hunting

Threat Hunting in Other Cloud Providers

What's In This Chapter

- Overview of threat-hunting capabilities by other key cloud platform providers, including:
  - Google cloud
  - IBM cloud
  - Oracle cloud
  - Alibaba cloud

The objective of this chapter is to explore the current threat-hunting capabilities in other leading cloud service providers (CSPs) such as Google, IBM, Oracle, and Alibaba.

There are three main service models of cloud computing—Infrastructure as a Service (IaaS), Platform as a Service (PaaS), and Software as a Service (SaaS). There are clear differences between the three and what they can offer a business in terms of storage and resource pooling, but they can also interact with each other to form one comprehensive model of cloud computing.

> **CAUTION**   Note that not all threat-hunting CSP capabilities are created equal. The primary rationale behind this is the underlying business model of CSP's value proposition (i.e., does the CSP offer IaaS, PaaS, or SaaS, or combinations of these?). The threat vectors that apply to SaaS, PaaS, and IaaS are very different. Hence, the defense mechanisms, tools, and approaches to combat these threats are also different.

Cloud platform providers of IaaS, PaaS, and SaaS have built or adopted threat-hunting capabilities to protect their customer's data residing on their platform. We went deeper into Microsoft Azure and AWS threat-hunting capabilities in previous chapters. Let's take a look at threat-hunting capabilities of some of the other leading cloud computing platform providers who offer all three main cloud service models—IaaS, PaaS, and SaaS—to enterprises and small to medium businesses. Note that key SaaS cloud capabilities such as Salesforce are not addressed, since the focus is on "pure cloud platform" providers who provide all IaaS, PaaS, and SaaS.

The Google Cloud Platform

The Google Cloud Platform is a suite of cloud computing services that runs on the same infrastructure that Google uses internally for its end-user products, such as Google Search, Gmail, file storage, and YouTube. Alongside a set of management tools, it provides a series of modular cloud services, including computing, data storage, data analytics, and machine learning.

Google's threat-hunting capability centers on the Chronicle platform (Figure 8.1). Chronicle is a cloud service, built as a specialized layer on top of core Google infrastructure, designed for enterprises to privately retain, analyze, and search the massive amounts of security and network telemetry they generate. Chronicle normalizes, indexes, correlates, and analyzes the data to provide instant analysis and context on risky activity. Chronicle is a global security telemetry platform for detection, investigation, and threat hunting within your enterprise network.

The key services that Chronicle provides include the following:

- **Threat Investigation:** VirusTotal Enterprise owns an extensive malware intelligence database that can link and visualize malware relationships across external files, domains, and internal assets. Chronicle takes advantage of the largest malware database in the world to provide enterprises with its threat investigation services. Chronicle's threat investigation services capabilities also include continuous automation and speed to ensure that threats are discovered in near real-time.

- **Threat Hunting and Detection:** Reducing false positives and eliminating the use of triaging in detecting threats speeds up the threat-hunting and detection processes for security analysts. Chronicle helps achieve this

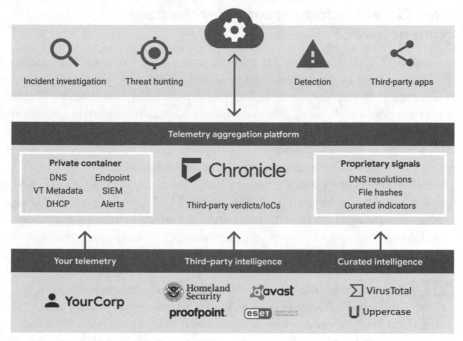

Figure 8.1: Chronicle overview

through retroactive correlation of enterprise security telemetry with backing from threat intelligence sources such as Avast and AVG. This process reduces the duration of security analysis by ensuring real threats are detected and providing a comprehensive analysis of discovered threats.

▪ **Security Analytics:** The Chronicle platform is capable of ingesting large datasets, indexing, correlating, and providing enterprise-grade security analyses in seconds. The high speed at which Chronicle executes security analytics means that teams can upload their security telemetry onto the platform and start analyzing it within seconds.

▪ **Security Operations on GCP with Security Command Center:** Security Command Center offers a single platform to aggregate and manage security findings on GCP. It was designed by Google to provide visibility into how resources are configured as well as the ability to reliably detect threats in real time. Security misconfigurations are often in and of themselves vulnerabilities. Therefore, monitoring for misconfigurations is one of its core capabilities in addition to monitoring for common web application vulnerabilities. Security Command Center offers near-real-time visibility into GCP resources and policies, as well as the detection of threats and compliance violations based on industry standards and benchmarks. You should consider using this service if you want to obtain a centralized view of your security and data attack surface.

Google Cloud Platform Security Architecture alignment to NIST

Google's NIST Cybersecurity Framework and Google Cloud whitepaper at `https://services.google.com/fh/files/misc/gcp_nist_cybersecurity_framework.pdf` mentions that NIST CSF complements, but does not replace, an organization's risk management process and cybersecurity program. It continues to elaborate that cloud computing allows organizations to leverage a shared security model (discussed in Chapters 4 and 6). Data security is still the responsibility of the organization's reference architecture.

The following section outlines categories and subcategories of the NIST Cybersecurity Framework. Corresponding to each NIST CSF category and subcategory are recommendations on how to meet and implement these requirements in Google Cloud. Organizations can leverage some or all of the suggested components to define, enforce, and manage cloud security and compliance.

> **NOTE** Note that some GCP services offer capability across multiple NIST pillars (i.e., the same service will accommodate multiple functions such as protect, detect, respond, etc.). We also provide a summary of the services capability in the following sections and provide further references for readers to be acquainted with more details. Unfortunately, this chapter acts as a summary and the objective is not to discuss CGP capability in detail, similar to Chapters 4 and 6 .

The Identify Function

The data, personnel, devices, systems, and facilities that enable the organization to achieve business purposes are identified and managed consistent with their relative importance to organizational objectives and the organization's risk strategy.

- **Cloud Identity:** Google's Identity as a Service (IDaaS). Manage users, groups, devices, and applications across your organization. `https://cloud.google.com/identity/`

- **Google Admin Console:** Manage and add users, devices, data regions, and security settings. `https://gsuite.google.com/products/admin/`

- **Cloud Resource Manager:** Get an org-wide snapshot of your GCP resources and policies. `https://cloud.google.com/resource-manager/docs/cloud-asset-inventory/overview`

- **Forseti Security:** Cloud Asset API to collect and store information about your GCP resources. (`https://forsetisecurity.org/docs/latest/configure/inventory/index.html`

- **Cloud Security Command Center (CSCC):** Enhance your security posture with centralized asset discovery and inventory, sensitive data identification, app vulnerability detection, access control monitoring, anomaly detection, and input from third-party security tools with real-time notifications. `https://cloud.google.com/security-command-center/`

- **Cloud Private Catalog:** Build out and manage a cloud catalog to manage your cloud resources and make them easily discoverable. `https://cloud.google.com/private-catalog/`

- **Cloud Data Catalog:** Fully managed metadata discovery and management platform. Helps organizations quickly discover, manage, secure, and understand their data assets. `https://cloud.google.com/data-catalog/`

- **Identity Platform:** Add Google-grade identity and access management to your apps. Identity Platform is a customer identity and access management (CIAM) platform that helps organizations add identity and access management functionality to their applications. `https://cloud.google.com/identity-cp/`

- **Cloud Identity & Access Management:** Maintain fine-grained control over who has access to what cloud resources. Define access roles and permissions while enforcing separation of duties and least privilege. `https://cloud.google.com/iam/`

- **Google Cloud Adoption Framework:** Determine your organization's cloud readiness and strategically map out your journey to the cloud. `https://cloud.google.com/adoption-framework/`

- **Professional Services:** Advisory capability to engage business leaders and users on innovating daily business processes with Google. `https://services.google.com/fh/files/misc/transformation_advisory.pdf`

- **Google's Security & Trust Center:** Understand and leverage Google's ISO, SOC, PCI, HIPAA, FedRAMP, FIPS GDPR, and other compliance standards, regulations, and certifications. `https://cloud.google.com/sec`

- **Cloud Security Scanner:** Automatically scan App Engine applications for common vulnerabilities such as XXS, flash injection, mixed HTTP(S) content, outdated and insecure libraries. `https://cloud.google.com/security-scanner/`

- **Container Registry Vulnerability Scanner:** Scan container images stored in Container Registry for common vulnerabilities. `https://cloud.google.com/container-registry/docs/container-analysis`

- **Cloud Armor:** Protect your infrastructure and web applications from Distributed Denial of Service (DDoS) attacks. `https://cloud.google.com/armor/`

- **Phishing Protection:** Quickly report unsafe URLs to Google Safe Browsing and view status in Cloud Security Command Center. `https://cloud .google.com/phishing-protection/`

The Protect Function

Access to physical and logical assets and associated facilities is limited to authorized users, processes, and devices, and is managed consistent with the assessed risk of unauthorized access to authorized activities and transactions.

- **Cloud Identity & Access Management:** Maintain fine-grained control over who has access to what cloud resources. Define access roles and permissions while enforcing separation of duties and least privilege. `https://cloud.google.com/iam/`

- **Cloud Identity Google's Identity as a Service (IDaaS):** Manage users, groups, devices, and applications across your organization. Also implements MFA and SSO. `https://cloud.google.com/identity/`

- **Google Admin Console:** Manage and add users, devices, data regions and security settings. `https://gsuite.google.com/products/admin/`

- **VPC Service Controls:** Define a security perimeter around specific GCP resources to help mitigate data exfiltration risks. `https://cloud.google .com/vpc-service-controls/`

- **Cloud Identity Aware Proxy:** Build an enterprise security model to control access to your applications and VMs. Verify user identities and access request context to determine if users should be allowed access to resources. `https://cloud.google.com/iap/`

- **Forseti Security:** Systematically monitor your GCP resources, create and enforce rule-based security policies. Codify your security stance to maintain compliance and governance. `https://forsetisecurity.org/about/`

- **Context Aware Access:** Manage access to apps and infrastructure based on a user's identity and context. `https://cloud.google.com/ context-aware-access/`

- **Identity Platform:** Add Google-grade identity and access management to your apps. Identity Platform is a customer identity and access management (CIAM) platform that helps organizations add identity and access management functionality to their applications. `https://cloud .google.com/identity-cp/`

- **Cloud VPC:** Manage network functionality and segmentation of cloud resources. Leverage Cloud Router, Cloud VPN, Firewalls, Routes, VPC Flow Logs, Shared VPC, and VPC peering for more granular network security. `https://cloud.google.com/vpc/`

- **Cloud Resource Manager:** Manage and separate GCP resource hierarchy across your organization, folders, and projects. `https://cloud.google.com/resource-manager/`

- **Google Cloud Training:** Leverage on-demand Coursera courses, hands-on qwiklabs, and Google or Partner-led classroom instruction to train your organization. `https://cloud.google.com/training/`

- **Google Cloud Adoption Framework:** Determine your organization's cloud readiness and strategically map out your journey to the cloud. `https://cloud.google.com/adoption-framework/`

- **Professional Services:** Advisory capability to engage business leaders and users on innovating daily business processes with Google. `https://services.google.com/fh/files/misc/transformation_advisory.pdf`

- **Google Encryption at Rest:** All data in Google is encrypted at rest by default using envelope encryption. `https://cloud.google.com/security/encryption-at-rest/`

- **Cloud Key Management Service:** Manage, generate, use, rotate, and destroy AES256, RSA 2048, RSA 3072, RSA 4096, EC P256, and EC P384 cryptographic keys on Google Cloud. `https://cloud.google.com/kms/`

- **Customer Supplied Encryption Keys (CSEKs):** In addition to Google's default encryption, supply your own AES256 encryption keys to encrypt GCP data. `https://cloud.google.com/storage/docs/encryption/customer-supplied-keys`

- **Cloud HSM:** Protect your encryption keys in the cloud using a fully hosted, FIPS 140-2 Level 3 compliant hardware security model. `https://cloud.google.com/hsm/`

- **Google Encryption in Transit:** Data encrypted in transit automatically at layer 7 and layer 3/4 in Google Cloud via TLS. `https://cloud.google.com/security/encryption-in-transit/`

- **GCP Quotas:** Set, enforce, and request quotas on resource usage to regulate how much of a particular GCP resource a project can use. `https://cloud.google.com/docs/quota`

- **Autoscaling:** Use GCE managed instance groups or managed compute services like Google App Engine to automatically scale capacity based on need or Cloud Monitoring metrics. `https://cloud.google.com/compute/docs/autoscaler/`

- **Cloud Data Loss Prevention:** Configure DLP to automatically discover, classify, and redact sensitive data in Google Cloud & G Suite. `https://cloud.google.com/dlp/`

- **Phishing Protection:** Quickly report unsafe URLs to Google Safe Browsing and view status in Cloud Security Command Center. `https://cloud.google.com/phishing-protection/`

- **Access Approval API:** Allows you to explicitly approve access to your data or configurations on GCP before it happens. `https://cloud.google.com/access-approval/docs/overview`

- **VPC Service:** Controls define a security perimeter around specific GCP resources to help mitigate data exfiltration risks. `https://cloud.google.com/vpc-service-controls/`

- **Titan Security Key:** Prevent account hacks, phishing attacks, and enforce MFA/2SV using Titan Security Keys. `https://cloud.google.com/titan-security-key/`

- **Shielded VMs:** Leverage hardened virtual machines on GCP that defend against rootkits, botkits, protect against remote attacks, privilege escalation, and malicious insiders. `https://cloud.google.com/shielded-vm/`

- **reCAPTCHA:** Protect your website from fraudulent activity, spam, and abuse. `https://cloud.google.com/recaptcha-enterprise/`

- **Binary Authorization:** Deploy-time security controls to ensure that only trusted container images are deployed on Kubernetes. Requires images to be signed by trusted authorities during development and enforces signature validation during deployment. `https://cloud.google.com/binary-authorization/`

The Detect Function

Anomalous activity is detected and the potential impact of events is understood.

- **Cloud VPC:** Manage network functionality and segmentation of cloud resources. Leverage Cloud Router, Cloud VPN, Firewalls, Routes, VPC Flow Logs, Shared VPC, and VPC peering for more granular network security. `https://cloud.google.com/vpc/`

- **Traffic Director:** Enterprise-ready traffic management for open service mesh. Delivers configuration and traffic control intelligence to sidecar service proxies. `https://cloud.google.com/traffic-director/`

- **VPC Service Controls:** Define a security perimeter around specific GCP resources to help mitigate data exfiltration risks. `https://cloud.google.com/vpc-service-controls/`

- **Cloud Armor:** Protect your infrastructure and web applications from Distributed Denial of Service (DDoS) attacks. `https://cloud.google.com/armor/`

- **G Suite Phishing & Malware Protection:** Advanced phishing and malware protection. Place emails in quarantine, protect against anomalous attachments, protect Google Groups from inbound email spoofing. `https:// support.google.com/a/answer/7577854`

- **Network Telemetry:** Enable firewall logging, VPC flow logs, performance monitoring and metrics, and log exports to keep your networks and services secure. `https://cloud.google.com/network-telemetry/`

- **Incident Response Management:** Leverage IRM with Monitoring to identify, manage, investigate, and resolve incidents. `https://cloud. google.com/incident-response/docs/`

- **Cloud Operations Suite:** Store, search, analyze, monitor, and alert on log data and events in Google Cloud. Includes error reporting, production application profiling, application tracing, alerting, debugging, and third-party integrations. `https://cloud.google.com/stackdriver/`

- **Cloud Security Scanner:** Automatically scan App Engine, Compute Engine, and Kubernetes Engine applications for common vulnerabilities such as XXS, flash injection, mixed HTTP(S) content, outdated and insecure libraries. `https://cloud.google.com/security-scanner/`

- **Container Registry:** Scan container images stored in Container Registry for common vulnerabilities. `https://cloud.google.com/container-registry/docs/container-analysis`

- **Cloud Security Command Center (CSCC):** Enhance your security posture with centralized asset discovery and inventory, sensitive data identification, app vulnerability detection, access control monitoring, anomaly detection, and input from third-party security tools with real-time notifications. `https://cloud.google.com/security-command-center/`

- **G Suite Security Center:** Actionable security insights for G Suite. Protect your organization with security analytics and best practice recommendations from Google. Get insights into external file sharing, visibility into spam and malware targeting users within your organization. `https:// gsuite.google.com/products/admin/security-center/`

- **Android Enterprise:** Provides multiple layers of security to prevent intrusions including built-in Titan Security Keys, Google Play Protect, Management APIs, hardened OS platform, and dedicated hardware. `https://www. android.com/enterprise/security/ https://blog.google/technology/ safety-security/your-android-phone-is-a-security-key/`

- **Google's Security & Trust Center:** Understand and leverage Google's ISO, SOC, PCI, HIPAA, FedRAMP, FIPS GDPR, and other compliance standards, regulations, and certifications. `https://cloud.google.com/sec`

■ **Event Threat Detection:** Uncover security threats in Google Cloud Platform environments. `https://cloud.google.com/event-threat-detection/`

■ **Cloud Pub/Sub:** Stream analytics, events, notifications, and messages. `https://cloud.google.com/pubsub/`

■ **Cloud Functions:** Event-driven serverless compute platform. `https://cloud.google.com/functions/`

■ **Policy Intelligence:** Smart access control for your GCP resources. Helps enterprises understand and manage their policies to reduce risk. `https://cloud.google.com/policy-intelligence/`

The Respond Function

Response processes and procedures are executed and maintained, to ensure response to detected cybersecurity incidents.

■ **Incident Response Management:** Leverage IRM with Monitoring to identify, manage, investigate, and resolve incidents. `https://cloud.google.com/incident-response/docs/`

■ **G Suite Security Center:** Actionable security insights for G Suite. Protect your organization with security analytics and best practice recommendations from Google. Get insights into external file sharing, visibility into spam and malware targeting users within your organization. `https://gsuite.google.com/products/admin/security-center/`

■ **Cloud Security Command Center (CSCC):** Enhance your security posture with centralized asset discovery and inventory, sensitive data identification, app vulnerability detection, access control monitoring, anomaly detection, and input from third-party security tools with real-time notifications. `https://cloud.google.com/security-command-center/`

■ **Cloud Identity & Access Management:** Maintain fine-grained control over who has access to what cloud resources. Define access roles & permissions while enforcing separation of duties and least privilege. `https://cloud.google.com/iam/`

■ **Cloud Identity Google's Identity as a Service (IDaaS):** Manage users, groups, devices, and applications across your organization. `https://cloud.google.com/identity/`

■ **Google Admin Console:** Manage and add users, devices, data regions and security settings. `https://gsuite.google.com/products/admin/`

■ **Identity Platform:** Add Google-grade identity and access management to your apps. Identity Platform is a customer identity and access management (CIAM) platform that helps organizations add identity and

access management functionality to their applications. `https://cloud`
`.google.com/identity-cp/`

■ **Cloud Operations Suite:** Store, search, analyze, monitor, and alert on log
data and events in Google Cloud. Includes error reporting, production
application profiling, application tracing, alerting, debugging, and third-
party integrations. `https://cloud.google.com/stackdriver/`

■ **Log Exports:** Export logs to GCS for storage and archival, to BigQuery
for analysis, or to external systems for broader integration and analysis.
`https://cloud.google.com/logging/docs/export/`

■ **BigQuery:** Serverless, highly scalable, and cost-effective cloud data ware-
house with an in-memory BI Engine and machine learning built in. Analyze
all your batch and streaming data. `https://cloud.google.com/`
`bigquery/`

■ **Event Threat:** Event Threat Detection to uncover security threats in Google
Cloud Platform environments. `https://cloud.google.com/`
`event-threat-detection/`

■ **Forseti Security:** Systematically monitor your GCP resources, create and
enforce rule-based security policies. Codify your security stance to maintain compliance and governance. `https://forsetisecurity.org/about/`

■ **Cloud Security Scanner:** Automatically scan App Engine, Compute Engine,
and Kubernetes Engine applications for common vulnerabilities such as
XXS, flash injection, mixed HTTP(S) content, outdated, and insecure
libraries. `https://cloud.google.com/security-scanner/`

■ **Cloud Armor:** Protect your infrastructure and web applications from
Distributed Denial of Service (DDoS) attacks. `https://cloud.google.`
`com/armor/`

■ **Container Registry Vulnerability Scanner:** Scan container images stored
in Container Registry for common vulnerabilities. `https://cloud.google.`
`com/container-registry/docs/container-analysis`

■ **Phishing Protection:** Quickly report unsafe URLs to Google Safe Browsing
and view status in Cloud Security Command Center. `https://cloud.`
`google.com/phishing-protection/`

The Recover Function

Recovery processes and procedures are executed and maintained to ensure
restoration of systems or assets affected by cybersecurity incidents.

■ **Google Cloud Disaster Recovery:** Build a disaster recovery architecture
and plan for data and applications in Google Cloud. `https://cloud.`
`google.com/solutions/dr-scenarios-planning-guide`

- **Global, Regional:** Build in high availability by leveraging global, zonal, and regional Google Cloud resources. `https://cloud.google.com/compute/docs/regions-zones/global-regional-zonal-resources`

- **Google Cloud Load Balancing:** Implement global network autoscaling, HTTP(S), TCP, SSL, and Internal Load Balancing. `https://cloud.google.com/load-balancing/`

- **Cloud CDN:** Deliver content across Google's global, low-latency network using cloud content delivery network. `https://cloud.google.com/cdn/`

- **Autoscaling:** Use GCE managed instance groups or managed compute services like Google App Engine to automatically scale capacity based on need or Cloud Monitoring metrics. `https://cloud.google.com/compute/docs/autoscaler/`

- **Google Deployment Manager:** Create and manage cloud resources with simple templates. Specify all the resources needed for your application in a declarative format, use templates to parameterize and reuse configurations. `https://cloud.google.com/deployment-manager/`

- **Incident Response Management:** Leverage IRM with Monitoring to identify, manage, investigate, and resolve incidents. `https://cloud.google.com/incident-response/docs/`

- **Contact Center AI:** Combine the best of Google AI with your customer contact center software to improve customer experience and operational efficiency. `https://cloud.google.com/solutions/contact-center/`

- **Google Cloud Status Dashboard:** View the current status of GCP services and uptime. `https://status.cloud.google.com/`

With capabilities in place to track and maintain security measures and controls, the CSF and Google Cloud make it possible for organizations to gain meaningful insights into how security configurations affect organizational objectives and business outcomes. Under a shared responsibility model (discussed in Chapters 4 and 6), companies can offload security components to be enforced by Google on trusted, validated, and accredited cloud services infrastructure. Secure by design, Google Cloud implements built-in, layered security measures across a global network to protect user information, identities, applications, and devices. Leveraging the robust set of security products and services made available to customers, organizations can protect critical assets while meeting compliance requirements for any industry on Google Cloud.

The IBM Cloud

IBM Cloud is a set of cloud computing services for business offered by International Business Machines (IBM). The IBM Cloud includes IaaS, SaaS, and PaaS offered through public, private, and hybrid cloud delivery models.

IBM Cloud Pak for Security is an open security platform that connects to customers' existing data sources to generate deeper insights and enables customers to act faster with automation. Whether the data resides on IBM or third-party tools, on-premises, or multiple cloud environments, the platform helps customers to find and respond to threats and risks—all while leaving the data where it is. Therefore, the customers can uncover hidden threats, make informed risk-based decisions, and respond to incidents faster.

IBM Cloud Pak for Security provides a platform to quickly integrate with customers' existing security tools and generate deeper insights into threats across hybrid, multi-cloud environments. The Cloud Pak for Security platform uses an infrastructure-independent common operating environment that can be installed and run anywhere (Figure 8.2).

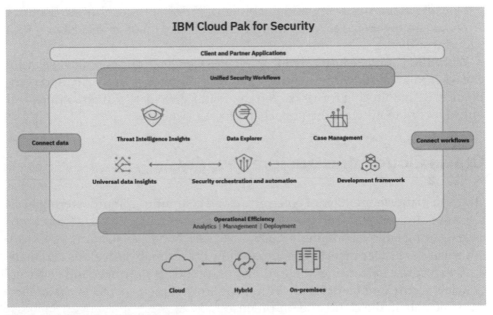

Figure 8.2: IBM Cloud Security

IBM Security Data Explorer for IBM Cloud Pak for Security enables federated investigations across IBM and third-party data sources. It connects insights from multiple security solutions, endpoint detection and response tools, and data stored in data lakes. It also gains insights from multi-cloud environments monitored by SIEM tools like Splunk and IBM QRadar.

IBM's QRadar Security Intelligence Platform is offered as an on-premises solution and delivers intelligent security analytics, enabling visibility, detection, and investigation for a wide range of known and unknown threats. Event analytics ingest, parse, normalize, correlate, and analyze log and event data to detect indicators of threats. Event analytics also identify anomalous activities, automatically connect related threat activity, and alert security teams to potential threats. Flow analytics collect, extract, and normalize valuable network flow data and packet metadata to augment log-based security insights. Flow analytics also identify network- and application-level threat activity, such as phishing, lateral movement, and data exfiltration.

IBM Security i2 helps cyberanalysts conduct cyber threat hunting by turning disparate datasets into comprehensive and actionable intelligence in near real-time. This cost-effective solution reduces training, maintenance, and deployment costs.

IBM Cloud Security Advisor is a security dashboard that provides centralized security management. The dashboard unifies vulnerability and network data as well as application and system findings from IBM services, partners, and user-defined sources.

By centralizing visibility and enabling drill down to resolution, Security Advisor empowers the security admin to cohesively manage security on IBM Cloud workloads.

With IBM Cloud Security and Compliance Center, you can embed security checks into your everyday workflows to help monitor for security and compliance. By monitoring for risks, you can identify security vulnerabilities and quickly work to mitigate the impact and fix the issue.

Oracle Cloud Infrastructure Security

Oracle, a platform provider of enterprise cloud computing, is empowering businesses of all sizes on their journey of digital transformation. Oracle Cloud provides leading-edge capabilities in SaaS, PaaS, IaaS, and DaaS (Data as a Service).

Oracle's security practices encompass how the company develops and manages enterprise systems, and cloud and on-premises products and services. Oracle's security-first approach with the following focus protects customers' valuable data in the cloud and on-premises:

- **Reduce Risk:** Strengthen security posture and reduce risk with security-first design principles that center on providing built-in security controls. These include isolated network virtualization in Oracle Cloud Infrastructure and strict separation of duties in Oracle Database.

- **Automate Security:** Automate security to reduce complexity, prevent human error, and lower cost with automated patching for Autonomous

Database and threat mitigation for Oracle Cloud Infrastructure provided by the Cloud Access Security Broker (CASB) cloud service and Identity Cloud Service.

- **Continuous Protection:** Keep the customer business protected using always-on encryption and continuous monitoring of user behavior with Autonomous Database and Oracle Cloud Infrastructure, further mitigating risk with the CASB Cloud Service and Identity Cloud Service.

Oracle's public cloud delivers high customer isolation and automated protections with data residency, sovereignty, and cloud security at the core of its innovation and operations.

Oracle SaaS Cloud Security Threat Intelligence

The Oracle SaaS Cloud Security (SCS) organization has significantly advanced and matured its threat intelligence program to align with the rapid adoption and growth of cloud-based SaaS applications. At a high-level, the SCS organization has three sustaining threat intelligence goals:

- Accurately and consistently identify and assess threats against Oracle SaaS.

- Adjust the prioritization of security DevSecOps engineering activities and projects based on findings from the threat intelligence program.

- Collaborate and share feeds, analysis, and insights with other security lines of business inside Oracle.

Threat intelligence has a continuous lifecycle, just like DevSecOps, that adapts and improves over time, based on results (Figure 8.3).

Figure 8.3: Oracle threat intelligence lifecycle

During the Analysis phase of the threat intelligence lifecycle, you can analyze the information and how a particular threat might potentially impact the customer environment. This analysis can include threat-hunting activities, which are the proactive search for signs of active or historical malicious activity in the infrastructure or applications. SCS uses both structured and unstructured threat-hunting approaches. Structured threat hunting determines what you want to look for and then detect if it is in place. Unstructured threat hunting is dependent on reviewing raw threat intelligence and signals to identify anomalies that may not have been detected in the past.

Oracle Cloud Guard is a unified security solution that provides a global and centralized approach to the protection of all the customers' assets. It works to analyze data, detect threats and misconfigurations automatically, then hunt down and kill those security threats without requiring human oversight. Oracle Cloud Guard continuously collects data from every part of the infrastructure and application stack, including audit logs, Oracle Data Safe, Oracle OS Management Service, as well as third-party products. Oracle Cloud Guard proactively detects and stops anomalous activity it identifies, shutting down a malicious instance automatically, and proactively revoking user permissions when it detects anomalous user behavior.

The Alibaba Cloud

The Alibaba Cloud is a multinational cloud computing company, a subsidiary of the Alibaba Group. Alibaba Cloud provides cloud computing services to online businesses and Alibaba's own e-commerce ecosystem.

Alibaba's Cloud Security Center is a unified security management system that identifies, analyzes, and alerts security threats in real time, helps organizations to achieve threat detection, response, traceability, automated security operations, protect assets and on-premises servers on the cloud, and meet regulatory compliance requirements through security capabilities such as anti-ransom, anti-virus, tamper-proof, mirror security scanning, and compliance checks.

Cloud Security Center helps you collect and present more than 10 types of logs and asset fingerprints on the cloud and expand security visibility with security posture analysis combined with network entity threat intelligence. Security Center integrates more than 250 threat detection models that are based on big data, six virus scan engines, seven webshell engines, and two threat detection engines for cloud services.

Security Center automatically collects various log data from your services on the cloud and implements control over found security threats. The threat detection and investigation and response capabilities include:

■ **Automated Alert Detection and Association:** Automatically associates alerts and identifies intrusions caused by low-risk anomalies to improve operational efficiency.

- **Custom Alerts:** The real-time analysis and aggregation of third-party data on the cloud. It also supports custom alert rules.

- **Security Overview:** Security screen to show network security from multiple dimensions with various metrics.

- **Automated Attack Traceability:** Automatically traces the sources and causes of attacks. This helps you understand the ins and outs of intrusion threats and make quick responses.

- **Log Analysis and Audit:** Provides the capability to analyze logs for threat anomalies and confirm to regulatory compliance for each geolocation.

The cloud threat detection feature provided by Security Center is also integrated with major antivirus engines. The feature detects threats based on large amounts of threat intelligence data provided by Alibaba Cloud. The feature also provides an exception detection module designed by Alibaba Cloud that detects threats based on machine learning and deep learning. These capabilities of the cloud threat detection feature enable both full-scale and dynamic antivirus protection for your assets.

The next chapter explores the future of threat hunting and the challenges we face as defenders against technology advances.

Summary

- Other cloud service providers, such as Google, IBM, Oracle, and Alibaba, facilitate threat-hunting capabilities through their capability stack aligned to the MITRE ATT&CK Framework.

- Google Cloud Platform offers extensive threat prevention capability similar to Azure and AWS. GCP offers threat protection across all five pillars of the NIST Framework (i.e., Identify, Protect, Detect, Respond, and Recover).

- Oracle and Alibaba Cloud platforms offer capability across major threat vectors. These platform security offerings are still evolving compared to Azure, AWS, and GCP.

References

NIST Cybersecurity Framework & Google Cloud (https://services. google.com/fh/files/misc/gcp_nist_cybersecurity_framework.pdf)

IBM Cloud Pak for Security (https://www.ibm.com/support/knowledgecenter/ en/SSTDPP_1.4.0/platform/docs/scp-core/overview.html)

CyberThreatHunting | IBM (https://www.ibm.com/security/cyber-threat-hunting)

How Threat Intelligence Complements Security Controls in Oracle SaaS Cloud | Oracle Cloud Security Blog (https://blogs.oracle.com/cloudsecurity/how-threat-intelligence-complements-security-controls-in-oracle-saas-cloud)

Security Center: Comprehensive and Intelligent Security Management System-AlibabaCloud (https://www.alibabacloud.com/product/security-center?spm=a3c0i.11071746.3212395230.6.5cce5db9eI8pkT)

Cloud Security: Secures Your Business, Operations, Network & Applications - Alibaba Cloud (https://www.alibabacloud.com/product/security?spm=a2c5t.10695662.1996646101.searchclickresult.22706cb6vU9hLw#J_3212395230)

Cloud threat detection - Threat Detection | Alibaba Cloud Documentation Center (https://www.alibabacloud.com/help/doc-detail/89379.htm)

The Future of Threat Hunting

What's In This Chapter

- The future of threat hunting, including:
  - Artificial intelligence and machine learning
  - Quantum computing
  - IoT
  - OT
  - Blockchain
  - Threat hunting as a service
  - The evolution of the threat-hunting tool
  - Potential regulatory guidance

If we look at the most recent SolarWinds breaches, the attackers evaded existing defenses for months. One of SolarWinds customers, FireEye, was the first to detect the breach, citing activity dating back to March 2020. The evasive hackers went undetected inside the victims' environments, giving them access to secure information over a long period of time. These are sophisticated actors that know the tripwires associated with simplistic rules and analytics people use to find them. The SolarWinds breach exemplifies organizations' need for effective and proactive threat hunting.

Legacy-based threat detection systems used heuristics and static signatures on a large amount of data logs to detect threats and anomalies. However, this meant that analysts needed to be aware of how normal data logs should look. The process included data being ingested and processed through the traditional extraction, transformation, and load (ETL) phase. The transformed data is read by machines and analyzed by analysts who create signatures. The signatures are then evaluated by passing more data. An error in evaluation meant rewriting the rules. Signature-based threat detection techniques, though well understood, are not robust, since signatures need to be created on-the-go for larger volumes of data.

The only path out of this quandary is to find solutions that enable threat hunters to effectively hunt faster. In order to allow hunters to do machine-assisted hunting, we need to automate the data mining process. Organizations need to allow machines to do what they are good at—mine through terabytes of data at machine speeds. With this assistance, hunters can trigger hunts based on interesting IoCs and behaviors, enabling them to effectively hunt an order of magnitude more than what they can today. Adding machine-assistance to aid human hunters will help organizations gain visibility into all of the attackers' steps, every lateral movement activity, usage of living off the land binaries, and persistence technique employed, ultimately showing the attackers' complete footprint across the entire environment.

Attackers are beginning to dynamically shift on the fly; for example, they no longer require an employee to click a phishing email to gain access to data. Next-generation attacks can execute from previews, shut off antivirus systems, escalate privileges, and even disable logs to hinder detection. Looking ahead, it is not only crucial for organizations and Managed Security Service Providers (MSSP) to prioritize the threat-hunting process in order to look for sophisticated threats, but to also equip the hunt team with machine-assisted hunting tools that will enable them to be as effective as possible.

Cybersecurity is a growth industry, and in our experience, there is a severe skills shortage in hiring cybersecurity professionals. Specifically, to single out the Security Operations Center (SOC) analysts who are tasked with analyzing the large datasets frequently on a daily basis. These SOC analysts are a "rare breed" with highly analytical skills to detect anomalies and to discard large sets of "false positives." These false positives (i.e., estimated to be in excess of 98% of all security alerts) drain a majority of the investigative resources. It is inconceivable to achieve the preceding level of insights with just human interactions. The secret weapon is artificial intelligence (AI) and the advances in machine learning (ML) algorithms. The SOC operators use machine learning extensively to reduce manual effort, reduce wasted effort on false positives, and speed up detection combatting cybercrime.

Artificial Intelligence and Machine Learning

This section discusses how threat hunting will evolve. Organizations and MSSPs can look into these technological trends and build their capabilities for more effective hunting in the future:

- Artificial intelligence and machine learning
- Quantum computing
- Internet of Things (IoT)
- Operational Technology (OT)
- Blockchain
- Threat hunting as a service
- The evolution of the threat-hunting tool
- Potential regulatory guidance

NOTE   Scale human expertise: Supervised machine learning can allow expertise by humans to extend far beyond what they could accomplish individually. As an example, we estimate on average 4,500 malicious antivirus samples are analyzed via next-gen technologies of machine learning, automation, and heuristics by the time a human analyst can evaluate a single malware sample.

There are numerous definitions of AI and a simple Internet search can provide many interpretations of this. As an academic and a researcher, the following definition of AI has always resonated with me. In essence, AI is the ability to provide:

- **Reasoning:** Learn and form conclusions with imperfect data
- **Understanding:** Interpret the meaning of data including text, voice, images, etc.
- **Interacting:** Interact with people in natural ways

AI is also often used interchangeably with the term machine learning (ML). ML is the ability to identify objects and data, such as files, images, etc., and to get better (or learn) as more diverse datasets are provided.

Machine intelligence approaches use machine learning that adapts and learns over time to react not only to the evolving threat, but also can be tuned based on human/analyst inputs as new insights are gleaned. Because threats evolve so rapidly, it's critical not to engage in a hunt with an outdated set of tools that will miss emerging threats. Additionally, machine intelligence can be used to consolidate a great deal of human-curated intelligence into robust, simplified machine-curated intelligence. Even though expert analysis is often required for intuition-based analysis, machine intelligence can help comb through large volumes of human intelligence or use human-defined frameworks to speed up the application of expert insight. This can alleviate the labor load on the human analyst, allowing them to focus only on tasks that demand their more complex thinking.

There are number of ML algorithms, and *deep learning* is a further subset of AI. We will specifically concentrate on ML advances in this chapter. The following are some examples of leveraging ML in the fight against cybercrime:

- **Unsupervised learning helps remove human bias:** ML algorithms can remove the human bias that comes with expertise to reveal unexpected insights.

- **Anomaly detection:** ML determines the norm for a variable and the average standard deviation, then identifies spikes that fall outside the standard. A couple of examples of anomaly detection are:

  - **Malicious User Profiling:** Malicious activity is often hard to detect with manually generated rules. These are due to complex attack patterns, diversity of valid virtual machine (VM) activities, and the rapid improvement in attacking tools. To overcome these challenges, we leverage ML capabilities to learn behavioral patterns of known malicious logins and execution sequences. The sources of malicious logins we use are GuardiCore honeypots, Brute Force scanners, and suspicious login–related alerts. These have the ability to dynamically adopt to new attacks and hacking tools. Later, these dynamically learned patterns are used to detect similar activities across cloud providers, such as Azure and AWS.

  - **Compromised VMs:** The defenders have the ability to detect and inform consumers that their VMs are compromised. These detections include outgoing port scanning from IP Flow Information Export (IPFIX) and outgoing spam and outgoing Distributed Denial of Service (DDoS). The outgoing spam detection is done in collaboration with cloud productivity tools such as Office 365 on Azure.

- **Cyber threat-hunting activities after a compromise:** Oftentimes, the window between compromise and detrimental effects is small, and hunt actors need to quickly identify where intrusions occurred, what likely attack vectors are moving forward, and how to quickly remediate exploited vulnerabilities. By utilizing machine intelligence, cyberthreat experts can deploy algorithms to sift through large amounts of data, bringing to the front the most applicable and important data. By training algorithms on historical data, machine intelligence can also rapidly uncover relationships in the data that are labor-intensive for a human to detect, helping to shrink the latency from compromise to remediation.

How ML Reduces False Positives

As mentioned earlier, false positives are the largest roadblock to attack disruption. The majority of Security Operations Centers (SOCs) are simply overloaded with false positive security signal data preventing (or at minimum distracting) resources to combat the "real threats." As per Figure 9.1, the traditional SOC approach has been to hand-craft rules by security professionals to combat impending threats. However, these static rules do not adapt to the changes in their environments. Specifically, they do not adapt to changing attack vectors and introduction of new malware. SOC analysts are also exposed to large volumes of data. For example, some our Azure services generate an estimated 1000+ API calls a minute. These high-dimensional data are very challenging for an SOC analyst to visualize and spot the outliers.

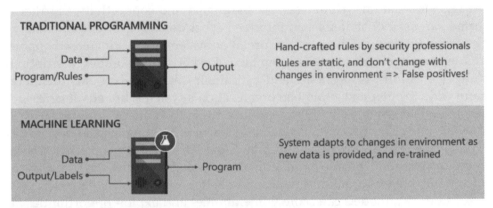

Figure 9.1: Traditional approach vs. ML approach

ML is assisting us to address these challenges. ML has the ability to retrain itself by adapting to new environments as new data is provided. Providing relevant and actionable large datasets is the key success factor here. These large datasets include industry threat-hunting research alerts, domain expert alerts, customer feedback alerts, labels from other product groups (AWS CloudTrail logs, O365, Windows Defender ATP, Azure, etc.), red team exercises, automated attack bots, and Bug Bounty programs. The combination of all these rich datasets enables us to successfully minimize the false positives and "give back more time" to SOC analysts. Hence, they can target and eradicate the real threats without getting drowned in a sea of security alerts.

How Machine Intelligence Applies to Malware Detection

Machine intelligence can identify potential malicious software by applying machine learning such as deep learning models that review and inspect the full software binaries. These models can detect actions that can be characteristic of malicious software and send them off for further review.

As the model reviews more software, the malware detection capability will continue to learn and detect other similar new attacks as well as completely new malware attacks that would be exposed as anomalies.

Those approaches have the potential to catch malware variants and zero-day attacks that traditional signature-based approaches will never detect. By no means are we suggesting eliminating a traditional antivirus from your security stack, but rather expanding your arsenal to achieve greater detection coverage.

How Machine Intelligence Applies to Risk Scoring in a Network

Cyber risk scoring uses context-defined predictive analytics to provide quantitative, data-driven outputs, allowing organizations to prioritize and focus remediation activities on network areas that are exposed to the greatest risk. As information systems increase in number and connectivity, the attack surfaces in need of strategic and informed cyber defense grow exponentially. The growing connectivity among information systems creates increased opportunities for adversaries to take advantage of cyber vulnerabilities, disrupting strategic missions, key systems, and critical infrastructure. Not only are there more ways to enter and exploit an organization's systems, but adversaries are becoming increasingly creative and innovative in their attack design.

By driving cyber risk assessments with machine learning instead of domain expert interpretation, risk scores are entirely data-driven and quantitative. These scores can offer both precise point estimates of scaled risk as well as data-driven uncertainty bounds around these scores to better inform decision makers.

Additionally, models can score vulnerabilities and exploit opportunities at scale and efficiently, covering the landscape of known risk in a matter of hours, rather than days, weeks, and months.

Advances in Quantum Computing

Paul Lipman says that quantum computing is based on quantum mechanics, which governs how nature works at the smallest scales. The smallest classical computing element is a bit, which can be either 0 or 1. The quantum equivalent is a qubit, which can also be 0 or 1 or in what's called a *superposition*—any combination of 0 and 1. Performing a calculation on two classical bits (which can be 00, 01, 10, and 11) requires four calculations. A quantum computer can perform calculations on all four states simultaneously. This scales exponentially: 1,000 qubits would, in some respects, be more powerful than the world's most powerful supercomputer.

WARNING   *Qubits* are inherently unstable. Interaction between a qubit and its surroundings degrades information in microseconds. Isolating qubits from the environment, for example, by cooling them close to absolute zero, is challenging and expensive. Noise increases with qubit count, requiring complex error correction approaches.

The other quantum concept central to quantum computing is *entanglement*, whereby qubits can become correlated such that they are described by a single quantum state. Measure one and you instantaneously know the state of the other. Entanglement is important in quantum cryptography and quantum communication.

The promise of quantum computing, however, is not speeding up conventional computing. Rather, it will deliver an exponential advantage for certain classes of problems, such as factoring very large numbers, with profound implications for cybersecurity.

Quantum computers are predicted to solve problems that are far too complex for classical computers according to the Quantum Exchange, a leading research body. This includes solving the algorithms behind encryption keys that protect data and the Internet's infrastructure. Much of today's encryption is based on mathematical formulas that would take today's computers an impractically long time to decode. To simplify this, think of two large numbers, for example, and multiply them together. It's easy to come up with the product, but much harder to start with the large number and factor it into its two prime numbers. A quantum computer, however, can easily factor those numbers and break the code. Peter Shor developed a quantum algorithm (aptly named Shor's algorithm) that easily factors large numbers far more quickly than a classical computer. Since then, scientists have been working on developing quantum computers that can factor increasingly larger numbers.

NOTE   Today's RSA encryption, a widely used form of encryption, particularly for sending sensitive data over the Internet, is based on 2048-bit numbers. Experts estimate that a quantum computer would need to be as large as 70 million qubits to break that encryption. Considering the largest quantum computer today is IBM's 53-qubit quantum computer, it could be a long time before we're breaking that encryption.

As the pace of quantum research continues to accelerate, though, the development of such a computer within the next three to five years cannot be discounted. As an example, according to *MIT Technology Review,* a 20 million-qubit computer could break a 2048-bit algorithm in 8 hours. What that demonstration means is that continued breakthroughs like this will keep pushing the timeline up. Quantum computing is expected to transform cybersecurity according to Paul Lipman in the following key areas:

- **Random number generation is fundamental to cryptography:** Conventional random number generators typically rely on algorithms known as pseudo-random number generators, which are not truly random and thus potentially open to compromise. Companies such as Quantum Dice and ID Quantique are developing quantum random number generators that utilize quantum optics to generate sources of true randomness.

- **Quantum-secure communications:** Sharing cryptographic keys between two or more parties to allow them to privately exchange information is at the heart of secure communications. Quantum-secure communications utilizes aspects of quantum mechanics to enable the completely secret exchange of encryption keys and can even alert to the presence of an eavesdropper. This is currently limited to fiber transmission over 10s of kilometers.

- **Breaking public-key cryptography, specifically the RSA algorithm, which is at the heart of the ecommerce industry:** RSA relies on the fact that the product of two prime numbers is computationally challenging to factor. It would take a classical computer trillions of years to break RSA encryption. A quantum computer with around 4,000 error-free qubits could defeat RSA in seconds. However, this would require closer to 1 million of today's noisy qubits. The world's largest quantum computer is currently less than 100 qubits; however, IBM and Google have road maps to achieve 1 million by 2030. A million-qubit quantum computer may still be a decade away, but that time frame could well be compressed. Additionally, highly sensitive financial and national security data is potentially susceptible to being stolen today—only to be decrypted once a sufficiently powerful quantum computer becomes available. The potential threat to public-key cryptography has engendered the development of algorithms that are invulnerable to quantum computers.

- **Machine learning has revolutionized cybersecurity, enabling novel attacks to be detected and blocked:** The cost of training deep models grows exponentially as data volumes and complexity increase. The emerging field of quantum machine learning may enable exponentially faster, more time- and energy-efficient machine learning algorithms. This, in turn, could yield more effective algorithms for identifying and defeating novel cyberattack methods.

As the future versions of quantum computers would have the power to crack passwords simultaneously, future cyber-physical systems must incorporate quantum computing–resistant designs of data security.

Quantum Computing Challenges

Quantum computing promises to transform cybersecurity, but there are substantial challenges to address and fundamental breakthroughs still required to be made.

The most immediate challenge is to achieve sufficient numbers of fault-tolerant qubits to unleash quantum computing's computational promise. Companies such as IBM, Google, Honeywell, and Amazon are investing in this problem.

Quantum computers are currently programmed from individual quantum logic gates, which may be acceptable for small quantum computers, but it's impractical once we get to thousands of qubits. Companies like IBM and Classiq are developing more abstracted layers in the programming stack, enabling developers to build powerful quantum applications to solve real-world problems.

Arguably, the key bottleneck in the quantum computing industry will be a lack of talent. While universities churn out computer science graduates at an accelerating pace, there is still too little being done to train the next generation of quantum computing professionals. It will take efforts from governments, universities, industry, and the broader technology ecosystem to enable the level of talent development required to truly capitalize on quantum computing.

Preparing for the Quantum Future

The quantum revolution is upon us. Although the profound impact of large-scale fault-tolerant quantum computers may be a decade off, near-term quantum computers will still yield tremendous benefits. We are seeing substantial investment in solving the core problems around scaling qubit count, error correction, and algorithms. From a cybersecurity perspective, while quantum computing may render some existing encryption protocols obsolete, it has the promise to enable a substantially enhanced level of communication security and privacy.

Organizations must think strategically about the longer-term risks and benefits of quantum computing and technology and engage in a serious way today to be ready for the quantum revolution of tomorrow.

Advances in IoT and Their Impact

The recent IDC report by MacGillivray and Wright (Worldwide Internet of Things Connectivity Forecast, 2017–2021, IDC, 2017) suggest that the next decade promises the universal democratization of connectivity to every device. Significant drops in the cost of connectivity mean that every form of electrical device—every child's toy, every household's appliances, and every industry's equipment—will connect to the Internet. This Internet of Things (IoT) will drive huge economic efficiencies; it will enable countless innovations as digital transformation reaches across fields from childcare to eldercare, from hospitality to mining, from education to transportation. Although no person can foresee the full impact of universal device connectivity, anticipation of this new frontier is widespread.

The Internet of Things can be used to interconnect various physical devices as well as virtual objects that can be accessed through the Internet. IoT is rapidly growing and changing our lives. There has been a massive surge in the use of IoT devices, mainly in the homes and manufacturing sectors. IoT has penetrated every aspect of our lives and everything from your water sprinkler to your security system, which is connected to the Internet. With the overwhelming amount of new technologies popping up every day, IoT security often tends to be overlooked, which makes the users of these devices particularly vulnerable to security threats.

IoT creates a network of the physical objects, whose data is stored on the cloud. The devices connect to the surrounding objects and the extensive data around them. Since the data is being passed back and forth on thousands of devices, hackers are just one vulnerability away from exploiting all your personal data stored on the network. This may not appear as a major risk when your home automation system and other IoT devices may have negligible personal information stored on these devices. However, IoT items may consist of a camera or microphone and they may be compromised. This will enable hackers to monitor all your movements thus leading to a breach of privacy and exfiltration of personal information. Cisco analysts estimated that more than 50 billion devices were connected to the Internet in 2020. This quantity is far more than the number of people on the planet and it only emphasizes the scale of this vulnerability and the urgency needed to tackle the issue.

> **NOTE**   According to *Business Insider*, spending on IoT devices, solutions, and support systems is expected to reach nearly $15 trillion. Consumers and businesses everywhere are getting used to the notion that critical data gathering, processing, and analysis are now being fulfilled at the far edge of technology infrastructure. IoT is the key driver of this trend, with 64 billion IoT devices estimated around the world by 2026.

According to Cyberie research, nearly 70% of IoT devices are riddled with serious vulnerabilities. Protecting organizations and individuals against the increasing risks isn't going to be easy, but we can't afford to have so many exposed weaknesses waiting to be exploited. First, one needs to be aware of the threats they are facing. The Open Web Application Security Project (OWASP) has provided us with the Internet of Things Project where they highlight the key susceptible areas. The project explains the vulnerabilities as well as discusses prevention. The list is as follows:

- Insecure web interfaces
- Insufficient authentications or authorizations
- Insecure network services
- Lack of transport encryption
- Privacy concerns
- Insecure cloud interfaces
- Insecure mobile interfaces
- Insufficient security configurations
- Poor physical security

Many good security practices have been theoretically considered. These include the use of secure protocols, using a VPN, using identity management, and by providing timely latest updates and patches for the gadgets. The Cyberie research expands on how IoT devices can impact cybersecurity:

- At a workplace, a savvy user may manipulate the ID access process to get into a restricted area.

- IoT security also includes public infrastructure such as traffic lights and power plants, which may be manipulated by malicious users and disrupt the day-to-day lives of the mass population.

- All the data generated by IoT devices is collected and stored for machine learning algorithms that use the data to create better business solutions and improve quality of life. The volume of this data produced is immense. This is another attack vector for adversaries.

Even though most IoT security challenges are yet to be overcome, the industry has recognized these weaknesses in the devices. Fortunately, cybersecurity professionals are already adjusting to the new demands of this widespread network.

Growing IoT Cybersecurity Risks

According to SimpliLearn, Deloitte recently outlined several key industries and market segments that are excelling at IoT utilization. The growing number of use cases is an indicator of not only how broad the impact of IoT is on society, but also how many entry points exist that hackers and cybercriminals can exploit. The list includes:

- **Healthcare and life sciences:** Patient care, remote diagnostics, bio wearables, food sensors, and equipment monitoring

- **Smart homes:** Wearables, smart thermostat, smoke alarm, refrigerator (and other appliances), and home security

- **Cities and infrastructure:** HVAC, smart cities and buildings, waste management, and electric vehicles

- **Transportation and urban mobility:** Traffic routing, telematics, smart parking, and public transport

- **Industrial systems and sensors:** Measuring speed, temperature, flow, pressure, light, and position of various systems

WARNING   The rapid growth of the IoT market also brings significant cybersecurity risk. Attacks on IoT devices tripled in the first half of 2019. The Symantec 2019 Internet Security Threat Report shows that cyberattacks on IoT environments are rapidly evolving in sophistication. This includes bots or worms that can compromise smart devices such as Linux-based Internet routers, for example, and leverage them to commit additional crimes such as the denial of service attacks or illicit mass marketing. Attacks on industrial control systems are also increasing, as are attacks on military and business infrastructure.

A key challenge in building security protocols for IoT is that there is a lack of standards available, thanks to the complexity of the IoT ecosystem and a huge number of devices from a wide range of vendors worldwide. The Department of Homeland Security's Science and Technology (S&T) Directive has recently created a set of best practices that enterprises can follow to secure their IoT systems. The directive breaks down security into three distinct segments:

- **Detection:** Understanding exactly which IoT devices and components are connected to a given network or system.
- **Authentication:** Verifying the identity and origin of IoT devices to detect and prevent spoofing.
- **Updating:** Continually maintaining, updating, and upgrading IoT security capabilities to stay ahead of hackers and cybercriminals.

With those basic guidelines in mind, companies are learning to tackle IoT security breaches with tangible new strategies, according to a recent list of solutions. Among the most effective strategies:

- Maintain accurate data on each IoT device to gauge the level of potential risk
- Proactively identify cyberthreats to anticipate and prevent breaches
- Restrict access to sensitive data
- Continually monitor who is accessing each device
- Frequently back up all the data the IoT device gathers

These core steps provide a roadmap that cybersecurity professionals can follow to create a comprehensive IoT security framework. Researches have taken into account these concerns and attempted to create a universal framework to address IoT security. There is a current draft NIST framework being authored.

Here are a few typical attack types that can be levied against enterprise IoT systems:

- **Authentication attacks:** Unfortunately, weak and default passwords continue to provide delicious targets to attackers.
- **Distributed Denial of Service (DDoS):** IoT devices can be controlled by a rogue command-and-control adversary to "overload" a system by initiating simultaneous requests. This will result in the system shutting down altogether.
- **Application security attacks:** IoT devices and connections can be exploited through attacks against application endpoints. Application endpoints

include web servers as well as mobile device applications (for example, iOS and Android) that have a role in controlling the device. Application code running on the device itself can also be directly targeted. Application fuzzing can find ways of compromising the application host and taking control of its processes.

■ **Wireless reconnaissance and mapping:** The majority of IoT devices on the market utilize wireless communication protocols such as ZigBee, ZWave, Bluetooth-LE, and Wi-Fi 802.11. Similar to the war dialing days of old, where hackers scanned through telephone switching networks to identify electronic modems, today researchers are successfully demonstrating scanning attacks against IoT devices.

■ **Security protocol attacks:** Many security protocols can sustain attacks against vulnerabilities introduced in the protocol design (specification), implementation, and even configuration stages (in which different, viable protocol options are set).

■ **Physical security attacks:** Physical security is a topic frequently overlooked by IoT vendors that are only familiar with designing equipment, appliances, and other tools historically not subject to exploitation. Physical security attacks include those in which the attackers physically penetrate the enclosure of a host, embedded device, or other type of IoT computing platform to gain access to its processor, memory devices, and other sensitive components.

Preparing for IoT Challenges

MacGillivray and Wright have identified seven properties that must be shared by all highly secure, network-connected IoT devices. They are detailed here. These guidelines should be followed to reduce IoT surface attacks and minimize the attack vectors.

■ **Highly secure devices have a hardware-based root of trust:** Device secrets are protected by hardware and the hardware contains physical countermeasures against side-channel attacks. Unlike software, hardware has two important properties that may be used to establish device security. First, single-purpose hardware is immune to reuse by an attacker for unintended actions. Second, hardware can detect and mitigate against physical attacks; for example, pulse testing the reset pin to prevent glitching attacks is easily implemented in hardware. When used to protect secrets and device correctness, hardware provides a solid root of trust upon which rich software functionality can be implemented securely and safely.

■ **Highly secure devices have a small trusted computing base:** The trusted computing base (TCB) consists of all the software and hardware that are used to create a secure environment for an operation. The TCB should be kept as small as possible to minimize the surface that is exposed to attackers and to reduce the probability that a bug or feature can be used to circumvent security protections. On the contrary, in less secure systems, all security enforcement is implemented in a software stack that contains no protection boundaries.

- **Highly secure devices have defense in depth:** In these devices, multiple mitigations are applied to each threat. In systems with only a single layer of defense, just a single error in design or implementation can lead to catastrophic compromise. Attackers are creative; threats are often not completely anticipated, so having multiple countermeasures often becomes the difference between a secure or compromised system.

- **Highly secure devices provide compartmentalization:** Compartments are protected by hardware-enforced boundaries to prevent a flaw or breach in one software compartment from propagating to other software compartments of the system. Compartmentalization introduces additional protection boundaries within the hardware and software stack to create additional layers of defense in depth. For example, a common technique is to use operating systems processes or independent virtual machines as compartments. On the contrary, many low-cost devices employed a design with no software separation.

- **Highly secure devices use certificate-based authentication:** Certificates, instead of passwords, are used to prove identities for mutual authentication when communicating with other local devices and with servers in the cloud. A certificate is a statement of identity and authorization that is signed with a secret private key and validated with a known public key. Unlike passwords or other authentication mechanisms that are based on shared secrets, certificates can't be stolen, forged, or otherwise used to authenticate an impostor.

- **Highly secure devices have renewable security:** A device with renewable security can update to a more secure state automatically even after the device has been compromised. Security threats evolve and attackers discover new attack vectors. To counter emerging threats, device security must be renewed regularly. In extreme cases, when compartments and layers of a device are compromised by zero-day exploits, lower layers must rebuild and renew the security of higher levels of the system. Remote attestation and rollback protections guarantee that once renewed, a device cannot be reverted to a known vulnerable state.

- **Highly secure devices have failure reporting:** When a failure occurs on these devices, a failure report is collected automatically and sent to a failure analysis system in a timely manner. In the best case, a failure is triggered by imperfect programming for an extremely rare sequence of events. In the worst case, a failure is triggered by attackers probing for new attack vectors. Whatever the case, a failure analysis system correlates failure reports that have similar root causes. With a sufficiently large reporting base, even extremely rare failure events can be diagnosed and corrected, and new attack vectors can be identified and isolated before they are widely exploited. Failure reporting creates a global "immune system" for highly secure devices. Without failure reporting, device manufacturers are left in the dark as to the device failures experienced by their customers and may be caught off guard by emerging attacks.

Operational Technology (OT)

ForcePoint defines Operational Technology (OT) as hardware and software that detects or causes a change through the direct monitoring and/or control of physical devices, processes, and events in the enterprises. Gartner describes OT as common in Industrial Control Systems (ICS) such as a SCADA (Supervisory Control and Data Acquisition) System. In the world of critical infrastructure, OT may be used to control power stations or public transportation. As this technology advances and converges with networked tech, the need for OT security grows exponentially.

For many years, industrial systems relied on proprietary protocols and software, were manually managed and monitored by operators, and had no connection to the outside world. For this reason, they were a fairly insignificant target for hackers as there was no networked interface to attack and nothing to gain or destroy. The only way to infiltrate these systems was to obtain physical access to a terminal and this was no easy task. OT and IT integrated little and did not deal with the same kinds of vulnerabilities.

Today, it's a very different story as we see more industrial systems brought online to deliver big data and smart analytics as well as adopt new capabilities and efficiencies through technological integrations. Information Technology (IT) and Operational Technology (OT) convergence gives organizations a single view of industrial systems together with process management solutions that ensure accurate information is delivered to people, machines, switches, sensors, and devices at the right time and in the best format. When IT and OT systems work in harmony together, new efficiencies are discovered, systems can be remotely monitored and managed and organizations can realize the same security benefits that are used on administrative IT systems. This transition from closed to open systems has generated a slew of new security risks that need to be addressed.

Importance of OT Security

As industrial systems become more connected, they also become more exposed to vulnerabilities. The high cost of industrial equipment and the devastation to communities and economies that an attack could generate are key factors for organizations looking to protect their industrial networks. Add legacy equipment, safety regulations that may prohibit any modifications being made to equipment, and compliance regulations that require sensitive data to be made available to third parties, and you have quite a challenge on your hands.

It is possible to secure industrial networks without disrupting operations or risking non-compliance. By using solutions that allow complete visibility of network control traffic and establishing the right security policies, you can put an effective OT strategy in place that will protect your processes, people, and profit and significantly reduce security vulnerabilities and incidents.

Blockchain

The decentralized communication system, *blockchain*, was implemented first to authenticate bitcoin transactions, but the technology has now emerged to be the future of cybersecurity. The most common challenges enterprises face with their existing systems include the ease to locate an availability of multiple avenues for hackers to attack and overtake the system.

A blockchain is basically a decentralized, digitized, public ledger of all cryptocurrency transactions and uses what is known as the distributed ledger technology. This could potentially help enhance cyber-defense as the platform can prevent fraudulent activities via consensus mechanisms and detect data tampering depending on its underlying characteristics of operational resilience, data encryption, auditability, transparency, and immutability.

Owing to their distributed nature, blockchains provide no "hackable" entrance or a central point of failure and, thereby, provide more security when compared with various present database-driven transactional structures.

Blockchain technology can be used for a variety of reasons across a slew of industries. It helps prevent cyberattacks, data breaches, identity theft, and unfairness in title transactions, and makes sure your data is private and safe. This is only the beginning for blockchain. As new technology, it's only going to get smarter and better.

> **NOTE**   For threat hunting, blockchain can monitor and predict attacks with artificial intelligence and provide a proactive response to incoming cyberthreats. It helps organizations reduce cost and puts their data at a much lower risk.

Another traditional weakness is eliminated through blockchain's collaborative consensus algorithm. It can watch for malicious actions, anomalies, and false positives without the need for a central authority. One pair of eyes can be fooled, but not all of them. That strengthens authentication and secures data communications and record management.

The Future of Cybersecurity with Blockchain

Cybersecurity is one of the most versatile industries in which businesses are witnessing a new breed of threat almost every other day. Although the future of cybersecurity will always be unpredictable for global leaders, it is critical to prepare an assessment of possible threats and potential security innovation to keep consistent customer and stakeholder trust.

The combination of block-building algorithms and hashing makes blockchain a great solution in the cybersecurity portfolio, by enhancing data security when transactions of any kind of value are being processed in the distributed network. Blockchain is changing the cybersecurity solution in several ways. After cloud computing and several other digital evolutions, it is obvious that organizations should use hundreds of applications (internal and cloud-based) for their business needs. This also gives rise to the level of data breaches for end users and organizations.

As per the new Breach Level Index (BLI) in 2017, more than 2.5 billion data records were compromised. As a result, it is expected that in the current digital age, comfort and flexibility will be overtaken by privacy and security. As has been clearly demonstrated, blockchain is all about providing data security and privacy for confidential information, and blockchain is likely to be a great attraction for several business applications to provide better security and privacy.

Threat Hunting as a Service

As discussed in the first chapter, the human element in threat hunting is foundational and one of the critical success factors. Threat hunting will continue to demand highly skilled and very experienced resources. And since these resources are hard to find, it seems like a lucrative upsell for managed services providers to offer "Threat Hunting as a Service." Today there are many players in the market that provide Threat Hunting as a Service.

More services providers are getting ready to capitalize the market potentials. Some of them offer Endpoint Detection and Response (EDR) products have great overlap with threat hunting tools, since they can detect and analyze whatever happens on the endpoint. As such, EDR companies that are under great stress to differentiate likely offer "hunting modules" to complement "regular" EDR functions.

The Evolution of the Threat-Hunting Tool

SIEM (Security Information and Event Management) is likely the reason that customers need threat-hunting tools in the first place. As a centralized platform, SIEM should have all information logs "hiding" indicators of compromise. Yet regular SIEM systems are not flexible enough to conduct true hunting operations. Product vendors will add incremental capability to their existing SIEM automation platform, which will allow analysts to build any type of complex query from any data source.

If threat hunting will become a product category of its own, do hunters really need dedicated tools to conduct their operations?

> **NOTE**   According to a SANS survey, "Most organizations are utilizing existing tools to understand their environment. Slightly more mature organizations are writing scripts to enhance their capabilities, and very mature organizations are utilizing third-party tools." Eighty-seven percent of respondents are using existing tools (such as SIEM, IDS/IPS) to aid in finding, tracking, and catching the adversary, while fewer than 50% are using specific source threat-hunting tools (from responders who actually conduct threat hunting).

Since threat hunting is mostly about sifting through communication data, it will be no surprise that network traffic analysis tools are offered as threat-hunting tools. Product vendors and services providers with a deep understanding of network traffic behavior can offer threat hunting as a by-product of their platform.

Potential Regulatory Guidance

Policymakers and authorities may consider providing threat-hunting guidelines for organizations to set forth a structured and a cyclic program of monitoring the organizational activity longitudinally (from organization to the outside world) and laterally (inside the organization). They can provide guidelines to leverage external intelligence, best practices to analyze and correlate information, and a consistent approach to responding to the threats, whether they were actually spotted in the context of the threat-hunting activity or as a preparatory measure for blocking even before it occurred.

Imagine having visibility into threats across all your resources, AI that stitches signals together and tells you what's most important, and the ability to respond swiftly across the organization. With SIEM and extended detection and response (XDR), defenders can be armed with all the context and automation needed to stop even the most sophisticated, cross-domain attacks.

Summary

- The future of threat hunting has multiple aspects. The advances of artificial intelligence and machine learning have introduced new attack vectors and created challenges to defenders. However, these advances can be also leveraged to prevent attacks to increase the security posture of organizations.

- The quantum computing advances are increasingly challenging the fundamentals such as cryptography algorithms that e-commerce is built on. However, researchers are not expecting this to materialize until 2030 at least. Also, there is significant research in play to create quantum-proof cryptography algorithms currently.

- The proliferation of IoT devices is increasing the attack surface for cyberattacks. The traditionally closed Operational Technology (OT) systems are increasingly getting connected to the Internet exposing critical infrastructure to cyber attackers. These IoT and OT systems are looming as key battlegrounds in cybersecurity in the next few years.

- The future of threat hunting will focus on bringing all relevant capabilities together from AI, ML, automation, IoT, quantum computing, blockchain, SIEM, XDR, and IR for a robust threat-hunting strategy, yet still using the same "assume breach" principle.

References

How Artificial Intelligence advances prevents Cybercrime (https://www.linkedin.com/pulse/how-artificial-intelligence-advances-prevents-dr-chris-peiris/)

How Quantum Computing Will Transform Cybersecurity (https://www.forbes.com/sites/forbestechcouncil/2021/01/04/how-quantum-computing-will-transform-cybersecurity/?sh=5353b6a7d3fb)

Worldwide Internet of Things Connectivity Forecast, 2017–2021 (https://www.marketresearch.com/IDC-v2477/Worldwide-Internet-Things-Connectivity-Forecast-10730165/)

IoT Business Opportunities, Models & Ideas for 2020 (https://www.businessinsider.com/iot-business-opportunities-models?r=AU&IR=T)

2021 cybersecurity challenges IoT-Internet of Things (https://www.cybervie.com/blog/cybersecurity-challenges-iot/)

Trends, Challenges, and Solutions With IoT Cybersecurity (`https://www.simplilearn.com/iot-cybersecurity-article`)

Internet Security Threat Report (ISRT) - 2019 (`https://www.phishingbox.com/news/phishing-news/internet-security-threat-report-irst-2019`)

Cybersecurity and the Internet of Things (`https://www.securitymagazine.com/articles/90793-cybersecurity-and-the-internet-of-things`)

What is OT Security? Defined, Explained, and Explored (`https://www.forcepoint.com/cyber-edu/ot-operational-technology-security`)

Part

V

Appendices

In This Part

Appendix A: MITRE ATT&CK Tactics
Appendix B: Privilege Escalation
Appendix C: Credential Access
Appendix D: Lateral Movement
Appendix E: Command and Control
Appendix F: Data Exfiltration
Appendix G: MITRE Cloud Matrix
Appendix H: Glossary

MITRE ATT&CK Tactics

The following appendixes contain an in-depth analysis of MITRE ATT&CK framework Tactics, Techniques, and Procedures (TTPs). They detail information that articulates the threat, treat actors, and the impact and remediation processes.

NOTE The appendixes in this part are extracts from publicly available MITRE ATT&CK Framework documentation. We have carefully crafted the relevant attack vector information that relates to multi-cloud attacks to assist the readers. Consult `https://attack.mitre.org/` for the latest revisions to ensure you're up to date with the latest TTP information.

ID	NAME	DESCRIPTION
TA0043	Reconnaissance	The adversary is trying to gather information they can use to plan future operations.
TA0042	Resource Development	The adversary is trying to establish resources they can use to support operations.
TA0001	Initial Access	The adversary is trying to get into your network.
TA0002	Execution	The adversary is trying to run malicious code.
TA0003	Persistence	The adversary is trying to maintain their foothold.

ID	NAME	DESCRIPTION
TA0004	Privilege Escalation	The adversary is trying to gain higher-level permissions.
TA0005	Defense Evasion	The adversary is trying to avoid being detected.
TA0006	Credential Access	The adversary is trying to steal account names and passwords.
TA0007	Discovery	The adversary is trying to figure out your environment.
TA0008	Lateral Movement	The adversary is trying to move through your environment.
TA0009	Collection	The adversary is trying to gather data of interest to their goal.
TA0011	Command and Control	The adversary is trying to communicate with compromised systems to control them.
TA0010	Exfiltration	The adversary is trying to steal data.
TA0040	Impact	The adversary is trying to manipulate, interrupt, or destroy your systems and data.

Privilege Escalation

Privilege escalation consists of techniques that adversaries use to gain higher-level permissions on a system or network. Adversaries can often enter and explore a network with unprivileged access but require elevated permissions to follow through on their objectives. Common approaches are to take advantage of system weaknesses, misconfigurations, and vulnerabilities. Examples of elevated access include:

➤ System/root level

➤ Local administrator

➤ User account with admin-like access

➤ User accounts with access to specific systems or the ability to perform specific functions

These techniques often overlap with persistence techniques, as OS features that let an adversary persist can execute in an elevated context.

ID	NAME	DESCRIPTION
T1134	Access Token Manipulation	Adversaries may modify access tokens to operate under a different user or system security context to perform actions and bypass access controls. Windows uses access tokens to determine the ownership of a running process. A user can manipulate access tokens to make a running process appear as though it is the child of a different process or belongs to someone other than the user that started the process. When this occurs, the process also takes on the security context associated with the new token.
	Token Impersonation/ Theft	Adversaries may duplicate then impersonate another user's token to escalate privileges and bypass access controls. An adversary can create a new access token that duplicates an existing token using `DuplicateToken(Ex)`. The token can then be used with `ImpersonateLoggedOnUser` to allow the calling thread to impersonate a logged-on user's security context, or with `SetThreadToken` to assign the impersonated token to a thread.
	Create Process with Token	Adversaries may create a new process with a duplicated token to escalate privileges and bypass access controls. An adversary can duplicate a desired access token with `DuplicateToken(Ex)` and use it with `CreateProcessWithTokenW` to create a new process running under the security context of the impersonated user. This is useful for creating a new process under the security context of a different user.
	Make and Impersonate Token	Adversaries may make and impersonate tokens to escalate privileges and bypass access controls. If an adversary has a username and password but the user is not logged onto the system, the adversary can then create a logon session for the user using the `LogonUser` function. The function will return a copy of the new session's access token and the adversary can use `SetThreadToken` to assign the token to a thread.
	Parent PID Spoofing	Adversaries may spoof the parent process identifier (PPID) of a new process to evade process-monitoring defenses or to elevate privileges. New processes are typically spawned directly from their parent, or calling, process unless explicitly specified. One way of explicitly assigning the PPID of a new process is via the `CreateProcess` API call, which supports a parameter that defines the PPID to use. This functionality is used by Windows features, such as User Account Control (UAC) to correctly set the PPID after a requested elevated process is spawned by SYSTEM (typically via svchost.exe or consent.exe) rather than the current user context.

ID	NAME	DESCRIPTION
	SID-History Injection	Adversaries may use SID-History Injection to escalate privileges and bypass access controls. The Windows security identifier (SID) is a unique value that identifies a user or group account. SIDs are used by Windows security in both security descriptors and access tokens. An account can hold additional SIDs in the SID-History Active Directory attribute, allowing inter-operable account migration between domains (e.g., all values in SID-History are included in access tokens).
T1574	Hijack Execution Flow	Adversaries may execute their own malicious payloads by hijacking the way operating systems run programs. Hijacking execution flow can be for the purposes of persistence, since this hijacked execution may reoccur over time. Adversaries may also use these mechanisms to elevate privileges or evade defenses, such as application control or other restrictions on execution.
	DLL Search Order Hijacking	Adversaries may execute their own malicious payloads by hijacking the search order used to load DLLs. Windows systems use a common method to look for required DLLs to load into a program. Hijacking DLL loads may be for the purpose of establishing persistence as well as elevating privileges and/or evading restrictions on file execution.
	DLL Side-Loading	Adversaries may execute their own malicious payloads by hijacking the library manifest used to load DLLs. Adversaries may take advantage of vague references in the library manifest of a program by replacing a legitimate library with a malicious one, causing the operating system to load their malicious library when it is called for by the victim program.
	Dylib Hijacking	Adversaries may execute their own malicious payloads by hijacking ambiguous paths used to load libraries. Adversaries may plant Trojan dynamic libraries, in a directory that will be searched by the operating system before the legitimate library specified by the victim program, so that their malicious library will be loaded into the victim program instead. MacOS and OS X use a common method to look for required dynamic libraries (`dylib`) to load into a program based on search paths.
	Executable Installer File Permissions Weakness	Adversaries may execute their own malicious payloads by hijacking the binaries used by an installer. These processes may automatically execute specific binaries as part of their functionality or to perform other actions. If the permissions on the file system directory containing a target binary, or permissions on the binary itself, are improperly set, then the target binary may be overwritten with another binary using user-level permissions and executed by the original process. If the original process and thread are running under a higher permissions level, then the replaced binary will also execute under higher-level permissions, which could include `SYSTEM`.

ID	NAME	DESCRIPTION
	LD_PRELOAD	Adversaries may execute their own malicious payloads by hijacking the dynamic linker used to load libraries. The dynamic linker is used to load shared library dependencies needed by an executing program. The dynamic linker will typically check provided absolute paths and common directories for these dependencies, but can be overridden by shared objects specified by `LD_PRELOAD` to be loaded before all others.
	Path Interception by PATH Environment Variable	Adversaries may execute their own malicious payloads by hijacking environment variables used to load libraries. Adversaries may place a program in an earlier entry in the list of directories stored in the `PATH` environment variable, which Windows will then execute when it searches sequentially through that `PATH` listing in search of the binary that was called from a script or the command line.
	Path Interception by Search Order Hijacking	Adversaries may execute their own malicious payloads by hijacking the search order used to load other programs. Because some programs do not call other programs using the full path, adversaries may place their own file in the directory where the calling program is located, causing the operating system to launch their malicious software at the request of the calling program.
	Path Interception by Unquoted Path	Adversaries may execute their own malicious payloads by hijacking vulnerable file path references. Adversaries can take advantage of paths that lack surrounding quotations by placing an executable in a higher-level directory within the path, so that Windows will choose the adversary's executable to launch.
	Services File Permissions Weakness	Adversaries may execute their own malicious payloads by hijacking the binaries used by services. Adversaries may use flaws in the permissions of Windows services to replace the binary that is executed upon service start. These service processes may automatically execute specific binaries as part of their functionality or to perform other actions. If the permissions on the file system directory containing a target binary, or permissions on the binary itself are improperly set, then the target binary may be overwritten with another binary using user-level permissions and executed by the original process. If the original process and thread are running under a higher permissions level, then the replaced binary will also execute under higher-level permissions, which could include `SYSTEM`.

ID	NAME	DESCRIPTION
	Services Registry Permissions Weakness	Adversaries may execute their own malicious payloads by hijacking the Registry entries used by services. Adversaries may use flaws in the permissions for registry to redirect from the originally specified executable to one that they control, in order to launch their own code at Service start. Windows stores local service configuration information in the Registry under `HKLM\SYSTEM\CurrentControlSet\Services`. The information stored under a service's Registry keys can be manipulated to modify a service's execution parameters through tools, such as the service controller, sc.exe, PowerShell, or Reg. Access to Registry keys is controlled through Access Control Lists and permissions.
	COR_ PROFILER	Adversaries may leverage the `COR_PROFILER` environment variable to hijack the execution flow of programs that load the `.NET CLR`. The `COR_PROFILER` is a .NET Framework feature, which allows developers to specify an unmanaged (or external of `.NET`) profiling DLL to be loaded into each `.NET` process that loads the Common Language Runtime (CLR). These profilers are designed to monitor, troubleshoot, and debug managed code executed by the `.NET CLR`.

Credential Access

Credential access consists of techniques for stealing credentials like account names and passwords. Techniques used to get credentials include keylogging or credential dumping. Using legitimate credentials can give adversaries access to systems, make them harder to detect, and provide the opportunity to create more accounts to help achieve their goals.

ID	NAME	DESCRIPTION
T1110	Brute Force	Adversaries may use brute force techniques to gain access to accounts when passwords are unknown or when password hashes are obtained. Without knowledge of the password for an account or set of accounts, an adversary may systematically guess the password using a repetitive or iterative mechanism. Brute forcing passwords can take place via interaction with a service that will check the validity of those credentials or offline against previously acquired credential data, such as password hashes.

ID	NAME	DESCRIPTION
	Password Guessing	Adversaries with no prior knowledge of legitimate credentials within the system or environment may guess passwords to attempt access to accounts. Without knowledge of the password for an account, an adversary may opt to systematically guess the password using a repetitive or iterative mechanism. An adversary may guess login credentials without prior knowledge of system or environment passwords during an operation by using a list of common passwords. Password guessing may or may not take into account the target's policies on password complexity or use policies that may lock accounts out after a number of failed attempts.
	Password Cracking	Adversaries may use password cracking to attempt to recover usable credentials, such as plaintext passwords, when credential material, such as password hashes is obtained. OS Credential Dumping is used to obtain password hashes; this may only get an adversary so far when Pass the Hash is not an option. Techniques to systematically guess the passwords used to compute hashes are available, or the adversary may use a pre-computed rainbow table to crack hashes. Cracking hashes is usually done on adversary-controlled systems outside of the target network. The resulting plaintext password resulting from a successfully cracked hash may be used to log into systems, resources, and services in which the account has access.
	Password Spraying	Adversaries may use a single or small list of commonly used passwords against many different accounts to attempt to acquire valid account credentials. Password spraying uses one password (e.g., `Password01`), or a small list of commonly used passwords, that may match the complexity policy of the domain. Logins are attempted with that password against many different accounts on a network to avoid account lockouts that would normally occur when brute forcing a single account with many passwords.
	Credential Stuffing	Adversaries may use credentials obtained from breach dumps of unrelated accounts to gain access to target accounts through credential overlap. Occasionally, large numbers of username and password pairs are dumped online when a website or service is compromised and the user account credentials accessed. The information may be useful to an adversary attempting to compromise accounts by taking advantage of the tendency for users to use the same passwords across personal and business accounts.

ID	NAME	DESCRIPTION
	Credentials from Password Stores	Adversaries may search for common password storage locations to obtain user credentials. Passwords are stored in several places on a system, depending on the operating system or application holding the credentials. There are also specific applications that store passwords to make it easier for users to manage and maintain. Once credentials are obtained, they can be used to perform lateral movement and access restricted information.
	Keychain	Adversaries may collect the keychain storage data from a system to acquire credentials. Keychains are the built-in way for macOS to keep track of users' passwords and credentials for many services and features, such as Wi-Fi passwords, websites, secure notes, certificates, and Kerberos. Keychain files are located in `~/Library/Keychains/`, `/Library/Keychains/`, and `/Network/Library/Keychains/`. The security command-line utility, which is built into macOS by default, provides a useful way to manage these credentials.
	Security Memory	An adversary may obtain root access (allowing them to read security's memory), then they can scan through memory to find the correct sequence of keys in relatively few tries to decrypt the user's logon keychain. This provides the adversary with all the plaintext passwords for users, Wi-Fi, mail, browsers, certificates, secure notes, etc.
	Credentials from Web Browsers	Adversaries may acquire credentials from web browsers by reading files specific to the target browser. Web browsers commonly save credentials, such as website usernames and passwords so that they do not need to be entered manually in the future. Web browsers typically store the credentials in an encrypted format within a credential store; however, methods exist to extract plaintext credentials from web browsers.
T1212	Exploitation for Credential Access	Adversaries may exploit software vulnerabilities in an attempt to collect credentials. Exploitation of a software vulnerability occurs when an adversary takes advantage of a programming error in a program, service, or within the operating system software or kernel itself to execute adversary-controlled code. Credentialing and authentication mechanisms may be targeted for exploitation by adversaries as a means to gain access to useful credentials or circumvent the process to gain access to systems. One example of this is MS14-068, which targets Kerberos and can be used to forge Kerberos tickets using domain user permissions. Exploitation for credential access may also result in Privilege Escalation depending on the process targeted or credentials obtained.

ID	NAME	DESCRIPTION
T1187	Forced Authentication	Adversaries may gather credential material by invoking or forcing a user to automatically provide authentication information through a mechanism in which they can intercept.
T1606	Forge Web Credentials	Adversaries may forge credential materials that can be used to gain access to web applications or Internet services. Web applications and services (hosted in cloud SaaS environments or on-premise servers) often use session cookies, tokens, or other materials to authenticate and authorize user access.
	Web Cookies	Adversaries may forge web cookies that can be used to gain access to web applications or Internet services. Web applications and services (hosted in cloud SaaS environments or on-premise servers) often use session cookies to authenticate and authorize user access.
	SAML Tokens	An adversary may forge SAML tokens with any permissions claims and lifetimes if they possess a valid SAML token-signing certificate. The default lifetime of an SAML token is one hour, but the validity period can be specified in the `NotOnOrAfter` value of the conditions . . . element in a token. This value can be changed using the `AccessTokenLifetime` in a `LifetimeTokenPolicy`. Forged SAML tokens enable adversaries to authenticate across services that use SAML 2.0 as an SSO (single sign-on) mechanism.
T1056	Input Capture	Adversaries may use methods of capturing user input to obtain credentials or collect information. During normal system usage, users often provide credentials to various different locations, such as login pages/portals or system dialog boxes. Input capture mechanisms may be transparent to the user (e.g., Credential API Hooking) or rely on deceiving the user into providing input into what they believe to be a genuine service (e.g., Web Portal Capture).
	Keylogging	Adversaries may log user keystrokes to intercept credentials as the user types them. Keylogging is likely to be used to acquire credentials for new access opportunities when OS Credential Dumping efforts are not effective, and may require an adversary to intercept keystrokes on a system for a substantial period of time before credentials can be successfully captured.
	GUI Input Capture	Adversaries may mimic common operating system GUI components to prompt users for credentials with a seemingly legitimate prompt. When programs are executed that need additional privileges than are present in the current user context, it is common for the operating system to prompt the user for proper credentials to authorize the elevated privileges for the task (e.g., Bypass User Account Control).

ID	NAME	DESCRIPTION
	Web Portal Capture	Adversaries may install code on externally facing portals, such as a VPN login page, to capture and transmit credentials of users who attempt to log into the service. For example, a compromised login page may log provided user credentials before logging the user in to the service.
	Credential API Hooking	Adversaries may hook into Windows application programming interface (API) functions to collect user credentials. Malicious hooking mechanisms may capture API calls that include parameters that reveal user authentication credentials. Unlike Keylogging, this technique focuses specifically on API functions that include parameters that reveal user credentials.
T1557	Man-in-the-Middle	Adversaries may attempt to position themselves between two or more networked devices using a man-in-the-middle (MiTM) technique to support follow-on behaviors, such as Network Sniffing or Transmitted Data Manipulation. By abusing features of common networking protocols that can determine the flow of network traffic (e.g., ARP, DNS, LLMNR, etc.), adversaries may force a device to communicate through an adversary-controlled system so they can collect information or perform additional actions.
	LLMNR/NBT-NS Poisoning and SMB Relay	By responding to LLMNR/NBT-NS network traffic, adversaries may spoof an authoritative source for name resolution to force communication with an adversary-controlled system. This activity may be used to collect or relay authentication materials.
	ARP Cache Poisoning	Adversaries may poison Address Resolution Protocol (ARP) caches to position themselves between the communication of two or more networked devices. This activity may be used to enable follow-on behaviors, such as Network Sniffing or Transmitted Data Manipulation.
T1556	Modify Authentication Process	Adversaries may modify authentication mechanisms and processes to access user credentials or enable otherwise unwarranted access to accounts. The authentication process is handled by mechanisms, such as the Local Security Authentication Server (LSASS) process and the Security Accounts Manager (SAM) on Windows or pluggable authentication modules (PAM) on Unix-based systems, responsible for gathering, storing, and validating credentials.
	Domain Controller Authentication	Adversaries may patch the authentication process on a domain controller to bypass the typical authentication mechanisms and enable access to accounts.

ID	NAME	DESCRIPTION
	Password Filter DLL	Adversaries may register malicious password filter dynamic link libraries (DLLs) into the authentication process to acquire user credentials as they are validated.
	Pluggable Authentication Modules	Adversaries may modify pluggable authentication modules (PAM) to access user credentials or enable otherwise unwarranted access to accounts. PAM is a modular system of configuration files, libraries, and executable files, which guide authentication for many services. The most common authentication module is `pam_unix.so`, which retrieves, sets, and verifies account authentication information in `/etc/passwd` and `/etc/shadow`.
	Network Device Authentication	Adversaries may use Patch System Image to hard-code a password in the operating system, thus bypassing native authentication mechanisms for local accounts on network devices.
T1040	Network Sniffing	Adversaries may sniff network traffic to capture information about an environment, including authentication material passed over the network. Network sniffing refers to using the network interface on a system to monitor or capture information sent over a wired or wireless connection. An adversary may place a network interface into promiscuous mode to passively access data in transit over the network, or use span ports to capture a larger amount of data.
T1003	OS Credential Dumping	Adversaries may attempt to dump credentials to obtain account login and credential material, normally in the form of a hash or a cleartext password, from the operating system and software. Credentials can then be used to perform Lateral Movement and access restricted information.
	LSASS Memory	Adversaries may attempt to access credential material stored in the process memory of the Local Security Authority Subsystem Service (LSASS). After a user logs on, the system generates and stores a variety of credential materials in LSASS process memory. These credential materials can be harvested by an administrative user or `SYSTEM` and used to conduct Lateral Movement using Use Alternate Authentication Material.
	Security Account Manager	Adversaries may attempt to extract credential material from the Security Account Manager (SAM) database either through in-memory techniques or through the Windows Registry where the SAM database is stored. The SAM is a database file that contains local accounts for the host, typically those found with the `net user` command. Enumerating the SAM database requires `SYSTEM`-level access.

ID	NAME	DESCRIPTION
	NTDS	Adversaries may attempt to access or create a copy of the Active Directory domain database in order to steal credential information, as well as obtain other information about domain members, such as devices, users, and access rights. By default, the NTDS file (`NTDS.dit`) is located in `%SystemRoot%\NTDS\Ntds.dit` of a domain controller.
	LSA Secrets	Adversaries with `SYSTEM` access to a host may attempt to access Local Security Authority (LSA) secrets, which can contain a variety of different credential materials, such as credentials for service accounts. LSA secrets are stored in the registry at `HKEY_LOCAL_MACHINE\SECURITY\Policy\Secrets`. LSA secrets can also be dumped from memory.
	Cached Domain Credentials	Adversaries may attempt to access cached domain credentials used to allow authentication to occur in the event a domain controller is unavailable.
	DCSync	Adversaries may attempt to access credentials and other sensitive information by abusing a Windows Domain Controller's application programming interface (API) to simulate the replication process from a remote domain controller using a technique called DCSync.
	Proc Filesystem	Adversaries may gather credentials from information stored in the Proc filesystem or `/proc`. The Proc filesystem on Linux contains a great deal of information regarding the state of the running operating system. Processes running with root privileges can use this facility to scrape live memory of other running programs. If any of these programs store passwords in cleartext or password hashes in memory, these values can then be harvested for either usage or brute force attacks, respectively.
	/etc/passwd and /etc/shadow	Adversaries may attempt to dump the contents of `/etc/passwd` and `/etc/shadow` to enable offline password cracking. Most modern Linux operating systems use a combination of `/etc/passwd` and `/etc/shadow` to store user account information including password hashes in `/etc/shadow`. By default, `/etc/shadow` is only readable by the root user.
	Steal Application Access Token	Adversaries can steal user application access tokens as a means of acquiring credentials to access remote systems and resources. This can occur through social engineering and typically requires user action to grant access.

ID	NAME	DESCRIPTION
	Steal or Forge Kerberos Tickets	Adversaries may attempt to subvert Kerberos authentication by stealing or forging Kerberos tickets to enable Pass the Ticket.
	Golden Ticket	Adversaries who have the KRBTGT account password hash may forge Kerberos ticket-granting tickets (TGT), also known as a golden ticket. Golden tickets enable adversaries to generate authentication material for any account in Active Directory.
	Silver Ticket	Adversaries who have the password hash of a target service account (e.g., SharePoint, MSSQL) may forge Kerberos ticket-granting service (TGS) tickets, also known as silver tickets. Kerberos TGS tickets are also known as service tickets.
	Kerberoasting	Adversaries may abuse a valid Kerberos ticket-granting ticket (TGT) or sniff network traffic to obtain a ticket-granting service (TGS) ticket that may be vulnerable to Brute Force.
	AS-REP Roasting	Adversaries may reveal credentials of accounts that have disabled Kerberos preauthentication by Password Cracking Kerberos messages.
T1539	Steal Web Session Cookie	An adversary may steal web application or service session cookies and use them to gain access web applications or Internet services as an authenticated user without needing credentials. Web applications and services often use session cookies as an authentication token after a user has authenticated to a website.
T1111	Two-Factor Authentication Interception	Adversaries may target two-factor authentication mechanisms, such as smart cards, to gain access to credentials that can be used to access systems, services, and network resources. Use of two or multi-factor authentication (2FA or MFA) is recommended and provides a higher level of security than usernames and passwords alone, but organizations should be aware of techniques that could be used to intercept and bypass these security mechanisms.
T1552	Unsecured Credentials	Adversaries may search compromised systems to find and obtain insecurely stored credentials. These credentials can be stored and/or misplaced in many locations on a system, including plaintext files (e.g., Bash History), operating system or application-specific repositories (e.g., Credentials in Registry), or other specialized files/artifacts (e.g., Private Keys).

ID	NAME	DESCRIPTION
	Credentials In Files	Adversaries may search local file systems and remote file shares for files containing insecurely stored credentials. These can be files created by users to store their own credentials, shared credential stores for a group of individuals, configuration files containing passwords for a system or service, or source code/binary files containing embedded passwords.
	Credentials in Registry	Adversaries may search the Registry on compromised systems for insecurely stored credentials. The Windows Registry stores configuration information that can be used by the system or other programs. Adversaries may query the Registry looking for credentials and passwords that have been stored for use by other programs or services. Sometimes these credentials are used for automatic logons.
	Bash History	Adversaries may search the bash command history on compromised systems for insecurely stored credentials. Bash keeps track of the commands user's type on the command-line with the "history" utility. Once a user logs out, the history is flushed to the user's `.bash_history` file. For each user, this file resides at the same location: `~/.bash_history`. Typically, this file keeps track of the user's last 500 commands. Users often type usernames and passwords on the command-line as parameters to programs, which then get saved to this file when they log out. Attackers can abuse this by looking through the file for potential credentials.
	Private Keys	Adversaries may search for private key certificate files on compromised systems for insecurely stored credentials. Private cryptographic keys and certificates are used for authentication, encryption/decryption, and digital signatures. Common key and certificate file extensions include: `.key`, `.pgp`, `.gpg`, `.ppk`, `.p12`, `.pem`, `.pfx`, `.cer`, `.p7b`, `.asc`.
	Cloud Instance Metadata API	Adversaries may attempt to access the Cloud Instance Metadata API to collect credentials and other sensitive data.
	Group Policy Preferences	Adversaries may attempt to find unsecured credentials in Group Policy Preferences (GPP). GPP are tools that allow administrators to create domain policies with embedded credentials. These policies allow administrators to set local accounts.

Lateral Movement

Lateral movement consists of techniques that adversaries use to enter and control remote systems on a network. Following through on their primary objective often requires exploring the network to find their target and subsequently gaining access to it. Reaching their objective often involves pivoting through multiple systems and accounts. Adversaries might install their own remote access tools to accomplish lateral movement or use legitimate credentials with native network and operating system tools, which may be stealthier.

ID	NAME	DESCRIPTION
T1210	Exploitation of Remote Services	Adversaries may exploit remote services to gain unauthorized access to internal systems once inside of a network. Exploitation of a software vulnerability occurs when an adversary takes advantage of a programming error in a program, service, or within the operating system software or kernel itself to execute adversary-controlled code. A common goal for post-compromise exploitation of remote services is for lateral movement to enable access to a remote system.

ID	NAME	DESCRIPTION
T1534	Internal Spear Phishing	Adversaries may use internal spear phishing to gain access to additional information or exploit other users within the same organization after they already have access to accounts or systems within the environment. Internal spear phishing is a multi-staged attack where an email account is owned either by controlling the user's device with previously installed malware or by compromising the account credentials of the user. Adversaries attempt to take advantage of a trusted internal account to increase the likelihood of tricking the target into falling for the phish attempt.
T1570	Lateral Tool Transfer	Adversaries may transfer tools or other files between systems in a compromised environment. Files may be copied from one system to another to stage adversary tools or other files over the course of an operation. Adversaries may copy files laterally between internal victim systems to support lateral movement using inherent file sharing protocols such as file sharing over SMB to connected network shares or with authenticated connections with SMB/Windows Admin Shares or Remote Desktop Protocol. Files can also be copied over on Mac and Linux with native tools like scp, rsync, and sftp.
T1563	Remote Service Session Hijacking	Adversaries may take control of preexisting sessions with remote services to move laterally in an environment. Users may use valid credentials to log into a service specifically designed to accept remote connections, such as telnet, SSH, and RDP. When a user logs into a service, a session will be established that will allow them to maintain a continuous interaction with that service.
	SSH Hijacking	Adversaries may hijack a legitimate user's SSH session to move laterally within an environment. Secure Shell (SSH) is a standard means of remote access on Linux and macOS systems. It allows a user to connect to another system via an encrypted tunnel, commonly authenticating through a password, certificate, or the use of an asymmetric encryption key pair.
	RDP Hijacking	Adversaries may hijack a legitimate user's remote desktop session to move laterally within an environment. Remote desktop is a common feature in operating systems. It allows a user to log into an interactive session with a system desktop graphical user interface on a remote system. Microsoft refers to its implementation of the Remote Desktop Protocol (RDP) as Remote Desktop Services (RDS).

ID	NAME	DESCRIPTION
T1021	Remote Services	Adversaries may use Valid Accounts to log into a service specifically designed to accept remote connections, such as telnet, SSH, and VNC. The adversary may then perform actions as the logged-on user.
	Remote Desktop Protocol	Adversaries may use Valid Accounts to log into a computer using the Remote Desktop Protocol (RDP). The adversary may then perform actions as the logged-on user.
	SMB/Windows Admin Shares	Adversaries may use Valid Accounts to interact with a remote network share using Server Message Block (SMB). The adversary may then perform actions as the logged-on user.
	Distributed Component Object Model	Adversaries may use Valid Accounts to interact with remote machines by taking advantage of Distributed Component Object Model (DCOM). The adversary may then perform actions as the logged-on user.
	SSH	Adversaries may use Valid Accounts to log into remote machines using Secure Shell (SSH). The adversary may then perform actions as the logged-on user.
	VNC	Adversaries may use Valid Accounts to remotely control machines using Virtual Network Computing (VNC). The adversary may then perform actions as the logged-on user.
	Windows Remote Management	Adversaries may use Valid Accounts to interact with remote systems using Windows Remote Management (WinRM). The adversary may then perform actions as the logged-on user.
T1091	Replication Through Removable Media	Adversaries may move onto systems, possibly those on disconnected or air-gapped networks, by copying malware to removable media and taking advantage of Autorun features when the media is inserted into a system and executes. In the case of Lateral Movement, this may occur through modification of executable files stored on removable media or by copying malware and renaming it to look like a legitimate file to trick users into executing it on a separate system. In the case of Initial Access, this may occur through manual manipulation of the media, modification of systems used to initially format the media, or modification to the media's firmware itself.
T1072	Software Deployment Tools	Adversaries may gain access to and use third-party software suites installed within an enterprise network, such as administration, monitoring, and deployment systems, to move laterally through the network. Third-party applications and software deployment systems may be in use in the network environment for administration purposes (e.g., SCCM, VNC, HBSS, Altiris, etc.).

ID	NAME	DESCRIPTION
T1080	Taint Shared Content	Adversaries may deliver payloads to remote systems by adding content to shared storage locations, such as network drives or internal code repositories. Content stored on network drives or in other shared locations may be tainted by adding malicious programs, scripts, or exploit code to otherwise valid files. Once a user opens the shared tainted content, the malicious portion can be executed to run the adversary's code on a remote system. Adversaries may use tainted shared content to move laterally.
T1550	Use Alternate Authentication Material	Adversaries may use alternate authentication material, such as password hashes, Kerberos tickets, and application access tokens, in order to move laterally within an environment and bypass normal system access controls.
	Application Access Token	Adversaries may use stolen application access tokens to bypass the typical authentication process and access restricted accounts, information, or services on remote systems. These tokens are typically stolen from users and used in lieu of login credentials.
	Pass the Hash	Adversaries may "pass the hash" using stolen password hashes to move laterally within an environment, bypassing normal system access controls. Pass the hash (PtH) is a method of authenticating as a user without having access to the user's cleartext password. This method bypasses standard authentication steps that require a cleartext password, moving directly into the portion of the authentication that uses the password hash. In this technique, valid password hashes for the account being used are captured using a Credential Access technique. Captured hashes are used with PtH to authenticate as that user. Once authenticated, PtH may be used to perform actions on local or remote systems.
	Pass the Ticket	Adversaries may "pass the ticket" using stolen Kerberos tickets to move laterally within an environment, bypassing normal system access controls. Pass the ticket (PtT) is a method of authenticating to a system using Kerberos tickets without having access to an account's password. Kerberos authentication can be used as the first step to lateral movement to a remote system.
	Web Session Cookie	Adversaries can use stolen session cookies to authenticate to web applications and services. This technique bypasses some multi-factor authentication protocols since the session is already authenticated.

Command and Control

Command and control consist of techniques that adversaries may use to communicate with systems under their control within a victim network. Adversaries commonly attempt to mimic normal, expected traffic to avoid detection. There are many ways an adversary can establish command and control with various levels of stealth, depending on the victim's network structure and defenses.

ID	NAME	DESCRIPTION
T1071	Application Layer Protocol	Adversaries may communicate using application layer protocols to avoid detection/network filtering by blending in with existing traffic. Commands to the remote system, and often the results of those commands, will be embedded within the protocol traffic between the client and server.
	Web Protocols	Adversaries may communicate using application layer protocols associated with web traffic to avoid detection/network filtering by blending in with existing traffic. Commands to the remote system, and often the results of those commands, will be embedded within the protocol traffic between the client and server.
	File Transfer Protocols	Adversaries may communicate using application layer protocols associated with transferring files to avoid detection/network filtering by blending in with existing traffic. Commands to the remote system, and often the results of those commands, will be embedded within the protocol traffic between the client and server.

ID	NAME	DESCRIPTION
	Mail Protocols	Adversaries may communicate using application layer protocols associated with electronic mail delivery to avoid detection/network filtering by blending in with existing traffic. Commands to the remote system, and often the results of those commands, will be embedded within the protocol traffic between the client and server.
	DNS	Adversaries may communicate using the Domain Name System (DNS) application layer protocol to avoid detection/network filtering by blending in with existing traffic. Commands to the remote system, and often the results of those commands, will be embedded within the protocol traffic between the client and server.
T1092	Communication Through Removable Media	Adversaries can perform command and control between compromised hosts on potentially disconnected networks using removable media to transfer commands from system to system. Both systems would need to be compromised, with the likelihood that an Internet-connected system was compromised first and the second through lateral movement by Replication Through Removable Media. Commands and files would be relayed from the disconnected system to the Internet-connected system to which the adversary has direct access.
T1132	Data Encoding	Adversaries may encode data to make the content of command and control traffic more difficult to detect. Command and control (C2) information can be encoded using a standard data encoding system. Use of data encoding may adhere to existing protocol specifications and includes use of ASCII, Unicode, Base64, MIME, or other binary-to-text and character encoding systems. Some data encoding systems may also result in data compression, such as gzip.
	Standard Encoding	Adversaries may encode data with a standard data encoding system to make the content of command and control traffic more difficult to detect. Command and control (C2) information can be encoded using a standard data encoding system that adheres to existing protocol specifications. Common data encoding schemes include ASCII, Unicode, hexadecimal, Base64, and MIME. Some data encoding systems may also result in data compression, such as gzip.
	Non-Standard Encoding	Adversaries may encode data with a non-standard data encoding system to make the content of command and control traffic more difficult to detect. Command and control (C2) information can be encoded using a non-standard data encoding system that diverges from existing protocol specifications. Non-standard data encoding schemes may be based on or related to standard data encoding schemes, such as a modified Base64 encoding for the message body of an HTTP request.

ID	NAME	DESCRIPTION
T1001	Data Obfuscation	Adversaries may obfuscate command and control traffic to make it more difficult to detect. Command and control (C2) communications are hidden (but not necessarily encrypted) in an attempt to make the content more difficult to discover or decipher and to make the communication less conspicuous and hide commands from being seen. This encompasses many methods, such as adding junk data to protocol traffic, using steganography, or impersonating legitimate protocols.
	Junk Data	Adversaries may add junk data to protocols used for command and control to make detection more difficult. By adding random or meaningless data to the protocols used for command and control, adversaries can prevent trivial methods for decoding, deciphering, or otherwise analyzing the traffic. Examples may include appending/prepending data with junk characters or writing junk characters between significant characters.
	Steganography	Adversaries may use steganographic techniques to hide command and control traffic to make detection efforts more difficult. Steganographic techniques can be used to hide data in digital messages that are transferred between systems. This hidden information can be used for command and control of compromised systems. In some cases, the passing of files embedded using steganography, such as image or document files, can be used for command and control.
	Protocol Impersonation	Adversaries may impersonate legitimate protocols or web service traffic to disguise command and control activity and thwart analysis efforts. By impersonating legitimate protocols or web services, adversaries can make their command and control traffic blend in with legitimate network traffic.
T1568	Dynamic Resolution	Adversaries may dynamically establish connections to command and control infrastructure to evade common detections and remediation. This may be achieved by using malware that shares a common algorithm with the infrastructure the adversary uses to receive the malware's communications. These calculations can be used to dynamically adjust parameters such as the domain name, IP address, or port number the malware uses for command and control.

ID	NAME	DESCRIPTION
	Fast Flux DNS	Adversaries may use Fast Flux DNS to hide a command and control channel behind an array of rapidly changing IP addresses linked to a single domain resolution. This technique uses a fully qualified domain name, with multiple IP addresses assigned to it, which are swapped with high frequency, using a combination of round robin IP addressing and short Time-To-Live (TTL) for a DNS resource record.
	Domain Generation Algorithms	Adversaries may make use of Domain Generation Algorithms (DGAs) to dynamically identify a destination domain for command and control traffic rather than relying on a list of static IP addresses or domains. This has the advantage of making it much harder for defenders to block, track, or take over the command and control channel, as there potentially could be thousands of domains that malware can check for instructions.
	DNS Calculation	Adversaries may perform calculations on addresses returned in DNS results to determine which port and IP address to use for command and control, rather than relying on a predetermined port number or the actual returned IP address. An IP and/or port number calculation can be used to bypass egress filtering on a C2 channel.
	Encrypted Channel	Adversaries may employ a known encryption algorithm to conceal command and control traffic rather than relying on any inherent protections provided by a communication protocol. Despite the use of a secure algorithm, these implementations may be vulnerable to reverse engineering if secret keys are encoded and/or generated within malware samples/configuration files.
	Symmetric Cryptography	Adversaries may employ a known symmetric encryption algorithm to conceal command and control traffic rather than relying on any inherent protections provided by a communication protocol. Symmetric encryption algorithms use the same key for plaintext encryption and ciphertext decryption. Common symmetric encryption algorithms include AES, DES, 3DES, Blowfish, and RC4.
	Asymmetric Cryptography	Adversaries may employ a known asymmetric encryption algorithm to conceal command and control traffic rather than relying on any inherent protections provided by a communication protocol. Asymmetric cryptography, also known as public key cryptography, uses a keypair per party: one public that can be freely distributed, and one private. Due to how the keys are generated, the sender encrypts data with the receiver's public key and the receiver decrypts the data with their private key. This ensures that only the intended recipient can read the encrypted data. Common public key encryption algorithms include RSA and ElGamal.

ID	NAME	DESCRIPTION
T1008	Fallback Channels	Adversaries may use fallback or alternate communication channels if the primary channel is compromised or inaccessible in order to maintain reliable command and control and to avoid data transfer thresholds.
T1105	Ingress Tool Transfer	Adversaries may transfer tools or other files from an external system into a compromised environment. Files may be copied from an external adversary controlled system through the command and control channel to bring tools into the victim network or through alternate protocols with another tool such as FTP. Files can also be copied over on Mac and Linux with native tools like scp, rsync, and sftp.
T1104	Multi-Stage Channels	Adversaries may create multiple stages for command and control that are employed under different conditions or for certain functions. Use of multiple stages may obfuscate the command and control channel to make detection more difficult.
T1095	Non-Application Layer Protocol	Adversaries may use a non-application layer protocol for communication between host and C2 server or among infected hosts within a network. The list of possible protocols is extensive. Specific examples include use of network layer protocols, such as the Internet Control Message Protocol (ICMP); transport layer protocols, such as the User Datagram Protocol (UDP); session layer protocols, such as Socket Secure (SOCKS); as well as redirected/tunneled protocols, such as Serial over LAN (SOL).
T1571	Non-Standard Port	Adversaries may communicate using a protocol and port pairing that are typically not associated. For example, HTTPS over port 8088 or port 587 as opposed to the traditional port 443. Adversaries may make changes to the standard port used by a protocol to bypass filtering or muddle analysis/parsing of network data.
T1572	Protocol Tunneling	Adversaries may tunnel network communications to and from a victim system within a separate protocol to avoid detection/network filtering and/or enable access to otherwise unreachable systems. Tunneling involves explicitly encapsulating a protocol within another. This behavior may conceal malicious traffic by blending in with existing traffic and/or provide an outer layer of encryption (similar to a VPN). Tunneling could also enable routing of network packets that would otherwise not reach their intended destination, such as SMB, RDP, or other traffic that would be filtered by network appliances or not routed over the Internet.

ID	NAME	DESCRIPTION
T1090	Proxy	Adversaries may use a connection proxy to direct network traffic between systems or act as an intermediary for network communications to a command and control server to avoid direct connections to their infrastructure. Many tools exist that enable traffic redirection through proxies or port redirection, including HTRAN, ZXProxy, and ZXPortMap. Adversaries use these types of proxies to manage command and control communications, reduce the number of simultaneous outbound network connections, provide resiliency in the face of connection loss, or to ride over existing trusted communications paths between victims to avoid suspicion. Adversaries may chain together multiple proxies to further disguise the source of malicious traffic.
	Internal Proxy	Adversaries may use an internal proxy to direct command and control traffic between two or more systems in a compromised environment. Many tools exist that enable traffic redirection through proxies or port redirection, including HTRAN, ZXProxy, and ZXPortMap. Adversaries use internal proxies to manage command and control communications inside a compromised environment, to reduce the number of simultaneous outbound network connections, to provide resiliency in the face of connection loss, or to ride over existing trusted communications paths between infected systems to avoid suspicion. Internal proxy connections may use common peer-to-peer (p2p) networking protocols, such as SMB, to better blend in with the environment.
	External Proxy	Adversaries may use an external proxy to act as an intermediary for network communications to a command and control server to avoid direct connections to their infrastructure. Many tools exist that enable traffic redirection through proxies or port redirection, including HTRAN, ZXProxy, and ZXPortMap. Adversaries use these types of proxies to manage command and control communications, to provide resiliency in the face of connection loss, or to ride over existing trusted communications paths to avoid suspicion.
	Multi-hop Proxy	To disguise the source of malicious traffic, adversaries may chain together multiple proxies. Typically, a defender will be able to identify the last proxy traffic traversed before it enters their network; the defender may or may not be able to identify any previous proxies before the last-hop proxy. This technique makes identifying the original source of the malicious traffic even more difficult by requiring the defender to trace malicious traffic through several proxies to identify its source. A particular variant of this behavior is to use onion routing networks, such as the publicly available TOR network.

ID	NAME	DESCRIPTION
	Domain Fronting	Adversaries may take advantage of routing schemes in Content Delivery Networks (CDNs) and other services, which host multiple domains to obfuscate the intended destination of HTTPS traffic or traffic tunneled through HTTPS. Domain fronting involves using different domain names in the SNI field of the TLS header and the Host field of the HTTP header. If both domains are served from the same CDN, then the CDN may route to the address specified in the HTTP header after unwrapping the TLS header. A variation of the technique, "domainless" fronting, utilizes an SNI field that is left blank; this may allow the fronting to work even when the CDN attempts to validate that the SNI and HTTP Host fields match (if the blank SNI fields are ignored).
T1219	Remote Access Software	An adversary may use legitimate desktop support and remote access software, such as Team Viewer, Go2Assist, LogMein, AmmyyAdmin, etc., to establish an interactive command and control channel to target systems within networks. These services are commonly used as legitimate technical support software, and may be allowed by application control within a target environment. Remote access tools like VNC, Ammyy, and Teamviewer are used frequently when compared with other legitimate software commonly used by adversaries.
T1205	Traffic Signaling	Adversaries may use traffic signaling to hide open ports or other malicious functionality used for persistence or command and control. Traffic signaling involves the use of a magic value or sequence that must be sent to a system to trigger a special response, such as opening a closed port or executing a malicious task. This may take the form of sending a series of packets with certain characteristics before a port will be opened that the adversary can use for command and control. Usually this series of packets consists of attempted connections to a predefined sequence of closed ports (i.e., Port Knocking), but can involve unusual flags, specific strings, or other unique characteristics. After the sequence is completed, opening a port may be accomplished by the host-based firewall, but could also be implemented by custom software.
	Port Knocking	Adversaries may use port knocking to hide open ports used for persistence or command and control. To enable a port, an adversary sends a series of attempted connections to a predefined sequence of closed ports. After the sequence is completed, opening a port is often accomplished by the host-based firewall, but could also be implemented by custom software.

ID	NAME	DESCRIPTION
T1102	Web Service	Adversaries may use an existing, legitimate external web service as a means for relaying data to/from a compromised system. Popular websites and social media acting as a mechanism for C2 may give a significant amount of cover due to the likelihood that hosts within a network are already communicating with them prior to a compromise. Using common services, such as those offered by Google or Twitter, makes it easier for adversaries to hide in expected noise. Web service providers commonly use SSL/TLS encryption, giving adversaries an added level of protection.
	Dead Drop Resolver	Adversaries may use an existing, legitimate external Web service to host information that points to additional command and control (C2) infrastructure. Adversaries may post content, known as a dead drop resolver, on Web services with embedded (and often obfuscated/encoded) domains or IP addresses. Once infected, victims will reach out to and be redirected by these resolvers.
	Bidirectional Communication	Adversaries may use an existing, legitimate external Web service as a means for sending commands to and receiving output from a compromised system over the Web service channel. Compromised systems may leverage popular websites and social media to host command and control (C2) instructions. Those infected systems can then send the output from those commands back over that Web service channel. The return traffic may occur in a variety of ways, depending on the Web service being utilized. For example, the return traffic may take the form of the compromised system posting a comment on a forum, issuing a pull request to development project, updating a document hosted on a Web service, or by sending a Tweet.
	One-Way Communication	Adversaries may use an existing, legitimate external Web service as a means for sending commands to a compromised system without receiving return output over the Web service channel. Compromised systems may leverage popular websites and social media to host command and control (C2) instructions. Those infected systems may opt to send the output from those commands back over a different C2 channel, including to another distinct Web service. Alternatively, compromised systems may return no output at all in cases where adversaries want to send instructions to systems and do not want a response.

Data Exfiltration

Exfiltration consists of techniques that adversaries may use to steal data from your network. Once they've collected data, adversaries often package it to avoid detection while removing it. This can include compression and encryption. Techniques for getting data out of a target network typically include transferring it over their command and control channel or an alternate channel and may also include putting size limits on the transmission.

ID	NAME	DESCRIPTION
T1020	Automated Exfiltration	Adversaries may exfiltrate data, such as sensitive documents, through the use of automated processing after being gathered during Collection.
	Traffic Duplication	Adversaries may leverage traffic mirroring in order to automate data exfiltration over compromised network infrastructure. Traffic mirroring is a native feature for some network devices and used for network analysis and may be configured to duplicate traffic and forward to one or more destinations for analysis by a network analyzer or other monitoring device.
T1030	Data Transfer Size Limits	An adversary may exfiltrate data in fixed-sized chunks instead of whole files or limit packet sizes below certain thresholds. This approach may be used to avoid triggering network data transfer threshold alerts.

ID	NAME	DESCRIPTION
T1048	Exfiltration Over Alternative Protocol	Adversaries may steal data by exfiltrating it over a different protocol than that of the existing command and control channel. The data may also be sent to an alternate network location from the main command and control server.
	Exfiltration Over Symmetric Encrypted Non-C2 Protocol	Adversaries may steal data by exfiltrating it over a symmetrically encrypted network protocol other than that of the existing command and control channel. The data may also be sent to an alternate network location from the main command and control server.
	Exfiltration Over Asymmetric Encrypted Non-C2 Protocol	Adversaries may steal data by exfiltrating it over an asymmetrically encrypted network protocol other than that of the existing command and control channel. The data may also be sent to an alternate network location from the main command and control server.
	Exfiltration Over Unencrypted/ Obfuscated Non-C2 Protocol	Adversaries may steal data by exfiltrating it over an unencrypted network protocol other than that of the existing command and control channel. The data may also be sent to an alternate network location from the main command and control server.
T1041	Exfiltration Over C2 Channel	Adversaries may steal data by exfiltrating it over an existing command and control channel. Stolen data is encoded into the normal communications channel using the same protocol as command and control communications.
T1011	Exfiltration Over Other Network Medium	Adversaries may attempt to exfiltrate data over a different network medium than the command and control channel. If the command and control network is a wired Internet connection, the exfiltration may occur, for example, over a Wi-Fi connection, modem, cellular data connection, Bluetooth, or another radio frequency (RF) channel.
	Exfiltration Over Bluetooth	Adversaries may attempt to exfiltrate data over Bluetooth rather than the command and control channel. If the command and control network is a wired Internet connection, an attacker may opt to exfiltrate data using a Bluetooth communication channel.
T1052	Exfiltration Over Physical Medium	Adversaries may attempt to exfiltrate data via a physical medium, such as a removable drive. In certain circumstances, such as an air-gapped network compromise, exfiltration could occur via a physical medium or device introduced by a user. Such media could be an external hard drive, USB drive, cellular phone, MP3 player, or other removable storage and processing device. The physical medium or device could be used as the final exfiltration point or to hop between otherwise disconnected systems.

ID	NAME	DESCRIPTION
	Exfiltration Over USB	Adversaries may attempt to exfiltrate data over a USB-connected physical device. In certain circumstances, such as an air-gapped network compromise, exfiltration could occur via a USB device introduced by a user. The USB device could be used as the final exfiltration point or to hop between otherwise disconnected systems.
T1567	Exfiltration Over Web Service	Adversaries may use an existing, legitimate external Web service to exfiltrate data rather than their primary command and control channel. Popular Web services acting as an exfiltration mechanism may give a significant amount of cover due to the likelihood that hosts within a network are already communicating with them prior to compromise. Firewall rules may also already exist to permit traffic to these services.
	Exfiltration to Code Repository	Adversaries may exfiltrate data to a code repository rather than over their primary command and control channel. Code repositories are often accessible via an API (e.g., `https://api.github.com`). Access to these APIs is often over HTTPS, which gives the adversary an additional level of protection.
	Exfiltration to Cloud Storage	Adversaries may exfiltrate data to a cloud storage service rather than over their primary command and control channel. Cloud storage services allow for the storage, edit, and retrieval of data from a remote cloud storage server over the Internet.
T1029	Scheduled Transfer	Adversaries may schedule data exfiltration to be performed only at certain times of day or at certain intervals. This could be done to blend traffic patterns with normal activity or availability.
T1537	Transfer Data to Cloud Account	Adversaries may exfiltrate data by transferring the data, including backups of cloud environments, to another cloud account they control on the same service to avoid typical file transfers/downloads and network-based exfiltration detection.

MITRE Cloud Matrix

The tactics and techniques covered in this appendix represent the MITRE ATT&CK Matrix for Enterprise covering cloud-based techniques. The Matrix contains information for the following platforms: Azure AD, Office 365, Google Workspace, SaaS, IaaS. Figure G.1 shows the framework.

Refer to `https://attack.mitre.org/matrices/enterprise/cloud/` for the latest information.

Initial Access

Drive-by Compromise

Adversaries may gain access to a system through a user visiting a website over the normal course of browsing. With this technique, the user's web browser is typically targeted for exploitation, but adversaries may also use compromised websites for non-exploitation behavior such as acquiring access to an application token. Multiple ways of delivering exploit code to a browser exist, including:

- A legitimate website is compromised where adversaries have injected some form of malicious code such as JavaScript, iFrames, and cross-site scripting.
- Malicious ads are paid for and served through legitimate ad providers.

Figure G-1: MITRE ATT&CK Framework Cloud Matrix

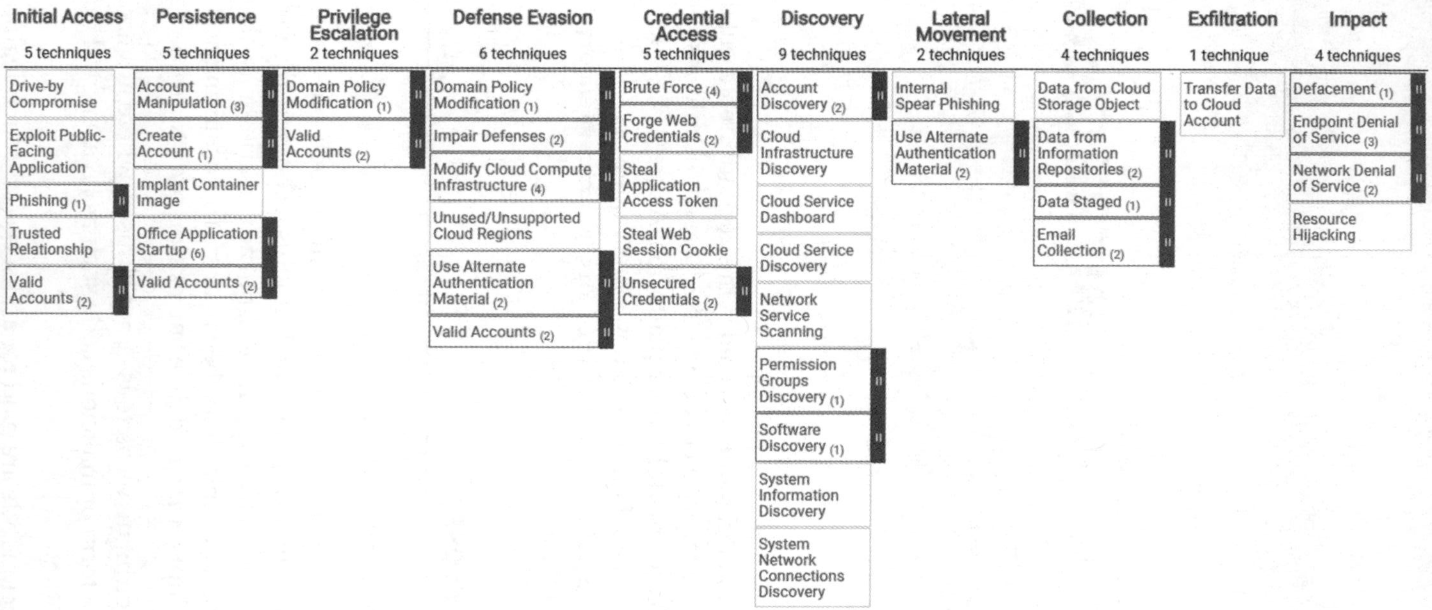

Initial Access (5 techniques)	Persistence (5 techniques)	Privilege Escalation (2 techniques)	Defense Evasion (6 techniques)	Credential Access (5 techniques)	Discovery (9 techniques)	Lateral Movement (2 techniques)	Collection (4 techniques)	Exfiltration (1 technique)	Impact (4 techniques)
Drive-by Compromise	Account Manipulation (3)	Domain Policy Modification (1)	Domain Policy Modification (1)	Brute Force (4)	Account Discovery (2)	Internal Spear Phishing	Data from Cloud Storage Object	Transfer Data to Cloud Account	Defacement (1)
Exploit Public-Facing Application	Create Account (1)	Valid Accounts (2)	Impair Defenses (2)	Forge Web Credentials (2)	Cloud Infrastructure Discovery	Use Alternate Authentication Material (2)	Data from Information Repositories (2)		Endpoint Denial of Service (3)
Phishing (1)	Implant Container Image		Modify Cloud Compute Infrastructure (4)	Steal Application Access Token	Cloud Service Dashboard		Data Staged (1)		Network Denial of Service (2)
Trusted Relationship	Office Application Startup (6)		Unused/Unsupported Cloud Regions	Steal Web Session Cookie	Cloud Service Discovery		Email Collection (2)		Resource Hijacking
Valid Accounts (2)	Valid Accounts (2)		Use Alternate Authentication Material (2)	Unsecured Credentials (2)	Network Service Scanning				
			Valid Accounts (2)		Permission Groups Discovery (1)				
					Software Discovery (1)				
					System Information Discovery				
					System Network Connections Discovery				

- Built-in web application interfaces are leveraged for the insertion of any other kind of object that can be used to display web content or contain a script that executes on the visiting client (e.g., forum posts, comments, and other user-controllable web content).

Often the website used by an adversary is one visited by a specific community, such as government, a particular industry, or region, where the goal is to compromise a specific user or set of users based on a shared interest. This kind of targeted attack is referred to a strategic web compromise or a *watering hole attack*. There are several known examples of this occurring. Typical drive-by compromise process is as follows:

- A user visits a website that is used to host the adversary-controlled content.
- Scripts automatically execute, typically searching versions of the browser and plugins for a potentially vulnerable version.
- The user may be required to assist in this process by enabling scripting or active website components and ignoring warning dialog boxes.
- Upon finding a vulnerable version, exploit code is delivered to the browser.
- If exploitation is successful, then it will give the adversary privileges to execute code on the user's system unless other protections are in place.

Unlike the Exploit Public-Facing application, the focus of this technique is to exploit software on a client endpoint upon visiting a website. This will commonly give an adversary access to systems on the internal network instead of external systems that may be in a DMZ.

Adversaries may also use compromised websites to deliver a user to a malicious application designed to steal Application Access Tokens, like OAuth tokens, to gain access to protected applications and information. These malicious applications have been delivered through popups on legitimate websites.

Detection

Firewalls and proxies can inspect URLs for potentially known-bad domains or parameters. They can also do reputation-based analytics on websites and their requested resources such as how old a domain is, who it's registered to, if it's on a known-bad list, or how many other users have connected to it before.

Network intrusion detection systems, sometimes with SSL/TLS MITM inspection, can be used to look for known malicious scripts (recon, heap spray, and browser identification scripts have been frequently reused), common script obfuscation, and exploit code.

Detecting compromises based on the drive-by exploit from a legitimate website may be difficult. Also look for behavior on the endpoint system that might indicate successful compromise, such as abnormal behavior of browser processes.

This could include suspicious files written to disk, evidence of Process Injection for attempts to hide execution, evidence of Discovery, or other unusual network traffic that may indicate additional tools transferred to the system.

Exploiting a Public-Facing Application

Adversaries may attempt to take advantage of a weakness in an Internet-facing computer or program using software, data, or commands in order to cause unintended or unanticipated behavior. The weakness in the system can be a bug, a glitch, or a design vulnerability. These applications are often websites, but can include databases (like SQL), standard services (like SMB or SSH), network device administration and management protocols (like SNMP and Smart Install), and any other applications with Internet-accessible open sockets, such as web servers and related services. Depending on the flaw being exploited, this may include Exploitation for Defense Evasion.

If an application is hosted on cloud-based infrastructure, exploiting it may lead to compromise of the underlying instance. This can allow an adversary a path to access the cloud APIs or to take advantage of weak identity and access management policies.

For websites and databases, the OWASP top 10 and CWE top 25 highlight the most common web-based vulnerabilities.

Detection

Monitor application logs for abnormal behavior that may indicate attempted or successful exploitation. Use deep packet inspection to look for artifacts of common exploit traffic, such as SQL injection. Web Application Firewalls may detect improper inputs attempting exploitation.

Phishing

Adversaries may send phishing messages to gain access to victim systems. All forms of phishing are electronically delivered social engineering. Phishing can be targeted, known as spear phishing. In spear phishing, a specific individual, company, or industry is targeted by the adversary. More generally, adversaries can conduct non-targeted phishing, such as in mass malware spam campaigns.

Adversaries may send victims emails containing malicious attachments or links, typically to execute malicious code on victim systems or to gather credentials for use of Valid Accounts. Phishing may also be conducted via third-party services, like social media platforms.

Detection

Network intrusion detection systems and email gateways can be used to detect phishing with malicious attachments in transit. Detonation chambers may also be used to identify malicious attachments. Solutions can be signature and behavior based, but adversaries may construct attachments in a way to avoid these systems.

URL inspection within email (including expanding shortened links) can help detect links leading to known malicious sites. Detonation chambers can be used to detect these links and either automatically go to these sites to determine if they're potentially malicious, or wait and capture the content if a user visits the link.

Because most common third-party services used for phishing via service leverage TLS encryption, SSL/TLS inspection is generally required to detect the initial communication/delivery. With SSL/TLS inspection, intrusion detection signatures or other security gateway appliances may be able to detect malware.

Antivirus can potentially detect malicious documents and files that are downloaded on the user's computer. Many possible detections of follow-on behavior may take place once user execution occurs.

Using Trusted Relationships

Adversaries may breach or otherwise leverage organizations who have access to intended victims. Access through a trusted third-party relationship exploits an existing connection that may not be protected or receives less scrutiny than standard mechanisms of gaining access to a network.

Organizations often grant elevated access to second- or third-party external providers in order to allow them to manage internal systems as well as cloud-based environments. Some examples of these relationships include IT services contractors, managed security providers, and infrastructure contractors (e.g., HVAC, elevators, and physical security). The third-party provider's access may be intended to be limited to the infrastructure being maintained, but may exist on the same network as the rest of the enterprise. As such, Valid Accounts used by the other party for access to internal network systems may be compromised and used.

Detection

Establish monitoring for activity conducted by second- and third-party providers and other trusted entities that may be leveraged as a means to gain access to the network. Depending on the type of relationship, an adversary may have access to significant amounts of information about the target before conducting an operation, especially if the trusted relationship is based on IT services. Adversaries may be able to act quickly toward an objective, so proper monitoring for behavior related to Credential Access, Lateral Movement, and Collection will be important to detect the intrusion.

Using Valid Accounts

Adversaries may obtain and abuse credentials of existing accounts as a means of gaining Initial Access, Persistence, Privilege Escalation, or Defense Evasion. Compromised credentials may be used to bypass access controls placed on various resources on systems within the network and may even be used for persistent access to remote systems and externally available services, such as VPNs, Outlook Web Access, and remote desktop. Compromised credentials may also grant an adversary increased privilege to specific systems or access to restricted areas of the network. Adversaries may choose not to use malware or tools in conjunction with the legitimate access those credentials provide to make it harder to detect their presence.

The overlap of permissions for local, domain, and cloud accounts across a network of systems is of concern because the adversary may be able to pivot across accounts and systems to reach a high level of access (i.e., domain or enterprise administrator) to bypass access controls set within the enterprise.

Detection

Configure robust, consistent account activity audit policies across the enterprise and with externally accessible services. Look for suspicious account behavior across systems that share accounts, such as user, admin, or service accounts. Examples include one account logged in to multiple systems simultaneously; multiple accounts logged in to the same machine simultaneously; and accounts logged in at odd times or outside of business hours. Activity may be from interactive login sessions or process ownership from accounts being used to execute binaries on a remote system as a particular account. Correlate other security systems with login information (e.g., a user has an active login session but has not entered the building or does not have VPN access).

Perform regular audits of domain and local system accounts to detect accounts that may have been created by an adversary for persistence. Checks on these accounts could also include whether default accounts such as Guest have been activated. These audits should also include checks on any appliances and applications for default credentials or SSH keys, and if any are discovered, they should be updated immediately.

Persistence

Manipulating Accounts

Adversaries may manipulate accounts to maintain access to victim systems. Account manipulation may consist of any action that preserves adversary access to a compromised account, such as modifying credentials or permission groups. These actions could also include account activity designed to subvert security policies, such as performing iterative password updates to bypass password duration policies and preserve the life of compromised credentials. In order to create or manipulate accounts, the adversary must already have sufficient permissions on systems or the domain.

Detection

Collect events that correlate with changes to account objects and/or permissions on systems and the domain, such as event IDs 4738, 4728, and 4670. Monitor for modification of accounts in correlation with other suspicious activity. Changes may occur at unusual times or from unusual systems. Especially flag events where the subject and target accounts differ or that include additional flags such as changing a password without knowledge of the old password.

Monitor for use of credentials at unusual times or to unusual systems or services. This may also correlate with other suspicious activity.

Monitor for unusual permissions changes that may indicate excessively broad permissions being granted to compromised accounts.

Creating Accounts

Adversaries may create an account to maintain access to victim systems. With a sufficient level of access, creating such accounts may be used to establish secondary credentialed access that does not require persistent remote access tools to be deployed on the system.

Accounts may be created on the local system or within a domain or cloud tenant. In cloud environments, adversaries may create accounts that only have access to specific services, which can reduce the chance of detection.

Detection

Monitor for processes and command-line parameters associated with account creation, such as `net user` or `useradd`. Collect data on account creation within a network. Event ID 4720 is generated when a user account is created on a Windows system and domain controller. Perform regular audits of domain and local system accounts to detect suspicious accounts that may have been created by an adversary.

Collect usage logs from cloud administrator accounts to identify unusual activity in the creation of new accounts and assignment of roles to those accounts. Monitor for accounts assigned to admin roles that go over a certain threshold of known admins.

Implanting a Container Image

Adversaries may implant cloud container images with malicious code to establish persistence. Amazon Machine Images (AMI), Google Cloud Platform (GCP) Images, and Azure Images as well as popular container runtimes such as Docker can be implanted or back-doored.

A tool has been developed to facilitate planting backdoors in cloud container images. If an attacker has access to a compromised AWS instance, and permissions to list the available container images, they may implant a backdoor such as a Web Shell. Adversaries may also implant Docker images that may be inadvertently used in cloud deployments, which has been reported in some instances of crypto-mining botnets.

Detection

Monitor interactions with images and containers by users to identify ones that are added or modified anomalously.

Office Application Startup

Adversaries may leverage Microsoft Office–based applications for persistence between startups. Microsoft Office is a fairly common application suite on Windows-based operating systems within an enterprise network. There are multiple mechanisms that can be used with Office for persistence when an Office-based application is started; this can include the use of Office Template Macros and add-ins.

A variety of features have been discovered in Outlook that can be abused to obtain persistence, such as Outlook rules, forms, and Home Page. These persistence mechanisms can work within Outlook or be used through Office 365.

Detection

Collect process execution information including process IDs (PID) and parent process IDs (PPID) and look for abnormal chains of activity resulting from Office processes. Non-standard process execution trees may also indicate suspicious or malicious behavior. If `winword.exe` is the parent process for suspicious processes and activity relating to other adversarial techniques, then it could indicate that the application was used maliciously.

Many Office-related persistence mechanisms require changes to the Registry and for binaries, files, or scripts to be written to disk or existing files modified to include malicious scripts. Collect events related to Registry key creation and modification for keys that could be used for Office-based persistence.

Microsoft has released a PowerShell script to safely gather mail forwarding rules and custom forms in your mail environment as well as steps to interpret the output. SensePost, whose tool Ruler can be used to carry out malicious rules, forms, and Home Page attacks, has released a tool to detect Ruler usage.

Using Valid Accounts

Adversaries may obtain and abuse credentials of existing accounts as a means of gaining Initial Access, Persistence, Privilege Escalation, or Defense Evasion. Compromised credentials may be used to bypass access controls placed on various resources on systems within the network and may even be used for persistent access to remote systems and externally available services, such as VPNs, Outlook Web Access, and remote desktop. Compromised credentials may also grant an adversary increased privilege to specific systems or access to restricted areas of the network. Adversaries may choose not to use malware or tools in conjunction with the legitimate access those credentials provide to make it harder to detect their presence.

The overlap of permissions for local, domain, and cloud accounts across a network of systems is of concern because the adversary may be able to pivot across accounts and systems to reach a high level of access (i.e., domain or enterprise administrator) to bypass access controls set within the enterprise.

Detection

Configure robust, consistent account activity audit policies across the enterprise and with externally accessible services. Look for suspicious account behavior across systems that share accounts—either user, admin, or service accounts. Examples include one account logged in to multiple systems simultaneously; multiple accounts logged in to the same machine simultaneously; and accounts logged in at odd times or outside of business hours. Activity may be from interactive login sessions or process ownership from accounts being used to execute binaries on a remote system as a particular account. Correlate other security systems with login information (e.g., a user has an active login session but has not entered the building or does not have VPN access).

Perform regular audits of domain and local system accounts to detect accounts that may have been created by an adversary for persistence. Checks on these accounts could also include whether default accounts such as Guest have been activated. These audits should also include checks on any appliances and applications for default credentials or SSH keys, and if any are discovered, they should be updated immediately.

Privilege Escalation

Modifying the Domain Policy

Adversaries may modify the configuration settings of a domain to evade defenses and/or escalate privileges in domain environments. Domains provide a centralized means of managing how computer resources (e.g., computers, user accounts) can act, and interact with each other, on a network. The policy of the domain also includes configuration settings that may apply between domains in a multi-domain/forest environment. Modifications to domain settings may include altering domain Group Policy Objects (GPOs) or changing trust settings for domains, including federation trusts.

With sufficient permissions, adversaries can modify domain policy settings. Since domain configuration settings control many of the interactions within the Active Directory (AD) environment, there are a great number of potential attacks that can stem from this abuse. Examples of such abuse include modifying GPOs to push a malicious Scheduled Task to computers throughout the domain environment or modifying domain trusts to include an adversary-controlled domain where they can control access tokens that will subsequently be accepted by victim domain resources. Adversaries can also change configuration settings within the AD environment to implement a Rogue Domain Controller.

Adversaries may temporarily modify domain policy, carry out malicious actions, and then revert the change to remove suspicious indicators.

Detection

It may be possible to detect domain policy modifications using Windows event logs. Group policy modifications, for example, may be logged under a variety of Windows event IDs for modifying, creating, undeleting, moving, and deleting directory service objects (Event IDs 5136, 5137, 5138, 5139, and 5141, respectively). Monitor for modifications to domain trust settings, such as when a user or application modifies the federation settings on the domain or updates domain authentication from Managed to Federated via ActionTypes Set federation settings on domain and Set domain authentication. This may also include monitoring for Event ID 307, which can be correlated to relevant Event ID 510 with the same Instance ID for change details.

Consider monitoring for commands/cmdlets and command-line arguments that may be leveraged to modify domain policy settings. Some domain policy modifications, such as changes to federation settings, are likely to be rare.

Using Valid Accounts

Adversaries may obtain and abuse the credentials of existing accounts as a means of gaining Initial Access, Persistence, Privilege Escalation, or Defense Evasion. Compromised credentials may be used to bypass access controls placed on various resources on systems within the network and may even be used for persistent access to remote systems and externally available services, such as VPNs, Outlook Web Access, and remote desktop. Compromised credentials may also grant an adversary increased privilege to specific systems or access to restricted areas of the network. Adversaries may choose not to use malware or tools in conjunction with the legitimate access those credentials provide to make it harder to detect their presence.

The overlap of permissions for local, domain, and cloud accounts across a network of systems is of concern because the adversary may be able to pivot across accounts and systems to reach a high level of access (i.e., domain or enterprise administrator) to bypass access controls set within the enterprise.

Detection

Configure robust, consistent account activity audit policies across the enterprise and with externally accessible services. Look for suspicious account behavior across systems that share accounts—either user, admin, or service accounts. Examples include one account logged in to multiple systems simultaneously; multiple accounts logged in to the same machine simultaneously; and accounts logged in at odd times or outside of business hours. Activity may be from interactive login sessions or process ownership from accounts being used to execute binaries on a remote system as a particular account. Correlate other security systems with login information (e.g., a user has an active login session but has not entered the building or does not have VPN access).

Perform regular audits of domain and local system accounts to detect accounts that may have been created by an adversary for persistence. Checks on these accounts could also include whether default accounts such as Guest have been activated. These audits should also include checks on any appliances and applications for default credentials or SSH keys, and if any are discovered, they should be updated immediately.

Defense Evasion

Modifying Domain Policy

Adversaries may modify the configuration settings of a domain to evade defenses and/or escalate privileges in domain environments. Domains provide a centralized means of managing how computer resources (e.g., computers, user accounts) can act, and interact with each other, on a network. The policy of the domain also includes configuration settings that may apply between domains in a multi-domain/forest environment. Modifications to domain settings may include altering domain Group Policy Objects (GPOs) or changing trust settings for domains, including federation trusts.

With sufficient permissions, adversaries can modify domain policy settings. Since domain configuration settings control many of the interactions within the Active Directory (AD) environment, there are a great number of potential attacks that can stem from this abuse. Examples of such abuse include modifying GPOs to push a malicious Scheduled Task to computers throughout the domain environment or modifying domain trusts to include an adversary-controlled domain where they can control access tokens that will subsequently be accepted by victim domain resources. Adversaries can also change configuration settings within the AD environment to implement a Rogue Domain Controller.

Adversaries may temporarily modify domain policy, carry out a malicious action, and then revert the change to remove suspicious indicators.

Detection

It may be possible to detect domain policy modifications using Windows event logs. Group policy modifications, for example, may be logged under a variety of Windows event IDs for modifying, creating, undeleting, moving, and deleting directory service objects (Event IDs 5136, 5137, 5138, 5139, and 5141, respectively). Monitor for modifications to domain trust settings, such as when a user or application modifies the federation settings on the domain or updates domain authentication from Managed to Federated via ActionTypes `Set federation settings on domain` and `Set domain authentication`. This may also include monitoring for Event ID 307, which can be correlated to relevant Event ID 510 with the same Instance ID for change details.

Consider monitoring for commands/cmdlets and command-line arguments that may be leveraged to modify domain policy settings. Some domain policy modifications, such as changes to federation settings, are likely to be rare.

Impairing Defenses

Adversaries may maliciously modify components of a victim environment in order to hinder or disable defensive mechanisms. This not only involves impairing preventative defenses, such as firewalls and antivirus, but also detection capabilities that defenders can use to audit activity and identify malicious behavior. This may also span both native defenses as well as supplemental capabilities installed by users and administrators.

Adversaries could also target event aggregation and analysis mechanisms, or otherwise disrupt these procedures by altering other system components.

Detection

Monitor processes and command-line arguments to see if security tools or logging services are killed or stop running. Monitor Registry edits for modifications to services and startup programs that correspond to security tools. Lack of log events may be suspicious.

Monitor environment variables and APIs that can be leveraged to disable security measures.

Modifying the Cloud Compute Infrastructure

An adversary may attempt to modify a cloud account's compute service infrastructure to evade defenses. A modification to the compute service infrastructure can include the creation, deletion, or modification of one or more components such as compute instances, virtual machines, and snapshots.

Permissions gained from the modification of infrastructure components may bypass restrictions that prevent access to existing infrastructure. Modifying infrastructure components may also allow an adversary to evade detection and remove evidence of their presence.

Detection

Establish centralized logging for the activity of cloud compute infrastructure components. Monitor for suspicious sequences of events, such as the creation of multiple snapshots within a short period of time or the mount of a snapshot to a new instance by a new or unexpected user. To reduce false positives, valid change management procedures could introduce a known identifier that is logged in with the change (e.g., tag or header) if supported by the cloud provider, to help distinguish valid, expected actions from malicious ones.

Using Unused/Unsupported Cloud Regions

Adversaries may create cloud instances in unused geographic service regions in order to evade detection. Access is usually obtained through compromising accounts used to manage cloud infrastructure.

Cloud service providers often provide infrastructure throughout the world in order to improve performance, provide redundancy, and allow customers to meet compliance requirements. Oftentimes, a customer will only use a subset of the available regions and may not actively monitor other regions. If an adversary creates resources in an unused region, they may be able to operate undetected.

A variation on this behavior takes advantage of differences in functionality across cloud regions. An adversary could utilize regions that do not support advanced detection services in order to avoid detection of their activity. For example, AWS GuardDuty is not supported in every region.

An example of adversary use of unused AWS regions is to mine cryptocurrency through Resource Hijacking, which can cost organizations substantial amounts of money over time depending on the processing power used.

Detection

Monitor system logs to review activities occurring across all cloud environments and regions. Configure alerting to notify of activity in normally unused regions or if the number of instances active in a region goes above a certain threshold.

Using Alternate Authentication Material

Adversaries may use alternate authentication material, such as password hashes, Kerberos tickets, and application access tokens, in order to move laterally within an environment and bypass normal system access controls.

Authentication processes generally require a valid identity (e.g., username) along with one or more authentication factors (e.g., password, PIN, physical smart card, token generator, etc.). Alternate authentication material is legitimately generated by systems after a user or application successfully authenticates by providing a valid identity and the required authentication factors. Alternate authentication material may also be generated during the identity creation process.

Caching alternate authentication material allows the system to verify an identity has successfully authenticated without asking the user to reenter authentication factors. Because the alternate authentication must be maintained by the system—either in memory or on disk—it may be at risk of being stolen through Credential Access techniques. By stealing alternate authentication material, adversaries are able to bypass system access controls and authenticate to systems without knowing the plaintext password or any additional authentication factors.

Detection

Configure robust, consistent account activity audit policies across the enterprise and with externally accessible services. Look for suspicious account behavior across systems that share accounts—either user, admin, or service accounts. Examples include one account logged in to multiple systems simultaneously; multiple accounts logged in to the same machine simultaneously; and accounts logged in at odd times or outside of business hours. Activity may be from interactive login sessions or process ownership from accounts being used to execute binaries on a remote system as a particular account. Correlate other security systems with login information (e.g., a user has an active login session but has not entered the building or does not have VPN access).

Using Valid Accounts

Adversaries may obtain and abuse credentials of existing accounts as a means of gaining Initial Access, Persistence, Privilege Escalation, or Defense Evasion. Compromised credentials may be used to bypass access controls placed on various resources on systems within the network and may even be used for persistent access to remote systems and externally available services, such as VPNs, Outlook Web Access, and remote desktop. Compromised credentials may also grant an adversary increased privilege to specific systems or access to restricted areas of the network. Adversaries may choose not to use malware or tools in conjunction with the legitimate access those credentials provide to make it harder to detect their presence.

The overlap of permissions for local, domain, and cloud accounts across a network of systems is of concern because the adversary may be able to pivot across accounts and systems to reach a high level of access (i.e., domain or enterprise administrator) to bypass access controls set within the enterprise.

Credential Access

Using Brute Force Methods

Adversaries may use brute force techniques to gain access to accounts when passwords are unknown or when password hashes are obtained. Without knowledge of the password for an account or set of accounts, an adversary may systematically guess the password using a repetitive or iterative mechanism. Brute forcing passwords can take place via interaction with a service that will check the validity of those credentials or offline against previously acquired credential data, such as password hashes.

Detection

Monitor authentication logs for system and application login failures of Valid Accounts. If authentication failures are high, then there may be a brute force attempt to gain access to a system using legitimate credentials. Also monitor for many failed authentication attempts across various accounts that may result from password spraying attempts. It is difficult to detect when hashes are cracked, since this is generally done outside the scope of the target network.

Forging Web Credentials

Adversaries may forge credential materials that can be used to gain access to web applications or Internet services. Web applications and services (hosted in cloud SaaS environments or on-premise servers) often use session cookies, tokens, or other materials to authenticate and authorize user access.

Adversaries may generate these credential materials in order to gain access to web resources. This differs from Steal Web Session Cookie, Steal Application Access Token, and other similar behaviors in that the credentials are new and forged by the adversary, rather than stolen or intercepted from legitimate users. The generation of web credentials often requires secret values, such as passwords, Private Keys, or other cryptographic seed values.

Once forged, adversaries may use these web credentials to access resources (e.g., use Alternate Authentication Material), which may bypass multi-factor and other authentication protection mechanisms.

Detection

Monitor for anomalous authentication activity, such as logons or other user session activity associated with unknown accounts. Monitor for unexpected and abnormal access to resources, including access of websites and cloud-based applications by the same user in different locations or by different systems that do not match expected configurations.

Stealing an Application Access Token

Adversaries can steal user application access tokens as a means of acquiring credentials to access remote systems and resources. This can occur through social engineering and typically requires user action to grant access.

Application access tokens are used to make authorized API requests on behalf of a user and are commonly used as a way to access resources in cloud-based applications and Software-as-a-Service (SaaS). OAuth is one commonly implemented framework that issues tokens to users for access to systems. An application desiring access to cloud-based services or protected APIs can gain entry using OAuth 2.0 through a variety of authorization protocols. One commonly used sequence is Microsoft's Authorization Code Grant flow. An OAuth access token enables a third-party application to interact with resources containing user data in the ways requested by the application without obtaining user credentials.

Adversaries can leverage OAuth authorization by constructing a malicious application designed to be granted access to resources with the target user's OAuth token. The adversary will need to complete registration of their application with the authorization server, for example Microsoft Identity Platform using Azure Portal, the Visual Studio IDE, the command-line interface, PowerShell, or REST API calls. Then, they can send a link through a spear-phishing link to the target user to entice them to grant access to the application. Once the OAuth access token is granted, the application can gain potentially long-term access to features of the user account through application access tokens.

Detection

Administrators should set up monitoring to trigger automatic alerts when policy criteria are met. For example, using a Cloud Access Security Broker (CASB), admins can create a "high severity app permissions" policy that generates alerts if apps request high severity permissions or send permissions requests for too many users.

Security analysts can hunt for malicious apps using the tools available in their CASB, identity provider, or resource provider (depending on the platform). For example, they can filter for apps that are authorized by a small number of users, apps requesting high-risk permissions, permissions incongruous with the app's purpose, or apps with old "Last authorized" fields. A specific app can be investigated using an activity log displaying activities the app has performed, although some activities may be mislogged as being performed by the user. App stores can be useful resources to further investigate suspicious apps.

Administrators can set up a variety of logs and leverage audit tools to monitor actions that can be conducted as a result of OAuth 2.0 access. For instance, audit reports enable admins to identify privilege escalation actions such as role creations or policy modifications, which could be actions performed after initial access.

Stealing Web Session Cookies

An adversary may steal web application or service session cookies and use them to gain access to web applications or Internet services as an authenticated user without needing credentials. Web applications and services often use session cookies as an authentication token after a user has authenticated to a website.

Cookies are often valid for an extended period of time, even if the web application is not actively used. Cookies can be found on disk, in the process memory of the browser, and in network traffic to remote systems. Additionally, other applications on the target machine might store sensitive authentication cookies in memory (e.g., apps that authenticate to cloud services). Session cookies can be used to bypasses some multi-factor authentication protocols.

There are several examples of malware targeting cookies from web browsers on the local system. There are also open source frameworks such as Evilginx 2 and Muraena that can gather session cookies through a man-in-the-middle proxy that can be set up by an adversary and used in phishing campaigns.

After an adversary acquires a valid cookie, they can then perform a Web Session Cookie technique to log in to the corresponding web application.

Detection

Monitor for attempts to access files and repositories on a local system that are used to store browser session cookies. Monitor for attempts by programs to inject into or dump browser process memory.

Using Unsecured Credentials

Adversaries may search compromised systems to find and obtain insecurely stored credentials. These credentials can be stored and/or misplaced in many locations on a system, including plaintext files (e.g., Bash History), operating system or application-specific repositories (e.g., Credentials in Registry), or other specialized files/artifacts (e.g., Private Keys).

Detection

While detecting adversaries accessing credentials may be difficult without knowing they exist in the environment, it may be possible to detect adversary use of credentials they have obtained. Monitor the command-line arguments of executing processes for suspicious words or regular expressions that may indicate searching for a password (e.g., password, pwd, login, secure, or credentials). See Using Valid Accounts section under Defence Evasion for more information.

Monitor for suspicious file access activity, specifically indications that a process is reading multiple files in a short amount of time and/or using command-line arguments indicative of searching for credential material (e.g., regex patterns). These may be indicators of automated/scripted credential access behavior.

Monitoring when the user's `.bash_history` is read can help alert to suspicious activity. While users do typically rely on their history of commands, they often access this history through other utilities like "history" instead of commands like `cat ~/.bash_history`.

Additionally, monitor processes for applications that can be used to query the Registry, such as Reg, and collect command parameters that may indicate credentials are being searched. Correlate activity with related suspicious behavior that may indicate an active intrusion to reduce false positives.

Discovery

Manipulating Account Discovery

Adversaries may attempt to get a listing of accounts on a system or within an environment. This information can help adversaries determine which accounts exist to aid in follow-on behavior.

Detection

System and network discovery techniques normally occur throughout an operation as an adversary learns the environment. Data and events should not be viewed in isolation, but as part of a chain of behavior that could lead to other activities, such as Lateral Movement, based on the information obtained.

Monitor processes and command-line arguments for actions that could be taken to gather system and network information. Remote access tools with built-in features may interact directly with the Windows API to gather information. Information may also be acquired through Windows system management tools such as Windows Management Instrumentation and PowerShell.

Manipulating Cloud Infrastructure Discovery

An adversary may attempt to discover resources that are available within an Infrastructure-as-a-Service (IaaS) environment. This includes compute service resources such as instances, virtual machines, and snapshots as well as resources of other services including the storage and database services.

Cloud providers offer methods such as APIs and commands issued through CLIs to serve information about infrastructure. For example, AWS provides a `DescribeInstances` API within the Amazon EC2 API that can return information about one or more instances within an account, as well as the `ListBuckets` API that returns a list of all buckets owned by the authenticated sender of the request. Similarly, GCP's Cloud SDK CLI provides the `gcloud compute instances list` command to list all Google Compute Engine instances in a project, and Azure's CLI command `az vm list` lists details of virtual machines.

An adversary may enumerate resources using a compromised user's access keys to determine which are available to that user. The discovery of these available resources may help adversaries determine their next steps in the cloud environment, such as establishing Persistence. Unlike in Cloud Service Discovery, this technique focuses on the discovery of components of the provided services rather than the services themselves.

Detection

Establish centralized logging for the activity of cloud infrastructure components. Monitor logs for actions that could be taken to gather information about cloud infrastructure, including the use of discovery API calls by new or unexpected users. To reduce false positives, valid change management procedures could introduce a known identifier that is logged with the change (e.g., tag or header) if supported by the cloud provider, to help distinguish valid, expected actions from malicious ones.

Using a Cloud Service Dashboard

An adversary may use a cloud service dashboard GUI with stolen credentials to gain useful information from an operational cloud environment, such as specific services, resources, and features. For example, the GCP Command Center can be used to view all assets, findings of potential security risks, and to run additional queries, such as finding public IP addresses and open ports.

Depending on the configuration of the environment, an adversary may be able to enumerate more information via the graphical dashboard than an API. This allows the adversary to gain information without making any API requests.

Detection

Monitor account activity logs to see actions performed and activity associated with the cloud service management console. Some cloud providers, such as AWS, provide distinct log events for login attempts to the management console.

Using Cloud Service Discovery

An adversary may attempt to enumerate the cloud services running on a system after gaining access. These methods can differ from Platform-as-a-Service (PaaS), to Infrastructure-as-a-Service (IaaS), or Software-as-a-Service (SaaS). Many services exist throughout the various cloud providers and can include Continuous Integration and Continuous Delivery (CI/CD), Lambda Functions, Azure AD, etc.

Adversaries may attempt to discover information about the services enabled throughout the environment. Azure tools and APIs, such as the Azure AD Graph API and Azure Resource Manager API, can enumerate resources and services, including applications, management groups, resources and policy definitions, and their relationships that are accessible by an identity.

Stormspotter is an open source tool for enumerating and constructing a graph for Azure resources and services, and Pacu is an open source AWS exploitation framework that supports several methods for discovering cloud services.

Detection

Cloud service discovery techniques will likely occur throughout an operation where an adversary is targeting cloud-based systems and services. Data and events should not be viewed in isolation, but as part of a chain of behavior that could lead to other activities based on the information obtained.

Normal, benign system and network events that look like cloud service discovery may be uncommon, depending on the environment and how they are used. Monitor cloud service usage for anomalous behavior that may indicate adversarial presence within the environment.

Scanning Network Services

Adversaries may attempt to get a listing of services running on remote hosts, including those that may be vulnerable to remote software exploitation. Methods to acquire this information include port scans and vulnerability scans using tools that are brought onto a system.

Within cloud environments, adversaries may attempt to discover services running on other cloud hosts. Additionally, if the cloud environment is connected to an on-premises environment, adversaries may be able to identify services running on non-cloud systems as well.

Detection

System and network discovery techniques normally occur throughout an operation as an adversary learns the environment. Data and events should not be viewed in isolation, but as part of a chain of behavior that could lead to other activities, such as Lateral Movement, based on the information obtained.

Normal, benign system and network events from legitimate remote service scanning may be uncommon, depending on the environment and how they are used. Legitimate open port and vulnerability scanning may be conducted within the environment and will need to be deconflicted with any detection capabilities developed. Network intrusion detection systems can also be used to identify scanning activity. Monitor for process use of the networks and inspect intra-network flows to detect port scans.

Discovering Permission Groups

Adversaries may attempt to find group and permission settings. This information can help adversaries determine which user accounts and groups are available, the membership of users in particular groups, and which users and groups have elevated permissions.

Detection

System and network discovery techniques normally occur throughout an operation as an adversary learns the environment. Data and events should not be viewed in isolation, but as part of a chain of behavior that could lead to other activities, such as Lateral Movement, based on the information obtained.

Monitor processes and command-line arguments for actions that could be taken to gather system and network information. Remote access tools with built-in features may interact directly with the Windows API to gather information. Information may also be acquired through Windows system management tools such as Windows Management Instrumentation and PowerShell.

Discovering Software

System and network discovery techniques normally occur throughout an operation as an adversary learns the environment. Data and events should not be viewed in isolation, but as part of a chain of behavior that could lead to other activities, such as Lateral Movement, based on the information obtained.

Monitor processes and command-line arguments for actions that could be taken to gather system and network information. Remote access tools with built-in features may interact directly with the Windows API to gather information. Information may also be acquired through Windows system management tools such as Windows Management Instrumentation and PowerShell.

Discovering System Information

An adversary may attempt to get detailed information about the operating system and hardware, including version, patches, hotfixes, service packs, and architecture. Adversaries may use the information from System Information Discovery during automated discovery to shape follow-on behaviors, including whether or not the adversary fully infects the target and/or attempts specific actions.

Tools such as Systeminfo can be used to gather detailed system information. A breakdown of system data can also be gathered through the macOS `systemsetup` command, but it requires administrative privileges.

Infrastructure as a Service (IaaS) cloud providers such as AWS, GCP, and Azure allow access to instance and virtual machine information via APIs. Successful authenticated API calls can return data such as the operating system platform and status of a particular instance or the model view of a virtual machine.

Detection

System and network discovery techniques normally occur throughout an operation as an adversary learns the environment. Data and events should not be viewed in isolation, but as part of a chain of behavior that could lead to other activities based on the information obtained.

Monitor processes and command-line arguments for actions that could be taken to gather system and network information. Remote access tools with built-in features may interact directly with the Windows API to gather information. Information may also be acquired through Windows system management tools such as Windows Management Instrumentation and PowerShell.

In cloud-based systems, native logging can be used to identify access to certain APIs and dashboards that may contain system information. Depending on how the environment is used, that data alone may not be useful due to benign use during normal operations.

Discovering System Network Connections

Adversaries may attempt to get a listing of network connections to or from the compromised system they are currently accessing or from remote systems by querying for information over the network.

An adversary who gains access to a system that is part of a cloud-based environment may map out Virtual Private Clouds or Virtual Networks in order to determine what systems and services are connected. The actions performed are likely the same types of discovery techniques depending on the operating system, but the resulting information may include details about the networked cloud environment relevant to the adversary's goals. Cloud providers may have different ways in which their virtual networks operate.

Utilities and commands that acquire this information include `netstat`, `net use`, and `net session` with Net. In Mac and Linux, `netstat` and `lsof` can be used to list current connections. `who -a` and `w` can be used to show which users are currently logged in, similar to `net session`.

Detection

System and network discovery techniques normally occur throughout an operation as an adversary learns the environment. Data and events should not be viewed in isolation, but as part of a chain of behavior that could lead to other activities, such as Lateral Movement, based on the information obtained.

Monitor processes and command-line arguments for actions that could be taken to gather system and network information. Remote access tools with built-in features may interact directly with the Windows API to gather information. Information may also be acquired through Windows system management tools such as Windows Management Instrumentation and PowerShell.

Lateral Movement

Internal Spear Phishing

Adversaries may use internal spear phishing to gain access to additional information or exploit other users within the same organization after they already have access to accounts or systems within the environment. Internal spear phishing is a multi-staged attack where an email account is owned either by controlling the user's device with previously installed malware or by compromising the account credentials of the user. Adversaries attempt to take advantage of a trusted internal account to increase the likelihood of tricking the target into falling for the phish attempt.

Adversaries may leverage spear phishing to deliver a payload or redirect to an external site to capture credentials through Input Capture on sites that mimic email login interfaces.

There have been notable incidents where internal spear phishing has been used. The Eye Pyramid campaign used phishing emails with malicious attachments for lateral movement between victims, compromising nearly 18,000 email accounts in the process. The Syrian Electronic Army (SEA) compromised email accounts at the Financial Times (FT) to steal additional account credentials. Once FT learned of the attack and began warning employees of the threat, the SEA sent phishing emails mimicking the Financial Times IT department and were able to compromise even more users.

Detection

Network intrusion detection systems and email gateways usually do not scan internal email, but an organization can leverage the journaling-based solution, which sends a copy of emails to a security service for offline analysis or incorporate service-integrated solutions using on-premise or API-based integrations to help detect internal spear phishing attacks.

Using Alternate Authentication Material

Adversaries may use alternate authentication material, such as password hashes, Kerberos tickets, and application access tokens, in order to move laterally within an environment and bypass normal system access controls.

Authentication processes generally require a valid identity (e.g., username) along with one or more authentication factors (e.g., password, PIN, physical smart card, token generator, etc.). Alternate authentication material is legitimately generated by systems after a user or application successfully authenticates by providing a valid identity and the required authentication factors. Alternate authentication material may also be generated during the identity creation process.

Caching alternate authentication material allows the system to verify an identity has successfully authenticated without asking the user to reenter authentication factors. Because the alternate authentication must be maintained by the system—either in memory or on disk—it may be at risk of being stolen through Credential Access techniques. By stealing alternate authentication material, adversaries are able to bypass system access controls and authenticate to systems without knowing the plaintext password or any additional authentication factors.

Detection

Configure robust, consistent account activity audit policies across the enterprise and with externally accessible services. Look for suspicious account behavior across systems that share accounts—either user, admin, or service accounts. Examples include one account logged in to multiple systems simultaneously; multiple accounts logged in to the same machine simultaneously; and accounts logged in at odd times or outside of business hours. Activity may be from inter-active login sessions or process ownership from accounts being used to execute binaries on a remote system as a particular account. Correlate other security systems with login information (e.g., a user has an active login session but has not entered the building or does not have VPN access).

Collection

Collecting Data from a Cloud Storage Object

Adversaries may access data objects from improperly secured cloud storage.

Many cloud service providers offer solutions for online data storage such as Amazon S3, Azure Storage, and Google Cloud Storage. These solutions differ from other storage solutions (such as SQL or ElasticSearch) in that there is no overarching application. Data from these solutions can be retrieved directly using the cloud provider's APIs. Solution providers typically offer security guides to help end users configure systems.

Misconfiguration by end users is a common problem. There have been numerous incidents where cloud storage has been improperly secured (typically by unin-tentionally allowing public access by unauthenticated users or overly broad access by all users), allowing open access to credit cards, personally identifiable information, medical records, and other sensitive information. Adversaries may also obtain leaked credentials in source repositories, logs, or other means as a way to gain access to cloud storage objects that have access permission controls.

Detection

Monitor for unusual queries to the cloud provider's storage service. Activity originating from unexpected sources may indicate improper permissions are set that are allowing access to data. Additionally, detecting failed attempts by a user for a certain object, followed by escalation of privileges by the same user, and access to the same object may be an indication of suspicious activity.

Collecting Data from Information Repositories

Adversaries may leverage information repositories to mine valuable information. Information repositories are tools that allow for storage of information, typically to facilitate collaboration or information sharing between users, and can store a wide variety of data that may aid adversaries in further objectives, or direct access to the target information.

The following is a brief list of example information that may hold potential value to an adversary and may also be found on an information repository:

- Policies, procedures, and standards
- Physical/logical network diagrams
- System architecture diagrams
- Technical system documentation
- Testing/development credentials
- Work/project schedules
- Source code snippets
- Links to network shares and other internal resources

Information stored in a repository may vary based on the specific instance or environment. Specific common information repositories include SharePoint, Confluence, and enterprise databases such as SQL Server.

Detection

As information repositories generally have a considerably large user base, detection of malicious use can be non-trivial. At minimum, access to information repositories performed by privileged users (for example, Active Directory Domain, Enterprise, or Schema Administrators) should be closely monitored and alerted upon, as these types of accounts should not generally be used to access information repositories. If the capability exists, it may be of value to monitor and alert on users that are retrieving and viewing a large number of documents and pages; this behavior may be indicative of programmatic means being used to retrieve all data within the repository. In environments with high maturity, it may be possible to leverage User-Behavioral Analytics (UBA) platforms to detect and alert on user-based anomalies.

The user access logging within Microsoft's SharePoint can be configured to report access to certain pages and documents. The user access logging within Atlassian's Confluence can also be configured to report access to certain pages and documents through AccessLogFilter. Additional log storage and analysis infrastructure will likely be required for more robust detection capabilities.

Collecting Staged Data

Adversaries may stage collected data in a central location or directory prior to Exfiltration. Data may be kept in separate files or combined into one file through techniques such as Archive Collected Data. Interactive command shells may be used, and common functionality within cmd and bash may be used to copy data into a staging location.

In cloud environments, adversaries may stage data within a particular instance or virtual machine before exfiltration. An adversary may Create Cloud Instances.

Adversaries may choose to stage data from a victim network in a centralized location prior to Exfiltration to minimize the number of connections made to their C2 server and better evade detection.

Detection

Processes that appear to be reading files from disparate locations and writing them to the same directory or file may be an indication of data being staged, especially if they are suspected of performing encryption or compression on the files, such as 7zip, RAR, ZIP, or zlib. Monitor publicly writeable directories, central locations, and commonly used staging directories (recycle bin, temp folders, etc.) to regularly check for compressed or encrypted data that may be indicative of staging.

Monitor processes and command-line arguments for actions that could be taken to collect and combine files. Remote access tools with built-in features may interact directly with the Windows API to gather and copy to a location. Data may also be acquired and staged through Windows system management tools such as Windows Management Instrumentation and PowerShell.

Collecting Email

Adversaries may target user email to collect sensitive information. Emails may contain sensitive data, including trade secrets or personal information, that can prove valuable to adversaries. Adversaries can collect or forward email from mail servers or clients.

Detection

There are likely a variety of ways an adversary could collect email from a target, each with a different mechanism for detection.

File access of local system email files for Exfiltration, unusual processes connecting to an email server within a network, or unusual access patterns or authentication attempts on a public-facing webmail server may all be indicators of malicious activity.

Monitor processes and command-line arguments for actions that could be taken to gather local email files. Remote access tools with built-in features may interact directly with the Windows API to gather information. Information may also be acquired through Windows system management tools such as Windows Management Instrumentation and PowerShell.

Detection is challenging because all messages forwarded because of an auto-forwarding rule have the same presentation as a manually forwarded message. It is also possible for the user to not be aware of the addition of such an auto-forwarding rule and not suspect that their account has been compromised; email-forwarding rules alone will not affect the normal usage patterns or operations of the email account.

Auto-forwarded messages generally contain specific detectable artifacts that may be present in the header; such artifacts would be platform-specific. Examples include `X-MS-Exchange-Organization-AutoForwarded` set to `true`, `X-MailFwdBy`, and `X-Forwarded-To`. The `forwardingSMTPAddress` parameter used in a forwarding process is managed by administrators and not by user actions. All messages for the mailbox are forwarded to the specified SMTP address. However, unlike typical client-side rules, the message does not appear as forwarded in the mailbox; it appears as if it were sent directly to the specified destination mailbox. High volumes of emails that bear the `X-MS-Exchange-Organization-AutoForwarded` header (indicating auto-forwarding) without a corresponding number of emails that match the appearance of a forwarded message may indicate that further investigation is needed at the administrator level rather than user-level.

Data Exfiltration

Detecting Exfiltration

There are likely a variety of ways an adversary could collect email from a target, each with a different mechanism for detection.

File access of local system email files for Exfiltration, unusual processes connecting to an email server within a network, or unusual access patterns or authentication attempts on a public-facing webmail server may all be indicators of malicious activity.

Monitor processes and command-line arguments for actions that could be taken to gather local email files. Remote access tools with built-in features may interact directly with the Windows API to gather information. Information may also be acquired through Windows system management tools such as Windows Management Instrumentation and PowerShell.

Detection is challenging because all messages forwarded because of an auto-forwarding rule have the same presentation as a manually forwarded message. It is also possible for the user to not be aware of the addition of such an auto-forwarding rule and not suspect that their account has been compromised; email-forwarding rules alone will not affect the normal usage patterns or operations of the email account.

Auto-forwarded messages generally contain specific detectable artifacts that may be present in the header; such artifacts would be platform-specific.

Examples include X-MS-Exchange-Organization-AutoForwarded set to true, X-MailFwdBy, and X-Forwarded-To. The forwardingSMTPAddress parameter used in a forwarding process is managed by administrators and not by user actions. All messages for the mailbox are forwarded to the specified SMTP address. However, unlike typical client-side rules, the message does not appear as forwarded in the mailbox; it appears as if it were sent directly to the specified destination mailbox. High volumes of emails that bear the X-MS-Exchange-Organization-AutoForwarded header (indicating auto-forwarding) without a corresponding number of emails that match the appearance of a forwarded message may indicate that further investigation is needed at the administrator level rather than user-level.

Detection

Monitor account activity for attempts to share data, snapshots, or backups with untrusted or unusual accounts on the same cloud service provider. Monitor for anomalous file transfer activity between accounts and to untrusted VPCs.

Impact

Defacement

Adversaries may modify visual content available internally or externally to an enterprise network. Reasons for Defacement include delivering messaging, intimidation, or claiming (possibly false) credit for an intrusion. Disturbing or offensive images may be used as a part of Defacement in order to cause user discomfort, or to pressure compliance with accompanying messages.

Detection

Monitor internal and external websites for unplanned content changes. Monitor application logs for abnormal behavior that may indicate attempted or successful exploitation. Use deep packet inspection to look for artifacts of common exploit traffic, such as SQL injection. Web Application Firewalls may detect improper inputs attempting exploitation.

Endpoint Denial of Service

Adversaries may perform Endpoint Denial of Service (DoS) attacks to degrade or block the availability of services to users. Endpoint DoS can be performed by exhausting the system resources those services are hosted on or exploiting the system to cause a persistent crash condition. Example services include websites, email services, DNS, and web-based applications. Adversaries have been observed conducting DoS attacks for political purposes and to support other malicious activities, including distraction, hacktivism, and extortion.

An Endpoint DoS denies the availability of a service without saturating the network used to provide access to the service. Adversaries can target various layers of the application stack that is hosted on the system used to provide the service. These layers include the Operating Systems (OS), server applications such as web servers, DNS servers, databases, and the (typically web-based) applications that sit on top of them. Attacking each layer requires different techniques that take advantage of bottlenecks that are unique to the respective components. A DoS attack may be generated by a single system or multiple systems spread across the Internet, which is commonly referred to as a distributed DoS (DDoS).

To perform DoS attacks against endpoint resources, several aspects apply to multiple methods, including IP address spoofing and botnets.

Adversaries may use the original IP address of an attacking system, or spoof the source IP address to make the attack traffic more difficult to trace back to the attacking system or to enable reflection. This can increase the difficulty defenders have in defending against the attack by reducing or eliminating the effectiveness of filtering by the source address on network defense devices.

Botnets are commonly used to conduct DDoS attacks against networks and services. Large botnets can generate a significant amount of traffic from systems spread across the global Internet. Adversaries may have the resources to build out and control their own botnet infrastructure or may rent time on an existing botnet to conduct an attack. In some of the worst cases for DDoS, so many systems are used to generate requests that each one only needs to send out a small amount of traffic to produce enough volume to exhaust the target's resources. In such circumstances, distinguishing DDoS traffic from legitimate clients becomes exceedingly difficult. Botnets have been used in some of the most high-profile DDoS attacks, such as the 2012 series of incidents that targeted major US banks.

In cases where traffic manipulation is used, there may be points in the global network (such as high-traffic gateway routers) where packets can be altered and cause legitimate clients to execute code that directs network packets toward a target in high volume. This type of capability was previously used for the purposes of web censorship where client HTTP traffic was modified to include a reference to JavaScript that generated the DDoS code to overwhelm target web servers.

Detection

Detection of Endpoint DoS can sometimes be achieved before the effect is sufficient to cause significant impact to the availability of the service, but such response time typically requires very aggressive monitoring and responsiveness. Typical network throughput monitoring tools such as Netflow, SNMP, and custom scripts can be used to detect sudden increases in circuit utilization. Real-time, automated, and qualitative study of the network traffic can identify a sudden surge in one type of protocol and can be used to detect an attack as it starts.

In addition to network-level detections, endpoint logging and instrumentation can be useful for detection. Attacks targeting web applications may generate logs in the web server, application server, and/or database server that can be used to identify the type of attack, possibly before the impact is felt.

Resource Hijacking

Adversaries may leverage the resources of co-opted systems in order to solve resource-intensive problems that may impact system and/or hosted service availability.

One common purpose for Resource Hijacking is to validate transactions of cryptocurrency networks and earn virtual currency. Adversaries may consume enough system resources to negatively impact and/or cause affected machines to become unresponsive. Servers and cloud-based systems are common targets because of the high potential for available resources, but user endpoint systems may also be compromised and used for Resource Hijacking and cryptocurrency mining.

Detection

Consider monitoring process resource usage to determine anomalous activity associated with malicious hijacking of computer resources such as CPU, memory, and graphics processing resources. Monitor for suspicious use of network resources associated with cryptocurrency mining software. Monitor for common crypto-mining software process names and files on local systems that may indicate compromise and resource usage.

APPENDIX

H

Glossary

This appendix is a collection of all terms used in the chapters. Note that they are alphabetically ordered so they are easier to find.

A

advanced persistent threat (APT)   An adversary that possesses sophisticated levels of expertise and significant resources, which allow it to create opportunities to achieve its objectives by using multiple attack vectors (e.g., cyber, physical, and deception). This term originated as a way to refer to nation state actors but has become a general term to describe organized adversaries.

adversary   An individual, group, organization, or government that conducts or has the intent to conduct cybersecurity attacks.

AI (artificial intelligence)   The simulation of human intelligence in machines that are programmed to think like humans and mimic their actions. The term may also be applied to any machine that exhibits traits associated with a human mind such as learning and problem-solving.

alert   A notification that a specific attack, anomaly, or suspicious activity has been detected or directed at an organization's information systems. Alerts frequently trigger investigations by security operations/analysts.

analyst   Also known as a cybersecurity analyst, a common role within an organization's SOC team that investigates, alerts, or hunts for adversarial activities.

asset   An entity or value that could take the form of a person, structure, facility, information and records, IT systems and resources, material, process, relationships, or reputations.

attachment (as in malicious email)   During phishing campaigns, cybercriminals attempt to trick users into clicking an email attachment, which then downloads a malicious executable, infecting the user's computer or mobile device, or, upon opening the attachment the user might be redirected to a fraudulent login site. Attachments can come in various forms, such as a Microsoft Office document, a PDF file, .zip files, etc.

attack   Any attempt to defeat the security assurances of a system or data, including confidentiality, integrity, or availability.

attack path   The steps that an adversary takes or might take to plan, prepare for, and execute an attack.

attack pattern   Similar cyber events or behaviors that might indicate that an attack has occurred or is occurring, resulting in a security violation or a potential security violation.

attack surface   An information system's characteristics that permit an adversary to probe, attack, or maintain presence in the information system.

attacker   An individual, group, or organization that executes an attack. An attacker might also refer to an adversary or an individual attack operator.

authentication   The process of verifying the identity of an entity (user, process, or device).

authorization   A process of determining whether a subject is allowed to have the specified types of access to a particular resource. This action is typically done by evaluating applicable access control information such as access control lists. In modern cybersecurity approaches, authorization could also incorporate other risk factors such as behavioral analytics and evaluation of threat intelligence.

availability   One of three primary cybersecurity assurances, the property of being accessible and usable upon demand. The other two are confidentiality and integrity.

B

banking Trojan   A type of malware designed to obtain credentials to banking and other financial services. These Trojans use a variety of techniques, including interception of web communications as users access financial services on infected devices. Many known banking Trojans are part of botnets that provide cybercrime organizations with persistent access to large numbers of devices.

blast radius   A machine learning method to identify the most impactful users, based on the level of risk to the organization if they become compromised.

botnet   A collection of computers compromised by malicious code and controlled across a network.

breach   Any incident that results in unauthorized access of data, applications, services, networks, and/or devices by bypassing their underlying security mechanisms. A security breach occurs when an individual or an application illegitimately enters a private, confidential, or unauthorized logical IT perimeter.

brownfield   Existing deployed IoT/IIoT devices that might not have modern hardware or functionality. For example, these devices might not have support for over-the-air updates or remote administration. Compare to *greenfield*.

brute force   An attack technique that uses systematic guessing, static or dynamic lists of passwords, dumped credentials from previous breaches, or other similar methods to forcibly authenticate to a device or service.

business email compromise (BEC)   A technology-facilitated social engineering scam that targets business email accounts and enables cybercriminals to unlawfully redirect and intercept money wires, exfiltrate documents, and launch other cybercrime. BEC is often initiated through some form of credential phishing.

C

ciphertext   Data or information in its encrypted form used primarily by cryptology experts. Sometimes referred to as *encrypted data*.

cleartext   Data that is unencrypted in its raw format. This format is highly discouraged due to lowering the security posture in light of not applying any encryption at rest or at transit.

Cloud Access Security Broker (CASB)   A software tool or service that sits between an organization's on-premises infrastructure and a cloud provider's infrastructure. They might also provide other services such as credential mapping when single sign-on isn't available.

confidentiality   An assurance that information isn't disclosed to unauthorized users, processes, devices, or other entities. One of the three primary cybersecurity assurances (confidentiality, integrity, and availability).

critical infrastructure   The systems and assets, whether physical or virtual, so vital to society that the incapacity or destruction of such might have a debilitating impact on the security, economy, public health or safety, environment, or any combination of these areas.

cybersecurity   The discipline of preserving and rapidly restoring the primary security assurances of confidentiality, integrity, and availability for systems, data, and identities.

D

dark web   The Internet content that operates using dark nets (i.e., networks that are not publicly accessible). They are accessed only by specialized closed-network protocols. Through the dark web, private computer networks can communicate and conduct business anonymously without divulging identity information. This term is associated with criminal activities in general.

data estate   The procedures, services, and infrastructure used to manage corporate data in the digital estate.

data loss prevention (DLP)   A set of procedures and mechanisms to stop sensitive data from leaving a security boundary.

denial of service   An attack that prevents or impairs the authorized use of information system resources or services. A distributed denial of service (DDoS) is a type of attack that uses multiple networked machines to overwhelm a host connected to the Internet, temporarily or permanently disrupting service or preventing access.

digital estate   An abstract reference to a collection of tangible owned assets. Those assets include virtual machines (VMs), servers, applications, data, containers, apps, and so on. Essentially, a digital estate is the collection of IT assets that powers business processes and supporting operations.

DLL   Dynamic link library is Microsoft's implementation of the shared library concept in the Microsoft Windows. In a conventional non-shared static library, sections of code are simply added to the calling program when its executable is built at the linking phase; if two programs call the same routine, the routine is included in both the programs during the linking stage of the two. With dynamic linking in DLLs, shared code is placed into a single, separate file.

drop account   An email account set up by a criminal to receive credentials provided by an unsuspecting victim.

E-F

encryption   The process of transforming plaintext into ciphertext.

event   An observable occurrence in an information system or network.

exfiltration   The unauthorized transfer of information from an information system.

exploit   A technique to breach the security of a network or information system in violation of security policy.

exposure   The condition of being unprotected, thereby allowing access to information or access to capabilities that an attacker can use to enter a system or network.

firewall   A capability to limit network traffic between networks and/or information systems.

fusion   A technology for finding threats that would otherwise fly under the radar. Fusion uses machine learning to combine disparate data from Enterprise and partner datasets, by combining low-fidelity "yellow" anomalous activities with high-fidelity "red" incidents.

G-K

greenfield   New or planned IoT/IIoT deployments that support the latest advances in security and technology management. Compare to *brownfield*.

honeypot   A computer or computer system intended to mimic likely targets of cybercriminals.

human-operated ransomware   A type of ransomware attack that's performed by human operators. During these attacks, human operators use various tools and techniques to compromise and traverse targeted networks, ultimately deploying ransomware on multiple devices on the compromised networks.

hunting   Proactively looking for active adversaries.

identity and access management (IAM)   The methods and processes used to manage subjects and their authentication and authorizations to access specific objects.

indicators of compromise (IOC)   Pieces of forensic data, such as data found in system log entries or files, that identify potentially malicious activity on a system or network.

insider threat   A person or group of persons within an organization who pose a potential risk through violating security policies.

integrity   The accuracy and completeness of data. Security controls focused on integrity are designed to prevent data from being modified or misused by an unauthorized party.

International Organization for Standardization (ISO)   An international standard-setting body composed of representatives from various national standards organizations. Founded in 1947, the organization promotes worldwide proprietary, industrial, and commercial standards.

intrusion   An unauthorized act of bypassing the security mechanisms of a network or information system.

Intrusion Detection Systems (IDS)   The process and methods for analyzing information from networks and information systems to determine if a security breach or security violation has occurred.

Intrusion Prevention Systems (IPS)   Intrusion Prevention Systems (IPS) also analyze packets, but they can also stop the packet from being delivered based on what kind of attacks it detects—helping to stop the attack.

just in time (JIT)   Provides temporary (measured in hours) elevated access to internal engineers to debug production issues or support customer cases to ensure limited access based on least privilege principles.

keylogging   Also referred to as *keyboard capturing*, this is the action of recording the keys struck on a keyboard, typically covertly, so that a person using the keyboard is unaware that their actions are being monitored by threat actors.

keypair   Consisting of a private key and a public key, is a set of security credentials that you use to prove your identity when connecting to an instance. The cloud provider stores the public key, and you store the private key. You use the private key, instead of a password, to securely access your instances.

kill chain   A cyber kill chain reveals the phases of a cyberattack: from early reconnaissance to the goal of data exfiltration. The kill chain is also a model for identification and prevention of cyber intrusions activity. The model identifies what the adversaries must complete in order to achieve their objective.

M-P

machine learning   A type of artificial intelligence focused on enabling computers to use observed data to evolve new behaviors that haven't been explicitly programmed.

macro virus   A type of malicious code that attaches itself to documents and uses the macro programming capabilities of the document's application to execute, replicate, and spread or propagate itself.

maintainer (as in GitHub)   Someone who manages a repository. This person might help triage issues and use labels and other features to manage the work of the repository. This person might also be responsible for keeping the README and contributing files updated.

malware   Software intentionally designed to cause damage to a computer, server, client, or computer network.

model inversion   An activity whereby an attacker uses careful queries to recover the secret features used in a machine learning model.

model stealing   An activity whereby an attacker constructs careful queries to recover a machine learning model.

nation state activity group   Cyberthreat activity that originates in a particular country with the apparent intent of furthering national interests.

National Institute of Standards and Technology (NIST)   A physical sciences laboratory and a nonregulatory agency of the U.S. Department of Commerce. Its mission is to promote innovation and industrial competitiveness.

npm (as in GitHub)   npm is the package manager for Node.js and the world's largest software registry.

obfuscation   A method used to hide or obscure an attack payload from inspection by information protection systems.

operator, or attack operator   An individual person who is executing an attack operation. This person might be acting alone, acting on behalf of an organization, or acting in concert with multiple other attack operators in a coordinated campaign.

password spray   High-volume attempts using a large number of common passwords to compromise sourced account information to authenticate and gain access to a network, often leveraging big data algorithms and extensive automation for rapid execution.

phishing   A digital form of social engineering to deceive individuals into providing sensitive information.

phishing kit   A collection of tools assembled to make it easier for individuals with little or no knowledge of phishing practices to launch a phishing exploit.

playbook   A set of rules that allows SOAR platforms to automatically take action when an incident occurs. Using SOAR playbooks, security teams can handle alerts, create automated responses for different incident types, and resolve issues more effectively and consistently.

poisoning attack   Contamination in the training phase of machine learning systems to get an intended result.

R

ransomware   A type of malware that uses cryptographic algorithms to encrypt a victim's data and block access. The bad actors threaten to publish the victim's data or block access perpetually unless a ransom is paid.

red team   A group authorized and organized to emulate a potential adversary's attack or exploitation capabilities against an enterprise's cybersecurity posture.

red team exercise or red team testing   An exercise, reflecting real-world conditions, that's conducted as a simulated attempt by an adversary to attack or exploit vulnerabilities in an enterprise's information systems.

remote desktop protocol (RDP)   A protocol for remotely connecting to computers running Windows.

resilience   The ability to adapt to changing conditions and prepare for, withstand, and rapidly recover from disruption.

reverse engineering   The reproduction of another manufacturer's product following detailed examination of its construction or composition.

S

secrets (as in GitHub secrets)   Tokens, credentials, private keys, or other authentication identifiers that might be used in a service at build or runtime. For example, secrets might be used by an application to access an external service.

Security Development Lifecycle (SDL)   The Microsoft SDL introduces security and privacy considerations throughout all phases of the development process, helping developers build highly secure software, address security compliance requirements, and reduce development costs. The guidance, best practices, tools, and processes in the Microsoft SDL are practices used internally to build more secure products and services. Since first shared in 2008, Microsoft has updated the practices as a result of its growing experience with new scenarios, like the cloud, IoT, and artificial intelligence.

Security Information and Event Management (SIEM)   An approach to security management that combines SIM (security information management) and SEM (security event management) functions into one security management system.

Security Operations Center (SOC)   A centralized function within an organization employing people, processes, and technology to continuously monitor and improve an organization's security posture while preventing, detecting, analyzing, and responding to cybersecurity incidents.

Security Orchestration, Automation, and Response (SOAR)   A solution stack of compatible software programs that allow an organization to collect data about security threats from multiple sources and respond to low-level security events without human assistance.

SMiShing (SMS phishing)   An attack method via a text or SMS message received on a mobile device. An attacker uses SMiShing to trick a user into downloading malware or revealing private information through a fraudulent link.

spoofing   Faking the sending address of a transmission to gain illegal (unauthorized) entry into a secure system. Website spoofing involves creating a duplicate version of a website that appears to be the original. Hackers use legitimate logos, fonts, colors, and functionality to make the spoofed site look realistic. Even the URL can appear genuine.

supply chain   A system of organizations, people, activities, information, and resources, for creating and moving products, including product components and/or services from suppliers through to their customers.

supply chain risk management   The process of identifying, analyzing, and assessing supply chain risk and accepting, avoiding, transferring, or controlling it to an acceptable level considering associated costs and benefits of any actions taken.

T-Z

threat variant   New or modified strains of an existing virus or malware program; malware family.

TTP   An acronym for the Tactics, Techniques, and Procedures that attackers use to infiltrate IT systems.

UEBA (user and entity behavior analytics)   Previously known as User Behavior Analytics (UBA). This mechanism uses large datasets to model typical and atypical behaviors of humans and machines within a network. By defining such baselines, it can identify suspicious behavior, potential threats, and attacks that traditional antivirus may not detect.

vishing (voice phishing)   The telephone equivalent of phishing. It's the act of using the telephone to scam the user into surrendering private information that will be used for identity theft. It can take shape as a phone call or voice message from a live or automated person.

Zero Trust   A security model based on the principle of maintaining strict access controls and not trusting anyone by default, even those already inside the network perimeter.

Index

2FA (Two Factor Authentication), 78

A

AAD (Azure AD), 113–114, 157
  B2B, 215
  B2C, 215
  Conditional Access, 210–211
  Domain Services, 114
  External Identities, 115–116
  Identity Governance, 215–216
  Identity Protection, 114, 212–213
  Kerberos/NTLM authentication, 114
  LDAP (Lightweight Directory Access
      Protocol), 114
  PIM (Privilege Identity Management),
      114, 213–214
    audit history, 157
  Zero Trust Access Architecture, 113
access control
  application access tokens, 462–463
  AWS IAM (Identity and Access
      Management), 337–338
  AWS RAM (Resource Access Manager),
      351–353
  Azure
    conditional access, 123–127
  Conditional Access, 210–211
  Credential Access, 73–74
    application access tokens, stealing, 462–463
    brute force, 461
    detection, 270

TTP detection, 137–139
    unsecured credentials, 464
    web credential forgery, 462
    web session cookie stealing, 463–464
  CSF, 324
  GCP (Google Cloud Platform)
    Access Approval API, 380
    Cloud Identity & Access Management,
        377, 378, 382
    Context Aware Access, 378
  Initial Access
    drive-by compromise, 447–450
    phishing, 450–451
    public-facing application exploit, 450
    trusted relationship, 451
    valid accounts, 452
  Initial Access TTP protection, 116–118
  LDAP (Lightweight Directory Access
      Protocol), 114
  Microsoft 365 Security, 187
  unauthorized access detection, 277–280
  Zero Trust Access Architecture, 113
account creation, 453
active defense, 28
AD (Active Directory), 456, 458
Advanced eDiscovery, 223–224
adversary, 479
AI (artificial intelligence), 479
  deep learning, 394
  definitions, 393–394
  ML (maching learning) and, 393–394

AIP (Azure Information Protection), Data Exfiltration TTP detection, 148–153
ALB (Application and Load Balancer), 342
alerts, 479
    AWS Security Hub, 254–255
Alibaba Cloud, 388–389
Amazon CloudWatch, 251–252, 360–361
    log sharing, 306–307
Amazon Detective, 356–357
Amazon DynamoDB, 247
Amazon EBS (Elastic Block Store), snapshots, 306
Amazon EC2, 247
    automated response, 292
    AWS Shield and, 340
    Command and Control server communication and, 281–282
Amazon Elastic Compute Cloud. *See* Amazon EC2
Amazon EventBridge, 302–304
Amazon Glacier, 366
Amazon GuardDuty, 253–254, 277–280, 328, 354
    AWS Security and, 355
    CloudTrail logging disable and, 310–317
Amazon Inspector, 328, 358–359
Amazon Macie, 270–276, 328, 357–358
Amazon Route 53, 363–364
Amazon S3, 247
Amazon S3 Glacier Vault Lock, 307
Amazon VPC (Virtual Private Cloud), 94, 342, 347–348
    Amazon VPC Flow Logs, 252–253
AMI (Amazon Machine Images), container images, 454
analysts, 480
anomalies
    CSF, 325
    detecting, 394
Antimalware, 19
API Gateway, SQL injection and, 256–263
API Management, 115
APN (AWS Partner Network), 328
application access tokens, 462–463
APT (advanced persistent threat), 47, 479
ASC (Azure Security Center), 113, 205
    automated response, 170–172
    versus Azure Defender, 105–108
    versus Azure Sentinel, 105
    Command and Control TTP detecting, 146–147

Credential Access TTP detection, 137–139
    CSPM (Cloud Security Posture Management), 106
    CWP (Cloud Workload Protection), 106
    Data Exfiltration TTP detection, 153–154
    Lateral Movement TTP and, 144–145
    prerequisites, 106–107
    Privilege Escalation TTP, 128–131
asset inventory, 37
asset management
    CSF (Cybersecurity Framework), 323
    Microsoft 365 Security, 186
assets, 480
assume breach mentality, 15, 51
    defense-in-depth, 84–86
ATT&CK, tags, 69
attachments, 480
attack operators, 485
attack paths, 480
attack patterns, 480
attack surfaces, 480
attackers, 480
attacks, 480
    denial of service attack, 482
    IoT and, 402–403
    malicious user profiling, 394
    poisoning attacks, 486
    threat-hunting activities after compromise, 394
    watering hole attack, 449
authentication, 480
    alternate authentication material, 460, 470–471
        theft detection, 277–280
    CSF, 324
    IoT and, 402
    Microsoft 365 Security, 187
    multi-factor, 338
authorization, 480
    GCP (Google Cloud Platform) binary authorization, 380
    multi-cloud environments, 38
    unauthorized access detection, 277–280
automation
    Amazon GuardDuty, 354
    Azure Sentinel, 90
    Exfiltration (TA0010), 79
    Microsoft Flow security response automation, 166–169
    MITRE ATT&CK Exfiltration (TA0010), 79

SOAR (Security Orchestration, Automation, and Response), 86, 487
Azure Sentinel, 108–109
availability, 480
Avast, GCP (Google Cloud Platform) and, 374–375
AVG, GCP (Google Cloud Platform) and, 374–375
awareness and training, CSF, 324
AWS Athena, 94
AWS Certificate Manager, 346
AWS Cloud Adoption Framework, 322
AWS CloudFormation, 366–367
AWS CloudHSM, 343–344
AWS CloudTrail, 93, 249–251, 359–360
  logging, disabled
    auto recovery, 310–317
    response, 295–304
  trails, creating, 296–299
AWS CloudWatch, 93
AWS Config, 329–330, 335
AWS Config Rules, automated response, 292
AWS Control Tower, 331–332
AWS Direct Connect, 349–350
AWS DRT (DDoS Response Team), 340
AWS ElasticSearch Service, 93
AWS Firewall Manager, 328, 342–343
AWS GuardDuty, 94
AWS IAM (Identity and Access Management), 328, 337–338, 483
  Credential Access detection, 270
AWS IoT Device Defender, 347
AWS KMS (Key Management Service), 343, 345–346
AWS Lambda, 93, 361–362
  automated response, 292
AWS Management and Governance services, 335
AWS OpsWorks, 368–369
AWS Organizations, 330–331
  service health, 365
AWS Personal Health Dashboard, 364–365
AWS PrivateLink, 349
AWS RAM (Resource Access Manager), 331
AWS Reference Architecture
  Amazon CloudWatch, 360–361
  Amazon Detective, 356–357
  Amazon Glacier, 366
  Amazon GuardDuty, 354–356

Amazon Inspector, 358–359
Amazon Macie, 357–358
Amazon Route 53, 363–364
Amazon VPC, 347–348
AWS Certificate Manager, 346
AWS CloudFormation, 366–367
AWS CloudHSM, 343–344
AWS CloudTrail, 359–360
AWS Config, 329–330
AWS Control Tower, 331–332
AWS Direct Connect, 349–350
AWS Firewall Manager, 342–343
AWS IAM (Identity and Access Management), 337–338
AWS IoT Device Defender, 347
AWS KMS (Key Management Service), 345–346
AWS Lambda, 361–362
AWS OpsWorks, 368–369
AWS Organizations, 330–331
AWS Personal Health Dashboard, 364–365
AWS PrivateLink, 349
AWS RAM (Resource Access Manager), 351–353
AWS Secrets Manager, 345
AWS Security Hub, 328–329
AWS Service Catalog, 334–335
AWS Shield, 340
AWS SSO (Single Sign-On), 338–339
AWS Step Functions, 362–363
AWS Systems Manager, 335–337
AWS Transit Gateway, 350–351, 352
AWS Trusted Advisor, 332–333
AWS WAF, 340–341
AWS Well-Architected Tool, 333–334
CloudEndure Disaster Recovery, 367–368
Detect and Respond
  Amazon CloudWatch, 360–361
  Amazon Detective, 356–357
  Amazon GuardDuty, 354–356
  Amazon Inspector, 358–359
  Amazon Macie, 357–358
  Amazon Route 53, 363–364
  AWS CloudTrail, 359–360
  AWS Lambda, 361–362
  AWS Personal Health Dashboard, 364–365
  AWS Step Functions, 362–363
Identify function, 326–328
Recover, 365

Amazon Glacier, 366
AWS CloudFormation, 366–367
AWS OpsWorks, 368–369
CloudEndure Disaster Recovery,
    367–368
AWS Secrets Manager, 345
AWS Security Hub, 254–255, 311–317,
    328–329
Amazon GuardDuty and, 355
AWS Security of the Cloud, 247
AWS Service Catalog, 334–335
AWS Shield, 340
AWS SSO (Single Sign-On), 338–339
AWS Step Functions, 362–363
automated response, 292
AWS Systems Manager, 328, 335–337
AWS Transit Gateway, 350–351, 352
AWS Trusted Advisor, 332–333
AWS VPC (Virtual Private Cloud), 94
AWS WA Tool (AWS Well-Architected
    Tool), 244
AWS WAF (Web Application Firewall),
    115, 200, 340–341
configuring, 259–263
Initial Access TTP protection, 116–118
SQL injection and, 256–263
AWS Well-Architected Framework,
    244–245, 322
Cost Optimization, 245–246
Operational Excellence, 245–246
Performance Efficiency, 245–246
Reliability, 245–246
Security, 245–246
AWS Well-Architected Labs, 244
AWS Well-Architected Tool, 333–334
Azure
conditional access, 123–127
DevOps, 115
WAF (Web Application Firewall), Initial
    Access TTP, 116–118
Azure AIP File Scanner, 222–223
Azure Application Gateway, 115
Azure Defender
    versus ASC (Azure Security Center),
        105–108
    dashboard, 108
    IoT (Internet of Things), 229
    plans, 109
Azure Defender for IoT, IoT (Internet of
    Things), 230
Azure Defender for SQL, 107

Azure Firewall, 114, 198–199
Azure Front Door, 114
Azure Identity Protection, Credential
    Access TTP detection, 132–137
Azure Information Protection, 115
Azure IoT Reference Architecture, 230–233
    Azure Defender for IoT
        agent-based solutions, 234–235
        agentless solutions, 233
Azure Key Vault, 114, 201–202
Azure Lighthouse, 197–198
Azure Marketplace, 194–195
Azure Monitor, 156–157
Azure Private Links, 114–115
    PaaS Services, 114
Azure Purview, 220–221
Azure Recovery, 204
Azure Secure Score, 205–206
Azure Sentinel, 105
    analytics, 88–89
    automation, 90
    Azure Logic Apps, 90
    Azure Monitor Workbooks, 88
    Command and Control TTP detection,
        146–147
    community, 92–93
    data collection, 86–87
    data connectors, 88
    Data Connectors gallery, 111
    Data Exfiltration TTP detection, 153–154
    enabling, 110–111
    incidents, 89
    investigation, 91
    Lateral Movement TTP detection,
        144–145
    overview, 108–112
    Privilege Escalation TTP, 128–131
    search, 110
    search-and-query tools, 92
    SIEM and, 108–109
    SOAR, 108–109
    workspace, 110
Azure Service Bus, 115
Azure Sphere, IoT (Internet of Things), 229
Azure Storage Service Encryption, 115
Azure WAF (Web Application Firewall),
    200
AzureArc, 196–197
AzureBackup, 115
AzureBastion, 202–204
AzureConfidential Computing, 115

AzureDatabricks ML, 174–181
AzureDDoS protection, 200–201
AzureDDoS Protection Standard, 114

B
banking Trojan, 480
BEC (business email compromise), 481
blast radius, 481
BLI (Breach Level Index), 407
blockchain, 406–407
Bot Control (AWS WAF), 341
botnets, 7, 481
breaches, 481
brownfields, 481
brute force, 481
brute force methods, 461
business email compromise, 119
business environment, CSF, 323

C
C2 (command and control). *See* Command
    and Control (MITRE ATT&CK)
CASB (Cloud Asset Security Broker),
    85, 216, 463, 481
castle defenses, 80
Chronicle (Google Cloud Platform)
    analytics, 375
    Avast, 374–375
    AVG, 374–375
    Security Command Center, 375
    VirusTotal Enterprise, 374
CI/CD (Continuous Integration and
    Continuous Delivery), 466
CIDRs (Classless Inter-Domain Routing),
    349
ciphertext, 481
CISO (Chief Information Security
    Officers), 5, 27
cleartext, 481
cloud matrix
    Collection
        cloud storage objects, 471
        email, 473–474
        information repositories, 471–472
        staged data, 472–473
    Credential Access
        application access tokens, stealing,
            462–463
        brute force, 461
        unsecured credentials, 464

web credential forgery, 462
web session cookie stealing, 463–464
Defense Evasion
    alternate authentication material, 460
    cloud compute infrastructure, 459
    cloud regions, unused/unsupported,
        459–460
    defenses, impairing, 458–459
    domain policy, 457–458
    valid accounts, 461
Discovery
    account discovery manipulation,
        464–465
    cloud infrastructure discovery
        manipulation, 465
    cloud service dashboards, 466
    cloud service discovery, 466
    network service scanning, 467
    permission groups, 467
    software, 468
    system information, 468
    system network connections, 469
Exfiltration, detecting, 474–475
Impact
    defacement, 475
    Endpoint DoS, 475–477
    resource hijacking, 477
Initial Access
    drive-by compromise, 447–450
    phishing, 450–451
    public-facing application exploit, 450
    trusted relationship, 451
    valid accounts, 452
Lateral Movement
    alternate authentication material,
        470–471
    spear phishing, internal, 469–470
Persistence
    account creation, 453
    account manipulation, 452–453
    container image implantation, 454
    office application startup, 454–455
    valid accounts, 455
Privilege Escalation
    domain policy modification, 456
    valid accounts, 457
CloudEndure Disaster Recovery, 367–368
CMS (Content Management Systems), 341
CNG (CryptoNG) libraries, 343
COBIT (Control Objectives for Information
    and Related Technology), 322

Collection (MITRE ATT&CK), 52, 414
  cloud storage objects, 471
  email, 473–474
  information repositories, 471–472
  staged data, 472–473
Command and Control, 8, 53, 77–78, 414,
    435–442
  case study, 77–78
  connection proxy, 77
  detecting, 145–147, 280–284
  one-way communication, 77
  ports, non-standard, 77
compliance
  AWS Config, 330
  shared responsibility model, 246–248
confidentiality, 481
container images, implanting, 454
controls, shared responsibility model, 248
cookies, stealing, 463–464
Cost Optimization, AWS Well-Architected
    Framework, 245–246
Credential Access, 52, 73–74, 414, 421–429
  Amazon Macie, 269–276
  application access tokens, stealing,
      462–463
  brute force, 461
  case study, 74
  credential dumping, 73
  detecting, 131–139, 269–276
  MiTM, 74
  password cracking, 73
  unsecured credentials, 464
  web credential forgery, 462
  web session cookie stealing, 463–464
credential phishing, 8
credentials, unsecured, 464
critical infrastructure, 482
cryptography
  public-key, breaking, 398
  random number generators, 397
CSF (Cybersecurity Framework), 321
  core, 322
  Detect function, 325
  GCP (Google Cloud Platform) and
    Detect function, 380–382
    Identify function, 376–378
    Protect function, 378–380
    Recover function, 383–384
    Respond function, 382–383
  Identify function, 323–324
  informative references, 322

MCRA comparison, 184–185
  profiles, 322
  Protect function, 324
  Recover function, 325–326
  Respond function, 325
  tiers, 322
CSPM (Cloud Security Posture
    Management), 105
  ASC (Azure Security Center), 106
CSPs (cloud service providers), 36–37
  Alibaba Cloud, 388–389
  Google Cloud Platform, 374–375
    NIST CSF and, 376–384
  IaaS (Infrastructure as a Service), 373–374
  IBM Cloud
    IBM Cloud Pak for Security, 385
    IBM Cloud Security Advisor, 386
    IBM QRadar, 385–386
    IBM Security Data Explorer, 385
    Security and Compliance Center, 386
  Oracle Cloud
    CASB (Cloud Access Security Broker), 387
    continuous protection, 387
    Guard, 388
    Oracle Cloud Infrastructure, 386
    SCS (SaaS Cloud Security), 387–388
  PaaS (Platform as a Service), 373–374
  SaaS (Software as a Service), 373–374
CTI (CyberThreat Intelligence), 26
Customer Access, AAD (Azure AD),
    External Identities, 115–116
CVE (Common Vulnerabilities and
    Exposures), 341
CWP (Cloud Workload Protection),
    ASC (Azure Security Center), 106
cyber resiliency, organizational culture
    and, 53–54
cyber risk awareness, 28
cybercrime
  increases in, 4–6
  WEF (World Economic Forum), 4
cybercriminals, 4
cybersecurity, 482
Cybersecurity Ventures, 4
cyberthreats. See threats

D
dark web, 482
Data & Application
  API Management, 115
  Azure Backup, 115

Azure Confidential Computing, 115
Azure DevOps, 115
Azure Information Protection, 115
Azure Storage Service Encryption, 115
data collection, 57
  Azure Sentinel, 86–87
data estate, 482
data exfiltration. *See* Exfiltration
data protection, 219
  Advanced eDiscovery, 223–224
  Azure, AIP File Scanner, 222–223
  Azure Purview, 220–221
  Microsoft Compliance Manager, 224–225
  MIP (Microsoft Information Protection),
    221–222
data security
  CSF, 324
  Microsoft 365 Security, 187
data-driven methods, 57
DDoS (distributed DoS), 476
  AWS DRT (DDoS Response Team), 340
  AWS Shield and, 340
  AzureDDoS protection, 200–201
  AzureDDoS Protection Standard, 114
  IoT and, 402
decision trees, 305
deep learning, 394
Defacement, 475
Defense Evasion (MITRE ATT&CK), 52, 414
  alternate authentication material, 460
  cloud compute infrastructure, 459
  cloud regions, unused/unsupported,
    459–460
  defenses, impairing, 458–459
  domain policy, 457–458
  valid accounts, 461
defense-in-depth
  assume breach mentality, 84–86
  external cloud security, 85
  internal cloud security, 85
denial of service attack (DoS), 482
Detect function (CSF), 325
Detect function (Microsoft 365 Security),
  188
detection features, 263
  CSF, 325
devices
  AWS IoT Device Defender, 347
  heterogeneity, 226
  IoT and, 401
    legacy devices, 227

DevOps, AWS CloudFormation and, 366
digital estate, 482
digital signing, AWS KMS, 346
Director's Handbook on Cyber-Risk Oversight
  (NACD), 29
Discovery (MITRE ATT&CK), 52, 414
  account discovery manipulation, 464–465
  cloud infrastructure discovery
    manipulation, 465
  cloud service dashboards, 466
  cloud service discovery, 466
  network service scanning, 467
  permission groups, 467
  software, 468
  system information, 468
  system network connections, 469
DLL (Dynamic Link Library), 482
DLP (Data Leakage Prevention), 19
DLP (data loss prevention), 482
DNS (Domain Name System), Amazon
  Route 53, 363
DNS protocol, Command and Control
  detection, 280–284
domains, Rogue Domain Controller, 456
DoppelPaymer, 10
Dridex, 10
drive-by compromise, 447–450
drop accounts, 482

E

EDR (Endpoint Detection Response),
  19, 407
ELB (Elastic Load Balancing), AWS Shield
  and, 340
email, data collection, 473–474
encrypted data, 481
encryption, 483
  AWS KMS, 345
  Azure Storage Service Encryption, 115
  GCP (Google Cloud Platform)
    CSEK (Customer Supplied Encryption
      Keys), 379
    Encryption at Rest, 379
    Encryption in Transit, 379
    RSA encryption, 397, 398
end-to-end integrated security, Microsoft,
  103
Endpoint DoS (Denial of Service), 475–476
EPP (Endpoint Protection Platform),
  207–208
EternalBlue tool, 16

event IDs, 456
events, 483
    CSF, 325
Execution (MITRE ATT&CK), 52, 413
Exfiltration, 53, 79–80, 414, 443–445, 483
    automation, 79
    case study, 79–80
    detecting, 147–155, 284–289, 474–475
    Exfiltration Over Alternative Protocol, 79
    Transfer Data to Cloud Account, 79
exploits, 483
exposure, 483
external cloud security, 85
Eye Pyramid campaign, 470

F
federated users, AWS IAM, 338
Firewall, 19
firewalls, 449–450, 483
fusion, 483

G
GCP (Google Cloud Platform)
    Access Approval API, 380
    Admin Console, 376, 378
    Android Enterprise, 381
    autoscaling, 379, 384
    BigQuery, 383
    binary authorization, 380
    Chronicle
        analytics, 375
        Avast, 374–375
        AVG, 374–375
        Security Command Center, 375
        VirusTotal Enterprise, 374
    Cloud Adoption Framework, 377, 379
    Cloud Armor, 377, 380, 383
    Cloud CDN, 384
    Cloud Data Catalog, 377
    Cloud Disaster Recovery, 383
    Cloud Functions, 382
    Cloud HSM, 379
    Cloud Identity, 376, 378
    Cloud Identity & Access Management,
        377, 378, 382
    Cloud Load Balancing, 384
    Cloud Operations Suite, 381, 383
    Cloud Private Catalog, 377
    Cloud Pub/Sub, 382
    Cloud Resource Manager, 376, 379

Cloud Security Scanner, 377, 381, 383
Cloud Status Dashboard, 384
Cloud Training, 379
Cloud VPC, 378, 380
Contact Center AI, 384
container images, 454
Container Registry Vulnerability Scanner,
    377, 381, 383
Context Aware Access, 378
CSCC (Cloud Security Command
    Center), 377, 381, 382
CSEK (Customer Supplied Encryption
    Keys), 379
CSF (Cybersecurity Framework) and
    Detect function, 380–382
    Identify function, 376–378
    Protect function, 378–380
    Recover function, 383–384
    Respond function, 382–383
Deployment Manager, 384
DLP (Data Loss Prevention), 379
Encryption at Rest, 379
Encryption in Transit, 379
Event Threat Detection, 382, 383
Forseti Security, 376, 378, 383
G Suite Phishing & Malware Protection, 381
G Suite Security Center, 381, 382
GCP Quotas, 379
Google Admin Console, 382
Google Security & Trust Center, 381
IDaaS (Identity as a Service), 378, 382
Identity Aware Proxy, 378
Identity Platform, 377, 378, 382
Incident Response Management,
    381, 382, 384
Key Management Service, 379
Log Exports, 383
network telemetry, 381
Phishing Protection, 378, 380, 383
Policy Intelligence, 382
Professional Services, 377, 379
reCAPTCHA, 380
Security & Trust Center, 377
Security Command Center, 375
Shielded VMs, 380
Titan Security Key, 380
Traffic Director, 380
VPC Service Controls, 378, 380
GDPR (General Data Privacy Regulation),
    Amazon Macie and, 357

GitHub
  AWS CloudFormation and, 366
  Azure Sentinel, 92–93
  maintainers, 485
  npm, 485
  secrets, 486
governance
  AAD (Azure AD)
    Identity Governance, 215–216
  AWS Management and Governance
    services, 335
  CSF, 323
  Identity Governance, 209
  Microsoft 365 Security, 186
GPOs (Group Policy Objects), 456, 458
graphs, Azure Sentinel, 91
greenfield, 483
GSOC (Global Security Operations
    Center), 43
GuardiCore honeypots, 394

H
HIPAA (Health Insurance Portability and
    Accountability Act), Amazon Macie
    and, 357
HMM (Hunting Maturity Model), 23
  Level 0 (Initial), 25
  Level 1 (Minimal), 25
  Level 2 (Procedural), 25
  Level 3 (Innovative), 25
  Level 4 (Leading), 25
  organization, 23–26
homoglyphs, 7
honeypot, 483
  GuardiCore, 394
HSM (hardware security module), 343
human-operated ransomware, 483
HUMINT (Human Intelligence), 26–27
hunting, 483
hypothesis-based methods, 57

I
IaaS (Infrastructure as a Service), 104,
    373–374
IBM Cloud
  IBM Cloud Pak for Security, 385
  IBM Cloud Security Advisor, 386
  IBM QRadar, 385–386
  IBM Security Data Explorer, 385
  Security and Compliance Center, 386

ICS (Industrial Control Systems), 405
ID Quantique, 397
Identify function (CSF), 323–324
Identify function (Microsoft 365 Security),
    186–187
Identity & Access Management
  AAD (Azure Active Directory), 113–114
    Identity Protection, 114
  ASC (Azure Security Center), 113
  CSF, 324
  Microsoft 365 Security, 187
identity protection
  AAD (Azure AD), 209, 211
    B2B, 209, 215
    B2C, 209, 215
    Privilege Identify Management, 209
  Azure MFA, 211–212
  Conditional Access, 209, 210–211
  Defender for Identity, 209
  Identity Governance, 209, 215–216
  Identity Protection, 212–213
  Microsoft Defender for Identity, 214–215
  Multi-Factor Authentication, 209
  PIM (Privilege Identity Management),
    213–214
IDPS (Intrusion Detection and Prevention
    Systems), 47
IDS (Intrusion Detection Systems), 19, 484
immutable storage, 307
Impact (MITRE ATT&CK), 53, 414
  defacement, 475
  Endpoint DoS, 475–477
  resource hijacking, 477
incident response
  Amazon EC2, 292
  automating, 290–294
  AWS Config Rules, 292
  AWS Fargate, 292
  AWS Lambda, 292
  AWS Step Functions, 292
  costs, scanning methods, 293
  event-driven responses, 294–304
  foundations, 289–290
  SSM Agent, 292
information repositories, data collection,
    471–472
Infrastructure & Network
  Azure Application Gateway, 115
  Azure DDoS Protection Standard, 114
  Azure Firewall, 114

Azure Front Door, 114
Azure Key Vault, 114
Azure Private Links, 114–115
Azure Service Bus, 115
Key Vault Managed HSM, 114
VPN Gateway, 114
WAF (Web Application Firewall), 115
Initial Access (MITRE ATT&CK), 52, 413
Azure Conditional Access, 123–127
Microsoft Defender for Endpoint,
121–123
Microsoft Defender for Office 365,
118–121
preventing, 256
WAF and, 116–118
insider threats, 483
integrity, 484
internal cloud security, 85
intrusion, 484
intuition-based analysis, machine
intelligence and, 394
investigation and remediation
Microsoft Defender for Endpoint,
157–158
Microsoft Threat Experts, 159–166
IOC (indicators of compromise), 23, 47, 483
IOC-based methods, 57
IoT (Internet of Things), 225, 399–401
attacks, 402–403
Azure Defender, 229
Azure Defender for IoT, 230
Azure Sphere, 229
denial of service, 228
devices, cybersecurity and, 401
elevation of privilege, 229
information disclosure, 228, 229
legacy devices, 227
OWASP (Open Web Application Security
Project) and, 400–401
preparedness, 403–404
risk growth, 401–403
security concerns, 226–227
spoofing, 228
threat models, 227–229
IPFIX (IP Flow Information Export), 394
IPS (Intrusion Prevention Systems), 484
ISO (International Organization for
Standardization), 484
ITSM (IT Service Management), 335
ITSM/ITOM, AWS Control Tower and, 335

J
JCE (Java Cryptography Extensions), 343
Jira Service Desk, 335
JIT (just in time), 484
Lateral Movement TTP and, 139–144

K
key management, AWS KMS, 346
Key Vault Managed HSM, 114
keylogging, 484
keypairs, 484
kill chains, 484
KPIs (key performance indicators), 25, 58
KRIs (key risk indicators), 58

L
Lambda functions, response and recovery,
314
Lateral Movement, 52, 75–76, 414, 431–434
alternate authentication material,
470–471
application access token, 75
case study, 75–76
detecting, 139–145, 276–280
pass the hash, 75
PtT (pass the ticket), 75
spear phishing, internal, 469–470
LDAP (Lightweight Directory Access
Protocol), 114
lifecycle
phishing, 9
ransomware, 11
logging
Amazon CloudWatch, 251–252
AWS CloudTrail, 249–251, 295–304
CloudTrail logging disable and, 310–317
VCP Flow Logs, 252–253

M
machine intelligence. *See* ML
(machine learning)
Machine Intelligence, 26
machine learning, 484. *See also*
ML (machine learning)
macro viruses, 485
maintainers, 485
maintenance
CSF, 324
Microsoft 365 Security, 188
malicious user profiling, 394

malware, 485
  Antimalware, 19
  detection, ML and, 395–396
  G Suite Phishing & Malware Protection,
    381
MCAS (Microsoft Cloud App Security),
  147, 157, 216–218
  dashboard, 148
  Microsoft Flow and, 166–169
MCRA (Microsoft Cybersecurity Reference
  Architecture), 184
  hybrid infrastructure
    ASC (Azure Security Center), 205
    Azure Arc, 196–197
    Azure Bastion, 202–204
    Azure DDoS protection, 200–201
    Azure Firewall, 198–199
    Azure Key Vault, 201–202
    Azure Lighthouse, 197–198
    Azure Marketplace, 194–195
    Azure Recovery, 204
    Azure Secure Score, 205–206
    Azure WAF, 200
    Private Link support, 195–196
  people security, 236
    attack simulator, 237
    Communication Compliance, 239–240
    IRM (Insider Risk Management),
      237–239
    SDL (Security Development Lifecycle),
      193–194
  Service Trust Portal, 192–193
  threat intelligence, 190–192
Microsoft
  end-to-end integrated security, 103
  Investigate and Response services,
    156–172
  security and prevention services, 112–127
Microsoft 365
  Defender, treat detection, 154–155
  Security
    Detect function, 188
    Identify function, 186–187
    NIST CSF and, 185
    Protect function, 187–188
    Recover function, 189–190
    Respond function, 189
  threat kill chain protection, 112
Microsoft Compliance Manager, 224–225
Microsoft Defender for Endpoint

attack surface reduction, 121
  enabling, 122–123
  Initial Access TTP protection, 121–123
  investigation and remediation, 157–158
Microsoft Defender for Office 365, 119–121
  Initial Access TTP protection, 118–121
Microsoft Detect services, 127–128
Microsoft Endpoint Manager, 206
  configuration manager, 207–208
  EPP (Endpoint Protection Platform),
    207–208
  Intune, 208–209
Microsoft Flow
  Cloud App security, 169
  MCAS and, 166–169
  security response automation, 166–169
Microsoft Intune, 208–209
Microsoft SDL (Security Development
  Lifecycle), 193–194
Microsoft Threat Experts
  alerts, 165, 166
  experts on demand, 161–165
  machine compromise, 165
  Targeted Attack Notification, 159–161
  threat intelligence, 166
migration, AWS PrivateLink, 349
MIP (Microsoft Information Protection),
  221–222
mitigation, CSF, 325
MITRE ATT&CK
  Collection (TA0009), 52, 67, 414
  Command and Control (TA0001), 53, 77,
    414, 435–442
  case study, 77–78
  connection proxy, 77
  detecting, 145–147
  one-way communication, 77
  ports, non-standard, 77
  Credential Access (T0006), 52, 73, 414,
    421–429
  case study, 74
  credential dumping, 73
  detecting, 131–139
  MiTM, 74
  password cracking, 73
  Defense Evasion (TA0005), 52, 67, 414
  Discovery, 52, 414
  Execution (TA0002), 52, 67, 413
  Exfiltration (TA0010), 53, 67, 79, 414,
    443–445

automation, 79
case study, 79–80
detecting, 147–155
Exfiltration Over Alternative Protocol, 79
Transfer Data to Cloud Account, 79
framework, 22
Impact, 53, 414
Initial Access (TA0001), 52, 67, 116–127, 413
Lateral Movement (TA0008), 52, 67, 75, 414, 431–434
application access token, 75
case study, 75–76
detecting, 139–145
pass the hash, 75
PtT (pass the ticket), 75
matrix, sub-techniques, 66
Persistence (TA0003), 52, 67, 413
New Service (T1050), 67–68
Privilege Escalation (TA0004), 52, 71–72, 128–131, 414, 415–419
access token manipulation, 72
case study, 72–73
DLL search order hijack, 72
New Service (T1050), 68
UAC bypassing, 72
reconnaissance, 413
resource development, 413
Tactic (TA0003), 67
tactics, 67, 70
techniques, 67–69, 70
AppInt (T1103), 67
New Service (T1050), 67
Spear Phishing Link, 68
Spear Phishing via Service, 68
testing, 65
threat modeling, 21–23
TTPs (Tactics, Techniques, and Procedures), 413–414
uses, 64–65
ML (machine learning), 172–173
AI and, 393–394
Azure Databricks ML, 174–181
deep learning, 394
false positives and, 395
fusion detections, 173–174
intuition-based analysis and, 394
malware detection and, 395–396
risk scoring and, 396
versus traditional approach, 395

unsupervised learning, 394
model inversion, 485
model stealing, 485
monitoring
Amazon GuardDuty, 253–254, 354
AWS Config, 329–330
Azure Monitor, 156–157
Azure Monitor Workbooks, 88
continuous, CSF, 325
MSSP (Managed Security Service Providers), 392
multi-cloud environment, 35–37
asset inventory, 37
authentication, 38
authorization, 38
configuration management, 37
CSPs (cloud service providers), 36–37
cyber resiliency, 53–54
multi-tenant environment, 38–40
SOC (Security Operations Center), 41–46
solutions, 38
threat modeling
assume breach mentality, 51
components, 19
hypothesis development, 52–53
methodologies, 20
MITRE ATT&CK, 21–23
proactive hunting team, 50–51
SDL (Security Development Lifecycle), 20–21
SOC and, 50–53
multi-factor authentication, AWS AIM, 338
multi-tenant environments, 38–40

N
NACD (National Association of Corporate Directors), 29
nation states
activity group, 485
threats, 10–14
actors, 14
adversaries list, 13
VPNs (virtual private networks), 11
NGOs (non-governmental organizations), 11
NIST (National Institute of Standards and Technology), 485. *See also* CSF (Cybersecurity Framework)
npm, 485

O

OAuth, 462–463
obfuscation, 485
Operational Excellence, AWS Well-Architected Framework, 245–246
operations, attack operators, 485
operators, 485
Oracle Cloud
  CASB (Cloud Access Security Broker), 387
  continuous protection, 387
  Guard, 388
  Oracle Cloud Infrastructure, 386
  SCS (SaaS Cloud Security), 387–388
organizations, cyber resiliency and, 53–54
OSINT (Open-Source Threat Intelligence), 26
OT (operational technology), 225, 405–406
  ICS (Industrial Control Systems), 405
  IoT and, 225–227
  legacy devices, 227
  SCADA (Supervisory Control and Data Acquisition) system, 405
OWASP (Open Web Application Security Project), 341
  IoT (Internet of Things) and, 400–401

P

PaaS (Platform as a Service), 104, 373–374
  Azure Private Links, 114
password spray, 485
PAW (Privilege Access Workstation), 139
Performance Efficiency, AWS Well-Architected Framework, 245–246
permissions, AWS IAM, 338
Persistence, 52, 413
  account creation, 453
  account manipulation, 452–453
  container image implantation, 454
  New Service (T1050), 67–68
  office application startup, 454–455
  valid accounts, 455
phishing, 7–8, 450–451, 485
  credential phishing, 8
  lifecycle, 9
  spear phishing, 6, 8, 118
    internal, 469–470
phishing kit, 485
PID (process IDs), 454

PII (personally identifiable information), Amazon Macie and, 357
PIM (Privileged Identity Management), 114
playbook, 485–486
poisoning attacks, 486
policy management, AWS Control Tower, 331
PPID (parent process IDs), 454
Private Link support, 195–196
Privilege Escalation, 52, 71–73, 414, 415–419
  access token manipulation, 72
  case study, 72–73
  detecting, 128–131, 263–268
  DLL search order hijack, 72
  domain policy modification, 456
  IoT, 229
  New Service (T1050), 68
  UAC bypassing, 72
  valid accounts, 457
Protect function (CSF), 324
Protect function (Microsoft 365 Security), 187–188
protective technology
  CSF, 324
  Microsoft 365 Security, 188
public-facing application exploit, 450

Q

quantum computing, 396
  challenges, 398–399
  entanglement, 397
  future, 399
  quantum-secure communications, 398
  qubits, 396
  Shor's algorithm, 397
Quantum Dice, 397
Quantum Exchange, 397
qubits, 396

R

random number generators, cryptography and, 397
ransomware, 8–10, 486
  human-operated ransomware, 483
  lifecycle, 11
  threats, 8–10
Ransomware-as-a-Service, 10
RDP (remote desktop protocol), 486

reconnaissance, 413
Recover function (CSF), 325–326
Recover function (Microsoft 365 Security),
     189–190
recovery. *See* response and recover
red team, 486
red team exercise, 486
red team testing, 486
regulatory issues, 408
Reliability, AWS Well-Architected
     Framework, 245–246
resilience, 486
resource development, 413
Resource Hijacking, 477
Respond function (CSF), 325
Respond function (Microsoft 365 Security),
     189
response and recover
     AI (artificial intelligence and), 317–319
     alternative accounts, 305–306
     Amazon EBS snapshots, 306
     automating response, 290–294
     CloudEndure Disaster Recovery,
          367–368
     CloudWatch log sharing, 306–307
     copying data, 306
     CSF, 325–326
     decision trees, 305
     event-driven responses, 294–304
     forensic workstations, 309
     immutable storage, 307
     incident response foundations, 289–290
     instances and, 309–310
     Lambda functions, 314
     ML (machine learning and), 317–319
     resource isolation, 308
     resource launch, 307–308
     viewing data, 306
reverse engineering, 486
risk assessment
     CSF, 324
     Microsoft 365 Security, 186
risk awareness, 28
risk management
     CSF, 324
     cybersecurity and, 28
     Microsoft 365 Security, 187
Rogue Domain Controller, 456
ROSI (Return of Security Investment), 58
RSA encryption, 397, 398

S
S3 bucket, 270
SaaS (Software as a Service), 104, 373–374
     SCS (SaaS Cloud Security), 387–388
SAML (Simple Access Mark-up
     Language), 14
     AWS SSO and, 339
SAW (Secure Access Workstation), 139
SCADA (Supervisory Control and Data
     Acquisition) system, 405
SCPs (service control policies), 331
SDL (Security Development Lifecycle),
     20–21, 486
SEA (Syrian Electronic Army), 470
SecOps, 47–48
     SOC, 235+236
secrets, 486
security, shared responsibility model,
     246–248
Security in the Cloud (customer), 247
Security of the Cloud (AWS), 247
Security section, AWS Well-Architected
     Framework, 245–246
service health, 364–365
ServiceNow, 335
shared responsibility model, 102–104
     AWS, 247–248
     controls, 248
     customer, 247–248
     IaaS (Infrastructure as a Service)
          solutions, 104
     on-premises solutions, 104
     PaaS (Platform as a Service) solutions,
          104
     SaaS (Software as a Service) solutions,
          104
     security and compliance, 246–248
SIEM (Security Information and Event
     Management), 41–42, 94–95, 408, 487
SIGINT (Signals Intelligence), 26
skillset requirements, 54
     analytical mindset, 56
     data analysis, 56
     outsourcing, 56–57
     programming languages, 56
     security analysis, 55
     soft skills, 56
SLAs (Service Level Agreements), 25
SMiShing (SMS phishing), 487
SNS, email topics, 299–301

SOAR (Security Orchestration, Automation, and Response), 86, 487
  Azure Sentinel, 108–109
SOC (Security Operations Center), 41, 487
  Azure Defender, 236
  Azure Sentinel, 235
  GSOC (Global Security Operations Center), 43
  hypothesis development, 52–53
  Microsoft DART (Detection and Response Team), 236
  Microsoft Defender XDR, 236
  Microsoft Threat Experts, 236
  model, 43–44
  MSSP/MDR providers, 236
  reference architecture, 48
  scope, 43
  services, 43
  SIEM (Security Information and Event Management), 41–42
  teams
    incident management, 45
    proactive hunting team, 50–51
    SOC analysts, 45
    specialized, 45–46
    threat intelligence, 45
  technologies, 44–45
  threat management, process, 44
  threat modeling, 50–53
  three-tier approach, 51
  tooling, 44–45
  type, 43
SOC analysts, 392
SolarWinds breaches, 391
Solorigate, 11
spear phishing, 6, 8, 118
  internal, 469–470
spoofing, 487
  homoglyphs, 7
SQL injection protection, 256–263
SREs (site reliability engineers), 360
SSL/TLS (Secure Sockets Layer/Transport Layer Security) certificates, 346
SSM Agent, automated response, 292
storage objects, data collection, 471
storage, immutable, 307
supply chain, 487
  Microsoft 365 Security, 187
  risk management, 487
    CSF, 324

T
testing, MITRE ATT&CK, 65
threat detection, 46–48
  legacy-based systems, 392
threat hunting, 6–7
  active defense, 28
  areas of study, 16
  board of directors, 27–30
  CISO (Chief Information Security Officers), 27
  data collection steps, 57
  desired outcome, 16
  foundational metrics
    functionality, 59
    scope, 58
    visibility, 58
  goals, 49–50
  human elements, 26–33
  hunter's role, 31–33
  methods
    data-driven, 57
    hypothesis-based, 57
    IOC-based, 57
    TTPS-based, 57
  multi-cloud environments, 35–37
    asset inventory, 37
    authentication, 38
    authorization, 38
    configuration management, 37
    multi-tenant environment, 38–40
    SOC (Security Operations Center), 41–46
    solutions, 38
  need for, 14–18
  objectives, 49–50
  operational metrics, 59–61
  organization size, 17–18
  program effectiveness, 61–62
  skillset requirements, 54
    analytical mindset, 56
    data analysis, 56
    outsourcing, 56–57
    programming languages, 56
    security analysis, 55
    soft skills, 56
  teams
    combined/hybrid team, 30
    dedicated internal team, 30
    periodic hunt teams, 30–31
threat hunting as a service, 407

threat intelligence, Zero Trust model
and, 83
threat kill chain, Microsoft 365, 112
threat management, SOC, process, 44
threat modeling
  assume breach mentality, 51
  components, 19
  hypothesis development, 52–53
  IoT cybersecurity, 227–229
  methodologies, 20
  MITRE ATT&CK, 21–23
  SDL (Security Development Lifecycle),
    20–21
  SOC and, 50–53
  teams, proactive hunting team, 50–51
threat variants, 487
threats
  nation state, 10–14
  phishing, 7–8
  ransomware, 8–10
Trojans, banking Trojans, 480
trusted relationships, 451
TTPs (Tactics, Techniques, and
  Procedures), 6, 70, 413–414, 487
  tactics, 67
  techniques, 67–69
TTPS-based methods, 57

U

UEBA (user and entity behavior analytics),
  109–110, 236–240, 487

V

VCP Flow Logs, 252–253
viruses, macro viruses, 485
VirusTotal Enterprise, 374
vishing (voice phishing), 488
VM (virtual machine)
  compromised, 394
  malicious user profiling, 394
VPN Gateway, 114
VPNs (virtual private networks), nation
  state threats, 11

W

WannaCry, 10
  EternalBlue tool, 16
watering hole attack, 449
WEF (World Economic Forum), 4
whaling attacks, 119
WRM (write once, read many), 307

X

XDR (extended detection and response),
  408

Z

Zapier, 166
Zero Trust, 488
Zero Trust Access Architecture, AAD
  (Azure Active Directory), 113
Zero Trust model, 80–83
  threat intelligence and, 83